Hᴇʟʟᴇɴɪᴄ Sᴛᴜᴅɪᴇs 25

King of Sacrifice

Ritual and Royal Authority in the *Iliad*

T0324458

Other Titles in the Hellenic Studies Series

Plato's Rhapsody and Homer's Music
The Poetics of the Panathenaic Festival in Classical Athens

Labored in Papyrus Leaves
Perspectives on an Epigram Collection Attributed to Posidippus
(P.Mil.Vogl. VIII 309)

Helots and Their Masters in Laconia and Messenia
Histories, Ideologies, Structures

Archilochos Heros
The Cult of Poets in the Greek Polis

Master of the Game
Competition and Performance in Greek Poetry

Greek Ritual Poetics

Black Doves Speak
Herodotus and the Languages of Barbarians

Pointing at the Past
From Formula to Performance in Homeric Poetics

Homeric Conversation

The Life and Miracles of Thekla

Victim of the Muses
Poet as Scapegoat, Warrior and Hero
in Greco-Roman and Indo-European Myth and History

Amphoterōglossia
A Poetics of the Twelfth Century Medieval Greek Novel

Priene (second edition)

Plato's Symposium
Issues in Interpretation and Reception

http://chs.harvard.edu/chs/publications

King of Sacrifice

Ritual and Royal Authority in the *Iliad*

SARAH HITCH

CENTER FOR HELLENIC STUDIES
Trustees for Harvard University
Washington, D.C.
Distributed by Harvard University Press
Cambridge, Massachusetts, and London, England
2009

King of Sacrifice: Ritual and Royal Authority in the *Iliad*
by Sarah Hitch
Copyright © 2009 Center for Hellenic Studies, Trustees for Harvard University
All Rights Reserved.
Published by Center for Hellenic Studies, Trustees for Harvard University, Washington, D.C.
Distributed by Harvard University Press, Cambridge, Massachusetts and London, England

LIBRARY OF CONGRESS CATALOGING-IN-PUBLICATION DATA
Hitch, Sarah.
   King of sacrifice : ritual and royal authority in the *Iliad* / Sarah Hitch.
      p.   cm. — (Hellenic studies ; 25)
   Includes bibliographical references and index.
   ISBN 978-0-674-02592-9 (alk. paper)
      1. Homer. Iliad. 2. Epic poetry, Greek—History and criticism.
   3. Achilles (Greek mythology) in literature. 4. Trojan War—Literature
   and the war. 5. Kings and rulers in literature. 6. Ritual in literature.
   7. Sacrifice in literature.   I. Title.
PA4037.H68 2009
883'.01—dc22   2009028063

Contents

Preface vii

Chapter 1. Defining Homeric Sacrifice 1
  1.1 Sacrifice and the Homeric Text 18
  1.2 The Unique Case of Homeric Sacrifice 39
  1.3 The Poetics of Sacrifice 59

Chapter 2. The Ritual Process 60
  2.1 Narrative Voices 68
  2.2 Pre-Kill 87
  2.3 Kill 92

Chapter 3. The Gift of Sacrifice 93
  3.1 The Reciprocity of Sacrifice 111
  3.2 The Pattern of Embedded Sacrifices 140

Chapter 4. The King of Sacrifice 141
  4.1 The Basis for Agamemnon's Ritual Authority 163
  4.2 Ritual Authority and Exclusion 176
  4.3 The Language of Sacrificial Authority 180
  4.4 Agamemnon's Sacrificial Authority in Akhilleus' Absence 189
  4.5 The Isolation of Akhilleus between Men and Gods 203

Bibliography 205

Index 227

Index Locorum 231

Preface

HOMERIC REPRESENTATIONS OF ANIMAL SACRIFICE have often been included in reconstructions and interpretations of Greek ritual practice, but the occurrence of this central action in Homer has not received its own independent, full-length study. As is the case with any 'type scene', no two Homeric sacrifices are identical. Within the poems, the emphasis placed on particular aspects of a sacrifice is carefully controlled according to the thematic needs of the context: the sacrificial process can be elaborate, such as the lengthy preliminary rites at ILIAD I 436–474, or abbreviated, such as at ILIAD I 313–317. This book seeks to provide an examination of animal sacrifice within the larger context of the ILIAD, identifying the function of the ritual within the poem's narrative design and illustrating how the epic's thematic goals shape the ritual's presentation.

In Chapter One, I discuss the possible approaches to sacrifice in the *Iliad* as both a ritual process and a typical compositional device in Homeric poetry. In order to facilitate this discussion, I propose a functional definition for sacrifice in the *Iliad*: the slaughter of animals in a ceremony dedicated to the gods, which is distinguished throughout the poem from preparations for meals without references to the gods. The focus on the sacrificer and on the sacrificial offering as an address to the gods becomes an emergent pattern among sacrifice scenes. Though three of the poem's seven enacted sacrifices are followed by shared meals, other meals are not associated with addresses to deities. While single words or whole verses may be shared between sacrifices and these other occasions for feasts, such as those describing the spitting of meat in Agamemnon's sacrifice in *Iliad* II or Akhilleus' feast with Priam in *Iliad* XXIV, the inclusion of specific rites shifts the meaning of a scene.

I distinguish, in Chapter Two, between 'enacted sacrifices', the primary narrator's descriptions of sacrifice, and 'embedded sacrifices', complex narrator and character-speech references to sacrifice. An analysis of enacted and embedded sacrifices generates a possible range of ritual procedures in the *Iliad*. It demonstrates, as well, that the performance of sacrifice within the primary narrative-text is designed to emphasize Agamemnon's dominance over the other troops in Akhilleus' absence; Agamemnon performs or provides for the primary narrative's enacted sacrifices, which cease upon Akhilleus' return in *Iliad* XIX, the point at which social relationships and hierarchical structures are no longer publicly contested. Other features of sacrifice, those most frequently attested in later literature and iconography, and considerations such as the practical requirements of slaughtering animals are either inconsistently represented or omitted.

A distinction between sacrifices described by the primary narrator and those referred to in character speech is created through their varying emphases on separate stages of the ritual performance. Whereas enacted sacrifices focus on the sacrificer, embedded sacrifices focus exclusively on the reciprocity between men and gods established through sacrificial offerings—the subject of Chapter Three. Embedded sacrifices call into question the efficacy of the ritual in the maintenance of mortal and immortal relations, revealing a tension between the descriptions of the sacrificial process in the primary narrative-text and the frustration of mortals and immortals expressed in character speech. For example, when the Akhaians are suffering, Agamemnon laments that Zeus favors the sacrifices of Hektor, while Zeus laments that Hektor and the numerous Trojan sacrifices cannot avert their own destruction. This tension between different perspectives on sacrifice is further complicated by the absence of descriptions of Hektor performing sacrifice in the primary narrative voice, which focuses exclusively on Agamemnon as the *Opferherr*.

This book concludes with a discussion, in Chapter Four, of the complex sacrificial framework that surrounds Akhilleus' withdrawal in *Iliad* I and return in *Iliad* XIX. The quarrel between Agamemnon and Akhilleus is expressed through sacrifice: Agamemnon's superiority over the Akhaians is demonstrated in the enacted sacrifices, while the embedded sacrifices highlight the contrast between the breakdown of communications between mortals and the gods and Akhilleus' ability to influence the gods through his mother, the goddess Thetis. Akhilleus' isolation from his community is marked by depictions of Agamemnon and the councilors taking part in sacrifices; after the death of Patroklos, his frustration over his impending death is signaled by both his abstinence from and disregard for animal sacrifice. Preferring to communicate with the gods through his mother's divine intervention, Akhilleus' semidivine status is reflected in his rejection of the standard pattern of mortal requests to the gods.

This project began as my dissertation at Harvard University, under the direction of Albert Henrichs; it is only thanks to his guidance, and the encouragement and inspiration provided by Gregory Nagy, that this book came into being. Many people provided invaluable support at various stages: I would like to especially thank Ian Rutherford, who helped me with the final draft, and to express my gratitude for the helpful comments from Stephen Instone, Robert Parker, Francesca Schironi, Richard Seaford, the late Christiane Sourvinou-Inwood, and Hans van Wees, as well as Leonard Muellner, Marian Demos, and the wonderful publication team at CHS. Invaluable support for this project was provided by Jonathan Katz and Shaun Hullis of Westminster School (London), my husband, Julian, and my parents, Bill and Lucy, to whom this book is dedicated.

Throughout the book, all Greek has been translated, based very loosely on Fagles' 1990 translation of the *Iliad* and Lattimore's 1967 translation of the *Odyssey*. I have endeavored to transliterate Greek words, except in cases where proper nouns are better known through their Latin spelling. The Greek text used is that of Monro and Allen (1920).

King of Sacrifice

Chapter One
Defining Homeric Sacrifice

1.1 Sacrifice and the Homeric Text

Rituals are actions performed in a repetitive pattern recognizable to members of a community that act as symbolic markers of the values underpinning a given society. Such actions can be both symbolic and functional, as is the case with the ritual of animal sacrifice: symbolic actions, such as scattering barley grains or wearing special clothing, elaborate the marked nature of the event as an expression of mortal relations with gods, while the shared meal after the ceremony often serves the function of providing food for the participants, binding them together as members of a community. This complex of ritual actions would have had meaning for the participants through their shared experience and traditions, but it can only be reconstructed by us through literary and artistic representations and archaeological remains. The lack of an official or written protocol for ancient Greek ritual, coupled with the vast variations attested in literature and inscriptions, has created something of a puzzle for modern scholars.

Often this ritual, because the term "sacrifice" is a modern construct largely colored by Roman and Christian perceptions, eludes interpretation. The Greeks themselves had no words for "religion" or "ritual," both terms derived from Latin. Drawing on our own cultural experience, we may be tempted to apply retroactively concepts of "sacred" and "secular," the former part of "religion" or "religious worship," but these words imply a distinction that would have been meaningless in antiquity.[1] There were also many types of offerings to the gods, a spectrum of actions with variations in meaning and context, perceived by ancient Greeks as obligatory, both as acts of devotion

---

[1] On modern attempts to distinguish between "sacred" and "secular" see Connor 1988 and Vernant 1991:273. Henrichs 2003 describes the tenuous connection between writing and ancient Greek ritual; as in the absence of sacred texts or professional clergy, ritual customs were transmitted orally, without sacred texts or a professional clergy (40). The accumulation of written testimonials about cults, temples, gods, and rituals lead to our modern concept of "Greek religion," and a distinction must be made between actual ritual practice and poetic representations in this regard (58). Gould 2001:203 has persuasively argued that there is no single thing as a "Greek religion." Bremmer 1998 describes the development of the terminology.

and as symbols of membership in a community. These actions varied from extending hospitality to dedicating statues in temples. Many gifts to the gods were ritually offered, sacrifice being only one variant among burnt offerings, bloodless offerings, libations, and dedications. The occasions on which gifts were offered determined the nature and function of the offering. Animal sacrifice, the grandest and most elaborate offering to the gods, is a specific part of this framework, and its meaning has comparable significance.

To date, there has yet to be a systematic, full-scale study of animal sacrifice in the *Iliad*. Scholars have looked at archaeological evidence for the descriptions of sacrifice in Homer, the influence of Homer on animal sacrifice in tragedy, and the impact of the Homeric representations of gods on Greek culture. Other rituals such as oath-making, supplication, and burial have been well studied.[2] Yet there has been no attempt to treat the circumstances, details, frequency, or significance of scenes of animal sacrifice in Homer. This book seeks to fill this void in Homeric studies by exploring the function of sacrifice within the context of the *Iliad* and the ways in which the goals of the poem shape the representation and meaning of sacrifice. I will focus exclusively on animal sacrifices performed with the intention of influencing gods and the outcome of events. Therefore, I will refer to the immolation of animals in contexts that include any address or ritual action directed toward the gods, whether or not it is followed by a meal, as "sacrifice." Libations poured and prayers made in conjunction with sacrifices will be discussed as part of the sacrificial process, but those performed without animal sacrifice, such as Akhilleus' libation and prayer for the safety of Patroklos (*Iliad* XVI 220–255), are best left for a separate study. I intend to consider sacrifice as a poetic construct in the *Iliad*, with respect both to the ways in which characters speak about sacrifice and its structural function within the poem. Through references to sacrifice, characters in the *Iliad* will present a remarkably consistent and, overall, negative view of the potential to create successful reciprocal relationships with the gods. On a structural level, the performance of sacrifice will frame Agamemnon's supremacy in the context of Akhilleus' withdrawal, while highlighting the isolation of the latter from his community.

The differences between the martial, Panakhaian society of the *Iliad*, dominated by questions of human/divine relationships and mortality, and the

---

[2] Archaeology: Vermeule 1974; oath-making: Kitts 1999, 2002, 2005; supplication: Thornton 1984; burial: Petropoulou 1988; Seaford 1994; Sourvinou-Inwood 1995; Saïd 1998; tragedy: Burkert 1966; Seaford 1994; Henrichs 2000, et al. The role of Homer in Greek culture, particularly in regard to concepts of the divine, was recognized already in antiquity: Herodotus 2.53, Jaeger 1965:39ff.

society of the *Odyssey*, with its emphasis on the *oikos* and intact social structures—as exhibited through the course of Odysseus' and Telemakhos' travels—radically affect the presentation of sacrifice. There are many similarities, but the overall conception of divine power is different in the two poems, particularly in the emphasis on justice in the *Odyssey*.[3] In the *Odyssey* sacrifice becomes a symbol of cultivation and civilization, the perversion or absence of which marks the suitors and other groups as excessive and sinister.[4] Whereas the sacrifices in the *Iliad* tend to focus on the role of individuals, different communities, such as the Pylians (*Odyssey* iii 5–9) and Phaiakians (*Odyssey* vii 186–190), are represented in the *Odyssey* performing sacrifice as a group. Athena, who is exceptionally involved in the plight of Odysseus, even attends the group sacrifice at Pylos disguised as Mentor (*Odyssey* iii 30–385), later provoking Nestor's own grateful sacrifice by her epiphanic departure (*Odyssey* iii 435–464), which in turn prompts yet another appearance (*Odyssey* iii 435–436). The portrait of relations between this goddess and her favorite mortals in the *Odyssey* seems idealized, reflected by the happy, communal sacrifices at Pylos and Athena's interactions with Nestor and Telemakhos.[5] However, similar interactions do not accompany the *Iliad*'s representations of sacrifice, which are often depicted by characters as a dubious attempt to bridge the immense gap between mortals and immortals. Such divergence in social and ethical concern can be seen in the representation of sacrifice in each poem, which necessitates an individual approach to both.

The representations of sacrifice in the *Iliad* cannot be appreciated as reflections of the practices of a particular society at a precise moment because of the lengthy and diffuse development of the Homeric tradition, by which I mean the versions of the *Iliad* and *Odyssey* that have come down to us. Homeric poetry derives from oral traditions, but how these poetic traditions became fixed as texts has been endlessly debated. Fortunately, the discourse begun in a sense by Friedrich August Wolf, developed by Milman Parry and Albert Lord, and enhanced and sophisticated by numerous scholars over recent decades, has advanced our understanding of the nature of Homeric epic. Since the groundbreaking work of Parry in the early part of the twentieth century, scholars have recognized that the composition and structure of Homeric poetry are the

---

[3] Kullmann 1985:6–7. Griffin 1980:144–178 gives a general discussion of the gods in both epics, highlighting differences between the two epics (164–167); see also Heubeck 1954; Jaeger 1960:16–33; Lloyd-Jones 1971; Kearns 2004:67–69.

[4] Vidal-Naquet 1986.

[5] Kullmann 1985:7.

result of the continual performance of inherited meter, diction, and themes.[6] This material, in its earliest stage, derives from an Indo-European tradition, as indicated by noun-epithet phrases in Vedic poetry cognate with such expressions as κλέος ἄφθιτον 'unfailing glory' and κλέος εὐρύ 'widespread glory'.[7] Additionally, the numerous and well observed parallels between the *Iliad* and the Babylonian epic *Gilgamesh* suggest that the initial Indo-European traditions are received and filtered through Near Eastern song culture before the Mycenaean period.[8] Many elements introduced at this time, on the level of both theme and diction, are maintained throughout the Iron Age and Archaic period until the poems reach the canonical, fixed shape that has been passed down to us in written form. The eighth century BCE witnesses an accelerated development of Panhellenic identity and shared culture, the trigger for the widespread diffusion of Homeric poetry and a result of the unifying power of its popularity. This trend of Panhellenism is evident in the presence of large regional and supra-regional cult centers developing concurrently with an increasing popularity of gift-offerings at Mycenaean tombs, both reflecting the widespread interest in the "age of heroes" also found in contemporary art.[9] The more widespread the diffusion, the more fixed the poetry becomes before its crystallization in a form similar to that which we possess.

This crystallization occurs in sixth-century Athens through a process that can be described, as posited by Gregory Nagy, diachronically, in terms of an evolutionary model consisting of five key stages. The first "age," approximately 2000 BCE–750 BCE, allows for the development of the poem through composition-in-performance using the building blocks of inherited formulas and themes. The ability of an *aoidos* to adapt the material would have ensured his success with whichever audience he sought to impress; this is possibly

---

[6] Parry 1971. The discussion of the origins and history of the hexameter begins with Meillet 1923; more recently Nagy 2003:42 discusses the lack of musical accompaniment and reduced melody, and West 1997a:235–236 summarizes the comparative evidence of Vedic meter. West 1988:159–160 treats the inheritance of diction, and Lord 1960 is still the best discussion of inherited themes. The bibliography is immense and most succinctly explained by Nagy 1979:42–43, 1996a, 2003:1–19.

[7] κλέος ἄφθιτον: *Iliad* IX 413 and *Rig-Veda* 1.9.7bc; see Nagy 1974:191–228 and his recent updating of the argumentation, 2003:48; West 1988:145. κλέος εὐρύ: *Iliad* I 344; III 83, 204; IV 726, 816; XIX 333; XXIII 137.

[8] Morris 1997:616–618 and Nagy 2005 detail the common heritage of Near Eastern and Homeric themes.

[9] Nagy 1979:7, 1990a:72–82; Snodgrass 1987: 159, 421; Morris 1988; Shapiro 1994 (specifically on art).

reflected in the depiction of bards in the *Odyssey*.[10] This very fluid period is followed by progressively more stable phases in the poems' development, first in a "Panhellenic" phase, 750–550 BCE, and then a "definitive" period, 550–300 BCE, in which the texts were created as part of the reforms of the Panathenaiac festival under the tyrants Peisistratos and Hipparkhos. The "definitive" phase was followed by a "standardizing" phase, 300–150 BCE, also triggered by reforms of Athenian performance customs, this time by Demetrios of Phaleron. Finally, the text becomes crystallized through Aristarkhos' production of a definitive version in the mid-second century BCE, after which the papyri showing significant variations disappears.[11]

This process of composition and transmission accounts for the mixture of dialects and cultural details that defy assignment to a specific region or isolated time period. Inconsistencies in the material culture of the Homeric epics, such as the variations in the size, shape, and use of shields, spears, and the armor of the heroes, also indicate varying periods of composition and stabilization, beginning with a probable time of "active generation"—the actual creation of the epics—in the pre-palatial and early palatial Mycenaean period (1600–1400 BCE), followed by a period of maintenance (1300–1200 BCE).[12] Similar evolutionary models account for the mixture of dialects and morphology found in the poems that, like the archaeological material, are drawn from long spans of time and never exist together in any form similar to that in the poems. A commonly adduced example is the loss of the digamma, probably in the eighth century, which is a necessary sound for some verses in the poems, while others are composed after this linguistic development.[13]

---

[10] Many scholars have explored the self-referential implications of song performance within the poems: see Nagy 1990b:21–24; Ford 1992:90–130; Segal 1994:113–141; Latacz 1996:28f.

[11] Nagy 1996a:41–42f.; 2003:2–3.

[12] The model proposed by Sherratt 1990, who focuses on the examples of the lump of iron given as a prize by Akhilleus (*Iliad* XXIII 826–835), the massive spears of Akhilleus (*Iliad* XIX 387–391) and Hektor (*Iliad* VIII 493f.), and the shield of Ajax (*Iliad* VII 219); see also Lorimer 1950:152ff.; Page 1959:232–235. Sherratt defends her model against those of Dickinson 1986:28–30, Kirk 1962:190–191, and Morris 1986:89ff., who explain these inconsistencies as deliberate "archaizing" or "heirlooms" (1990:84–85). Helpful diagrams of elements "less susceptible to adaptation," such as formulas and main characters and plots, and "more susceptible," such as speeches and incidental details, are found at Sherratt 1990:86. West 1988:151, Latacz 1996:49, and Lesky 1967:695 also trace the origins of the Greek epic tradition back to Mycenaean times.

[13] Hoekstra 1965:42–58 discusses the digamma; see also Janko 1992:8–19; Horrocks 1997; West 1997a. Five stages of linguistic development have been discerned: Indo-European, pre-Mycenaean Greek, Mycenaean Greek, Aeolic Greek, and Ionic Greek; see Ruijgh 1957; West 1988. Sherratt 1990:89 finds linguistic evidence less convincing because of the natural linguistic changes in a lengthy process of oral transmission.

The combined force of these independently determined evolutionary models is overwhelming.

The Homeric tradition's ability to transform itself into poetry appropriate for diffusion over a wide area guarantees its survival through such a long transmission process.[14] But the Panhellenic consciousness that enables the *Iliad*'s wide diffusion makes the expectations of any particular audience impossible to reconstruct with certainty, such as we might do with Athenian tragedy, since the poem develops over such a long period of time. The identification of a Homeric audience, the particular performance context, and the impact of the *Iliad*'s reception are all debatable.[15] Performances in palaces after meals seem likely during an early stage of epic development on the basis of the portrayal of bards in the *Odyssey*, and Plato's *Ion* describes the performance of Homeric poetry in rhapsodic contests in the fifth century, but the complete picture is impossible to reconstruct and, therefore, so is the potential response of material in the poem to the expectations of a particular audience.[16] The wide diffusion of the poems is particularly relevant to the representations of sacrifice, a ritual variously practiced throughout Hellenic cities, depending on the context and participants, as part of a polytheistic system that could accommodate innumerable local deities and rites alongside well-established Panhellenic practices. The localized variations in cult practice that are such an important and defining characteristic of the epigraphic evidence for Greek ritual are not emphasized. Instead, the epic provides a picture of ritual practice that is universally recognizable to the diverse audiences of the *Iliad* throughout its long period of development and transmission.

[14] Nagy 1996a:42.

[15] This topic is covered by Foley 1990, Latacz 1996, and Scodel 2002; Taplin 1992:2–39 also discusses probable performance contexts at length. On the problems of reconstructing the Homeric audience, see Lord 1960:14–17; Doherty 1995:24–25; Taplin 1992:2–3. Latacz has argued, from the time of composition up through the fifth century BCE, for an aristocratic audience, demonstrable through the ranking of singers within the poems and the general themes of the poems, which marginalize the lower classes. On this basis, he argues for a mid-eighth-century date, during the revival and *floruit* of the Greek aristocracy (1996:32–35). On the identification of Homer as an aristocrat himself, see Bowra 1930:410; Fränkel 1975:9f.; Schadewaldt 1944:63; et al. Hesiod's praise of kings in the *Theogony*, which is probably due to the performance context at the funeral games of Amphidamas, may be comparable (West 1966:44).

[16] *Odyssey* i 325–359; viii 61–83, 266–369, 471–543; Plato *Ion* 530a–b, 533c; *Hipparkhos* 228b–c; Nagy 1996a:80–81; 2002; 2003:3–7, 41–45. Discussions of performance and singers in the poems can be found in Ford 1992 and Segal 1994:113–141. Kitts 2005:125–187, drawing on the work of Stanley Tambiah, proposes that descriptions of rituals in the *Iliad* were experienced by the audience as part of the ritual performance of epic; Scodel 2002:12 is skeptical about 'ritual' performances by bards.

As the *polis* emerges as the dominant political structure, Panhellenic religious centers, such as the sanctuaries of Zeus at Olympia and Apollo at Delphi, develop. These centers promote cults and deities recognizable to and worshipped by all communities while incorporating local ritual concepts into a broader framework.[17] The portrait of ritual in the *Iliad* reflects this transition: while there are echoes of localized practices, such as particular divine epithets, the Olympian gods are conceptualized in a generalizing way appropriate for mass diffusion.[18] The presentation of sacrifice in the poems would have been familiar to different audiences, not because of a basis in historical practice or as a reflection of "real" ritual, but because of a shared, idealized conceptualization of sacrifice as a recurrent theme in epic poetry.

An understanding of the *Iliad*'s portrayal of sacrifice must be grounded in an appreciation of its structural, thematic, and lexical complexity, for which working definitions and terminology will be briefly established here before moving on to a discussion of repeated verses in Homeric epic and the repetition of 'typical' elements in sacrifice scenes. As early as Aristotle, the *Iliad* and the *Odyssey* are admired for having a central focus, the wrath of Akhilleus and the homecoming of Odysseus, respectively, despite their remarkable length.[19] This 'central action' is presented through a vast network of actions and speeches, enacted and embedded stories that inform the audience of past and future events and indicate a cohesive context in which the action takes place. These enacted and embedded speeches and actions are built from traditional, inherited material, from the smallest elements of diction to the grandest themes. The formula is the building block of oral poetry, defined as "a group of words which is regularly employed under the same metrical conditions to express a given essential idea."[20] "Formula" can refer to either phrases of two or three words or whole verses or groups of verses, repeated markers for the audience and an aid to performance for the bard, postulated by some scholars as a defining feature of oral composition.[21] As tools available to the singer, formulas work to express ideas in units of thought; the more relevant

---

[17] West 1973:182; Nagy 1979:7; Morris 1992:35; Snodgrass 1971:421–423; and Sourvinou-Inwood 2005:34.

[18] Nagy 1979:6f. A similar tendency has been observed by van Straten 1995:24f. in the iconography of sacrifice in the Classical period, which frequently presents a universal picture without any features specifically tied to particular festivals or sanctuaries.

[19] Aristotle *Poetics* 1459a30.

[20] Parry 1971:80. Hainsworth 1969:19, 24–25 lists ten possible definitions of "formula"; he defines the necessary conditions in 1993:4–6. Russo 1997:242 details the difficulties in finding one working definition for such a widely functional unit of Homeric poetry.

[21] Ong 1982:23–27; Bakker 1997:24.

an idea is to the poem's themes, the more often it is repeated.[22] These phrases and verses form an arsenal of poetic expressions suitable to different thematic and metrical needs.[23] Through repetition over time, they become fixed in the tradition, expanding from individual phrases or verses to longer blocks of repeated formulas. Thus the poems gradually develop through constant adaptation of and innovation upon episodic, traditional material.[24] The singer could insert the inherited material as best suited the representation of the central action, which allows the narrative to develop over centuries of performance.

Of Parry's many important contributions to Homeric studies, the most important is his demonstration of the economy of the formula: the singer has at his disposal only one formula with a given meaning at a given space in the verse.[25] The formula, used by the singer as a building block for composition-in-performance through a mental process that has been likened by Michael Nagler to a pre-verbal *Gestalt,* is newly expressed in every application of the "ready-made phrase." This allows for traditional material to be innovative and particular to context: each recurrence of a formula is the result of spontaneous generation.[26] Therefore, there is no contrast between scenes described with similar or identical vocabulary and those without parallel in the poems: they are part of the same process of poetry-in-performance. Over the course of the twentieth century, the formula has been reexamined and is now recognized as a consequence of certain recurrent contexts for which a given expression is required. If an expression becomes very useful, it can become standardized and applied to similar but not necessarily identical situations through a process of "routinization." The essential ideas are composed of a nuclear word and peripheral elements, the former fulfilling semantic needs while the latter completes the verse. This process is most easily recognized in the 'A killed

---

[22] Hainsworth's "cola" (1993); this theory of "cola" is questioned by Nagy 1990a; cf. Ong 1982: 39–41.

[23] Bakker and Fabbricotti 1991: "The formula is a ready-made phrase which accommodates what the poet wants to say to the metrical space available" (63). Bakker 1997:24 describes the formula as "stylized everyday speech."

[24] Heubeck 1974:149; Nagy 1996a:113–146. Jones 1992:78 with examples 79–81, describes three different types of innovation: (1) *de novo*; (2) application of 'typical' epic material to new contexts; (3) adaptation of traditional stories from other contexts to new or different epics.

[25] Parry 1971:64, 195. This theory has been re-evaluated and re-interpreted often, the results of which are summarized by Russo 1997.

[26] Nagler 1974:11–14, 271; he dismisses the notorious argument of the misapplied formula (35–36) with his theory of the verbal *Gestalt,* which is "pregnant with meaning" beyond the factual simplicities of a passage such as *Odyssey* ix 473–491; cf. Nagy 1990b:23. Edwards 1997:264–277, Bakker 1988:189 and Lowenstam 1993 are good discussions of the application of formulas in the poems.

B' verses, where the changing names determine the choice of verb, which is metrically reactive.[27] The meter is not the organizing principle of a formula; it is a precondition for an expression appropriate to a context. This context, owing to its meaningful significance to the story, is repeated often enough to become familiar through the "communicative economy" created in a performance arena.[28] Parts of formulaic verses may be used elsewhere as formulas on their own, but they will carry the associations of the entire verse formula for an audience. These associations create an "aura of meaning which has been put there by all the contexts in which [the formula] has occurred in the past."[29]

Formulaic phrases and verses are the fundamental units of composition, used with varying frequency in proportion to the importance of the ideas they express. "Themes" are groups of ideas regularly used to describe actions.[30] Themes can express specific actions on the micro-level of repetition, such as arming before battle, or macro-level structural mechanisms, such as wrath and retribution.[31] Composition by theme is characterized by the tendency to express repeatedly recurrent actions, termed "type scenes," in a recognizable, fixed order with similar vocabulary. The "type scene," first studied in depth by Walter Arend, is commonly considered to be an action repeated at least twice with the same order of events, variable in length but not in structure.[32] The singer of the story draws from an immense inherited tradition of vocabulary and recurring scenes suited to his description of the central action, which becomes both recognizably traditional and meaningful within the specific context.

Sacrificial ritual in the *Iliad* is a repeated thematic action, a type scene, described in traditional, formulaic language in a fixed pattern. It has often been

---

[27]   Bakker 1997:186. Visser 1988; Russo 1997:254–256; Bakker and Fabbricotti 1991.

[28]   Foley's terminology (1997:172). The reciprocal relationship between meter and formula has been demonstrated by Lord 1960:35–36; O'Nolan 1969:14, 17; Whallon 1969; Nagy 1974:140–149; 1990a:37; 1990b:18–35, esp. 29–32; Austin 1975:11–80; Tsagarakis 1982:34–39; Lowenstam 1993:13–57; et al. Cantilena 1982:82–89 thinks that the epics are 54 percent formulaic.

[29]   Lord 1960:148.

[30]   Lord 1960:68, 146–147. "Theme" and "motif" are used interchangeably by Lord 1960:68, Segal 1971:1, Gunn 1971, Nagler 1974:64, and Edwards 1975. Stanley 1993:n97 distinguishes between "universal themes", such as "quarrel," and "subsidiary motifs," of which sacrifice is one.

[31]   Lord 1960:130; Lowenstam 1993:2.

[32]   Arend 1933. The list of type scenes occurring in Homer includes arrival scenes, visits, embassies, sacrifice, dreams, boat and wagon journeys, arming and dressing, sleep, meetings, oaths, and baths. His work on repetition is developed in the study of battle scenes by Fenik 1968; cf. the discussions of Edwards 1980, 1987:72–74, 1997. Taplin 1992:10 has suggested the concepts of "scene shapes" and "sequences" to replace the difficult "type scene."

discussed in the context of the considerable modern dialogue on the creation, use, and significance of repetition in Homer.[33] Although repetition in Homer is not as emphatically significant as a repeated quotation or reminiscence might be in a modern literary text, the repetition of actions in a recognizably similar form creates a pattern that links scenes together in relation to the central poetic aims of the work.[34] Composition by theme during the performance of material necessitates some repetition, which becomes part of the process of interpretation and representation of traditional material. Repetition helps to create and relay themes to the audience, yet it remains proportional to the importance of the action; recurrence is motivated by poetic needs.[35] Because "a significant detail, a pattern of events, or a series of narrative details might be presented within a work to present a comparison or contrast with the preceding material or foreshadow an upcoming event,"[36] the repeated scene must be considered as both individually significant in its immediate context and as part of a larger pattern running throughout the work. In a discussion of the different models for audience participation and reception, Ruth Scodel writes:

> The implied audience of Homeric epic has heard epic before. A poet could expect that almost all adults would know one of the things we mean when we speak of 'the tradition'—the generic conventions of language and style. They would all know the meter and could understand the particular dialect, which was widely diffused and largely, though not completely, standardized. Many formulae would surely be familiar to everyone, and many members of the audience would understand their significance beyond the denotative meaning. Listeners would be comfortable with those epithets so fossilized that their denotative meaning was lost. They would also know the narrative conventions—the most important type scenes, for example—so that everybody who had any interpretative skill would be

---

[33] Fenik 1968:229 describes the lack of a sound method of distinguishing between type scenes, patterns, and variations therein. Lowenstam 1993 and Kahane 1994 are two very important full-length studies of the poetics of repetition. Shive 1987 draws attention to the importance of the lack of repetition where it might be expected.

[34] Lord 1960:148; Hainsworth 1969:30. Austin 1975:19–20, Ong 1982:57–68, Lynn-George 1988:61, Lowenstam 1993:2, and Nagy 1996a discuss the problems of applying literary aesthetics to orally derived texts. Snodgrass 1974:170 may be representative of the contrasting analytical approach: "We can neither assume that the elements in a given passage are deliberately designed to be consistent, nor transfer our deductions from that passage to others."

[35] Bakker 1997:119.

[36] Lowenstam 1993:9; see also Austin 1975:115.

able to estimate the importance of a feast, a journey, or an arrival by comparing its level to the level of elaboration of other sequences in the performance.[37]

Variations on themes occurred within a context of numerous performances, contextualized in regard to the individual's experience with the entire tradition.[38] Lord explains that the theme exists "at one and the same time in and for itself and for the whole song."[39] Themes may have a number of regularly occurring details that identify a scene, but these details may take on "specific coloring" singular to their context.[40] The process of thematic composition-in-performance limits the size and range of this inherited material, highlighting the importance of such recurrent scenes. The reception of such repetition would have been dependent on the frequency of the audience's exposure to these songs. Comparative studies of other cultures in which oral poetry is performed indicate that audiences have a preexisting repertoire of shared knowledge on both the level of theme and diction. Frequent exposure to oral performance allows an audience to develop an advanced perception of traditional material through individual presentations, both from within the poem, in the form of variations of repeated actions or phraseology, and from outside the poem, based on the degree to which the song differs from or adapts known themes and patterns.[41]

The repetition of significant actions is crucial to the performance context and better enables the audience to listen and understand and the singer to recall and create. Scenes refer back and forth to each other to amplify the effect of variation.[42] Although it is difficult to know *exactly* how much detail,

---

[37] Scodel 2002:12–13; cf. Pucci's discussion of possible audience responses to repetition (1998: 97–112).

[38] Foley's principle of traditional referentiality (1991:6–8). Foley 2002: "Just as the audience comes to expect an overall sequence of events, so each event itself tends towards a traditional, idiomatic, and therefore expectable shape" (13). The *tradition* of Greek epic poetry comprises the process of transmission among singers, the generic conventions of meter and formula, and, most importantly, the themes and artistic conventions of presentation (Scodel 2002:3).

[39] Lord 1960:94.

[40] Foley 1997:169.

[41] Martin 1993:227–228 describes the traditional audience of oral poetry as having a memory like a "CD-ROM." This comparison is questioned by Scodel 2002:5–11, who raises the issue of reception of variations on well-known stories, for example the allusion to the death of Akhilleus at the hands of Apollo at *Iliad* XXII 358–360. She concludes that this extra knowledge provides "narrative pleasure" and "narrative profit" (5). For a discussion of the competent audience, see Pucci 1987 and Ahl and Roisman 1996:21–22. Ford 1992:90–130 describes the circuitous engagement of representations of singing in the poems and the oral tradition.

[42] So Thornton 1984:100, 103.

11

expansion, or repetition a scene would need in order for it to become familiar to the audience, large blocks of repeated material would certainly have been recognizable throughout the poem.[43] These large blocks of repeated material, type scenes, must not be treated as isolated from the central action or as less significant by virtue of their familiar, repetitive content. Rather, they should serve as clear markers of the contextual relevance of the actions, such as animal sacrifice, that they describe, providing identifiable additions, variations, and omissions by which it is possible to understand the progress of the central action. Type scenes have enough in common to be identifiable, but no two are exactly identical.[44]

The small variations in typical representations depend on the contextual needs of the narrative and are the key to the essential meaning of the recurrent idea. For instance, there are four arming scenes in the poem, each signaled with the same three verses near the beginning of the scene. These scenes, much smaller in number than sacrifice scenes, have been analyzed in depth by James Armstrong as an example of the importance of variable details within individual type scenes as well as within the larger narrative.[45] In all of the arming passages except that of Akhilleus, the formulaic leitmotif is followed by a descriptive verse particular to the individual hero. For example, Paris dons a breastplate in the standard way (*Iliad* III 332), and the breastplate is then described as belonging to his brother, Lukaon (*Iliad* III 333), a detail specific to Paris' arming scene. The significance of such variation is perhaps best evidenced in Patroklos' omission of Akhilleus' spear, where the variables point both to his and Akhilleus' impending doom. Patroklos picks up two spears that fit his grip (*Iliad* XVI 139), described with a verse that is a combination of Paris and Agamemnon's spear-grasping (*Iliad* III 338 and XI 43). This

---

[43] Lord 1960:65–66. Hainsworth 1993:19 proposes that repetitions of three or more verses would have been familiar; cf. Nagler 1974:200. Definition and comparison of typical verses in the modern reception of the poems have been much debated: Edwards 1987:71 sees every verse in *Iliad* I as part of a "typical" action, Lord 1960:148 finds *Iliad* I 1–15 to be 90 percent formulaic, while Hainsworth 1993, examining the formulas in IX 434f., concludes that a significant portion of the epic is composed of *hapax legomena* and unique grammatical forms; cf. Tsagarakis 1982:80–86. Edwards 1997:270–271 summarizes the discussion.

[44] Parry 1971:380 notes the tendency toward variation. See also Chantraine 1932:127, Arend 1933:8f., and Fenik 1968:229f.

[45] Armstrong 1958:342, although he is careful to emphasize that it is not identical verses but the identical structure of all arming scenes that makes them "typical" (344). Arming scenes: *Iliad* III 328–338; XI 15–46; XVI 130–144; and XIX 364–391. Each scene has the exact repetition of two verses: *Iliad* III 330–332 = XI 17–19 = XVI 131–133 = XIX 369–371. On arming, see also Lord 1960:90f. Arming and sacrifice are often cited together as the best examples of type scenes; cf. Hainsworth 1993:21.

traditional verse is followed by the unique detail that Patroklos will not take the spear because Akhilleus is the only man who can lift it (*Iliad* XVI 140–144). Armstrong persuasively argues that the inclusion of the unique detail after a series of recognizably repetitive verses emphasizes the significance of the spear as a signal of Patroklos' inability to perform as a substitute Akhilleus, incorporating the small-scale detail of armor carried into battle into the large-scale narrative movement of the poem, which at this stage is building up to the death of Patroklos: "Working within the fixed limitations of his formula without embellishment for eight lines, Homer ... heightens the effect of the reversal which comes at the end ... The meaning of this reversal can only be ... to lift the range of our perspective and relate the arming of Patroklos with the main stream of the poem."[46]

These conclusions about the meaning of variations in typical patterns are essential when considering sacrifice scenes, which have been regarded by Arend to be the most typical of all recurrent scenes, owing to the fixity and standardization of cult ritual.[47] Arend is intent upon an "ideal schema," of which sacrificial scenes are all variations because of their expansion or contraction of formulaic material, most notably *Iliad* I 440–470 and II 402–431. He suggests that the poet's motivation for including these "filler scenes" is to expand the time for important events, but does not fully explore the relationship between individual ritual details and the contexts in which they occur.[48] Arend identifies a pattern of sacrifice in Homer on the basis of repeated verses in seven scenes in the *Iliad* and *Odyssey*, which form for him the clearest examples of standardized verse repetition creating a type scene, but this emphasis on similarity between sacrifice scenes obscures the important differences which illuminate the meaning of these procedures within the poems.[49] The difficulty in studying the sacrifice scenes is that, while they can feature large

---

[46] Armstrong 1958:346–347.

[47] Arend 1933:64; see also Parry's 1936 review. Cf. Edwards 1987: "The sacrifice scene is the most complex (not, of course, the most expanded), no doubt because it describes the actions of a major religious ritual" (71). An interesting parallel between features of ritual language and oral poetry is drawn by Tambiah 1979:131–142, followed by Kitts 2005:148–149. Both ritual language and oral poetry can be characterized by redundancy, parallelism, and formulas.

[48] For instance, he concludes that *Iliad* II 402–431 is included as preparation for battle (1933:65). On the basis of the use of formulaic material, he maintains that *Iliad* I 440–470 is dependent on the sacrifice in *Iliad* II. Seaford 1994:43 agrees to a large extent with Arend's conclusions: sacrificial details are always related in the same order; they often open or conclude a dangerous activity.

[49] Arend's sacrifice scenes: *Iliad* I 447; II 410; VII 314; XXIV 621; *Odyssey* iii 419; xii 353; and xiv 419. As I will show, not all of these scenes in the *Iliad* are depictions of animal sacrifice: see below page 42f.

sections of formulaic material, they do not share many ritual features. The apparent consistency, which forms the focus of Arend's study, arises from the repetition, in the two most detailed sacrifices in the *Iliad*, of large blocks of formulaic verses in the first two *books* of the poem:

αὐτὰρ ἐπεί ῥ' εὔξαντο καὶ οὐλοχύτας προβάλοντο,
αὐέρυσαν μὲν πρῶτα καὶ ἔσφαξαν καὶ ἔδειραν,
μηρούς τ' ἐξέταμον κατά τε κνίσῃ ἐκάλυψαν
δίπτυχα ποιήσαντες, ἐπ' αὐτῶν δ' ὠμοθέτησαν·

(Iliad I 458–461 = II 421–424)

Once the men had prayed and flung the barley,
first they lifted back the heads of the victims, slit their throats,
    and skinned them,
and carved out the thigh bones and wrapped them in a double
    layer of fat,
and topped them with strips of raw flesh.

αὐτὰρ ἐπεὶ κατὰ μῆρε κάη καὶ σπλάγχνα πάσαντο,
μίστυλλόν τ' ἄρα τἆλλα καὶ ἀμφ' ὀβελοῖσιν ἔπειραν,
ὤπτησάν τε περιφραδέως, ἐρύσαντό τε πάντα.
αὐτὰρ ἐπεὶ παύσαντο πόνου τετύκοντό τε δαῖτα
δαίνυντ', οὐδέ τι θυμὸς ἐδεύετο δαιτὸς ἐΐσης.

(Iliad I 464–468 = II 427–431)

Once the thigh bones were burned and they tasted the *splankhna*,
they cut the rest into pieces, pierced them with spits,
roasted them to a turn and pulled them off the spits.
The work done, the feast laid out, they ate well
and no man's hunger lacked an appropriate share of the feast.

The innovative use of traditional material, repeated language, and story patterns through extension, by means of a combination of repetition and variation, is the goal of oral poetry. Repeated formulas do not act as restrictive structures within the poems; they rather reflect the importance of an action: the more often a particular goal is desired, the more regularized the expression of that action will become, giving the poems a degree of repetition.[50] The quick repetition of a large amount of material from Book I in Book II would have signaled the importance of sacrifice within the poem

---

[50] Bakker 1997:157.

to the audience, but the different contexts in which these sacrifices occur is signaled by two dissimilar verses that interrupt the large block of repetition:

καῖε δ' ἐπὶ σχίζῃς ὁ γέρων, ἐπὶ δ' αἴθοπα οἶνον
λεῖβε· νέοι δὲ παρ' αὐτὸν ἔχον πεμπώβολα χερσίν.

(*Iliad* I 462–463)

And the old man burned these over dried, split wood and over
them poured out glistening wine
while young men at his side held five-pronged forks.

καὶ τὰ μὲν ἄρ σχίζῃσιν ἀφύλλοισιν κατέκαιον,
σπλάγχνα δ' ἄρ' ἀμπείραντες ὑπείρεχον Ἡφαίστοιο.

(*Iliad* II 425–426)

And they burned these on a cleft stick, peeled and dry,
spitted the *splankhna*, and held them over Hephaistos' flames.

These scenes demonstrate the way in which variations in the typical pattern create meaning specific to the context. In *Iliad* I, Khruses performs a sacrifice at the behest of Agamemnon's ambassador, Odysseus, and is helped by young men; the group participation responds to the large-scale damage inflicted upon the Akhaian army by Apollo's plague, but Khruses is carefully differentiated from the Akhaian youths who assist him. As will be discussed at length in Chapter Three, Agamemnon leads a sacrifice for the councilors in *Iliad* II, who together roast the meat and the *splankhna*, the internal organs of the victims; the emphasis on the intimate ceremony, in contrast to the anonymous group of young men attending Khruses, is heightened with the expanded description of the roasted *splankhna*.

The singer can use whole verses or parts of them to create new meanings, and, although sacrificial ritual contexts dictate a high degree of similarity, as noted by Arend, sacrificial procedures are widely variable. These variations of details in sacrificial scenes frustrate Jean Stallings's attempt to demonstrate the aesthetics of the formula in scenes of eaten sacrifice, and lead Arend to define the Homeric pattern of sacrifice with a tabulation of twenty-one or more typical details, most of which only occur once in Homer.[51] For instance, barley grains are scattered as part of the preparation of the sacrifice only in

---

[51] Stallings 1984:238. She is aware of other organizational principles such as context, but rejects them in favor of an analysis according to length of the scenes. Arend 1933:64–70 lists 21 different elements of sacrifice, an approach critically reexamined by Kirk 1981, but encouraged by Edwards 1987:71, who wants this list to be expanded.

Khruses' sacrifice in *Iliad* I and Agamemnon's sacrifice in *Iliad* II. The half-verse describing the picking up of the grains is identical, as is a subsequent verse describing the scattering of the grains, though in *Iliad* I they wash their hands and scatter barley, while in *Iliad* II they stand around the ox:

χερνίψαντο δ' ἔπειτα καὶ οὐλοχύτας ἀνέλοντο.

(*Iliad* I 449)

Then they rinsed their hands and took up barley.

βοῦν δὲ περιστήσαντο καὶ οὐλοχύτας ἀνέλοντο.

(*Iliad* II 410)

They stood in a ring around the ox and took up barley.

αὐτὰρ ἐπεί ῥ'εὔξαντο καὶ οὐλοχύτας προβάλοντο...

(*Iliad* I 458 = II 421)

Once the men had prayed and flung the barley...

Similar to the verses describing the *splankhna* and libations in these scenes, hand washing is replaced with the stance of the group in *Iliad* II to shift the emphasis from purification—important because the sacrifice in the *Iliad* I is performed to relieve the plague—to more intimate social bonding—important for Agamemnon and the councilors. Changes to the ritual procedure, even on the smallest level, are made to adapt the material to the individual context as well as to alter the meaning of the scene. Shared formulas are found almost entirely in and immediately following the kill sections of sacrifices, and some scholars have assumed that the missing pre-kill details are omitted from the shorter scenes for the sake of brevity.[52] If we were to approach Homeric descriptions of sacrifice as typical actions with a fixed structure and traditional phrases, only a handful of sacrificial scenes would fall into this category, as there is no consistently used terminology for sacrifice that would link all of these scenes together. For example, most of the repeated verses that link Khruses' sacrifice in *Iliad* I to Agamemnon's sacrifice in *Iliad* II are not found in other scenes of animal sacrifice in Homer, and even these two sacrifices have very different occasions and goals. Khruses sacrifices a hecatomb to alleviate the plague and propitiate Apollo, while Agamemnon sacrifices one ox to Zeus

---

[52] First proposed by Arend 1933, followed by Stallings 1984 and, to some extent, Sherratt 2004.

in hopes for success in the forthcoming battle. From the standpoint of ritual detail, these sacrifices have significant differences. The degree of repetition has been overestimated, as has the influence of "fixed" ritual.

A very similar block of verses describes the roasting and spitting of meat for the feast between Priam and Akhilleus in *Iliad* XXIV, a scene with a very different thematic meaning for the audience than those previously cited, another example of the ways in which repeated material is adapted to each context in which it occurs. The repetition of blocks of verses reminds the audience of previous sacrifice scenes, but the variations signaled by comparison with the other contexts in which these repeated verses occur create a very different impression. In every instance, significant changes have been made to suit the individual context:[53]

"ἀλλ᾽ ἄγε δὴ καὶ νῶϊ μεδώμεθα, δῖε γεραιέ,
σίτου· ἔπειτά κεν αὖτε φίλον παῖδα κλαίοισθα
Ἴλιον εἰσαγαγών· πολυδάκρυτος δέ τοι ἔσται."
ἦ καὶ ἀναΐξας ὄϊν ἄργυφον ὠκὺς Ἀχιλλεὺς
σφάξ᾽· ἕταροι δ᾽ ἔδερόν τε καὶ ἄμφεπον εὖ κατὰ κόσμον.
μίστυλλόν τ᾽ ἄρ᾽ ἐπισταμένως πεῖράν τ᾽ ὀβελοῖσιν,
ὤπτησάν τε περιφραδέως, ἐρύσαντό τε πάντα.
Αὐτομέδων δ᾽ ἄρα σῖτον ἑλὼν ἐπένειμε τραπέζῃ
καλοῖς ἐν κανέοισιν· ἀτὰρ κρέα νεῖμεν Ἀχιλλεύς.
οἳ δ᾽ ἐπ᾽ ὀνείαθ᾽ ἑτοῖμα προκείμενα χεῖρας ἴαλλον.
αὐτὰρ ἐπεὶ πόσιος καὶ ἐδητύος ἐξ ἔρον ἕντο ...

(*Iliad* XXIV 619–628)

"So come—we too, old king, must think of food.
Later you can mourn your beloved son once more
taking him to Troy, and you'll weep many tears."
Having spoken, swift Akhilleus sprang to his feet and slaughtered
  a white sheep
and comrades skinned the carcass and dressed the quarters well.
Expertly they cut the meat into pieces, pierced them with spits,
roasted them to a turn and pulled them off the spits.
Automedon brought the bread, set it out on the board
in ample wicker baskets. Akhilleus served the meat.
They reached out for the good things that lay at hand
and when they had put aside desire for food and drink ...

---

[53] Cf. *Odyssey* iii 457–463 and xii 359–361.

Although the verses describing the treatment of the carcass are almost identical to those in *Iliad* I and II, and the same verb describes the slaughter in all three scenes (σφάζειν), this scene exclusively emphasizes the preparations for eating. The sacrificial ritual details, such as barley grains and prayer, which both sacrifice scenes in *Iliad* I and II share, are lacking. Though sacrifice may not be implied in every use of the verb σφάζειν, the audience's attention may be directed to the differences as much as to the similarities of the verb's usage, generating gradations of signification aptly expressed by Lord's phrase "aura of meaning."[54] The repetition of verses describing the skewering of meat recalls very important sacrifices in *Iliad* I and II, but as the audience is reminded of these scenes, they are made to notice the manifest difference in the current situation caused by the substitution of two crucial verses (625–626):

> Αὐτομέδων δ' ἄρα σῖτον ἑλὼν ἐπένειμε τραπέζῃ
> καλοῖς ἐν κανέοισιν· ἀτὰρ κρέα νεῖμεν Ἀχιλλεύς.

> Automedon brought the bread, set it out on the board
> in ample wicker baskets. Akhilleus served the meat.

These verses interrupt the pattern, which is then resumed with familiar verses describing the conclusion of the meal. Whereas the variations in ritual details between *Iliad* I and II emphasize different occasions for sacrifice, those ritual details (libations, roasting *splankhna*) have been supplanted in *Iliad* XXIV with Automedon and Akhilleus' preparation of food; nourishment is now given prominence. The emphasis shifts to Akhilleus' renouncement of his fast, which concludes the representation of his isolation and semi-divine status by his abstinence from food and sacrifice, as will be discussed in Chapter Four. We will return to the meal shared by Akhilleus and Priam in a discussion of the distinction between sacrifice and eating below.

In order to classify sacrifice scenes in the *Iliad*, which do not fit the prominent theoretical models for the context of Greek sacrifice, a general overview of modern interpretations of ancient Greek animal sacrifice must be established. We must then examine the ritual content of representations of sacrifice in the *Iliad* and create a working definition for 'sacrifice scenes'.

1.2 The Unique Case of Homeric Sacrifice

Having outlined the major approaches to the Homeric texts, as well as the way in which sacrifice scenes are representative of the incorporation of 'type

---

[54] See above page 9.

scenes' within the poem, we will now determine how Homeric sacrifices fit into the wider scope of ancient Greek sacrificial practices. Sacrifice, as a ritual action, would have been identifiable to the participating members of a community through a series of symbolic and highly visible activities, varied to match particular contexts. The lengthy and elaborate process of Greek animal sacrifice allows for great variation, as does the polytheistic nature of Greek cult, which accommodates numerous localized, community-specific deities alongside Panhellenic deities. Because they reflect the customs and beliefs of the participants performing the ceremony, the choices of victim, location, and sacrificial procedure are variable, but not optional, as the meticulous records of victims in numerous *leges sacrae* demonstrate.[55] To facilitate the analysis of this symbolic action and its range of variables, the practice of sacrifice is often reconstructed with a model that accommodates the full spectrum of ritual possibilities. Homeric sacrifice scenes are most often discussed as part of these diachronic overviews of sacrificial practice, which are compiled of evidence drawn from literary and artistic sources throughout the Classical period.[56] This approach is partly necessitated by a lack of direct evidence concerning animal sacrifice. Though bolstered by recent archaeological field work and the growing study of inscriptions that regulate specific details of local practices, scant evidence otherwise limits the accessibility of the topic to the perspective of poets and artists, whose bias must be taken into consideration.[57]

[55] For example, the careful specification of a variety of victims in an Athenian cult calendar, IG II² 1358. *Leges sacrae* is the modern terminology for the surviving inscriptions of laws found throughout the Greek world that pertain to cult practices; they are most easily accessible in the collections produced by von Prott and Ziehen 1896–1906, Sokolowski 1955, 1962, 1969 and Lupu 2005. See page 101f. below on the typology of victims in sacrifice.

[56] This is a common approach in handbooks on Greek cult, e.g. Burkert 1983:3–12 and 1985:56–57; cf. Ziehen 1939; Rudhardt 1958; Bremmer 1996; Graf 2002:114–116. Burkert 1983: "Thanks to descriptions in Homer and tragedy, we can reconstruct the course of an ordinary Greek sacrifice to the Olympian gods almost in its entirety" (3); cf. Rudhardt 1958:253. Graf 2002:119, observing that the numerous variations in extant accounts of sacrifice make reconstruction of the ritual difficult, argues that an ideal type of sacrifice should be reconstructed on the basis that an "ideal form, or a grammar of sacrifice must have existed in the heads of the Greeks and Romans." Hermary et al. 2004:65–67 focuses on the longest extant descriptions, including *Iliad* I 447–468 and *Odyssey* iii 382–384, 430–463, with cautionary notes about the inconsistency between ancient accounts of sacrifice.

[57] Numerous osteoarchaeological studies are published annually. A relatively early study is Reese 1989:63–70, who discusses the finds of animal bones in the Athenian *agora*. Isaakidou et al. 2002:86–92 discusses the implications of bones found in the Mycenaean palace at Pylos in relation to the Homeric sacrifice scenes. A recent overview is provided by Hermary et al. 2004, which includes archaeozoologic evidence for sacrifice, along with literature, epigraphy, and art. The limitations of literary representations of sacrifice are well recognized, for instance Sourvinou-Inwood 1997:162. Van Straten 1995 and Peirce 1993 discuss the idealized bias in iconography.

Literary representations of sacrifice, like much of the iconography, are not mirror images of reality; they are the images chosen and shaped by the poet or performer. In order to illuminate the relatively restricted presentation of sacrificial ritual in the *Iliad*, which lacks most of the essential features of large-scale, public sacrifices in the Classical period, I will briefly outline the principal components of the reconstructed Greek sacrificial process and the more prominent scholarship regarding its function and significance. The distinction between Homeric sacrifice and the evidence of the ritual in the Classical period draws attention not only to the relative focus of the Homeric narrator on certain aspects of the ritual, but also to the differing implications of sacrificial terminology, which we will explore fully in Section 1.3. Having established the distinct presentation of sacrifice within the *Iliad*, we will concentrate on its depiction of commensal sacrificial meals as opposed to feasts in Section 1.3.

Greek animal sacrifice is essentially a series of symbolic actions leading up to the violent killing of one or more animals, followed by the practical actions of transforming the sacrifice into a feast or disposing of the carcass, actions that can be divided into the tripartite categories of pre-kill, kill, and post-kill.[58] The pre-kill rites involve highly artificial signs, which mark the ceremony, participants, and victim(s) as extraordinary. Herodotos' description of Scythian sacrifice, in which the animal is dragged forward and killed "without lighting a fire, making a first offering from the victim, or pouring libations," may attest to the significance attached by Greeks to their pre-kill rites.[59] The ceremony begins with a *pompê* 'procession' to the altar, led by the *kanêphoroi* 'basket-carriers', well-born maidens carrying the *kanoun* 'sacrificial basket' and accompanied by music. This celebratory scene is a favorite on vase paintings, in which context it is often used as a universal symbol for the entire ritual, "the defining marker of *thusia*."[60] The most vivid example of this practice is the

---

[58] The organizing principle in van Straten 1995, which he compares to the tripartite division utilized by Rudhardt 1958, who distinguishes the moment of kill, the division of the carcass, and the distribution of meat (290). Mauss 1968:193–307 describes the same stages in the process of sacralization as 'entry', 'culmination', and 'exit'. Cf. 'before the kill' and 'the kill' in Bremmer 1996. Other divisions are possible: Graf 2002 divides the process into the procession, the prayer, and the treatment of the carcass.

[59] Herodotos IV 60: οὔτε πῦρ ἀνακαύσας οὔτε καταρξάμενος οὔτ' ἐπισπείσας·

[60] Peirce 1993, esp. 228, 251. *Thusia* is a common Greek term for sacrifices followed by a commensal meal; see page 25 below. In vase painting, the *pompê* is the most popular stage of the ritual, followed by the roasting of the *splankhna*: Peirce 1993:228; see also van Straten 1995:13–35, Burkert 1983:38, and Hermary et al. 2004:113–116. The honor of serving as a *kanêphoros* seems to have been one of the most important religious duties for girls; cf. Aristophanes *Lysistrata* 638–647. It is interesting to note that the procession plays a prominent role in the decoration of the main

Panathenaic festival in Athens, which centers around an elaborate *pompê*, in which representatives from virtually every social group, including maidens, ephebes, hoplites, and male and female metics, escort the offering of a hecatomb of cattle for the goddess.[61] Once the *pompê* reaches the altar, on top of which a fire is built, the *khernips* 'water basin' and the *kanoun*, containing barley grains and the *'makhaira'* sacrificial knife, are both carried clockwise around the altar. The participants, whose involvement bonds them as members of the group, and the officiant, customarily a household leader, community leader, religious official, or honorand, wash their hands. The animal is sprinkled with water. *Euphêmia* 'ritual silence' is followed by a prayer, and the participants then scatter barley grains. The person performing the sacrifice, the "sacrificer," cuts hairs from the forehead of the animal and throws them into the fire, the first offering from the victim (καταρξάμενος 'beginning').[62] The throat of the animal is slit, perhaps accompanied by a *ololugê* 'female ritual cry', and the blood is collected in a *sphageion* 'bowl'.[63] In such commensal sacrifices, the animal is carved up into different portions, some of which are burned for the god, others given to special participants, especially the religious officials, and the leftover portions distributed for general consumption or even sale.[64] In Classical sources, the priest's portion is substantial and closely regulated. For instance, a mid-fifth-century inscription records the 50 drakhmai, legs, and skins of "public" sacrificial victims awarded to the priestess of Athena Nikê.[65] The god's portion differs slightly in literary accounts, but is always the *mêria* 'thigh bones' and other inedible parts of the animal.[66] While the god's portion

---

building of the "Palace of Nestor," alongside representations of feasting in Room 6, and can be interpreted as evidence for state-sponsored religious processions in the Mycenaean period (Bennet and Davis 1999:115).

[61] No single source describes the Panathenaic procession, which has been reconstructed by scholars from a combination of scenes on the Parthenon frieze and literary sources. Parke 1977:38–50 is a detailed reconstruction; see also Parker 1996:89–92 and Rosivach 1994:70 on the hecatomb.

[62] Very detailed representations of sacrifices can be found in Aristophanes *Peace* 956–1016, Euripides *Elektra* 784–843. A sacrifice to Zeus is described in detail in an inscription from Cos (LSCG 151); the pre-kill actions are generally discussed by Rudhart 1958:259–261; Burkert 1983:5f.; and van Straten 1995.

[63] The *ololugê* is described at *Odyssey* iii 450; Aeschylus *Agamemnon* 595, 1118; *Seven Against Thebes* 269; Herodotos IV 189; on which Burkert 1983:5.

[64] This is a difficult issue because of inconsistencies in epigraphic and literary sources and the vague nature of artistic depictions of this stage of the ritual. Hermary et al. 2004:118–129 details the evidence and the focus on the priest's portion (120), and the sale of sacrificial meat is discussed by Berthiaume 1982; Rosivach 1994; Parker 2005:66n63.

[65] IG I³ 35; Hermary et al. 2004:120; Parker 1996:125–126; Burkert 1985:386n16.

[66] On the differences in Greek literary accounts of the god's portion throughout antiquity, see Burkert 1985:57; van Straten 1995:127; Henrichs 1998:42–43; on the epigraphic evidence, Gill

is burnt, the *splankhna* 'vitals' (the heart, lungs, liver, spleen and kidney) are roasted and then eaten by special participants, a highly significant action emphasizing their bond and special role.[67] The rest of the animal is butchered, burnt on spits, and consumed at a celebratory feast.[68]

The sacrificer and the participants, on whose behalf he acts, perform sacrifice in order to gain divine favor. This is part of an exchange, a process of barter in which men honor the gods so that the gods will respond to their requests. Theophrastos divides the function of sacrifice into three categories, reflecting the different purposes intended for this one action: to thank the gods, to honor them, and to ask them for something.[69] Yet the recognition that the sacrificial meal provides obvious benefits to mortal participants, in contrast to the intangible benefit offered to the gods, also underlies much of ancient discourse concerning sacrifice, from the earliest etiology of the ritual to the theological discussions of late antiquity. The practical benefit of sacrifice as a bonding experience and occasion for benefaction and patronage for the community would have been very clear, whereas its emotional and theological motivations and its value as a gift for the divinities would be much harder to gauge.[70] The origins of sacrifice, as set out in Hesiod's *Theogony*, the earliest extant attempt to explain this custom, reveal the innate contradictions in the act. Prometheus, as he distributes the portions of meat, attempts to deceive Zeus by giving him the thigh bones wrapped in fat.[71] Zeus, undeceived, decrees that henceforth men will feast separately and present the gods with thigh bones. Hesiod's portrayal is concerned with the seeming imbalance

---

1974:125. For instance, in Aristophanes *Peace* 1020–1115 the *mêria* are burned, and cakes, *splankhna*, tongue, and tail are roasted and eaten by the officiant and his helper; incense, cakes, tail, and gall-bladder are offered in Menander *Duskolos* 447–453.

[67] Aristotle *On the Gait of Animals* 665a28 describes the components of *splankhna*; cf. Aristophanes *Acharnians* 738–796.

[68] Van Straten 1995:115–160 provides a good overview of this lengthy process.

[69] Theophrastos *On Piety*, as quoted by Porphyry *On Abstinence* 2.24.1, on which see Obbink 1988: 282–283.

[70] On social bonding, Aristotle, when describing his ideal state, describes *thusiai*, groups that sacrifice together, as a pre-condition for the city, along with families and *phratries* (*Politics* 1280b 36-8). On gifts for the gods, in Plato's *Euthyphro*, Socrates queries the belief that sacrifice is a gift to the gods: "Is it then the case that sacrificing is making a gift to the gods and praying is making a request?" (14c); see Parker 1998b. Knemon complains that meager offerings for the gods at sacrifices prove that people only care about the feast (Menander *Duskolos* 442–455).

[71] Hesiod *Theogony* 507–616, see pages 93–94 below. The seminal discussions of this scene may be found in Meuli 1975:907–1021 and Vernant 1989. Kirk 1974:138 interprets this as a reversal of the typical folk tale motif of the outwitted human offered a tricky choice by gods as well as a unique attempt to account for a real problem: the god's portion of the sacrifice.

between the mortal benefit from this supposed gift to the gods, the consumption of meat, and the divinities' enjoyment of only the smoke and inedible parts. Similar questions about the pleasure afforded to gods by such offerings are posed in Xenophon: Socrates' relatively humble sacrifices are defended against the proposition that gods might prefer larger offerings, an issue also raised by Theophrastos.[72] In Greek inscriptions referring to animal sacrifice, the recurrent emphasis on the priest's portion is remarkable, given the almost total silence on that given to gods.[73] Approximately 800 years after Hesiod, the first-century CE philosopher Dio Chrysostom tries to incorporate divine pleasure into the human feast when he remarks, "What sacrifice is pleasing to the gods without the fellow-banqueters?"[74] In many ways, the social importance and emotional pleasure of the shared feast overwhelm the notion of reciprocity with divinities; the meal is a tangible benefit of the performance, whereas the pleasure the gods may take in the sacrifice and the hoped-for divine favor cannot be as immediately obvious.

Such difficulty in interpreting the significance of the offering to the gods has skewed some modern discussions on sacrifice toward the ritual actions, irrespective of the sacrificers' motives. Anthropological studies of the ritual practices in many different cultures have found that faith and piety often seem overshadowed by the emphasis in different sacrificial rituals on the kill and the social importance of the shared meal. In reference to the custom of sacrifice among the Nuer tribe and in Bantu, Africa, the anthropologist J. H. M. Beattie observes that, aside from the necessary recognition of higher powers behind the act of sacrifice, the notion of giving gifts to the higher powers can be secondary or even expendable.[75] The work of Emile Durkheim has been particularly influential in changing modern understanding of rituals, showing

---

[72] Xenophon *Memorabilia* 1.3.3. Theophrastos concludes that the gods are more pleased by the *ethos* of the sacrificer than the cost of the victim, presumably an attempt to account for the meager victims offered by most people (*On Piety* f. 7.52–54 and f. 8.8–10 Pötscher 1964).

[73] For example, Hermary et al. 2004:118–125, although not a comprehensive database, found only seven descriptions of the gods' portion in texts and inscriptions, compared to 28 sources for gifts to priests and other participants.

[74] Dio Chrysostom *Oration* 3.97. Burkert 1985:57 notes that there are countless jokes in comedy about "food for the gods and men."

[75] Beattie 1980:31. However, in these African rituals the idea of gift-giving is supplanted by an emphasis on change for the better (riddance of pollution, evil, or sin), which is not apparent as such in Greek sacrifice. In a study on sacrifice as a cultural institution, Bourdillon 1980:6 concludes: "On the relationship between the effects of ritual and what participants expect to achieve through them, anthropologists have on the whole retained an embarrassed silence." Cautions about overstating the social importance of the meal have been raised by Bremmer 1996:268, 281; Parker 1998b.

how they identify social groups and even make participants aware of their own collective experience.[76] Building on this premise, sacrificial ritual has evoked two major interpretations, both focusing on the violent slaughter of the animal at the center of the act and the ways in which the ritual addresses the death of the animal. Jean-Pierre Vernant and the so-called "Paris School" have approached sacrifice as a ritual expression of man's place between gods and beasts.[77] Vernant questions the interpretation of Henri Hubert and Marcel Mauss, who propose that sacrifice represents a process of consecration that functions as a ritualized gift-offering: the pre-kill rites, culminating in the slaughter of the animal by the sacrificer, who acts as intermediary, achieve sacralization, while the post-kill process represents a return to the normal, de-sacralized world.[78] In this scenario, the crucial moment is the consecration of the victim, which, in death, moves from a profane to a sacred state, symbolic of the officiant and/or the group.[79]

For the Paris School, the act of killing is necessitated by man's need to eat, and their innovative work on the intersection between myth, ritual, and culture places the emphasis in studies of Greek sacrifice on the social significance of the meal. For these scholars, the ritual must be understood in its cultural context, as part of a social system, which for Greek sacrifice can be best understood through Hesiod's etiology of sacrifice and its focus on the gap between mortal and immortal.[80] The way in which sacrifice attempts to bridge this gap is a recurring theme in the *Iliad*, which we will discuss fully in Chapter Three. Animal sacrifice reinforces man's place in the cosmic order, an interme

---

[76] Durkheim 1912, reprinted in 2001:46f. On Durkheim's contribution to the study of Greek sacrifice, see Burkert 1983:24; cf. Bremmer 1998 and Versnel 1993:26. Morris 1992 gives a survey of the history of sacrificial theory, as does Beattie 1980 (though not specifically Greek sacrifice).

[77] Vernant 1991: "In a ritual that seeks to join the mortal with the immortal it consecrates the unattainable distance that henceforth separates them. Through an alimentary code it seats man in his proper place, between beasts and gods..." (297). The "Paris School" refers to the collective contribution of scholars working with Vernant at the Centre pour Recherches Comparées sur les Sociétés Anciennes in Paris, whose treatments of sacrifice have been collected in Detienne and Vernant 1989.

[78] Hubert and Mauss 1964; Mauss 1968:193–307.

[79] Mauss 1968:193–307; Hubert and Mauss present a comparative study partly based on Indic and Biblical accounts of sacrifice. Their approach has been criticized as inapplicable to ancient Greece by Rudhardt 1958:295–296; see also Vernant 1991:292; Kirk 1981:42; Burkert 1981:121; and Graf 2002:122. Seaford 1994:44–45 and García López 1970 refute this approach specifically in regard to Homeric accounts of sacrifice, which neither seem to recognize any such transformation on the part of the sacrificer, nor are concerned with the pre-kill and post-kill accounts as establishing sacred boundaries. Finley 1977:23, 64 reinterprets their theory of ritualized gift-giving as a social principle in his study of Homeric society.

[80] Hesiod *Theogony* 535–560; page 93f. below.

diate stage between animals and gods, primarily signified by agriculture and the consumption of cooked food.[81] One ancient term for sacrifice, *thusia*, has been defined as "alimentary blood sacrifice" on the premise that the "absolute coincidence of meat eating and sacrificial practice" is the "first characteristic that justifies the central place of the blood sacrifice in Greek social and religious thought."[82] This is further established by the use of domesticated animals as sacrificial victims, which to some scholars negates the possible connection between sacrifice and hunting prominent in other structuralist interpretations.[83] In the model of the Paris School, the pre-kill rites symbolize the distance between sacrifice and murder, between sacrificer and hunter: according to Vernant, "[sacrifice] admits that we must slaughter animals to eat, yet at the same time it aims to banish acts of murder and savagery from what is human."[84] Considering this distance, Richard Martin interprets the sacrifice of Helios' cattle in the *Odyssey* as demonstrative of the "realistic basis for sacrifice: it is the literal means of salvation for humans, by providing meat in time of starvation."[85]

Drawing on a similar theory regarding the centrality of the slaughter, a more psychological interpretation has been elaborated by Walter Burkert, who raises questions about the ways in which the violent butchering of the animal elevate the importance of sacrifice in maintaining social structures. Burkert, drawing on the work of anthropologist Karl Meuli and animal psychologist Konrad Lorenz, extensively explores the emotional drive to kill an animal and the act's emotional impact as forms of tension control within groups or as outlets for innate aggression. Meuli believes that animal sacrifice descended from hunting rites in primitive cultures, particularly in Siberia, where animal bones received special treatment.[86] Such special treatment, generally of the thigh bones, preserves the animal from complete destruction so that the hunters may be confident of future successes. For Meuli, the ritual process leading up to the sacrifice, attested in elaborate descriptions such as Nestor's sacrifice (*Odyssey* iii 418–472), is an attempt to mask and atone for the violent

---

[81] Vernant 1989:74; questioned by Bremmer 1996:277–278.

[82] Detienne 1989:3. The noun *thusia* is not used in Homer; see below page 49. Theoretical criteria for the comprehension of ritual are given by Detienne 1989:4–5 and Vernant 1991:291.

[83] So Detienne 1989:5; Vernant 1991:298.

[84] Vernant 1991:301; cf. Detienne 1989:9 and Durand 1989:87–118.

[85] *Odyssey* xii 353–365; Martin 1983:38.

[86] Meuli 1946, summarized and interpreted by Burkert 1979:50f. and 1983:13–21; see esp. 13n1–5 on the research contributing to the discussion of hunting societies. More recently, Hamerton-Kelly 1987. Bremmer 1996:273–275 positively incorporates Meuli's work into a revision of sacrificial theory.

act of slaughter. The pre-kill actions are performed like an *Unschuldskomödie* 'comedy of innocence', an expression of the guilty conscience of the participants and an effort to reconstitute the animal symbolically.[87]

Burkert expands Meuli's findings with an emphasis on the role of sacrifice, via the shared experience of slaughter, in the creation and maintenance of communities: "Community is defined by participation in the bloody work of men.... The power to kill and respect for life illuminate each other."[88] Just as the purpose of hunting is to eat, "*Töten zum Essen*," so the same is true for sacrifice.[89] As in the interpretations of Hubert and Mauss, the sacrificial killing allows the participants to experience the "sacred," to form a relationship with the divine provided through slaughter, but for Burkert, animal sacrifice also helps to bring natural aggression under control.[90] Aggression can be alleviated through the violence of sacrifice, particularly when it is triggered by situations of anxiety. Observations by cultural anthropologists of the widespread tendency for ritual action in response to crisis support this theory. Bronislaw Malinowski describes the psychological security provided by ritual actions in dangerous situations, a theory similar to that proposed by Victor Turner concerning Ndembu sacrifices, which are encouraged by the cognizance of social antagonism.[91] Of particular importance for the present study is Burkert's emphasis on the visibility of the performance of sacrifice and the distinctive roles played by the participants according to their status in the community. The sacrificer, for example the *arkhōn basileus* in Classical Athens, demonstrates his authority, both economic and social, through the performance of certain sacrifices. While the onerous task of dismembering the animal is left to slaves, the responsibility for the distribution of the meat indicates high social rank, as does the reception of choice bits of meat. Burkert summarizes: "The sacrificial community is thus a model of society as a whole, divided according to occupation and rank. Hence, the hierarchies manifested in the ceremony are given great social importance and are taken very seriously."[92] We will return to

---

[87] Meuli 1946:224–252; Burkert 1985:58.

[88] Burkert 1983:20–21.

[89] Burkert 1976:172.

[90] Burkert 1976:172; 1983: "The worshipper experiences the god most powerfully not just in pious conduct or in prayer, song, or dance, but in the deadly blow of the axe, the gush of blood and burning of thigh-pieces" (2).

[91] Malinowski 1948; Turner 1967:196, 208–209; see Beattie 1980. Equally important in the development of the field of modern social anthropology is the work of Alfred Radcliffe-Brown, who postulates that "the ceremonial customs of a society are a means by which the sentiments in question are given collective expression on the appropriate occasion" (1933:234).

[92] Burkert 1983:37. The role of the *arkhōn basileus* is described in Aristotle *The Constitution of the Athenians* 3.3, 47.4, 57.1, Demosthenes 59.74–77.

the importance of the *Opferherr* and the way in which sacrificial ritual provides a visible demonstration of social hierarchy in the discussion of Agamemnon and Akhilleus in Chapters Three and Four.

For Meuli and Burkert, the experience of the "sacred" through the act of killing is the focus of the ancient Greek experience of sacrifice rather than the desire for reciprocal relations with divinities.[93] Emphasis on the moment of death plays a central role in other interpretations of sacrifice as well: René Girard expresses a similar notion that, through a feeling of exhilaration subsequent to a heightened awareness of life and death, sacrifice affects a transition from the human sphere to the divine.[94] Van Straten's lucid terminology of pre-kill, kill, and post-kill reflects this modern emphasis on the kill as the central action. Vernant, in his theoretical model for sacrifice, has also written of "a central dramatic moment in the sacrificial scenario: the slaying of the animal."[95] For the Paris School as well as for Burkert, the centrality of the kill explains much of Greek sacrificial procedure. For Vernant, the symbolic pre-kill rituals distinguish the slaughter of the sacrificial victim from murder (*phonos*), while, for Burkert, they evolve from a feeling of guilt evoked by the killing.[96] In this regard, pre-kill rites such as the scattering of barley grains, the concealment of the *makhaira* in the *kanoun*, actions taken to prove the willingness of the victim, and the *ololugê* all stand as markers of the anxiety of the participants regarding the necessary violence.[97] Detienne and Vernant describe the symbolic assent of the animal as both a representation of the animal's domestication and a disclaimer for any injustice in the killing, whereas Burkert sees an attempt to dispel the guilt of the participants.[98] For both interpretations,

---

[93] Burkert 1966:106.

[94] Girard 1977:152, similar to Burkert's "epiphany" (1983:38).

[95] Vernant 1991:292.

[96] Vernant 1991:294; Burkert 1966:87–121, esp. 105; 1976:172; 1979:54–56; 1983:1. The premise that Greeks felt guilt over the instinctual urge to kill has rightly been questioned as a projection of idealized Christian values, which would have been alien to Greeks. Responses to Burkert: Kirk 1981:126–128; Henrichs 1987:29–30 and 2000:58–60.

[97] Detienne 1989:20; Vernant 1991:294; Durand 1989.

[98] Detienne 1989:9; Vernant 1991:294; Burkert 1966:107–108. Cf. the instructions for the victim to shake itself in Aristophanes *Peace* 960 and the scholiast's comments; Naiden 2007 provides a skeptical look at the question of the animal's assent, which is never described in Homer. The enigmatic Classical Athenian festival of the *Bouphonia*, although admittedly rare and already considered 'old-fashioned' in the fifth century, is a favorite example for both the Paris School and Burkert. Burkert emphasizes the 'trial' of the axe (1983:136–143). Vernant 1991:298–300 discusses the same ritual with emphasis on the reconstitution of the ox, stuffed with barley, as a symbol of sacrificial ritual's inherent provision of food: "A provider of meat for men and of bones and fat burned for the gods once it has been ritually slaughtered, the animal, now associated with agricultural labor, appears also as a producer of grain" (301). See also Deubner 1932:158–174; Meuli 1946:275–276; and Detienne 1989:12.

the relative silence of the ancients on this topic is significant: for example, the slaying of the animal is not described in Hesiod's etiology of sacrifice.[99] Even greater emphasis is given by these scholars to the seeming aversion to the moment of death in surviving vase paintings: the kill is only represented in 4.5 percent, as compared to 55.5 percent for pre-kill and 40 percent for post-kill.[100]

The work of Meuli, Burkert, Vernant, and Detienne, among others, has been instrumental in expanding modern perceptions of ancient Greek ritual, to the extent that any study of Greek sacrifice must either "agree" or "disagree" with their compelling interpretations. However, the theoretical arguments made by Burkert and the Paris School are drawn largely from evidence from the Classical period, which is, in many ways, different from the Homeric representations. Homeric representations of sacrifice are idealized and adapted to the thematic needs of the poem. The pre-kill details outlined above, which seem to have been the defining characteristics of Classical Athenian sacrifices, do not appear in the *Iliad*. The relative significance attached to such pre-kill rites can again be demonstrated by an observation in Herodotos, who remarks that Persian sacrifices do not include an altar, fire, libations, flute music, garlands, or sprinkled barley, features he seems to consider to be expected parts of sacrifice.[101] But many of these elements, which we might consider to be important features of a large-scale sacrifice in the Classical period, never occur in the *Iliad*. For example, no sacrifice in the *Iliad* begins with a procession, nor is any accompanied by music. Though we have observed the importance of the *kanêphoros* to the performance of sacrifice in Classical Athens, the *kanoun* is never used in the *Iliad*, in spite of the fact that barley grains are scattered in several sacrifices.[102] The animals and participants are never decorated with wreaths, garlands, or crowns, all consistent features of Classical sacrifices in the iconography and literary sources. Inscriptions and recent osteoarchaeological studies have revealed that in the Classical period, in contrast to vase paintings that depict cattle as sacrificial victims in over 60 percent of existing examples, the most commonly offered victims would have been the cheapest:

---

[99] Vernant 1991:294 and 1989.

[100] Burkert 1983:38; Durand 1989; Vernant 1991:294. The absence of 'kill' images in extant iconography is evaluated by van Straten 1995:186–187 and Peirce 1993:232.

[101] Herodotos I 132.1: Θυσίη δὲ τοῖσι Πέρσῃσι περὶ τοὺς εἰρημένους θεοὺς ἥδε κατέστηκε· οὔτε βωμοὺς ποιεῦνται οὔτε πῦρ ἀνακαίουσι μέλλοντες θύειν, οὐ σπονδῇ χρέωνται, οὐκὶ αὐλῷ, οὐ στέμμασι, οὐκὶ οὐλῇσι.

[102] Nestor's son carries a *kanoun* with barley grains (*Odyssey* iii 442) and Penelope puts barley grains into a *kanoun* before praying (*Odyssey* iv 761).

sheep.[103] The *Iliad* does not spare any expense in sacrificial victims, which function as status symbols of the wealth and power of the sacrificer; sheep are sacrificed only on one occasion, when Priam provides the victims for the oath sacrifice between the armies before the duel of Paris and Menelaos (*Iliad* III 245f.). Due to their relatively cheap cost, pigs seem to have been the most common purificatory victims in Classical Athens, but Agamemnon sacrifices a hecatomb to Apollo to purify the army.[104]

The emphasis placed on violence in the above interpretations of pre-kill and kill rites does little to inform our understanding of sacrifice in the *Iliad*, since no actions are taken that could be interpreted as disguising anxiety over the slaughter of the animal, such as hiding the knife before the kill or taking care that the animal willingly assents. Only three pre-kill rites are represented in the *Iliad*, and they do not occur consistently in every sacrifice scene: hand-washing (*Iliad* I 449, III 270), scattering barley (*Iliad* I 449, II 410), and cutting the "first hairs" (*Iliad* III 273, XIX 254).[105] Fundamental necessities, such as lighting the fire to roast the meat or restraining the animals, are not mentioned. The victim's sympathetic adornment and inclusion in the ceremony, followed by its symbolic separation—being pelted with barley grains—and the process of sacralization—indicated in Classical accounts by special clothing and the *pompê*—are entirely missing from Homer.[106] Richard Seaford distinguishes Homeric sacrifice from later accounts precisely by the lack of elements suggesting feelings of guilt or anxiety. The barley grains thrown at *Iliad* I 449 = II 410 are not directed at the animal, a gesture in some Classical accounts interpreted as a symbolic distancing of the animal, destined for death, from the group.[107] The ritual cry performed by women (*ololugê*), a defining feature of Meuli's "comedy of innocence," is performed at a sacrifice by the female members of Nestor's family (*Odyssey* iii 450); it accompanies a prayer given by Penelope (*Odyssey* iv 767), and at the gift-offering of a *peplos* in Athena's

---

[103] Van Straten 1995:170–186.

[104] *Iliad* I 313; on pig sacrifices in Classical Athens, see Burkert 1985:81; Rosivach 1994:15; Bremmer 1996:251; and Clinton 2005.

[105] Burkert 1985:56 believes that the features not present in Homer are later additions, as does Bremmer 1996. Graf observes the differences in Homer in his reconstruction of an "ideal" sacrifice (2002:121–122). Kirk 1981 responds to Meuli's theories in light of the Homeric representations.

[106] Seaford 1994:44–45, in response to Burkert 1966:106–113; 1981:126–127; 1983:5–6, 21, 40; and Detienne 1989:9. He acknowledges a trace of anxiety in the libations of wine, which are poured out as a symbolic expression of the penalty for transgressing the oath at *Iliad* III 292–301 (1994:46–47). On special clothing in ritual contexts, Stengel 1920:47–48; on the iconography, van Straten 1995:168, Peirce 1993:231.

[107] Seaford 1994:45n59; Burkert 1983:4–5 describes the act of distancing, as does Foley 1985:31.

temple by the Trojan women (*Iliad* VI 301); but these are the only ceremonies at which women are present. Their relative exclusion from Homeric sacrifices, which are never performed on set occasions or as part of a larger framework of regulated ritual performance, is critically distinct from the important and conspicuous roles they play in many public sacrifices in the Classical period.[108]

In the *Iliad*, the portion for the gods consists of the *mêria* 'thigh bones', *knisê* 'the pleasing smoke produced by the cooking meat', and, in some descriptions, the otherwise unattested rite of ὠμοθετεῖν, which seems to refer to the process of putting bits from each limb on the bones before burning them. Meuli and Burkert place great emphasis on the symbolic reconstitution of the animal signified by this action.[109] However, ὠμοθετεῖν is offered to gods in only two sacrifices in the *Iliad*, and the significant meaning conferred upon this action by Meuli is not generally accepted.[110] If ὠμοθετεῖν originally signified anxiety over the death of the victim, this detail would have stood alone among the other aspects of the Homeric sacrificial process, which do not otherwise suggest guilt provoked by the physical violence of slaughter. In fact, far from concealing the weapon, Agamemnon always hangs his *makhaira* 'sacrificial knife' on his belt (*Iliad* III 271–272, XIX 252–253). There is no reluctance in the narrative to describe the death of the animal, as the following graphic description from an oath sacrifice of lambs demonstrates:

> ἦ, καὶ ἀπὸ στομάχους ἀρνῶν τάμε νηλέϊ χαλκῷ·
> καὶ τοὺς μὲν κατέθηκεν ἐπὶ χθονὸς ἀσπαίροντας,
> θυμοῦ δευομένους· ἀπὸ γὰρ μένος εἵλετο χαλκός.

> (*Iliad* III 292–294)

> He spoke and dragged his ruthless dagger across the lambs'
>   throats
> and let them fall to the ground, dying, gasping away
> their life breath, their strength cut short by the sharp bronze.

In fact, far from obscuring the violence of sacrifice, the narrative, as Margo Kitts has observed, draws deliberate connections between the slaughter of sacrificial victims and of warriors on the battlefield, such as Lukaon,

---

[108] Deubner 1982 (reprint of 1941) is still the definitive study on the *ololugê*; see also Rudhardt 1958:178–180. Osborne 2000 discusses the complex evidence for women's participation in ancient Greek sacrifice.

[109] Meuli 1946:218, 256, 262; Burkert 1985:6, 16, 25. This will be discussed in more detail in Chapter Three.

[110] *Iliad* I 461 = *Iliad* II 424 = *Odyssey* iii 458, xii 361, and xiv 427; Pulleyn 2000 *ad Iliad* I 461; Heubeck, West, and Hainsworth 1988 *ad Odyssey* iii 458. Seaford 1994:46 believes, not that these elements are developments in the ritual, but that they reflect narrative purposes.

whose violent death is described in language reminiscent of the other oath sacrifice in *Iliad* XIX.[111] A further distinction in Classical and Homeric sacrifices must be noted here. Ritual oath sacrifices involve particular actions in the Classical period that do not feature in the two Homeric representations: participants often grasp the entrails or stand on the testicles or entrails of the victim.[112]

The ritual practices in many Classical communities are characterized by group participation, to the extent that communal identity is formed through festivals and in sanctuaries in which ritual activity is very closely regulated and mediated by the *polis*.[113] The exact type and function of the political system represented in the *Iliad* is a question that we will address in Chapter Four; however, sacrifice is not performed as part of festivals sponsored collectively by a city or community group, so the social importance of *polis* festivals as happy occasions marked by sacrifice and subsequent feasts bears no similarity to the presentation of sacrifice in the *Iliad*, in which sacrifices are either signs of increased anxiety and despair or attempts to relieve social crises.[114] Seaford finds that Homeric sacrifices open or conclude dangerous activities, at which point the narrative seeks to impose order on the chaos and unpredictability of battle, while they also function as a symbol of group unity. In his opinion, sacrifices play a positive architectonic role in Homer, as opposed to their connection to murder in Attic tragedy.[115] That sacrifice is performed in response to crisis and anxiety is not surprising in a poem entirely set during the siege of a city; in this sense, all actions in the *Iliad* are responses to

---

[111] Kitts 2005:155–156; 2002:103–124; 1999:42–57; we will return to this thesis in Chapter Four, page 193. Contrast Seaford 1994:47, who believes that the violence of sacrificial ritual is not likened to battlefield slaughter, with the possible exception of the bellowing bull simile (*Iliad* XX 403), despite the numerous similes comparing warriors to wild animals and the later prevalence of sacrificial metaphor in tragedy. Burkert draws many parallels between war and sacrifice, which he sees as interchangeable symbols of outlet for instinctual male aggression; see Burkert 1983:47–48; Pindar fr. 78, Snell-Maehler.

[112] See Chapter Two below, page 89. Bremmer 1996:266 notes the "curious" absence of these elements from the Homeric scenes. Burkert 1983:35–36 discusses the importance of blood in the forging of oaths as described in Demosthenes 23.68 and Pausanias III 20.9, IV 15.8, V 24.9; see also Burkert 1985:250–254.

[113] Sourvinou-Inwood 2000:11, a very important description of the make-up of *polis* religion.

[114] *Odyssey* iii 4 is perhaps a representation of a community-wide festival. Thomson 1943:57n40 identifies an allusion to a calendar feast, the *Hecatombaia*, in *Odyssey* xiv 162 and xix 306, but he also notes the lack of localized cult details in the poems. Happy *polis* sacrifices: Peirce 1993:219–266, supported by Graf 2002:123, *contra* Burkert 1979:50ff.

[115] Seaford 2004: "The sacrifice performed by Agamemnon at *Iliad* II 402–432 is a peaceful preliminary to the warfare that starts immediately afterwards and continues, interrupted only by ritual, throughout the *Iliad*" (40).

crisis situations. Yet sacrifices are infrequent and do not open or conclude all dangerous activities, nor are they closely linked to the start and end of battles.

Moreover, sacrifices in the *Iliad* are unlike those found in military contexts of the Classical period. While on the march, Xenophon describes the frequent performance of sacrifice before any significant undertaking and, in the battle-lines, immediately before fighting. In this context, *sphagia* sacrifices are performed at the start and conclusion of battle, the taking of oaths, the crossing of rivers, the assuaging of winds, for some types of purification, and as rites for the dead and for heroes.[116] Sacrifices are performed at the start of battle to provide an opportunity for interpreting omens and at the end to thank the gods, two practices not attested in the *Iliad*, where, except for the oath sacrifice in *Book* III, sacrifices are not performed before battle, for divination purposes, or as thanks-offerings.[117] For example, Nestor recalls how, upon his arrival at the river Alpheios, the scene of a battle with the Epeians on the following day, he made sacrifices to Zeus, Athena, Poseidon, and the river Alpheios. Though the sacrifice marks the conclusion of the march to the river, the danger of the expedition lay presumably in the forthcoming engagement with the enemy, which, nevertheless, is not preceded by a sacrifice in Nestor's recollection of events:

> ἔνθεν πανσυδίῃ σὺν τεύχεσι θωρηχθέντες
> ἔνδιοι ἱκόμεσθ' ἱερὸν ῥόον Ἀλφειοῖο.
> ἔνθα Διὶ ῥέξαντες ὑπερμενεῖ ἱερὰ καλά,
> ταῦρον δ' Ἀλφειῷ, ταῦρον δὲ Ποσειδάωνι,
> αὐτὰρ Ἀθηναίῃ γλαυκώπιδι βοῦν ἀγελαίην,
> δόρπον ἔπειθ' ἑλόμεσθα κατὰ στρατὸν ἐν τελέεσσι,
> καὶ κατεκοιμήθημεν ἐν ἔντεσιν οἷσιν ἕκαστος
> ἀμφὶ ῥοὰς ποταμοῖο. ἀτὰρ μεγάθυμοι Ἐπειοὶ
> ἀμφίσταντο δὴ ἄστυ διαρραῖσαι μεμαῶτες·
> ἀλλά σφι προπάροιθε φάνη μέγα ἔργον Ἄρηος·
> εὖτε γὰρ ἠέλιος φαέθων ὑπερέσχεθε γαίης,
> συμφερόμεσθα μάχῃ, Διί τ' εὐχόμενοι καὶ Ἀθήνῃ.

(*Iliad* XI 725–736)

"Then, with all haste, harnessed in battle armor,
our army reached the Alpheios' holy ford at noon.

---

[116] E.g. Xenophon *Hellenika* IV 7.7; Jameson 1991:198.

[117] Stengel observes that Homeric sacrifices are not thanks-offerings: they are performed by anxious people who fear angering the gods or want something (1910:59–65); cf. the discussion in Adkins 1972 on the *timê* of the gods.

There we slaughtered fine victims to mighty Zeus,
a bull to Alpheios, a bull to lord Poseidon
and a cow from the herd to blazing-eyed Athena.
And then through camp we took our evening meal by rank
    and file,
and caught what sleep we could, each in his gear
along the river rapids. And all the while those vaunting
    Epeians
were closing round the fortress, burning to tear it down.
But before they got the chance a great work of the War-god
    flashed before their eyes!
Soon as the sun came up in flames above the earth
we joined battle, praying to Zeus and Pallas."

Nestor is very specific in his recollection: they reached the river at noon, sacrificed different victims appropriate to the individual divinities, ate dinner, slept, and met the enemy at sunrise. Henrichs has interpreted the pre-battle *sphagia* sacrifices in Xenophon as taking place before battle, in a "liminal period," being performed by the *mantis* to cope with the anxiety triggered by warfare.[118] In Nestor's battle with the Epeians, there are prayers to Zeus and Athena immediately before the battle, but they neither release any pre-battle tension through sacrifice nor do they employ a *mantis* 'seer'. In fact, sacrificial victims are never used in the *Iliad* for divination. Nestor never describes the crossing of the river or sacrifices before the battle or in front of the approaching enemy. Interestingly, he does refer to the offerings to Zeus as *hiera kala*, a phrase which Michael Jameson has linked to the pre-battle sacrifices producing good omens in the Classical period: "the ostensible purpose of all rites before victory was achieved was to obtain from the gods favorable signs (*kallierein*, from the phrase *hiera kala*) for the next step in the campaign."[119] *Hiera kala* does not carry these mantic connotations in the *Iliad*; for instance, in the narrator's description of Akhilleus' promise of *hiera kala* to the winds in return for kindling the fire of Patroklos' pyre (*Iliad* XXIII 195), the term does not refer to divination. Although Zeus and Athena are invoked before the battle and, in Nestor's opinion, the success in battle is attributed to them, no thanks-offering is described.[120]

---

[118] Henrichs 1981:216; cf. Xenophon *The Constitution of the Lakedaimonians* 13.2. Burkert 1983:57, 66 observes the comparison between the sacrificial victim and the hoped-for disaster for the enemy; Seaford 1994:47 discusses this in the Homeric context.

[119] Jameson 1991:199.

[120] *Iliad* XI 753, 758, see page 119f. below.

The *mantis* is an essential part of the Classical Greek army, primarily tasked with performing sacrifices before battle and pronouncing the will of the gods based on the visual appearance of the victims' inner organs.[121] Various other kinds of ritual experts could be consulted in the Classical period, but in Homer there are only a few types, which do not correspond with the professionals depicted in Xenophon or other Classical sources.[122] People who perform religious offices in the *Iliad* are called *hiereus* or *arêtêr*, generally translated as 'priest', who can be described as custodians of traditions. Khruses is referred to with both of these terms (*Iliad* I 11, 94, 370); Kalkhas is consistently described as a *mantis*.[123] Odysseus remembers the *mantis* Kalkhas' interpretation of a bird sign, the only method of divination present in the *Iliad*. During an Akhaian sacrifice, they are interrupted when a serpent devours a sparrow and her babies just before it turns to stone (*Iliad* II 306–330). Kalkhas interprets the scene as an indication that the Akhaians will defeat Troy. This kind of divination is very different from the so-called 'Xenophontic system', where the divine signs resulting from the sacrifice are interpreted, a practice that seems to have been *de rigeur* in the Classical period.[124] In historical sources, the *mantis* almost always performs the sacrifices in the context of war for this reason.[125] However, in Homer *manteis* are not consulted in any standardized or consistent fashion. Kalkhas interprets the bird signs at Aulis, but he is not specifically linked with the act of sacrificing, nor are the bird signs expected or resultant from the sacrifice. Instead, they interrupt the ritual.[126] In fact, Kalkhas is not involved in any sacrifice performed in the narrative. Passing mention is made of other seers—a *theopropos* 'seer', an

---

[121] Thucydides VI 69.2 describes seers "bringing out the traditional *sphagia*," and the sacrifices performed by *manteis* are also described by Xenophon *Anabasis* 6.5.7–8; Jameson 1991:204; Parker 1998a:300; see also Pritchett 1979:47–90.

[122] There are dozens of sacred officials described in the extant *leges sacrae*: those serving Eleusis have been cataloged by Clinton 1974 and those for Athens are partially covered by Garland 1984.

[123] Pulleyn 2000 *ad Iliad* I 11 argues that, in Homer, the *hiereus* is specifically connected to sacrifice, and *arêtêres* to prayer, but the textual evidence is not consistent enough to support such observations. The translation "priest" is misleading, but is the commonly used designation for this complex role. The difference between the professionals was slight, but it seems that *manteis* alone had the skills to divine: see Henrichs 2008.

[124] The 'Xenophontic system' is called so because of the frequency of this kind of divination in Xenophon's writings. E.g. Xenophon *Hellenika* IV 8.36, VI 5.49 and Jameson 1991:198; see also Aeschines 3.131, 152, Parker 1998a:300n3.

[125] Jameson 1991:204 and n19 in support of his argument, in contrast to Pritchett's theory that *sphagia* were not performed for divination (1979:110). Rudhardt 1958:275 argues for a propitiatory and divinatory purpose.

[126] See page 73f. below on this scene.

oiônistês 'bird-diviner', a *thuoskoos* 'observer of sacrificial smoke', and an *oneiropolos* 'dream-interpreter'—but they never figure directly in the narrative.[127] Akhilleus proposes that the army consult a *mantis, hiereus,* or *oneiropolos* to learn the cause of the plague (*Iliad* I 62–63: ἀλλ' ἄγε δή τινα μάντιν ἐρείομεν ἢ ἱερῆα / ἢ καὶ ὀνειροπόλον). These categories puzzled the Hellenistic commentators: Zenodotos athetized this verse and Aristarkhos attempted to explain that *mantis* was the generic type of diviner, while *hiereus* and *oneiropolos* were subcategories of those who prophesy by sacrifice and dreams, respectively. Akhilleus suggests that these experts can interpret whether the god is angry about a lack of sacrifice, exactly what Kalkhas does on this crucial occasion. Priests, otherwise, do not play much of a role in ritual performance in the *Iliad.* As we will see, religious authority is entirely centered on Agamemnon, and Akhaian priests and diviners play correspondingly small roles.

There are only two other sacred officials in the *Iliad* who perform religious duties, Khruses and Theano, and the prominence given to these priests outside of the Akhaian community furthers the marginalization of Akhaian cult-practitioners in the narrative.[128] Khruses is a priest of Apollo who maintains a cult site at Khruse, near Troy, where the Akhaians return his daughter; he officiates at the propitiatory sacrifice occasioned by her return in *Iliad* I, a scene which we will discuss in full in Chapter Four. Priam refers to diviners and priests to cast doubt upon their predictions:

εἰ μὲν γάρ τίς μ' ἄλλος ἐπιχθονίων ἐκέλευεν,
ἢ οἳ μάντιές εἰσι θυοσκόοι ἢ ἱερῆες

(*Iliad* XXIV 220–221)

"If someone else had commanded me, some mortal man,
either some prophet staring into the smoke, or some priest..."

Priam assures Hekabe that it was the messenger of the gods, Iris, who commanded him to go to the Akhaian camps, not a diviner or priest, whose knowledge of the divine seems to be the object of scorn or at least skepticism. The contrast in the poem between direct communication with the gods, such as Akhilleus has through his mother, and ineffectual attempts to appease the

---

[127] These terms are only very rarely found outside of Homer. *Theopropos: Iliad* XII 228. This term can refer to public messengers sent to consult oracles in the Classical period; cf. Aeschylus *Persae* 659. *Oiônistês: Iliad* II 858, XIII 70, XVII 218; also Hesiod *Scutum* 185, and a few instances in late prose. *Thuoskooi: Iliad* XXIV 221; also *Odyssey* xxi 145, xxii 318, 321; this term is used elsewhere only twice in Euripides (*Rhesos* 68, *Bakkhai* 224). *Oneiropolos: Iliad* I 63, V 149; also in Herodotos I 128, V 56 and Philo 1.664.

[128] *Iliad* I 436–474, VI 297–310. At *Iliad* I 37, Khruses remembers sacrifices and refers to a temple he has 'roofed' in the past.

gods through mortal activities, such as prophecy, is a prominent theme to which we will return in Chapter Four. Priam's reference to *thuoskooi manteis* is unique in the *Iliad*. Despite the numerous battles, the practice of *hepatoscopy* is not performed in the *Iliad*, and since *thuein* refers, not to animal sacrifice in the *Iliad*, but to 'burning', Priam's reference probably alludes to "scrutineers of incense smoke" rather than to the *thuoskooi* of the Classical era, professionals who examine livers.[129]

There is one priestess in the *Iliad*, the Trojan Theano, who opens the temple and leads the women's offering of a *peplos* and sacrificial vow to Athena. Although sacred officials in the *Iliad* bear much resemblance to their Classical counterparts, Theano, who bears some resemblance to the role of priestesses in the Mycenaean and Classical periods, provides an interesting exception. A link can be drawn between the description of Theano and that of the Mycenaean priestesses attested in the Linear B tablets. The Trojans have appointed Theano (ἔθηκαν, *Iliad* VI 300); she has a key to the temple (*Iliad* VI 89, 298); and she dedicates a textile to Athena (*Iliad* VI 303). A Mycenaean priestess (*i-je-re-ja*) is described on a tablet from Pylos (Un 6) as a "key-bearer" (*ka-ra-wi-po-ro*: κλαιϝφορος), in conjunction with textiles in a dedicatory context.[130] Although the ritual practices of the Classical period have often been compared to Homeric scenes, the evidence for Mycenaean cult practice, which seems to have included sacrificial banquets on special occasions and festivals, frequent offerings to a variety of local and supra-regional deities, and a well-established priesthood, is not often used as *comparanda* for Homer. Mycenaean cult practice, as we can reconstruct it, provides a parallel to the representations of sacrifice in Homeric poetry for the three following reasons: many of the deities are the same, and the coincidence between the prominence of Poseidon in the Pylian tablets and the Pylian offerings to Poseidon in *Odyssey*

---

[129] West 1997b:46; Stengel 1910:4–12. Mackie 1996:33–36 outlines the tense relationship between Hektor and Poludamas, who acts in an advisory capacity to the prince similar to Nestor for Agamemnon, as does Helenos, another Trojan seer. In reference to Poludamas and Hektor (*Iliad* XII 195–250), Parker 1998a:300 remarks that the conflicts characteristic of Classical depictions of seers are already brewing in Homer.

[130] The "key-bearer" is also recorded on PY Jn 829, recording the requisitioning of temple bronze for spear points, and Ep 704, a record of land tenure (Killen 2001:440; Ventris and Chadwick 1973:484). Nosch and Perna 2001:475–476 identify the 'keybearer' as Karpathia, a well-known Pylian woman also found in Ep 388. Kirk 1990:165 summarizes some of the more prominent interpretations on the "appointment" of Theano. Keys are a distinctive attribute of priestesses in the Classical period: Parker 2005:93–95 and Connelly 2007 (ch. 3); a general discussion of priestesses is given by Dillon 2002:73–106 as well as pp. 57–60f. on presentations of the *peplos* to goddesses.

iii has been well noted;[131] recent archaeological findings suggest a tantalizing similarity with the Homeric treatment of thigh bones;[132] and there is sufficient evidence to suggest that religious offerings and sacrificial feasts were organized and controlled by the elites, primarily the highest-ranking people living in the palace, as manipulative tools for both consolidation and intimidation. I will argue for a comparable purpose for Agamemnon's use of sacrifice in the *Iliad*. We will periodically return to evidence from the Mycenaean period for sacrificial practices resembling those in the *Iliad*. Although the evidence is fragmentary and connections between historic Mycenaean practices and the creative, idealized representations in Homer can never be proven, Mycenaean evidence can provide analogous cult practices useful to our study. We will return to the Mycenaean evidence again in Chapter Four. As I have stated, much of the scholarship on sacrifice does not illuminate the sacrifice scenes in the *Iliad* because of the differences between the Homeric representations and practices in the Classical period. Both G. S. Kirk and Seaford have noted the need for more serious work on the topic of sacrifice in Homer.[133] In one of the few recent treatments of Homeric sacrifice, Kirk wisely observes, "Too little consideration is given to the process of the self-consistency or otherwise of the Homeric picture, and to possible motives for the addition of new ritual acts or the revaluation of old ones."[134] By using the

---

[131] The names of Ares, Artemis, Athena, Eileithuia, Enyalius, Erinys, Hera, Hermes, Paion, Poseidon, Zeus, and perhaps Dionysus occur in the tablets, as well as scores of otherwise unattested deities, particularly Potnia, who receives more offerings than any other individual god at Knossos and is excelled only by Poseidon at Pylos. *Pa-ki-ja-ne* is a well-recorded shrine for the palace at Pylos, as was Amnisos for Knossos. On religion in the tablets: Ventris and Chadwick 1973:172–208; Chadwick 1976:88–101; Killen 2001:437–442. Burkert 1985:43–47 argues against continuity in cult practice between Mycenaean and later Greek cultures.

[132] A team of archaeologists, following the initial conclusions of Carl Blegen, has reexamined groups of bones found in the "Palace of Nestor" in Pylos. In summary, they found six distinct groups of almost exclusively cattle bones. These Pylos groups contained only the right and left mandible, humerus, and femur bones, a collection inexplicable in terms of either taphonomic processes or carcass processing. The bones were first scraped clean of meat before being burned; then most were moved to carefully chosen locations within the palace, as evidenced by the lack of burnt matrices underneath the piles of bones. The special treatment of thigh bones is similar to the Homeric burnt offerings of *mêria*, such as those offered to Apollo and Zeus in *Iliad* I and II (αὐτὰρ ἐπεὶ κατὰ μῆρε κάη, *Iliad* I 464 = II 427). See Isaakidou et al. 2002; Halstead and Isaakidou 2004; and the articles by Stocker, Davis, and Palaima in Wright 2004; the original archaeological findings are described by Blegen and Rawson 1966:93. Isaakidou et al. 2002 give a summary of archaeological finds from Archaic and Classical sites suggestive of animal sacrifice, as well as the Late Bronze Age sanctuary at Kato Syme on Crete, where burnt deposits, including animal bones, have been found.

[133] Kirk 1981:63; Seaford 1994:42.

[134] Kirk 1981:63, though he seems to contradict this in Kirk 1990:9, which states that animal sacrifice "is described in typical scenes and is more or less automatic (although sometimes abbre-

models of Mauss and Meuli, Kirk analyzes six scenes to identify the recurrent elements of sacrifice in Homer, which he contrasts with the evidence from the Classical period.[135] Finding that crucial symbolic details for interpretations of "sacralization" are missing from Homer, he does not offer an alternative approach, yet he successfully highlights the problems with modern approaches to the Homeric material. The comprehensive bibliographies of publications on ritual have only one entry for "sacrifice in Homer"—Seaford's article on the influence of Homer on scenes of sacrifice in Greek tragedy.[136] The *Cambridge Companion to Homer* includes a thoughtful essay on "The Gods in Homer," but neglects ritual.[137] Wace and Stubbings' *Companion to Homer* includes a good, if brief, discussion of relationships between men and gods, including sacrifice, in the chapter "Polity and Society," whereas the chapter entitled "Religion" confines itself exclusively to archaeological material. Morris and Powell, in their *New Companion to Homer*, do not treat cult practice in Homer at all.[138] Jean Stallings, in an unpublished dissertation, attempts to analyze the aesthetics of formulaic language in scenes of "eaten sacrifice" in the *Iliad,* but she is frustrated by divergent details and the limitations placed on her own study, which excludes the "uneaten" oath sacrifices and includes feast scenes without explicit animal sacrifice.[139] Kitts's recent book stands out as a good study on the oath sacrifices, but it does not address the wider context of animal sacrifice.[140]

While Homeric sacrifices may not be easily clarified by many of the prevailing theories of sacrifice, partly because the ritual process varies within the poem, partly because the ritual details do not exactly correspond

---

viated) as far as the human participants are concerned." Equally, Kirk 1985 *ad Iliad* I 447–468: "a few ritual actions have been omitted ... but occur elsewhere in Homer: gilding the victim's horns (as at *Od.*3.436-8), paralyzing it with an axe blow, accompanied where appropriate by the ritual female shriek, before slitting its throat (*Od.*3.449), cutting hair from its head (*Il.*3.273) and throwing this on the fire (*Od.*3.446, 14.442). Some of these further actions belong to any formal sacrifice but happen not to be mentioned in our passage, or in other particular versions of the typical scene...." Bremmer 1996:249 admits that modern scholars do not often differentiate between Homeric and post-Homeric accounts, even though the ritual developed. Parker 1983:13–15 describes the problems of discussing ritual in different genres. Kitts 2005:26 concludes that Homeric sacrifices should be analyzed on their own. Berthiaume 1982:5–9, 64–67 discusses Homeric contexts for eating and food preparation.

[135] Kirk 1981:65f. His scenes are *Iliad* I 447, II 410, and III 268; *Odyssey* iii 5, 419, and xiv 419. Seaford 1994:43 notes the inaccuracy of his tabulation.

[136] Motte et al. 1992; 1998.

[137] Kearns 2004.

[138] Rose 1962; Morris and Powell 1997.

[139] Stallings 1984: "It may be objected that the scenes of eaten sacrifice have proved less than satisfactory as a test case of Homeric aesthetics" (338).

[140] Kitts 2005, building on earlier articles (1999, 2000). See Ready's important review (2006).

with Classical evidence, and partly because the Homeric poems are creative representations never intended to mirror reality,[141] if we are able to successfully separate them from other poetic and literary descriptions, we will be in a better position to explore their specific presentation. My analysis of sacrifice in the *Iliad* rests upon two principles: the important distinction between sacrifices and feasts, which are unmarked and lack references to gods, and the difference in perspective on sacrifice offered by the primary and secondary narrative voices. I will now discuss a few different approaches to commensal sacrifice in Homer, offering a new classification of Homeric sacrifice based on its thematic emphasis on gift-offerings to deities, before turning to the different narrative 'voices' in Chapter Two.

1.3 The Poetics of Sacrifice

The function of sacrifice in the *Iliad* is complicated by a lack of consensus on a definition of 'sacrifice'. Occasions for sacrifice and feasting in the *Iliad* cannot be explicated by comparisons with evidence from the Classical period, as discussed above, or by theoretical interpretations suggesting that, with few exceptions, the only livestock consumed in ancient Greek communities were sacrificial animals. In such a model, feasting and animal sacrifice become inextricable. Uneaten sacrifices (*sphagia*), often burnt entirely, fall into a sepa rate category, usually excluded from specific studies of *thusia* sacrifices.[142] In regard to both literary and epigraphic sources from the Classical period, Marcel Detienne has asserted "the absolute coincidence of meat eating and sacrifice."[143] Inscriptions have provided a wealth of evidence for the number

---

[141] As Henrichs 2003 notes regarding literary depictions of Greek ritual: "Greek poets and prose authors wrote religion with their own agendas in mind" (58); so also Parker 1983:13–16. Van Straten 1995:2, concerning the iconography of sacrifice, writes that the images depict not how the Greeks sacrificed, but how they *visualized* themselves sacrificing.

[142] Cf. Rosivach 1994:4; Jameson 1991:201f., in an essay on the different contexts and uses for *sphagia* sacrifices, observes that the emphasis on violence and slaughter in *sphagia* sacrifices is still present but "subordinated" in *thusia* sacrifices. Kirk 1981:42 remarks that much scholarship oversimplifies sacrifice into either a simple gift or meal.

[143] Detienne 1989:3; the conclusions of Berthiaume 1982:79–93 are similar, although he admits rare instances of meat consumption without sacrifice; so also Graf 2002:120, while observing the priority of gift-giving to the gods in the ritual, states "animal sacrifice has a practical aim, the provision of edible meat." With regard to the *Iliad*, this approach has been questioned recently by Kitts 2005:30. A notable exception is the study on women as participants in sacrifice by Osborne 2000: if all available meat came from sacrifices, as proposed by Detienne and Berthiaume, women would then necessarily be excluded from most or all occasions for eating meat (298n11). In a lengthy footnote, Osborne draws attention to LSCG 96, a sacred law providing for the purchase of multiple potential victims, from which

39

and type of animals sacrificed, but these documents are primarily concerned with finance and procedures of public record keeping, and they vary among the *poleis* that produced them in the Classical period. Although vastly important to an understanding of how communities practiced sacrifice, the interpretative models drawing on epigraphic sources cannot entirely explain literary representations of sacrifice, which are creative expressions subject to the manipulations of artists.[144] Attempts to identify the absolute coincidence of meat eating and sacrifice have encouraged similar generalizations in the interpretation of iconography as well. For example, the same image of meat on a chopping block can be identified as a representation of sacrificial procedure by one scholar, excluded from being termed a 'sacrifice' by another because of its absence of the clear indications of religious performance found in many other images, such as garlands or a *kanoun*, and discussed without reference to sacrifice at all by a third.[145] This kind of contradiction, a result of the fragmentary and often inconsistent nature of the evidence, leads not only to a lack of consensus on the evidence among modern audiences but also to too little attention being paid this lack of consensus.

Analyses of Homeric sacrifice are equally inconsistent. B. C. Dietrich has argued strongly for secular eating divorced from religious practices in the poems:

> Homer cannot be held to account for varying what we know to have been standard procedure from other sources. Homer had his own views and could adapt ritual quite substantially to suit his particular purpose. The impression of consistency in Homeric sacrifice is due to the conventions of epic formular composition. In fact the Homeric hero was not strictly bound to any particular place or

---

only one is chosen for sacrifice; the implication is that others are eaten without a preliminary sacrifice. Osborne also questions the insistence that most images of meat preparation are also images of sacrifice on the basis of theories of exclusive consumption of sacrificial meat.

[144] One such model is proposed by Rosivach 1994, whose valuable study of fourth-century public sacrifice in Athens finds only one Classical reference (Plato *Laws* 849D), suggesting that non-sacrificial meat might have been available, and this only for *xenoi* and others who would have been excluded from *polis* sacrifices (84, 88; cf. 3n5). Bowie has observed the anecdote in Aelian *On the Nature of Animals* 2.47, which describes kites stealing the sacrificial meat and leaving "secular" meat (1995:481n164). See also Burkert 1976:172 and the response to Burkert in Henrichs 2000:60.

[145] Osborne 2000:298–299n11 discusses the conflicting interpretations of an Attic black figure *oinochoë* (Boston 999527, Boardman 1974:fig. 287); Durand 1989:122, disputed by Osborne, discusses this scene as identifying the importance of trees in scenes of sacrifice, while Sparkes's interpretation does not refer to sacrifice (1975:132).

format in offering sacrifice. Sometimes he killed to eat without a thought for the gods. The act was purely secular.[146]

However, in a discussion of Homeric sacrifice, Susan Sherratt describes feasting as one of the most frequent and regularly formulaic activities in the *Odyssey*, which can be expanded or abbreviated without change in meaning. This abbreviation implies that the "distinctive features of the fully described Homeric feast" are part of a "continuum."[147] She allows no distinction between feasting and sacrifice in the epics, partly because of the remoteness of the gods as beneficiaries of such events:

> In terms of practice, however, no very clear dividing line exists between these two types of feast (sacrificial and secular), and the differences lie principally in the amount of detail in which the elements of the feast, from slaughter to consumption, are described. When they are not described, we are given no reason to believe that there is any substantial difference in the basic methods and procedures involved.[148]

Similarly, George Calhoun and Emily Vermeule have insisted upon an implicit link between sacrifice and feasting, so that any reference to one is also to the other.[149] Stallings tries to link all references to sacrifice in the *Iliad* to feasting, stating that "there are no grounds in the Homeric text for supposing that any sacrifice dedicated to a specific god or hero is uneaten; the references are too brief, and our knowledge of cult practice too limited."[150] However, the shared meal cannot be used as the definitive criterion for animal sacrifice in the *Iliad*, as some sacrifices are not followed by meals, and there are numerous occasions on which the heroes eat without any reference to gods. Nagy, in his seminal examination of concepts of heroism, while recognizing the usefulness of the type of generalizing method favored by Sherratt, has described the theory of "every-meal-a-sacrifice" as an "overly one-dimensional" approach to epic

---

[146] Dietrich 1988:36, citing Ziehen 1939:598 and Kirk 1981:62–80 in support. A similar perspective, based on a study of "religious utterances" in Homer, is offered by Tsagarakis 1977.

[147] Sherratt 2004:182–183.

[148] Sherratt 2004:182. Kitts 2005:28 makes a helpful distinction between commensal and oath sacrifices, but Dietrich 1988:35 does not find any difference in the representation of *thusia* and uneaten sacrifice in Homer.

[149] Stallings 1984:102; Sherratt 2004:182; Calhoun 1962:446, following Wilamowitz-Moellendorff 1931:283; Nilsson 1967:145; Meuli 1946:215–216. Vermeule 1974:98 describes the link between sacrifice and feasting as "*gewöhnlich*."

[150] Stallings 1984:103.

action.[151] The poetic narrative focuses on different stages of the ritual pattern of sacrifice, with variations suited to particular contexts: the context sometimes requires emphasis on the theme of nourishment, sometimes on a ritual offering to the gods. Shared feasts conclude some representations of sacrifice, which include all three pre-kill, kill, and post-kill phases, but without pre-kill details the shared feast can also have a different thematic significance. In his discussion of the oral nature of Homeric discourse, Egbert Bakker has argued that the even the smallest details are added for a purpose: "The detail may be the very reason why the frame has been set up at all."[152] The variations in the descriptions of sacrifice and feasting alter the presentation and therefore the function of the action.

The inclusion or exclusion of ritual details must be considered carefully within the context of Homeric narrative. In some scenes, the characters state clearly their intention to kill an animal for food, whereas other scenes describe the same actions as directed toward the gods. Differences between the description of sacrifice and dinner preparations would have been meaningful for the audience. For example, in the *Odyssey*, Eumaios' sacrifice is signaled by the praise for his piety, which precedes a description of his performance of a lengthy sacrifice (*Odyssey* xiv 419-432). This is in contrast to an earlier meal (*Odyssey* xiv 74-80), in which there are no references to pre-kill actions or divinities.[153] A brief discussion of these scenes from the *Odyssey*, which seem designed to echo each other in order to signal the thematic importance of the inclusion of sacrificial details in the latter description, will help set the stage for our study of sacrifice in the *Iliad*.

In Eumaios' first meal with Odysseus, the emphasis is placed firmly on his generous hospitality. The careful actions of preparing food for his guest highlight his good nature and anticipate his role as a trustworthy helper, but they do not refer to the gods or identify this meal with a thematic use of sacrifice in the poem. He kills the pigs to provide nourishment for his guest:

> ἔνθεν ἑλὼν δύ' ἔνεικε καὶ ἀμφοτέρους ἱέρευσεν,
> εὗσέ τε μίστυλλέν τε καὶ ἀμφ' ὀβελοῖσιν ἔπειρεν.
> ὀπτήσας δ' ἄρα πάντα φέρων παρέθηκ' Ὀδυσῆϊ
> θέρμ' αὐτοῖς ὀβελοῖσιν· ὁ δ' ἄλφιτα λευκὰ πάλυνεν·

---

[151] Nagy 1979:127–128.

[152] Bakker 1997:90.

[153] Stengel 1910:61–62 presents a similar argument for the distinction between the two meals. On Eumaios' sacrifice, Kadletz 1984 and Petropoulou 1987 are the primary studies. Petropoulou 1987:145 does not think ἔσφαξαν means 'sacrifice' in the latter scene (*Odyssey* xiv 426), although she maintains that it still retains a "sacral aspect" through Eumaios' 'first fruit' offerings. Cf. Stanford 1947–1948 *ad Odyssey* xiv 28: "the sacrificial implications of ἱερεύω are almost lost here."

ἐν δ' ἄρα κισσυβίῳ κίρνη μελιηδέα οἶνον,
αὐτὸς δ' ἀντίον ἷζεν, ἐποτρύνων δὲ προσηύδα·
"ἔσθιε νῦν, ὦ ξεῖνε, τά τε δμώεσσι πάρεστι."

(*Odyssey* xiv 74–80)

And [Eumaios] picked out a pair and brought them in and killed
them,
and singed them, and cut them into little pieces, and spitted them.
Then he roasted all and brought it and set it before Odysseus
hot on the spits as it was, and sprinkled white barley over it,
and mixed the wine, as sweet as honey, in a bowl of ivy,
and himself sat down facing him, and urged him on, saying:
"Eat now, stranger, what we serving men are permitted to eat."

The slaughter of the pigs is described with ἱέρευσεν (*Odyssey* xiv 74), a verb which can be used of sacrifice in Homer, and which has the exclusive meaning 'sacrifice' in the Classical period. In this scene, although a verb with sacrificial connotations describes the kill, there are no other indications that this action is dedicated to gods or is part of an animal sacrifice. Arend points out that the *Odyssey* often depicts meals without sacrifices, and Vermeule, in her primarily archaeological study of gods and cult in Homer, decides that ἱερεύειν does "not always" have a "sacred" meaning.[154] Stengel thinks that the definition 'sacrifice' is impossible in most cases for ἱερεύειν.[155] The meat from the pigs is put on spits, an act that occurs in sacrificial feasts, but without the pre-kill rites which would mark the scene as sacrificial, this need not imply any more than food preparation.[156] Instead, the act of eating is prioritized by Eumaios' command to the stranger: ἔσθιε νῦν 'eat now' (*Odyssey* xiv 80). The narrative identifies Eumaios as a loyal servant and as the antithesis of the suitors through his generosity and hospitality, a characterization made explicit with his lengthy diatribe about the suitors' behavior following his command to Odysseus to eat (*Odyssey* xiv 81–108). So ἱέρευσεν, in this context, would seem to mean not 'sacrifice', but 'kill'. However, in the second meal prepared for Odysseus, the emphasis shifts to highlight Eumaios as not only a good host and

---

[154] Arend 1933:64. Vermeule 1974:95. However, she also states that some meat or wine is set aside for the gods at every meal, unless it is specifically excluded (97).

[155] Stengel 1910: "*In der Merhzahl der Stellen, an denen das Wort (*ἱερεύειν*) sich findet, ist die Übersetzung 'opfern' unmöglich*" (1). However, Casabona 1966:22–23 describes two types of actions represented by ἱερεύειν, which he believes always has an associative sacred meaning: those where the offering is the primary motivation and those where eating is the goal. Cunliffe 1924 lists 'sacrifice' as the primary meaning of ἱερεύειν, followed by 'to kill an animal for a meal': he cites *Iliad* II 402; XVIII 559; and XXIV 125.

[156] On the spitting of meat, see below page 104.

therefore antithetical to the suitors, who are bad guests, but also as a person attuned to the gods. The performance of sacrifice in the second meal ties in with the oaths and prayers Odysseus and Eumaios describe in their creation of a trusting relationship (*Odyssey* xiv 149–198, 390–409) and their exchange of 'life stories' (*Odyssey* xiv 199–389).

As the characterization of Eumaios develops and the bond with Odysseus strengthens, the narrative emphasizes his good relations with the gods, as well as his performance as a good host, through a sacrificial meal:

> οἱ δ' ὖν εἰσῆγον μάλα πίονα πενταέτηρον.
> τὸν μὲν ἔπειτ' ἔστησαν ἐπ' ἐσχάρῃ· <u>οὐδὲ συβώτης</u>
> <u>λήθετ' ἄρ' ἀθανάτων· φρεσὶ γὰρ κέχρητ' ἀγαθῆσιν·</u>
> ἀλλ' ὅ γ' ἀπαρχόμενος κεφαλῆς τρίχας ἐν πυρὶ βάλλεν
> ἀργιόδοντος ὑός, καὶ ἐπεύχετο πᾶσι θεοῖσι
> νοστῆσαι Ὀδυσῆα πολύφρονα ὅνδε δόμονδε.
> κόψε δ' ἀνασχόμενος σχίζῃ δρυός, ἣν λίπε κείων·
> τὸν δ' ἔλιπε ψυχή. τοὶ δ' <u>ἔσφαξάν</u> τε καὶ εὖσαν,
> αἶψα δέ μιν διέχευαν· ὁ δ' ὠμοθετεῖτο συβώτης,
> πάντων ἀρχόμενος μελέων, ἐς πίονα δημόν.
> καὶ τὰ μὲν ἐν πυρὶ βάλλε, παλύνας ἀλφίτου ἀκτῇ,
> μίστυλλόν τ' ἄρα τἆλλα καὶ ἀμφ' ὀβελοῖσιν ἔπειραν
> ὤπτησάν τε περιφραδέως ἐρύσαντό τε πάντα,
> βάλλον δ' εἰν ἐλεοῖσιν ἀολλέα.
>
> (*Odyssey* xiv 419–432)

And the men brought in a pig, five years old and a very fat one,
and made it stand in front of the fireplace, <u>nor did the swineherd</u>
<u>forget the immortal gods, for he had the uses of virtue;</u>
but he cut off hairs from the head of the white-toothed pig to start
    the rite, and threw them
into the fire as a dedication, and prayed to all the gods
that Odysseus of the many designs should have his homecoming.
He hit the beast with a split of oak that he had lying by him.
The breath went out of the pig; then they <u>sacrificed</u> and singed
    him.
They jointed the carcass, and the swineherd laid pieces of raw
    meat
with offerings from all over the body upon the thick fat,
and sprinkled these with meal of barley and threw them in the
    fire, then

they cut all the remainder into pieces and spitted them,
and roasted all carefully and took off the pieces,
and laid them all together on platters.

The different emphasis in the scenes, from food for a hungry guest to a gift-offering to the gods followed by a shared meal, is striking, all the more so given the overlap of cooking details and the quickness with which the second meal follows the first: in between the first and second meals, the men have exchanged life stories, though they do not seem to have moved from their lunch table. The two meals have many details in common, but the sacrificial context of the second meal changes its meaning within the poem. Here, the verb ἔσφαξαν 'butchered', found in sacrificial contexts, is used (*Odyssey* xiv 426), but it is the combination of this verb with pre-kill rites, prayer, and the narrative insight into Eumaios' actions as directed toward the gods ("nor did the swineherd forget the immortal gods, for he had the uses of virtue," οὐδὲ συβώτης λήθετ' ἄρ' ἀθανάτων· φρεσὶ γὰρ κέχρητ' ἀγαθῇσιν, *Odyssey* xiv 420-421) that designates this scene as an animal sacrifice. Although verses similar to those in the non-sacrificial lunch describe the roasting of meat (*Odyssey* xiv 75-77, 430-431), this sacrificial scene is elaborated with the offering of hairs, cut and thrown into the fire, and the prayer for Odysseus' safety (*Odyssey* xiv 422-424). Both meats are sprinkled with barley (*Odyssey* xiv 77, 429), the former presumably for taste, the latter before being thrown into the fire as a preliminary offering.

The sacrificial performance elevates this meal as a sign of the swineherd's devotion to Odysseus. Eumaios' emphasizes his devotion by directly appealing to the gods with the prayer for his master's homecoming that accompanies the preliminary offerings (*Odyssey* xiv 422-424). Recalling the initial description of Eumaios as one "not forgetful of the gods," the swineherd's piety is highlighted by the narrator's description of his "fair-mindedness." Further, with his setting aside special portions for gods and the honorific portion of meat for his guest, his honoring of Odysseus is explicitly linked to worship of the gods:[157]

ἂν δὲ συβώτης
ἵστατο δαιτρεύσων· περὶ γὰρ φρεσὶν αἴσιμα ᾔδη.
καὶ τὰ μὲν ἔπταχα πάντα διεμοιρᾶτο δαΐζων·

---

[157] Kearns 1982 notices that the descriptions of Odysseus' arrival in Ithaka and encounter with Telemakhos allude to visits from disguised gods, which are associated with the practice of *theoxenia*, setting out food for gods. This discussion could be usefully expanded with Eumaios' setting aside of portions in this sacrificial meal.

τὴν μὲν ἴαν Νύμφῃσι καὶ Ἑρμῇ, Μαιάδος υἱεῖ,
θῆκεν ἐπευξάμενος, τὰς δ' ἄλλας νεῖμεν ἑκάστῳ·
νώτοισιν δ' Ὀδυσῆα διηνεκέεσσι γέραιρεν
ἀργιόδοντος ὑός, κύδαινε δὲ θυμὸν ἄνακτος.

(*Odyssey* xiv 432–438)

The swineherd
stood up to divide the portions, for he was fair-minded,
and separated all the meat into seven portions.
One he set aside for the Nymphs and Hermes, the son of Maia,
with a prayer, and the rest he distributed to each man,
but he gave Odysseus in honor the long cuts of the chine
of the white-toothed pig, and so exalted the heart of his master.

Here Eumaios' sacrifice is clearly distinguished from the earlier unmarked meal because of his specific gestures toward gods and prayers. Yet, due to the lack of a clear definition of sacrifice in Homer, some would exclude this as a sacrificial meal, while others would describe both meals as 'sacrificial'. Eumaios' division of the meat into portions is a unique offering, while the consumption of *splankhna* found in some Homeric sacrificial scenes, frequently referred to in Classical descriptions of sacrifice, is not part of this ritual performance. Berthiaume, following the definition of sacrificial ritual offered by Rudhardt, defines the difference between ritual killing and butchery in Homer as the consumption of the *splankhna*, therefore disqualifying Eumaios' offerings.[158] However, no single detail can be used in Homer to define an action, even a 'typical action', since the variation between scenes is an essential part of the creation of meaning and the composition-in-performance of the poems. *Splankhna* are only consumed on six occasions in all of Homer, including once by the suitors in the *Odyssey*, who serve as symbols of the perversion of normative ritual, so this cannot be considered a defining criterion.[159] A similar attempt to define sacrifice on the basis of a single ritual action is made by Stengel, who proposes that prayer identifies sacrificial scenes in Homer, being a clear marker that the action is directed at the gods; this assertion is also supported by José García-López in a book on Mycenaean and Homeric sacrifice.[160] Yet not every sacrificial scene includes prayer, for

---

[158] Berthiaume 1982:65–67, Rudhardt 1958:255. Burkert 1985: the consumption of the *splankhna* is the "privilege and duty of the innermost circle of participants" (57). See above, page 22.

[159] The *splankhna* are eaten at *Iliad* I 464, II 426; *Odyssey* iii 9, 461, xii 364, and xx 252 (suitors). The suitors' failure to offer sacrifice is part of their "disordered violence" and a perversion of hospitality; see Nagy 1990b:271; Seaford 1994:30; 2004:44; and Saïd 1979.

[160] Stengel 1910:65;/García-López 1970:53. So Graf 2002: "The prayer is the one unequivocal

instance Agamemnon's hecatomb for Apollo (*Iliad* I 313–317), and the prayers themselves exhibit a great deal of variation. Rather than a single detail or action defining sacrifice, it is an accumulation of details and specific references in the narrative to gift-offerings to the gods that create the thematic meaning of sacrifice in Homer. Some details in Eumaios' sacrifice are unique in Homer, others may be found elsewhere, but the accumulation of pre-kill rites, the prayer, special offerings for the gods, and the twice-repeated observation of Eumaios' pious nature mark this meal as 'sacrificial', in contrast to the earlier scene, which focuses on hospitality and nourishment.

This implies not a division between "religious" and "non-religious" actions, a meaningless distinction in antiquity, but a range of possible traditional actions adaptable to different contexts.[161] The marked occasion is an animal sacrifice, preceded by recognizable pre-kill rites directed toward divinities. To avoid confusion, I will refer to the unmarked descriptions at the farthest end of the spectrum from communication with the gods, those of animals slaughtered without pre-kill rites, as "feasting." This does not exclude feasting as a ritual action or, when included in sacrifice, render it a meaningless part of sacrifice. It merely illustrates a different emphasis created by the selective process of artistic representation. The slaughter of the animal is described in both scenes of feasting and sacrifice, but pre-kill or post-kill details are expanded to suit the needs of the context. The focus can shift from sacrifice with a commensal meal, or sacrifice without a commensal meal, to a commensal meal without sacrifice. Sacrifice is marked by the intention of communicating with the gods, which is not always equated with a shared meal. At the other end of the spectrum, the narrative emphasizes the meal in scenes that do not call attention to mortal/immortal relations, or in which the theme of mortal nourishment is prominent, symbolizing revitalization and survival. In the *Iliad* this spectrum ranges from grand sacrifices to the gods as performed by Agamemnon to Akhilleus' complete exclusion of such actions in his preparation of food.

Many scholars of ritual have struggled with the connection between Homeric sacrifice and feasting. Kirk refers to 'secular meals' in Homer, as do Dietrich and Angeliki Petropoulou.[162] Stallings, constrained by her definition

---

communicative act with the divinity" (121). Kirk 1985 *ad Iliad* II 400–402 notes that sacrifices accompanied by prayers (apparently here his working definition of sacrifice) normally occur in the context of aristocratic, heroic dinners.

[161] However, to scholars such as Durkheim (19121, 2001:36f.), the essence of the "sacred" is the separation between secular and sacred: it is something set apart.

[162] Kirk 1981; Petropoulou 1987, who considers Eumaios' meal with Odysseus as "secular"; and Dietrich 1988. Gunn 1971:22 describes feasting as "closely connected with sacrifice," but he

of sacrifice as part of a feast, is unable to identify a significant theme in the formulas of animal sacrifice: "In the first place, the automatic significance conferred by religious action is not shared by all type scenes, in the second place, the eaten sacrifices are exceedingly diverse in diction, so that they may hardly constitute a single type."[163] Sharing a similar state of frustration, Calhoun concludes that the poems describe ritual "incidentally," "circumstantially," and "incompletely."[164] The lack of "automatic religious significance" comes from the tendency to group together scenes from opposite ends of the previously described spectrum, which results from a strict categorization of "every-meal-a-sacrifice" and the similarly confining view that the varying length of sacrificial scenes is only a matter of insignificant reduction or expansion. Studies on the Classical iconography of sacrifice have reached similar conclusions. Sarah Peirce's discussion of scenes of *thusia* in Classical vase painting, while denying any distinction between "sacred" killing and "secular" eating, only considers images with explicit "ritual" details, such as wreaths or altars, to be snapshots of a particular stage of a *thusia* sacrifice.[165] Similarly, van Straten considers a combination of features, such as the altar, the divine recipient, and decorations on the animal, to be indicative of sacrificial contexts.[166]

The quantity and diversity of words used to describe Homeric sacrifice complicate attempts at its interpretation, in contrast to the relatively consistent later usage of verbs describing animal sacrifice. In the Classical period, verbs as such as θύειν, ἱερεύειν, and σφάζειν are used so frequently in connection with particular circumstances that they can be assigned, with few exceptions, meanings specific to different types of sacrifice.[167] Homeric poetics necessitates that a variety of different words and phrases be used for important actions. For example, in a relatively short number of verses, six different

---

does not consider these actions to be inseparable.

[163] Stallings 1984:338.

[164] Calhoun 1962:445.

[165] Peirce 1993:236–237 uses the medium of sympotic cups to substantiate her evidence for scenes of *thusia*. She figures the Homeric material into her theory of the continuum of sacrifice, describing the elaborate dedications of thigh bones and *splankhna* as "the *thusia* that appears in Homer and Classical literature" (236).

[166] Van Straten 1995:10.

[167] On the different meanings of these verbs and the contrast between *sphagia*, which emphasizes blood-letting, and the sacrificial feast, *thusia*, often respectively interpreted as "khthonic" and "Olympian," see Benveniste 1973:486–487; Jameson 1991:201; Bowie 1995:466; Bremmer 1998:29n87; and Henrichs 2005. Other important Homeric sacrificial terms are not found in later authors, such as ὠμοθετεῖν and δαίς, although these do occur in tragedy. On the latter, see Sherratt 2004:189, who discusses the possible Mycenaean attestation of *e-pi-de-da-to* (PY Vn 20).

expressions are used to describe the deaths of six heroes in battle.[168] Similarly, there are numerous ways to indicate animal sacrifice in Homer, with combinations of nouns and verbs expressing a range of meanings appropriate to each individual context. Though there is some continuity from the sacrificial terminology used in the *Iliad* to that found in the Classical period, many terms and concepts found in later authors are not yet established by the time of Homer.

The most commonly used designation for sacrifice in later authors is θύειν. However, in Homer, θύειν expresses burning, which includes, but is not restricted to, parts of animals.[169] This original meaning of 'go up in smoke' is reflected in the Homeric noun-epithet phrase "smoky altar" (βωμὸς θυήεις), such as the one for Zeus on Mount Ida.[170] That this verb becomes the technical term for animal sacrifice in later periods is due to a process of verbal evolution, described by Jean Casabona as "accidental."[171] In addition to the adjective θυήεις, there are only four other occurrences in the *Iliad* of either the verb θύειν or related nouns, in all instances referring to smoke or the act of burning rather than animal sacrifice.[172] Hektor describes the gift-offerings the women will take to Athena, in addition to the *peplos*, as θυέεσσι (*Iliad* VI 270), also used by Phoinix as one of three offerings to the gods, along with libations and the smoke of sacrificial meat (*knisē, Iliad* IX 499–501). Akhilleus initiates a very abbreviated offering to the gods when preparing dinner for the embassy: he reportedly orders an offering to be made to the gods (θῦσαι) by Patroklos, who then throws θυηλαί into the fire (*Iliad* IX 219–220). The verb and derivative noun, a *hapax legomenon*, in this context describe a burnt offering to the gods. Akhilleus' burnt offering is unique in the poem, a deviation from Agamemnon's idealized enacted sacrifices that will be discussed fully in Chapter Four. In the *Iliad*, θύειν does not depict animal sacrifice, the slaughter of victims with pre-kill actions dedicated to the gods. Likewise, θύειν, which in this context seems

---

[168] Muellner 1976:25 gives a tabulation of the deaths of six heroes described in six different ways within 42 verses (*Iliad* VI 42–83); Visser 1988 lists the eleven different verbs used in killing scenes.

[169] Stengel 1910:4–12; Burkert 1966:103; West 1997b:46. Kadletz 1984:101 defines it as "the burning of some food product," echoed by Petropoulou 1986:137.

[170] *Iliad* VIII 48; XXIII 148; and *Odyssey* viii 363. The issue is discussed by Burkert 1985:62; Casabona 1966:69–72; and Stengel 1910:7–12, who cites the famous distinction made by Herodian (fragment 48). It is interesting that σφάζειν is derived from Mycenaean *sa-pa-ka-te-ri-ja*, which seems to refer to sacrifice in the tablets (see page 54 below), whereas θύειν comes from *tu-we-ta*, which seems to be profane. On the latter see Burkert 1985:370n64, writing before the discovery of *sa-pa-ka-te-ri-ja*; see also Killen 2001.

[171] Casabona 1966:127; cf. Burkert 1966:103.

[172] Benveniste 1973: "Its origin is certain: *thúô* goes back to a present tense *dhu-yô*, the root of which properly means 'to produce smoke'" (486).

to mean 'burn for the gods', as noted by Aristarkhos, rather than 'slaughter for the gods', is used four times in the *Odyssey*.[173]

The myriad connotative and denotative meanings implicit in sacrificial terminology are scarcely covered by our word 'sacrifice'. This range of meaning is particularly an issue with the verbs ἱερεύειν and σφάζειν, which have been the subject of much confusion in modern studies of sacrifice in Homer.[174] The confusion stems from the lack of an accepted definition of sacrifice in the Homeric poems, leading to varying tabulations of sacrificial scenes on the basis of shared terminology rather than on a combination of terminology and meaning generated by context.[175] Arend proposes that ritual reality imposes restrictions on the use of sacrificial terminology. However, the thematic needs of the poetry overrule any possible "fixity" that ritual actions may have. The poems use the same language to describe different actions in different contexts, but the gradual semantic development of these words must also be taken into account, considering that the meanings of these words are not clearly established until the Classical period. As words develop meaning over time, they may either gain or lose sacral meanings. For example, τέμενος begins as a secular term for a tract of land, but comes to denote exclusively a sanctuary, and εὔχομαι, which seems originally to have meant 'boast', develops into 'pray'.[176] Such linguistic development is sure to be found in a poem with as lengthy a process of transmission as the *Iliad*.

A thorough investigation of the different applications and contexts evoked by these words further reinforces the distinction between sacrifices, which are directed toward the gods, and feasts, in which the killing of the animal is described by σφάζειν or ἱερεύειν, but without reference to divinities. These verbs are *nuanced* according to context.[177] We may compare Stephen Lowenstam's discussion of the infamous "irrational epithets," the occurrence of adjectives in Homeric verse that defy the usual definitions assigned to them in individual contexts, such as the description of the beggar Iros' mother as πότνια (*Odyssey* xviii 5). If one insists upon a definition of this word as 'queenly',

---

[173] *Odyssey* ix 231; xiv 446; xv 222, and 261. Scholiast A *ad Iliad* IX 219 = Lehrs 1964:82; Scholiast A *ad Odyssey* XIV 446; Benveniste 1973:486; Burkert 1966:103; Casabona 1966:72.

[174] Calhoun 1962:446; Kadletz 1984:102f.; Stallings 1984:102; and Sherratt 2004:182.

[175] Thirty sacrifices are listed by Stallings 1984:102f. Casabona found 28 (1966:19), and Stengel 17 (1910:1): a good example of the lack of consensus on ritual terminology in Homer.

[176] Arend's views on type scenes are discussed above, pages 13–15. On εὔχομαι, see Muellner 1976:10, 25.

[177] A comparable example of this nuance may be drawn from the *Odyssey*: Telemakhos' ritual offering is twice described with θύειν (*Odyssey* xv 222, 260), but then with σπένδειν (*Odyssey* xv 258), a verb normally used of liquid libations: Kadletz 1984:102, disputed by Petropoulou 1986; cf. Casabona's definition of σπένδειν (1966:236).

this specific usage becomes "irrational," but if one allows for context's influence over meaning, as Lowenstam suggests, meanings that fit all contexts, such as 'lawfully wedded', emerge.[178] An analysis of the range of meanings expressed by σφάζειν and ἱερεύειν will lead to some preliminary conclusions about the role of sacrifice in the presentation of the quarrel between Akhilleus and Agamemnon, which will be developed further in Chapter Four.

ἱερεύειν is probably attested in Linear B: John Chadwick has translated the verb *i-je-to-qe*, on the famous sacrificial tablet from Pylos (Tn 316), as 'sacrifice'.[179] On the obverse of this tablet, probably recording last-minute offerings before the destruction at Pylos, the first line reads: "Pylos *sacrifices* at the shrine of Poseidon" (*PU-RO i-je-to-qe po-si-da-i-jo a-ke-que wa-tu*). This statement is followed by a list of the offerings, which seem to include gold vessels and women. Much of the controversy in Homeric scholarship stems from the use of ἱερεύειν nine times in the *Odyssey* to describe the suitors' consumption of Odysseus' livestock. In these instances, sacrifice cannot be meant; the thematic emphasis lies in the suitors' perversion, through their greedy appetites, of social behavior rather than in their expressing of piety toward the gods.[180] For instance, they are described as slaughtering animals simply to eat, "so that killing (ἱερεύσαντες) the pigs, they might satisfy their spirits with meat" (*Odyssey* xiv 28). As discussed above, there has been little consensus on the meaning of this word in Homer.

There are ten occurrences of ἱερεύειν in the *Iliad*, in contexts that vary from sacrificial meals to the unmarked killing of animals for consumption.[181] Twice, in very important scenes to which we shall return throughout this study, ἱερεύειν describes Agamemnon's sacrifices to Zeus (*Iliad* II 402; VII 314), both full-range descriptions featuring prayers and pre-kill rites. ἱερεύειν also describes the promised sacrifice vowed to Athena: "Then promise to sacrifice twelve heifers in her shrine, yearlings never broken, if only she'll pity Troy, the Trojan wives and all our helpless children," (καί οἱ ὑποσχέσθαι δυοκαίδεκα βοῦς ἐνὶ νηῷ / ἤνις ἠκέστας ἱερευσέμεν, αἴ κ' ἐλεήσῃ / ἄστυ τε καὶ Τρώων ἀλόχους καὶ νήπια τέκνα, *Iliad* VI 93–95), suggested first by Helenos (*Iliad* VI 94) and then repeated by Hektor (*Iliad* VI 275) and Theano (*Iliad* VI 309).

---

[178] Lowenstam 1993:24–25.

[179] Ventris and Chadwick 1973:462; Palmer 1994.

[180] *Odyssey* ii 56; xiv 9; xvii 180, 181, 535; and xx 3, 250, 251, 391. The LSJ gives the definition 'slaughter generally for a feast' for *Odyssey* ii 56; viii 59; xiv 414; xix 198; and xxiv 215, explaining that the two senses of 'slaughter' and 'sacrifice' are combined at *Odyssey* xiii 24.

[181] Agamemnon's performance of sacrifice: *Iliad* II 402; VII 314; the Trojan vow: (Helenos) VI 94; (Hektor) VI 275; (Theano) VI 309; Glaukos on feasting: VI 174; in the context of Akhilleus' rejection of sacrifice: XVIII 559; XXI 131; XXIII 147; XXIV 125.

However, complications arise in the usage of the same verb in Glaukos' digression on Bellerophon, in which the verb describes the Lycian king's reception of the hero: "For nine days he showed him hospitality and slaughtered nine oxen" (ἐννῆμαρ ξείνισσε καὶ ἐννέα βοῦς ἱέρευσεν, *Iliad* VI 174). There are no references here to divinities, but rather a description of the generous reception of Bellerophon before the king commands him to kill the Khimaira (*Iliad* VI 179). The feasting, a symbol of social harmony, is designed to contrast with the king's reaction to the revelation of the baneful signs Bellerophon carries with him (*Iliad* VI 168, 178). Although the verb ἱερεύειν, associated with animal sacrifice, is used in this description, the lack of other indications of a ceremony addressing the gods and the clear emphasis on hospitality for guests (ξείνισσε) differentiate its meaning in this instance from the descriptions of Agamemnon's sacrifices and the Trojan vow to Athena. Similarly, a banquet without reference to divinities is depicted on the shield made by Hephaistos for Akhilleus:

βασιλεὺς δ' ἐν τοῖσι σιωπῇ
σκῆπτρον ἔχων ἑστήκει ἐπ' ὄγμου γηθόσυνος κῆρ.
κήρυκες δ' ἀπάνευθεν ὑπὸ δρυῒ δαῖτα πένοντο,
βοῦν δ' ἱερεύσαντες μέγαν ἄμφεπον· αἱ δὲ γυναῖκες
δεῖπνον ἐρίθοισιν λεύκ' ἄλφιτα πολλὰ πάλυνον.

(*Iliad* XVIII 556–560)

And there in the midst the king, in silence,
scepter in hand at the head of the reaping-rows, stood, rejoicing
    in his heart.
And off to the side, beneath an oak, the heralds were setting out
    the feast,
they were dressing a great ox <u>they had slaughtered</u>, while women
poured out white barley, generous, for the reaper's midday meal.

The scene on Akhilleus' shield depicts preparations for supper for a king, who holds a scepter and, as such, recalls Agamemnon as chief king of the Akhaians.[182] The heralds who set out the harvest for the king anticipate the role of Talthubios in setting up Agamemnon's oath sacrifice in *Iliad* XIX, which will mark Akhilleus' reintegration into the group—the last sacrifice in the

---

[182] On the shield of Akhilleus as a microcosm of the themes expressed throughout the poem, particularly the prosperity of a peaceful life that Akhilleus will never be able to enjoy, see Nagy 2003:72–87 and Taplin 2000. Taplin 2000:352 interprets this scene as a dinner for hungry harvesters, challenging Kirk's reading of the meat as prepared exclusively for the king (1976: 12).

epic. That there are no references to divinities on the shield of Akhilleus is significant. The emphasis of the verb ἱερεύειν has shifted to create an image of feasting unlike those found in the Trojan vow or Agamemnon's sacrifices. Because Thetis brings Akhilleus this divinely made armor, a gift from the gods to a semi-divine hero, its echo of Agamemnon's sacrifices serves to highlight Akhilleus' isolation. Throughout the poem, sacrifice will remain central to thematic opposition between Akhilleus and the methods of communicating with the gods used by the mortal heroes. Akhilleus himself twice uses ἱερεύειν in his rejection of animal sacrifice as a meaningful act. Over the corpse of Lukaon he vaunts that the Trojan sacrifices to the Skamandros did not avail him ("the many bulls you sacrificed," πολέας ἱερεύετε ταύρους, *Iliad* XXI 131). In a very poignant moment, standing over the pyre of Patroklos, he revokes the vow his father made to the river Sperkheios for sacrifices upon his return home ("to sacrifice sheep into your waters," μῆλ' ἱερεύσειν ἐς πηγάς, *Iliad* XXIII 147–148). Akhilleus' emphatic rejection of sacrifice as he approaches his own death will be discussed in detail in Chapter Four. Suffice it for now to say that the language of sacrifice adapts to the context of the speaker: when Akhilleus speaks of sacrifice, it is resoundingly negative.

A final usage of ἱερεύειν occurs in the primary narrative description of the preparation of Akhilleus' breakfast, which serves as a backdrop for Thetis' approach to the gods to discuss their anger over Akhilleus' perversion of burial ritual and mistreatment of Hektor's corpse:

> εὗρ' ἁδινὰ στενάχοντα· φίλοι δ' ἀμφ' αὐτὸν ἑταῖροι
> ἐσσυμένως ἐπένοντο καὶ ἐντύνοντο ἄριστον·
> τοῖσι δ' ὄϊς λάσιος μέγας ἐν κλισίῃ ἱέρευτο.
>
> (*Iliad* XXIV 123–125)

> [Thetis] found him groaning hard. Around him trusted comrades
> busily swung to the work, preparing breakfast,
> for them a large fleecy sheep lay slaughtered in the shelter.

At this moment, the narrative describes the animals slaughtered for Akhilleus' meal with a verb associated with animal sacrifice. However, not only are the expected features of animal sacrifice absent, but the sacrificers are also unspecified: the sheep is, exceptionally, the nominative subject of the passive verb.[183] This impersonal usage emphasizes Akhilleus' distance from normative animal sacrifice. Akhilleus' refusal to eat has been a hallmark of his grief for

---

[183] The passive is also used by Telemakhos concerning the suitors slaughtering sheep and drinking wine, another type of deviant feasting behavior: μήλων σφαζομένων οἴνοιό τε πινομένοιο (*Odyssey* xx 312).

Patroklos; his neglected breakfast, which is only referred to here and is never eaten in the narrative, further emphasizes his social removal.

The individual context of ἱερεύειν is important for the poem's characterization of Agamemnon and of his the quarrel with Akhilleus. Its meanings can range from "sacrifice animals to the gods as a gesture of power" to "kill animals to eat them without pre-kill rites as an expression of deviance from expected behavior,"[184] but it is through the recollection of other scenes in the poem that ἱερεύειν generates audience expectations of animal sacrifice, expectations to be either fulfilled or frustrated according to the thematic needs of the context. When the expectation of sacrifice is introduced, if the verb is used without reference to the gods or other sacrificial details, the audience notices the *lack* of sacrifice to the gods. This destabilization of audience expectation heightens the significance of the descriptions of Akhilleus' shield and his uneaten breakfast as divergent from Agamemnon's animal sacrifices.

σφάζειν has a similar range of applications. This verb is also attested in Linear B: *sa-pa-ka-te-ri-ja* (*sphakteria*), occurring on tablets from Knossos.[185] The LSJ and Cunliffe's *Lexicon* define σφάζειν as 'slaughter' in Homer, but it becomes 'sacrifice' in later authors, for example Pindar and Xenophon, and in tragedy. In tragic poetry, but not in Homer, σφάζειν can be applied to the killing of people.[186] In the Classical period, it is even possible to broadly categorize different types of sacrifice according to the use of this verb: *thusia* sacrifices are followed by a feast on the basis of the frequent use of the verb θύειν, and *sphagia* sacrifices are uneaten on the basis of the use of the verb σφάζειν, which refers only to the kill and need not be followed by sacrifice. Thus Casabona believes that σφάζειν, with a few exceptions, represents an uneaten sacrifice, as seems to be its meaning in the Classical period.[187] As opposed to

---

[184] Compare Muellner's distinction in his separation of sacral and secular uses of εὔχομαι (1976: 31–34) and Visser's important work on formulas in battle scenes. The verbs ἐναίρειν and ἐναρίζειν mean 'to strip the armor, despoil', but are more often used to mean 'kill', without reference to armor (Visser 1988:30).

[185] Killen 1994. *sa-pa-ka-te-ri-ja* occurs on a tablet from Knossos, C(2) 941, in reference to ten female sheep given by *a-pi-qo-ta*, the name for 'collector', which seems to have been a group of individuals, probably members of the royal family or high-ranking palace officials. Two other tablets from Knossos probably record the *sphakteria* of animals: KN C 1561 recording an unknown number of ewes, and KN X 9191, the arrangement of which is suggestive of a sheep record. *sa-pa* is not the usual reflex for σφα-, which is *p-* (for example, *pe-mo* for *sperma*), but it is possible; Killen 1994:75 provides comparanda.

[186] Seaford 1989, 1994:47n71.

[187] Casabona 1966:155–156. See above, note 167; Henrichs 2000: "From Homer on θύειν tends to be associated with the gods and σφάζειν with the sacrificial animal" (180).

the happy contexts for feasting provided by most *thusia* sacrifices, *sphagia* sacrifices are performed in the Classical period at the taking of oaths, in purification rites, and before battle for divination purposes.[188]

However, no sacrifices are performed before battle for divination in Homer, nor does σφάζειν have a special connection with 'uneaten sacrifice', as it is always used of animals killed for feasts in Homer. Similar to the use of ἱερεύειν, σφάζειν is used in reference only to Agamemnon, Akhilleus, and, on one other occasion, in Phoinix's autobiography. Therefore, it becomes part of the thematic use of sacrifice to exemplify the special status of Akhilleus in regard to mortal/immortal dynamics. Agamemnon's enacted sacrifices are twice described in this way (*Iliad* I 459 = II 422); these sacrifices, to which we will return in Chapters Two and Four, demonstrate the full range of pre-kill rites and prayers to the gods. After bringing Hektor's mutilated corpse to his camp, a blood-spattered Akhilleus and the Myrmidons lament Patroklos, and Akhilleus has a funeral feast prepared for them (ὁ τοῖσι τάφον μενοεικέα δαίνυ, *Iliad* XXIII 29). Akhilleus' attendants butcher (σφαζόμενοι) bulls, sheep, goats, and swine for the mourners (*Iliad* XXIII 30–31). However, despite the stated intention to prepare a feast, the consumption of the meal is not depicted; rather, the slaughter and destruction of the animals is dramatically emphasized: the 'quivering' (ὀρέχθεον) animals are killed and burnt ("They singed the bristles, splaying the porkers out across Hephaistos' fire," θαλέθοντες ἀλοιφῇ / εὐόμενοι τανύοντο διὰ φλογὸς Ἡφαίστοιο, *Iliad* XXIII 32–33), and they provide copious amounts of blood, in which everyone could dip cups (πάντη δ' ἀμφὶ νέκυν κοτυλήρυτον ἔρρεεν αἷμα, *Iliad* XXIII 34). In this context, no divinities are mentioned, nor are there any indications that these actions are part of a ceremony directed toward the gods. Instead, the gory tone established by Akhilles' grim treatment of Hektor continues. There is no feast, and Akhilleus is brought to Agamemnon still covered in gore, which he refuses to wash until Patroklos is buried. This usage of σφάζειν closely recalls that in the speech of Phoinix, which exhibits many of the same features found in Akhilleus' funeral feast, even repeating a verse that describes animals being burnt:

> αὐτοῦ λισσόμενοι κατερήτυον ἐν μεγάροισι,
> πολλὰ δὲ ἴφια μῆλα καὶ εἰλίποδας ἕλικας βοῦς
> ἔσφαζον, πολλοὶ δὲ σύες <u>θαλέθοντες ἀλοιφῇ</u>

---

[188] Stengel 1920:92–102, Rudhardt 1958:272–281, Casabona 1966:180–193, Burkert 1983:59–60, Pritchett 1979:83–90. Peirce has determined that most representations of *sphagia* in Classical visual art are of the pre-battle type (1993:253n143).

εὐόμενοι τανύοντο διὰ φλογὸς Ἡφαίστοιο,
πολλὸν δ' ἐκ κεράμων μέθυ πίνετο τοῖο γέροντος.

(*Iliad* IX 465–469)

Holding me in the house, begging me to stay,
<u>they butchered</u> plenty of fat sheep, and shambling crook-horned
    cattle,
droves of pigs, <u>succulent, rich with fat—</u>
<u>they singed the bristles, splaying them out across Hephaistos' fire,</u>
then a great amount of wine was poured from the old man's jars.

This description is part of Phoinix's autobiographical story of betrayal and withdrawal: he was persuaded to sleep with his father's concubine by his jealous mother, and after 'one of the immortals' stops him from killing his father, he decides to leave home (*Iliad* IX 444–463). There are numerous striking parallels between Phoinix's experience and Akhilleus' own wrath and withdrawal, but the object of his speech is to persuade the young hero to heed his advice not to abandon the Akhaian army.[189] The description of Phoinix's friends and relatives beseeching him and killing numerous animals is not meant to imply sacrifice, since there are no references to divinities or pre-kill rites. Therefore, it belongs to a different end of the spectrum of meaning implied by ἔσφαζον than the commensal feasts arranged by Agamemnon. Phoinix's apparent lack of participation in this feast may anticipate Akhilleus' thematic opposition to sacrifice, which will become so important in the latter half of the poem. He goes on to describe the power of sacrifice in his paradigm of the *Litai* and in Oineus' neglected sacrifices to Artemis, to which we will return below. Phoinix presents a range of eating and sacrificial activities, all anecdotes about the anger of gods: Artemis is angry about neglected sacrifices; the anger of the gods can generally be appeased by sacrifices. His speech is, of course, unsuccessful, and Akhilleus remains withdrawn.

To conclude this Chapter, we will return to Akhilleus' meal with Priam, which has been variously interpreted as both a "sacrificial meal" and a "non-sacrificial" meal.[190] Building on our discussion of the creation of sacrificial

[189] Scodel 1982b:132 likens the feasting described here to the suitors' revels in the *Odyssey*, in contrast to the pathetic appeals in the Meleagros paradigm and the embassy to Akhilleus. Rosner 1976:317 describes Phoinix's description as a "noisy and repeated sacrifice."

[190] Sacrificial: Arend 1933; Heubeck et al. 1988 ad *Odyssey* iii 445f.; Stallings 1984. Non-sacrificial: Kirk 1981:63. Edwards 1987:71–72 cites this as one of two meals in the epic (the other is *Iliad* IX 219) without explicit mention of sacrifice. Richardson 1993 note *ad loc.* does not mention "sacrifice" and describes it as a "meal" following "conventional patterns." In two articles on this scene in Seaford's volume on reciprocity, Zanker 1998:85 calls it a "meal," and Postlethwaite 1998:99 describes the "ritual slaughter of sheep." Kitts 2005:30 notes that Akhilleus' meals

ritual through an accumulation of ritual details, we can see that Akhilleus describes the meal to Priam without referencing gift-offerings to divinities or other rites which mark sacrifice scenes. He first makes known his intention to provide a feast for Priam with the remark, "now, at last, let us turn our thoughts to supper" (νῦν δὲ μνησώμεθα δόρπου, *Iliad* XXIV 601), followed by his digression on the fate of Niobe (*Iliad* XXIV 602–617), after which he again reiterates his intention to eat: [191]

"ἀλλ᾽ ἄγε δὴ καὶ νῶι μεδώμεθα, δῖε γεραιέ,
σίτου· ἔπειτά κεν αὖτε φίλον παῖδα κλαίοισθα
Ἴλιον εἰσαγαγών· πολυδάκρυτος δέ τοι ἔσται."
Ἦ, καὶ ἀναΐξας ὄιν ἄργυφον ὠκὺς Ἀχιλλεύς
σφάξ᾽· ἕταροι δ᾽ ἔδερόν τε καὶ ἄμφεπον εὖ κατὰ κόσμον,
μίστυλλόν τ᾽ ἄρ᾽ ἐπισταμένως πεῖράν τ᾽ ὀβελοῖσιν,
ὤπτησάν τε περιφραδέως, ἐρύσαντό τε πάντα.
Αὐτομέδων δ᾽ ἄρα σῖτον ἑλὼν ἐπένειμε τραπέζῃ
καλοῖς ἐν κανέοισιν· ἀτὰρ κρέα νεῖμεν Ἀχιλλεύς.
οἳ δ᾽ ἐπ᾽ ὀνείαθ᾽ ἑτοῖμα προκείμενα χεῖρας ἴαλλον.
αὐτὰρ ἐπεὶ πόσιος καὶ ἐδητύος ἐξ ἔρον ἕντο,

(*Iliad* XXIV 618–628)

"So come—we too, old king, must think of food.
Later you can mourn your beloved son once more
when you bear him home from Troy, and you'll weep many tears."
Having spoken, swift Akhilleus sprang to his feet
and slaughtered a white sheep as comrades moved in
to skin the carcass quickly, dress the quarters well.
Expertly they cut the meat into pieces, pierced them with spits,
roasted them to a turn and pulled them off the spits.
Automedon brought the bread, set it out on the board
in ample wicker baskets. Akhilleus served the meat.
They reached out for the good things that lay at hand
and when they had put aside desire for food and drink...

When Akhilleus tells Priam, "we too, old king, must think of food," the audience is given clear indication that eating, as an act of nourishment, is a priority, just as it is in Eumaios' first meal. Like *dorpon* (*Iliad* XXIV 601), *sitos* is an unmarked

---

in *Iliad* IX and XXIV do not represent "sacrificial killing," but argues that the shared verses describing the feast create the idea of sacrifice for the audience.

[191] On the innovations to the Niobe story designed to convince Priam to eat, see Seaford 1994:174–176.

term for food, which does not carry associations of sacrificial performance or gift-offerings to the gods.[192] Akhilleus' lack of dedicatory actions or addresses to divinities is even emphasized by the narrative description of his jumping up and slaughtering the animal (ἀναΐξας ὄϊν ἄργυφον ὠκὺς Ἀχιλλεὺς σφάξ', *Iliad* XXIV 617–618), a complete inversion of the slow solemnity exhibited in the pre-kill rites that precede sacrifices. Although the same verb, σφάζειν, is used here as it is in Eumaios' sacrificial dinner, the lack of actions directed toward gods, such as pre-kill rites or prayer, distinguish this killing from the sacrificial ritual performed by Eumaios before his second meal. The narrative emphasis in this feast with Priam is on human nourishment, as twice stated by Akhilleus himself and further clarified in his paradigmatic digression about Niobe.

As discussed in section 1.1, the same verses describe the spitting and roasting of meat as in the sacrifice scenes in *Iliad* I and II. The audience will have been reminded of the sacrifice scenes in *Iliad* I and II by the repetition of familiar material, but the different emphasis on nourishment is made clear through the variations unique to this scene: burning thigh bones for the gods and consumption of the *splankhna*, ritual details found in the sacrifice scenes in *Iliad* I and II, are replaced with the description of Akhilleus and Automedon preparing dinner. The resonance of the earlier sacrifice scenes resumes at the end of Akhilleus' meal with Priam, which concludes: "when they had put aside desire for food and drink" (αὐτὰρ ἐπεὶ πόσιος καὶ ἐδητύος ἐξ ἔρον ἕντο, *Iliad* I 469 = II 432 = XXIV 628).[193] However, the description of the satisfied diners having partaken of their appropriate share of the feast (δαίνυντ', οὐδέ τι θυμὸς ἐδεύετο δαιτὸς ἐΐσης, *Iliad* I 468 = II 431), a crucial indication of the success of sacrifice in social maintenance, is missing.[194] The description of partaking in the equally distributed feast, this essential communicative event, has actually been replaced in *Iliad* XXIV with verses that emphasize both the unique nature of the meal and Akhilleus' role as distributor of meat. The significance of the verses that distinguish this scene at the end of the poem from the sacrifice scenes in *Iliad* I and II is part of the expression of Akhilleus' unique heroic

---

[192] Rundin 1996:185–186 exlains that *deipnos, ariston,* and *dorpon* are the three nouns which designate meals "whose principle purpose is nourishment"; cf. Saïd 1979:14. Berthiaume 1982:5 lists three categories of Homeric food: *les céréales* (*sitos*), meat, and "the rest" (fruit, cheese, beans, fish and poultry).

[193] This verse is found seven times in the *Iliad* to refer to the conclusion of a variety of different feast occasions (*Iliad* I 469; II 432; VII 323; IX 92, 222; XXIII 57; XXIV 628). It links Akhilleus' meal to a pattern of feasting established throughout the poem, but does in itself not carry connotations specifically of sacrifice. A further discussion can be found below, page 202.

[194] Nagy 1979:128 defines δαιτὸς ἐΐσης as the proper share of meat at sacrificial feasts. See also Motto and Clark 1969:118–119; Bowie 1995:467n44 and Seaford 2004:50 discuss the equal share as a sign of citizenship.

status through the theme of the *dais* in the *Iliad*, a complex issue to which we will return throughout this book.[195]

As opposed to the sacrifices in *Iliad* I and II, which are motivated by mortal desires to influence the gods—to assuage the anger of Apollo and to win the favor of Zeus, respectively—the marked emphasis in this scene is on eating. In this study of sacrifice, we will see that Akhilleus' reciprocal relationship with Zeus is not established by or dependent on sacrifice, the normative mortal method of communicating with the gods. Instead, he relies on his divine mother's reciprocal relationship with Zeus. The distinction between sacrifice and feasting on this occasion, established by variations upon the typical representation of sacrifice, demonstrates a pattern found throughout the poem: the use of sacrifice to identify Akhilleus' semi-divine status and unique relationship with the gods. Before further analyzing this role for sacrifice within the poem, we will explore the ways in which sacrifice is represented as establishing reciprocity between gods and men in the *Iliad*.

---

[195] This serves as a reversal of his earlier representation in connection with either the hideous aspects of eating or abstinence from food. We will return to this topic in Chapter Four, page 189f. below.

Chapter Two

The Ritual Process

T HE THEMATIC RESONANCE OF SACRIFICE in the *Iliad* depends on the combination of individual ritual actions, each appropriate to context, which produce a pattern of significance throughout the poem.[1] To better illuminate this pattern, we can catalog the range of possible ritual details in Homeric sacrifices and thus clarify the restricted focus on certain actions according to the needs of the context. For example, when Nestor convinces Patroklos to enter the battle in *Iliad* XI, he gives a long speech in which he remembers Peleus making sacrifice at home. In Nestor's memory, the burning of thigh bones for Zeus encapsulates the sacrificial process (γέρων δ' ἱππηλάτα Πηλεὺς πίονα μηρία καῖε βοός, *Iliad* XI 772-773), but we are given much more information, which indicates that the narrative lens has zoomed in on specific moments in a long procedure. The participants are in the courtyard (αὐλῆς ἐν χόρτῳ, *Iliad* XI 774); libations are poured from a golden cup on the burning offerings, which implies a fire (χρύσειον ἄλεισον, σπένδων αἴθοπα οἶνον ἐπ' αἰθομένοις ἱεροῖσι, *Iliad* XI 774-775); and Akhilleus and Patroklos are busy dismembering the carcass to prepare a feast (*Iliad* XI 776-777). Some of these details are unique; others are frequently included in sacrificial descriptions. In order to understand the significance of the inclusion of these particular details in Nestor's memory, we must determine how often locations are described, the frequency and type of libations made in sacrifice, and the different representations of the post-kill stage of the process.

2.1 Narrative Voices

Many different "voices" transmit the story of the *Iliad* to the audience.[2] The primary narrative voice, inspired by the Muses and therefore omniscient, pre-

---

[1]   Even Arend admits this, while maintaining that sacrificial scenes are the most repetitive of all type- scenes (1933:8). Seaford 1994: "The Homeric selection of sacrificial elements is determined, consciously or unconsciously, by the function of the description in the overall poetic conception" (46).

[2]   Chatman 1978 establishes a theory of the structure of narrative transmission, which can be identified by the following criteria: the number of narrating voices; the relation of these voices to the audience; the characterization of the voices; the identification of a narratee or an internal listener; the standpoint offered to the audience; the elements of discourse used in transmission; and the assumptions of values and experience with other texts placed on the audience.

sents a largely detached, 'eyewitness' perspective.[3] Characters, on the other hand, describe events as they perceive them to be, colored by their personas and experiences. Plato observes the multiplicity of Homeric narrative voices, distinguishing between the simple narrative (διήγησις ἁπλῆ), in which the omnipresent/omniscient narrator describes an event, and mimesis (μίμησις), in which the narrator describes an event through the persona of a character, a dichotomy persuasively applied to modern narrative theory in the ground-breaking work of Gérard Genette.[4] Genette emphasizes the point of view that transmits information, a voice that can range from an analytic or omniscient narrator to any of the characters; the narrator and the "focalizer," the perspective presented to the external audience, must be distinguished within any given narrative section.[5] Such distinctions help illuminate the enormous complexity of narrative strategy in the *Iliad* and *Odyssey*. The work of Irene de Jong has provided the most prominent exploration of this kind of literary analysis to the *Iliad*. In her interpretation, the omniscient narrator provides a "primary" narrative perspective, while the speech of characters and the subjective perspective, which can also be expressed by the omniscient narrator, form the "secondary" narrative voice.[6] In other words, we can distinguish between the *primary narrator*, who presents an eyewitness perspective, and the *secondary narrators*, who focalize the story. The story related by the primary narrator can be said to take place in primary narrative time, the chronological unfolding of events at Troy, while characters and the complex narrator refer to the past and future, as well as current events and actions not described by the primary narrator.[7]

---

[3]   On the perspective of texts, Bal 1985:100–101.

[4]   Plato *Republic* 3.392c–395; Genette 1980:162–172. Using the example of Plato's rewriting of *Iliad* I 33–36, he distinguishes between three types of narrative speech (narratized, transposed, and mimetic). De Jong discusses the flaws in Genette's translation of *diêgêsis*, 1987b:2–4, see also 1999:481–482. The scholia *ad Iliad* II 494–877, XV 116, XVI 605, and XVIII 282–302 comment upon this difference, describing the "narrator text" as ἀμίμητον, διηγηματικόν, or (ἀπ)αγγελία, and the "character text" as δραματική or μιμητικόν (de Jong 1987b:10–11).

[5]   Genette 1980:186f.

[6]   An overview of narrative theory is provided by de Jong and Nünlist 2004: the terminology "primary," "secondary," and "complex" narrator/narrative-text/voice are some of many possible designations for these techniques, as discussed by de Jong 1987a:8; 1987b:31f. Richardson 1990 is another full-length study of narrative voices in Homer. Chatman 1978:33 explains that the "[narrator] should mean only the someone—person or presence—actually telling the story to an audience no matter how minimally evoked his voice or the audience's listening ear."

[7]   Zieliński 1899–1901 proposes that the Homeric (primary) narrative never strays from a linear progression of events, even when describing different events occurring simultaneously. The relevance of this very early and important theory is evident first in Bassett 1938:33–34, and more recently in Richardson 1990:89–98, a re-evaluation suggesting that Homer conceals his

The subjective perspective expressed by the primary narrator can be termed the *"complex" narrator*, a secondary narrative voice in which the linear progression of the primary narrative is slightly altered. The primary narrator relates an objective, visualized presentation of the story, whereas the complex narrator applies a subjective perception or imparts special knowledge. For instance, in *Iliad* IV, a direct address to Menelaos interrupts the linear, eyewitness style of the primary narrator to introduce a subjective, sympathetic perspective:[8] "But you, Menelaos, the blessed deathless gods did not forget you" (οὐδὲ σέθεν, Μενέλαε, θεοὶ μάκαρες λελάθοντο / ἀθάνατοι, *Iliad* IV 127–128). Apostrophes, such as this address to Menelaos, "if-not" suppositions, similes, prolepses and analepses, summaries, pauses (such as ekphrasis), bird's eye views, and narratorial comments, in which a subjective voice intrudes upon the objective perspective of the primary narrator, can be collectively described as the complex narrative voice.[9] Furthermore, the complex narrative voice can present speech acts indirectly, while still representing the words spoken, or reports of speech, when the speech act is summarized.[10]

Speech is itself a typical action, like sacrifice, but with a much greater number of variables, ranging from single speeches to conversations, which the primary narrative constructs by joining speeches together in a systemized fashion (through introductory and concluding signposts).[11] There are seventy speakers that deliver 677 speeches in the *Iliad*, accounting for nearly one-half of the poem. These speeches initiate conversation, respond to the speech of others, or are 'single speeches' not intended to engage with another person.[12] Every speech act is framed in the narrative by introductory and concluding statements, which form a fixed pattern like that exhibited in other typical

---

manipulation of temporal sequence to give the impression of continuity; see also Stanley 1993:6. On the time of character speech, page 63 below.

[8]   Block 1982:11 gives a list of instances of apostrophe.

[9]   De Jong's categories (1997:308); see also Richardson 1990 and Scully 1986. Bassett 1938:59 identifies three categories of presentation as "objectively narrative," "subjectively explanatory," and "dramatically imitative." Stanley 1993:7 provides a good typology of the complex narrator, which he calls "digressive interruptions."

[10] Richardson 1990: "When the narrator informs us of spoken words without availing himself of direct speech, he is manipulating the story and leaving his mark on the text" (71).

[11] Beck's model of "conversational analysis": the social context of the speech affects the rules that govern the conversation (2005:21).

[12] The number of speakers given by Lateiner 1997:257 and, of speeches, by de Jong 1987b:115; Beck 2005:29 counts 678. Nine speeches are given by anonymous people, the *tis*-speeches (*tis* 'someone') analyzed by de Jong 1987a, 1987b:69. Griffin 1986:37 estimates that 7,018 verses of a total 15,690 in the *Iliad* are direct speech, accounting for 45 percent of the poem. 'Single speeches' are identified by Bassett 1938:63, who qualifies such speeches as "the most undramatic." He counts 357 in the *Iliad* and 72 in the *Odyssey*.

actions: never are speeches interrupted with phrases that function as post-positives such as the Latin *inquit*.[13] Character speeches differ in genre, style, and significance within the poem and have been described with an extensive array of terminology created by modern scholars in an attempt to reflect these differences.[14] Genette proposes approaching narrative voices as representative of internal and external perspectives, both in terms of person and time. A speech describing events in the first person (for example, that of the characters—the secondary narrators in the *Iliad*) is internal or homodiegetic, while descriptions in which the voice of the narrator is "absent" from his own story (the primary narrator in the *Iliad*), is external or heterodiegetic. Speeches about events within the time of the poem are intradiegetic; those outside the time of the poem are extradiegetic. The same processes can be further specified by references to prior events within the poem (internal analepsis) or future events within the poem (internal prolepsis/foreshadowing), descriptions of events outside the timeline of the poem (external analepsis or narration from memory), and anticipation of events outside the poem (external prolepsis/foreshadowing).[15] Moreover, within these categories, speeches may again be categorized according to the content of the speech: 90 percent of character speech falls into the genres of prayer, lament, supplication, command, insult, and narration from memory, henceforth called 'digressions', which serve a persuasive, hortatory, or apologetic function; in addition, there are speeches which repeat information already given (mirror stories).[16] Many different layers create the complex meaning of speech in the *Iliad*, ranging from the persona of the speaker, content of the speech, reaction to the speech

---

[13] Beck 2005:1–45. Scully 1986: "all speeches in the *Iliad* and the *Odyssey* are fully set apart from the narrative" (137n4); similar to Beck's conclusions, he observes that the speeches are framed with narrative markers and never interrupted by narrative voice or ending in the middle of a line, making them exclusive metrically as well. Speeches may be further categorized according to the number of people addressed (Beck 2005:49f).

[14] This area of Homeric scholarship in particular suffers from a lack of agreed terminology. De Jong 1987b:82–83 gives a list of terms and definitions, as does Dickson 1995.

[15] Genette 1980:212–262. Auerbach 1953:6, 13 describes the invisibility of the Homeric narrator, whose presentation of events is completely externalized.

[16] Bassett's estimation (1938:70–71). Austin 1966:298 defines 'digression' as an "anecdote which describes action outside the time of the poem" and which relate "personal experience, family history, or myths outside of the Trojan legend"; he observes the three possible intentions, which are not exclusive, of the speaker in giving this particular type of speech. Martin 1989:47f. organizes the speeches in Homer designated as *muthoi* into the categories of "command," "flyting," and "memory." Beck 2005:26 suggests that some speech acts can be roughly categorized as "non-conversational speeches," most frequently commands, instructions to messengers, prayers, vaunts, and other kinds of boasts, all of which are hierarchical and involve an imbalance of power.

by other characters, different designations for speech, and methods of speech-making.[17]

Typically, the primary narrator avoids directly imparting background information to the audience, preferring to place this information in the mouths of characters that reference events outside of the poem's narrative chronology. The secondary narrators tell stories relevant to the specific context in which they are speaking rather than filling in missing background information, of which a general knowledge is assumed.[18] These external analepses create a dual level of significance—first, for the addressee within the poem (the "argument" function), and, second, for the audience of the poem (the "key" function).[19] For example, when Nestor remembers how he was asked to fight against the centaurs (*Iliad* I 259–274), his speech has an "argument" function, exhorting Agamemnon and Akhilleus to heed his advice, and a "key" function, establishing his role as a wise advisor. The "argument" function makes a comparison between a mythological exemplum and the context of the speech. The "key" function, which is part of a larger pattern, compares the digressive story to its context within the poem: Phoinix's digression on Meleagros, who accepts gifts, foreshadows the wrath of Akhilleus, who refuses them.[20]

Descriptions of sacrifice are embedded in characters' commands, insults, digressions, prayers, and vows. In addition, there are sacrifices embedded in the complex narrative-text, points at which the usually impersonal primary narrative voice interrupts the presentation of the story with a specialized, subjective viewpoint. Of particular interest for our study is the potential for contrast between the version of events given by the primary narrator and accounts given by different characters: divergences from the primary narrative voice are apparent to the audience, but are never commented upon by

---

[17] There are numerous studies, a few of which are listed here, that are relevant to our discussion: Lohmann 1970 is one of the seminal studies. Latacz 1975:395–422 gives a bibliography of scholarship on speech in Homer. Martin 1989 treats the relationship between speaker, type of speech, and context; Beck 2005 is a full-length study of conversation techniques. Parry 1956 studies the language of Akhilleus as does Dickson 1995 for Nestor. Gaisser 1969 analyzes the technique of ring composition and the structure of these speeches. On mythological *paradeigma*, Andersen 1987; Pedrick 1983; and Willcock 1964.

[18] For example, Austin 1966:298 notes that we are told more about Nestor's youthful exploits than about the cause of the Trojan War.

[19] Andersen 1987.

[20] Andersen 1987:6–7. Scodel 2002:25 points out that the digressions encourage listeners not to consider innovations, but to concentrate on the similarities and differences between Niobe and Priam. I do not address the issue of chronology—the hypothesis that speeches are 'older' or 'newer' insertions into the poem—on which see Griffin 1986:37; Kirk 1990:29–30.

characters or the primary narrator. A particularly poignant example of this contrast can be found in the multiple descriptions of Hektor's sacrifices from the perspective of the gods and of the Akhaians. Agamemnon imagines that Zeus favors Hektor's sacrifices, while Zeus laments that he cannot save Hektor despite his sacrifices.[21]

The different narrative levels are essential tools for interpreting the meaning of sacrifice scenes in the *Iliad*: the representation of sacrifice in the secondary and complex narrative voices, which present a relatively restricted picture of sacrificial ritual, diverge from that of the primary narrative voice. I shall henceforth refer to descriptions of the performance of sacrifice in the primary narrative text as *enacted sacrifices*. Those presented through a secondary voice, either by the complex narrator or in character speech, I will designate as *embedded sacrifices*. This terminology reflects Seymour Chatman's recasting of Plato's original distinction between narrative voices as "narration," the "recounting of an event," and "enactment," which is the "unmediated presentation."[22] The term 'enacted' is potentially misleading in reference to performance poetry, as everything in the poem can be said to be 'enacted' in the singer's performance. However, if referring specifically to sacrifice as transmitted through the different voices of the narrative, 'enacted' emphasizes the eyewitness presentation of sacrifice by the primary narrator, and 'embedded' signals the focalization of secondary perspectives by the complex narrator and in character speech. Though focusing on elements important to the thematic meaning in a particular context, the narrative agenda in both embedded and enacted sacrifices alludes to a much more elaborate process, and it is this process in enacted and embedded sacrifices, and the emphasis constructed through the restricted focus on different elements of this process, that we will consider in this chapter.

There are seven enacted sacrifices described by the primary narrator as part of the chronological unfolding of events at Troy. These sacrifices are not as frequent as one might expect: enacted sacrifices seem to be motivated not by fear of the gods, by desire to thank gods, or in order to offset the anxiety caused by warfare; rather, they occur as part of the quarrel between Agamemnon and Akhilleus. In *Iliad* I, two enacted sacrifices frame Akhilleus'

---

[21] The contrast between primary and secondary narrator perspectives is discussed by Andersen 1990:26f., the related issue of "mirror stories" by de Jong 1987b:210–218. We will return to Hektor's sacrifices below, page 122.

[22] Chatman 1978:32. In a different context, Hammer 2002:147 describes Homeric social interactions as "enacted in a public space," a useful working definition for the sacrifices described in the primary narrative.

withdrawal. Akhilleus argues with Agamemnnon and announces his intention
to withdraw (*Iliad* I 148–307), at which point Agamemnon arranges for Odysseus
to take the hecatomb to Khruse and then himself enacts a purificatory sacrifice (*Iliad* I 308–317). The narrative shifts its focus to the events in the camp
of Akhilleus, who surrenders Briseis and complains to Thetis (*Iliad* I 318–429),
after which the hecatomb arrives at Khruse. Then the narrative resumes with
the embarkation at Khruse and sacrifice to Apollo (*Iliad* I 430–474). Before the
first day of battle, Agamemnon sacrifices an ox to Zeus (*Iliad* II 402–432); this
long day ends in *Iliad* VII, at which point Agamemnon again sacrifices an ox
to Zeus and gives the best part of the meat to Ajax, Akhilleus' replacement
(*Iliad* VII 313–323). Between Agamemnon's sacrificial feasts, he performs the
oath sacrifice before the duel between Paris and Menelaos (*Iliad* III 264–313).
Iliad VIII encompasses the second day of battle, which elapses without sacrifice.[23] The third day of battle begins in *Iliad* XI with Agamemnon's *aristeia*
and ends with the production of Akhilleus' shield; again there are no enacted
sacrifices. The fourth and final day of battle, beginning in *Iliad* XIX, follows the
reintegration of Akhilleus into the army, which is marked by an oath sacrifice performed by Agamemnon (*Iliad* XIX 249–268). This is the final enacted
sacrifice of the poem. The thematic prominence of sacrifice in the *Iliad* reflects
the social breakdown caused by the crisis between Agamemnon and Akhilleus.
Therefore, the primary narrator ceases to describe sacrifice once Akhilleus
returns to the battlefield. Although the sacrifice in *Iliad* II precedes battle, the
primary narrator focuses on Agamemnon's authority, since the start of battle
is postponed by the Catalogue of Ships until *Iliad* III. No sacrifice marks the end
of battle in *Iliad* XXII. Since the inclusion of non-martial scenes throughout
the poem has been said to aid in creating a varied and multi-dimensional
plot,[24] we might expect sacrifice to be utilized as a possible extension device,
a break for the audience from the tedium of warfare, as Arend indeed argues
for the lengthy sacrifices in *Iliad* I and II.[25] However, the overriding principle
for the structural role of sacrifice in the primary narrative is the expression of
Agamemnon's authority during Akhilleus' withdrawal.

---

[23] Except perhaps the Trojan sacrifice at nightfall (*Iliad* VIII 548–552), which has been excluded
from this discussion and omitted from the texts of Monro and Allen 1920 (3rd edition) and
West 1998, on the grounds that verses 548 and 550–552 are only found in (Plato) *Alcibiades* II
149d.

[24] On the shifting perspective of Homeric narrative around battle events, see Bakker 1997:116;
Beye 1993:346–347; Fenik 1968:16–17; and Kirk 1985:12. Stanley 1993:29–32 rehearses the
history of scholarship on the structure of the *Iliad*.

[25] Arend 1933:65.

There are 39 *embedded* references to sacrifice in the *Iliad*, spoken by 17 different characters,[26] in contrast to the consistent and restricted presentation of the seven *enacted* sacrifices performed by Agamemnon or at his behest. The *Iliad* is largely composed of character speeches, so the increased number of embedded sacrifices is not surprising in this regard. However, we will see that the emphasis on Agamemnon in enacted sacrifices is marked in comparison to the number of characters who describe sacrifices, and there are a number of other significant differences according to the primary or secondary narrative perspectives. Embedded sacrifices often only focus on one moment in the sacrificial process, such as the burning of thigh bones, to represent a lengthy ritual procedure. Enacted sacrifices describe a continual sacrificial *process*, in which the role of the sacrificer is made prominent. A broad view of the different emphases established by recurrent ritual details in embedded and enacted scenes, as well as meanings created by unique variations, will lay the groundwork for a similar approach to descriptions of the post-kill phase (Chapter Three) and the thematic associations of Agamemnon and Akhilleus to sacrificial performances (Chapter Four).

Animal sacrifices are described with a combination of details drawn from the elements of ritual procedure, including location, preliminary rites, sacrificer, victims, recipient, prayer, details of the kill, offerings to the gods, divine response, and shared feast. These recurrent elements, included in multiple sacrifices in the *Iliad*, and the fixed order in which they occur allow for the emergence of general trends, which in turn reveal the importance of sacrifice to the design of the *Iliad*. As established in Chapter One, type-scenes are "typical" because their importance to the overall design of the poem merits repetition. The long enacted sacrifices are composed of enough repetitive actions to portray a carefully fixed ritual process, creating in the mind of the audience a concept of "typical" sacrificial practice, which is then altered according to each individual context. For this reason, we will outline the ritual process in the order of events: first the pre-kill stage, encompassing

---

[26] Embedded sacrifices (in alphabetical order by speaker): *Iliad* I 140–147, VIII 236–244, X 46 (Agamemnon); *Iliad* V 177–178 (Aineias); *Iliad* I 62–67, IX 357, XXI 130–132, XXIII 144–150 (Akhilleus); *Iliad* XXIV 33–34 (Apollo); IV 101–103 (Athena); *Iliad* X 283–294 (Diomedes); *Iliad* VI 110–115, 274–278 (Hektor); *Iliad* VI 93–98 (Helenos); *Iliad* XXIII 205–207 (Iris); *Iliad* I 93 (Kalkhas); *Iliad* I 40–42 (Khruses); *Iliad* XI 706–707, 727–729, 772–775, XV 371–376 (Nestor); *Iliad* I 305–321 (Odysseus); *Iliad* IX 499–501, 535–537 (Phoinix); *Iliad* VII 450 (Poseidon); *Iliad* VI 308–310 (Theano); *Iliad* IV 48–49, XXII 170–172, XXIV 69–70 (Zeus). In the complex narrative-text: *Iliad* II 550–551, IV 119–121, VIII 250, X 571, XII 6, XX 403–405, XXII 159–160, XXIII 195, 863–864, 872–873. Enacted sacrifices: *Iliad* I 308–317, 430–474; II 398–401, 402–432; III 264–311; VII 313–323; XIX 249–268.

the preliminary rituals performed at the altar while the animal is still alive; followed by the kill phase, the slaughter of the victims. The post-kill stage, including the treatment and disposal of the carcass, which is either discarded or divided into portions for god and men, cooked, and eaten, will be covered in Chapter Three.[27] These three stages are performed in a fixed order to honor the gods in expectation of divine favor and aid. An analysis of the range of ritual details will establish that the focus on different stages of the ritual process, as well as the language used to describe individual rites, varies in the primary narrator and character speech. Sacrifice, as described by the characters in the poem, is perceived almost exclusively as a method of appeasing or communicating with the gods, while the primary narrative voice focuses on the performance of sacrifice among a group, highlighting the actions of the sacrificer rather than its divine reception and intended outcome. Further, the gap between these perspectives creates a complex tension between the uncertainty expressed by characters and the time and effort expended on sacrifice by Agamemnon in the primary narrative voice.

2.2 Pre-Kill

Pre-kill rites can be extended to involve a *pompê* 'procession' or abbreviated to hand washing and a prayer. Indeed the extension of the ceremony marks the significance of the event for the participants and increases the splendor of the occasion. We will look at the opening verses introducing enacted sacrifices, followed by preliminary actions (*katarkhesthai*) and prayers before the kill, none of which are described in embedded sacrifices. The importance of the *pompê* in the Classical period has been discussed in Chapter One: there are no processions to the altar in the *Iliad* that resemble the Classical model of basket carrying, flute playing, or concomitant visual demonstration of social participation that this action provides for the community. The only lengthy movement *toward* a place of ritual action is Odysseus' docking, unloading, and leading of the hecatomb to the altar at Khruse (*Iliad* I 430–439), a procedure emphasized by the repetition of ἐκ at the start of each verse (*Iliad* I 436–439). Although victims are procured for the oath sacrifices, this is the only reference in the poem to the transportation of animals, a practical necessity otherwise unacknowledged. The movement of the hecatomb is more suggestive of a typical, if exaggerated, boat anchorage scene, having many elements also found in nautical representations in the *Odyssey*, rather than a ritual proces-

---

[27] I discuss this approach on page 27 above; see van Straten 1995:9f.

sion in honor of the gods.[28] In the context of enacted sacrifices, the prolonged arrival of the ship and the relatively detailed description of standing around the altar heighten the anticipation of the return of Khruseis (*Iliad* I 430–448).

Just as the visual demonstration of community accord provided by processions in the Classical period is not a feature of sacrifice in the *Iliad*, other visible markers such as special clothing or wreaths worn by participants in sacrifices do not appear. Nor are the victims decorated with other ornamentation such as garlands, which are so frequent in Classical iconography that Peirce considers them to be a defining feature of sacrifice.[29] An exception may be the ribbons on Khruses' staff, described as *stemmata* (*Iliad* I 14), the term used to describe the decorative garlands in the Classical period, but victims in the *Iliad* are never decorated in this fashion.[30]

Although the sacrificial procession and festive decorations do not feature in the *Iliad*, the location is always carefully described, though not fixed or specifically designated for sacrifice. The question of sacred space in Homer is complicated. In the Bronze Age, sacrifices would probably have been performed at home or in open-air enclosures, a practice which seems to have continued from the ninth century until the development of temples in the eighth century. The evolution of the *polis* seems to have created a distinction of sorts between private sacrifices performed at home and those sponsored by the *polis* in the public spaces dedicated to the gods—temples and sanctuaries.[31] The practice of the *Iliad* does not seem particularly representative of either Bronze Age or Classical *polis* practices. In the *Iliad*, gods have sacred *temenê* 'enclosures', but these spaces are never used for enacted sacrifices, and the term is used more frequently of allotments of land to heroes.[32] The only

---

[28] On the scene in general, Arend 1933:79–81, who classifies *Iliad* I 430–439 as part of a typical "arrival by ship" scene; so too Latacz 2002:120. Lord 1960:190 proposes that the emphasis on the hecatomb and the simultaneous presentation of the sacrificial victims and Khruseis has suppressed an original myth of human sacrifice. There has been some discussion of this episode as a late insertion; see Edwards 1980:19.

[29] Peirce 1993:228n30; see also Parker 1983:153.

[30] Pulleyn 2000 *ad Iliad* I 14 gives the ancient testimonia on *stemmata*, which seem to have been made of laurel wreaths or wool.

[31] Coldstream 1985:67–97 and Rutkowski 1986 outline the evidence for the development of independent temples in Geometric Greece. On the Dark Age, see Mazarakis Ainian 1988. 'Polis religion' is defined and explored by Sourvinou-Inwood 2000, and for general discussion of 'private' and 'public' sacrifice, cult places in Attika are examined by Rosivach 1994 and Parker 2005:50–78, and Parker 2005:155f. on the Attic festivals.

[32] In the *Iliad, temenos* is a sacred space for Demeter (*Iliad* II 696), and, with an altar, for Zeus (*Iliad* VIII 48) and Sperkheios (*Iliad* XXIII 148). *Temenê* are honorary gifts for heroes in Lycia (*Iliad* VI

connection between a *temenos* and sacrifice is found in Akhilleus' memory of his father's vow to sacrifice rams to the river Sperkheios, where its *temenos* and altar are located, which he seems to imply is actually in the water (μῆλ' ἱερεύσειν ἐς πηγάς, ὅθι τοι τέμενος βωμός τε θυήεις, *Iliad* XXIII 147–148). The river water of the Skamandros is also described by Akhilleus as a location where the Trojans would sacrifice (*Iliad* XXI 132).

Neither sacred spaces for the gods nor temples are regularly connected with sacrifice, although temples are described in other contexts throughout the poem.[33] Three dedicated to Apollo are described: Khruses remembers modifying a temple for Apollo, Aineias is safely placed in a temple of Apollo, and Hektor imagines dedicating Akhilleus' armor in Apollo's temple. Athena has a temple in Athens and Troy, and the latter is imagined exceptionally as the location for sacrifice in the Trojan vow, but this vow is never to be fulfilled. In the Catalogue of Ships, a description of the sacrifices received by Erekhtheus at Athens, related in the context of Athena's establishment of Erekhtheus in her *naos*, may at least loosely connect the sanctuary with the offerings, but nowhere else in the poem are temples depicted as locations for sacrifice.[34] Certainly the Akhaian army does not have access to temples in which to sacrifice to their gods, but it is noticeable that temples do not feature even in Akhaian remembrances of sacrifice at home or sacrificial vows for the future. Other, more general locations are described in two of Nestor's embedded sacrifices in his speech to Patroklos: the banks of a river (*Iliad* XI 726) and the courtyard of Peleus' house (*Iliad* XI 774).

In the *Iliad* temples occur more frequently in the role of honoring the gods or, more rarely, as places in which material offerings can be placed than as locations for sacrifice.[35] For instance, Khruses refers to the temple of Apollo as

---

194, XII 313), Meleagros (*Iliad* IX 578), and Aineias (*Iliad* XX 184). The word is used to describe the king's estate on Akhilleus' shield (*Iliad* XVIII 550) and for the ancestral estate of Iphition (*Iliad* XX 391).

[33] Sourvinou-Inwood 1993:2–5 discusses cult places in Homer; see also Lorimer 1950. On temples in the *Odyssey*, see Heubeck, West, and Hainsworth 1988:38n15. Burkert 1985:88 believes that the temple (*naos*) in Homer refers to the dwelling place of the god. That temples are not consistently described and are not often used in ritual practice probably reflects the gradual composition and transmission of the poem over centuries.

[34] Apollo: *Iliad* I 39; V 445–446; VII 83. Athena: *Iliad* II 549; VI 93 = 274, 308.

[35] Morris 1992:33–35 gives a brief summary on the related development of votive offerings and temples. Votive offerings are generally very marginalized in Homer: Seaford 2004:54–56 discusses the issues. He finds only five votive offerings in the *Iliad*: the Trojan *peplos* to Athena (VI 302–303), Hektor's wish to dedicate to Apollo the armor of his opponent (VII 81–83), Hera's description of gifts at Poseidon's sanctuaries (VIII 203–204), Odysseus' promise to dedicate the arms of Dolon (X 462–464, 570–571), and Akhilleus' lock of hair (XXIII 141–146). According to Seaford 2004:56, the only explicit reference to wealth in a temple is found in Akhilleus'

evidence of his past favors to the god: "If I ever roofed a shrine to please your heart" (εἴ ποτέ τοι χαρίεντ' ἐπὶ νηὸν ἔρεψα, *Iliad* I 39). Yet the building roofed by Khruses is not described in his enacted sacrifice to Apollo at Khruse, and he revokes his request with another prayer without referencing these former honors. At Khruse, an altar is used for sacrifice (βωμός, *Iliad* I 448), but is not located in a sanctuary, and no building or dwelling of any sort is described. The *Iliad* does not even closely associate sacrificial practice with altars, though they seem to have been well-established features in Mycenaean cult practice, and in the Classical period altars (or *bothroi* 'sacred ditches') seem to be a defining feature of sacrifice.[36] For example, the victim and the altar are the essential requirements for Trugaios' sacrifice in Aristophanes' *Peace*:

ἴθι νυν, ἄγ' ὡς τάχιστα τὸ πρόβατον λαβών·
ἐγὼ δὲ ποριῶ βωμὸν ἐφ' ὅτου θύσομεν.

(Aristophanes *Peace* 937–938)

Come on, get a sheep as quickly as possible.
I'll fetch an altar on which we will sacrifice.

However, in the *Iliad* the sacrifice at Khruse is the only enacted sacrifice to utilize any such established object, carefully mentioned when the men "quickly set up the sacred hecatomb for the god in order around the well made altar" (τοὶ δ' ὦκα θεῷ ἱερὴν ἑκατόμβην ἑξείης ἔστησαν ἐΰδμητον περὶ βωμόν, *Iliad* I 447–448).[37] This sacrifice has many unique features. Along with Athena's temple in Troy, it is the only cultic place attended by a priest, and Khruses is the only priest who attends a sacrifice. This location also stands out in the larger pattern of movement and travel within the poem, being the only

---

dismissal of Agamemnon's gifts, which are no more preferable to him than all the wealth in Apollo's temple at Delphi (*Iliad* IX 401–405).

[36] Archaeologists have generally agreed that raised structures occurring in sacral contexts in the Bronze Age, such as the bench-like platforms in the cult rooms of most Mycenaean shrines, are suggestive of 'altars' (Bergquist 1988). Yavis 1949 gives the typology of altars.

[37] Sourvinou-Inwood 1993:2 proposes that "altars by the sea, on the beach, are well known in Homer" on the basis of two citations (*Iliad* VIII 238–240; XI 806–808). Sourvinou-Inwood, like many scholars, incorporates evidence from Homer into a larger argument about historical ritual practice; however, if one considers the context of these two references to altars, it does not seem that a clear pattern emerges that may be applied to the whole poem. Seaford 2004:53 observes that "there is no description of an altar in Homer." βωμός describes 11 altars in the *Iliad*: altars for Apollo (I 440, 448) and Zeus (VIII 48) are mentioned by the primary narrator; altars for Zeus (VIII 249) and the gods (XI 808) are described by the complex narrator. Zeus describes his own altars: *Iliad* IV 48; XXIV 69. Odysseus describes an altar at Aulis without reference to the gods: *Iliad* II 238, 305, 310. Akhilleus refers to Sperkheios' altar: *Iliad* XXIII 305. Altars used by Trojans and Akhilleus' dedication to Sperkheios will be discussed below, pages 197f.

place outside of Troy that is visited at any length.[38] These unique details (altar, priest, and travel location) stress the foreign context of this sacrifice and its relative removal from Agamemnon's ritual sphere, as we shall see. Otherwise, the primary narrator localizes the performance of sacrifice not with altars, temples, or other specialized sacred locations, but in terms of the social hierarchy of the army. The lack of consistent attention to the place of sacrifice has bothered scholars, but the focus in enacted scenes on Agamemnon and his role as leader of the army clarifies this seeming variety:[39] two sacrifices are performed in Agamemnon's quarters (*Iliad* II 402; VII 313); he leads two "in the middle" space in front of the army *en masse* (*Iliad* III 265; XIX 248); and one takes place at a seashore location under his direction (*Iliad* I 312).

The substitution of altars with spaces linked to Agamemnon's hegemony over the army in the enacted sacrifices is highlighted by the frequent description of altars in secondary and complex narrative voices, often in reference to divine pleasure and positive examples of reciprocity between mortals and immortals. Although they are never used in the poem, there are two Akhaian altars described in complex narrative pauses; these brief references to a larger picture of ritual practice demonstrate the restricted focus and complicated integration of enacted and embedded sacrifices. Agamemnon prays fervently to Zeus for help, invoking all the past sacrifices made on altars during the journey to Troy (*Iliad* VIII 238–242). In response, Zeus sends the sign of an eagle dropping a fawn on his altar, "where the Akhaians always sacrificed to Zeus whose voice rings clear with omens" (ἔνθα πανομφαίῳ Ζηνὶ ῥέζεσκον Ἀχαιοί, *Iliad* VIII 250). ῥέζεσκον 'they continually sacrificed' is the only past iterative form used in the poem, which implies repeated use of the altar, though the altar is not mentioned again. This contrast is part of the tension between narrative voices: inconsistent or even contradictory perceptions of ritual practice are presented according to the differing points of view. The description of continual sacrifice is also unusual in that ῥέζεσκον is not followed by a noun, such as *hiera* or hecatombs, which is the more typical expression for sacrifice in the poem.[40]

The poem occasionally pauses for such descriptions of setting, which, because they break the linear progression of events, become part of the

---

[38] Taplin 1992:85.

[39] In this regard, Seaford 2004:52f. describes the "lack of objective continuity" in Homeric sacrifice. Cf. Vermeule 1974: "*man opfert, wo man geht und steht*" (95), and Kirk 1981:68, not entirely consistent with his note *ad loc. Iliad* VI 87–94.

[40] Similarly, the iterative form ἐπιρρέζεσκον is found only once in the *Odyssey*, describing the altar of the nymphs where passersby sacrifice (*Odyssey* xvii 210–211). On the language of sacrifice, see below pages 48–59.

complex narrative voice.[41] In the first instance, Zeus sends his omen to the altar where the Akhaian army often sacrifices in response to the complaint that Agamemnon's sacrifices on Zeus' altars have gone unnoticed. However, this altar is only described in the complex narrative; Agamemnon's prayer describes altars used on the way to Troy, but he never sacrifices on this altar or any other in the enacted sacrifices.[42] The contrast between Agamemnon's memory of using Zeus' altars *en route* to Troy and the complex narrator's description of the god's altar, next to which Agamemnon seems to be standing but to which he does not refer, is typical of the differing perspectives between the narrative voices. To complicate matters further, this altar is dedicated to Zeus *Panomphaios*, an epithet found only here in Homeric poetry. The epithet fits the context of an omen, although Agamemnon has requested not an omen, but the opportunity for flight. We will explore the pattern of using these types of variables to create tension between representations of sacrifice in narrative voices throughout this study.

The second description of an altar by the complex narrator alludes, again, to a much larger picture of ritual practice than that offered by the primary narrator. Patroklos has met Eurupulos by Odysseus' ships, where there is an *agora* and altars built for the gods (θεῶν ἐτετεύχατο βωμοί, *Iliad* XI 808).[43] Presumably, Odysseus and his troops use this altar near their ships, but the agenda of the primary narrative-text and the tendency of characters to refer to sacrifice as suits the occasion of their speech restrict the scene's focus without specifying. In other words, this reference to an altar is surprising since Odysseus neither makes sacrifices in primary narrative time nor does he refer to any such ritual activities or this altar in his speeches. Such abbreviated references to altars and sacrifice indicate a larger picture of ritual practice, which is pared down to a small and limited sample relevant to the thematic needs of the context.

Although he does not describe the altars near his ships, Odysseus does repeatedly emphasize an altar in his memory of Aulis, the most extended description of the location of sacrifice in an embedded sacrifice:

χθιζά τε καὶ πρωΐζ', ὅτ' ἐς Αὐλίδα νῆες Ἀχαιῶν
ἠγερέθοντο κακὰ Πριάμῳ καὶ Τρωσὶ φέρουσαι,
ἡμεῖς δ' ἀμφὶ περὶ κρήνην ἱεροὺς κατὰ βωμοὺς
ἔρδομεν ἀθανάτοισι τελήεσσας ἑκατόμβας,

---

[41] On complex narrative pauses, see Richardson 1990:50–61.
[42] Agamemnon's prayer is discussed at length at pages 97–98 below.
[43] Kirk 1990 *ad Iliad* VIII 249–250 identifies these altars with the aforementioned altar of Zeus.

καλῇ ὑπὸ πλατανίστῳ, ὅθεν ῥέεν ἀγλαὸν ὕδωρ·
ἔνθ᾽ ἐφάνη μέγα σῆμα·

(*Iliad* II 303-308)

Why, it seems like only yesterday or the day before when the ships
    of the Akhaians gathered at Aulis,
freighted with slaughter bound for Priam's Troy.
We were all milling round a spring and on the holy altars
offering perfect hecatombs to the immortals,
under a spreading plane tree where the glittering water flowed,
when a great omen appeared.

When Odysseus tries to persuade the troops to stay at Troy, he recalls the interruption of a sacrifice at Aulis, which provides an austere backdrop for the focus of his speech: the propitious omens interpreted by Kalkhas (*Iliad* II 305-321). The location of the sacrifice at Aulis, a suitably tranquil environment for the climactic appearance of the snake portent, is intricately described, but the other details of the ritual process are only briefly summarized. Odysseus describes how "we" stood around a spring, offering hecatombs to the immortals (*Iliad* II 305-307). No specific details are given about the victims, the sacrificer, the divinities, or the purpose of the sacrifice, but Odysseus does dwell on the location at some length, which anticipates a lengthy description of the snake devouring the sparrow and her chicks. Odysseus follows this recollection of the portent with a concluding reference to the interrupted sacrifices: "and so when the terrible portent interrupted the hecatombs of the gods then Kalkhas immediately spoke this prophecy" (ὡς οὖν δεινὰ πέλωρα θεῶν εἰσῆλθ᾽ ἑκατόμβας / Κάλχας δ᾽ αὐτίκ᾽ ἔπειτα θεοπροπέων ἀγόρευε, *Iliad* II 321-322). On the basis of the omen, Kalkhas predicts that the Akhaians will take Troy in the tenth year (*Iliad* II 305-321), and Odysseus presents the Akhaian victory as a type of divine response to the sacrifices.[44] This is the only description of divine signs accompanying or interrupting sacrifices.

Odysseus deliberately elides details of the sacrifice itself, which is left unfinished in his description. The focus on the site leaves only a vague sketch of the sacrificer and victims, perhaps evincing Odysseus' diplomatic censorship of the well-known story of the sacrifice of Iphigenia at Aulis.[45] The

---

[44] Gaisser 1969:8.

[45] The Iphigenia sacrifice is told in the *Kupria* as paraphrased by Proklos, where she is saved at the last minute (Bernabé 1987:41). In Aeschylus *Agamemnon* 218-249 it is suggested that she was killed at the altar, on which see Seaford 1989; Aretz 1999; and Henrichs 2000:183n37-38. Odysseus' diplomacy in speechmaking in his appeal to Akhilleus in *Iliad* IX has been well observed by Griffin 1995.

suspense created through the accumulation of details of location, and perhaps the audience expectation of details of the sacrifice of Iphigenia, gives more weight to the climactic portent, which foretells that the Akhaians will conquer Troy, a bitter irony for an audience recently informed of Zeus' assent to Thetis' request. Odysseus' digression is intended to inspire the troops to rejoin battle rather than sail for home. The possibility of retreat, suggested by Agamemnon to be a way of testing them (*Iliad* II 110–141), creates strife among the troops similar to that in *Iliad* I. The notion of sacrifice is used in this digression to recall and ameliorate the damage caused by the complicated discussions of sacrifice in *Iliad* I, in which Agamemnon's decision to send the sacrificial embassy to Khruse is formulated in conjunction with his plan to remove Briseis, putting sacrifice at the very heart of the quarrel. This positive recollection of Kalkhas' prophecies is a subtle resolution of the problem created by Agamemnon's accusation in *Iliad* I against the *mantis* for lying and giving only bad prophecies.

Preliminary actions performed before the kill, often described as *katarkhesthai* 'to begin' in Classical sources, tend to be briefly described and only one or two in number in the *Iliad*. This tendency is in stark contrast to the large range of preliminary rites attested in other literary sources; the pre-kill phase is also the most frequently depicted in iconography.[46] By comparison, pre-kill details are quite limited in the *Iliad* and are found exclusively in enacted sacrifices, as embedded sacrifices give only skeletal or very restricted details of the entire process. These details are specially included to reflect the occasion for sacrifice: the sacrifices to Apollo during the plague include purification and hand washing, which also marks the oath sacrifice before Paris and Menelaos' duel. Only those sacrifices associated with pollution, including the potential for pollution incurred through the violation of oaths, include this ritual detail. The two oath sacrifices feature the cutting of hairs before the kill, but the Trojan/Akhaian oath sacrifice also includes the mixing of wine, which is poured out after the kill when the soldiers make their prayers.[47]

Though barley grains may have played an important role in the Mycenaean religious experience and are a central part of the pre-kill rites in the

---

[46] See page 28 above. Interesting comparisons can be made with the *leges sacrae*, which always specify deity and victim, but lack details about the procedure (Parker 1996:53).

[47] Purification: *Iliad* I 313; hand washing: *Iliad* I 449; III 270; cutting of hairs: *Iliad* III 273; XIX 254; wine: *Iliad* III 269; see further page 89 below. Because hand washing occurs more frequently before libations are poured, Gillies 1925:71 suggests that the action is a primarily physical cleansing without much emotional significance: Hektor refuses to pour libations with unclean hands (*Iliad* VI 266–269), and the embassy and councilors (*Iliad* IX 174–177), Akhilleus (*Iliad* XVI 230), and Priam (*Iliad* XXIV 305) wash their hands before pouring libations. On the inconsistent representation of purification in Homer, see Parker 1983:66–70, 140–143f.

Classical period, they are used in the *Iliad* only in the longest two enacted sacrifices, in which they are distributed before the prayer and thrown afterwards.[48] These sacrifices are the most detailed in the poem, and it is not surprising to find expanded pre-kill rites in this context. None of the scenes that include preliminary rites exhibit exactly the same process, even when the ritual is ostensibly the same (the oath sacrifices) or when large sections of the kill and post-kill are exactly repeated (*Iliad* I 447f. and II 402f.). So the two descriptions of the distribution of barley grains are combined with different ritual actions: hand washing in *Iliad* I (χερνίψαντο δ' ἔπειτα καὶ οὐλοχύτας ἀνέλοντο, 449); standing around the victim in *Iliad* II (βοῦν δὲ περιστήσαντο καὶ οὐλοχύτας ἀνέλοντο, 410). The former sacrifice, featuring hand washing, is occasioned by the plague, whereas the latter focuses more on the society of Agamemnon's councilors, emphasized by their collective stance around the victim. No pre-kill rites are described in embedded sacrifices, which, given the length of Odysseus' and Nestor's embedded sacrifices (*Iliad* II 305–321, XI 772–780), should be attributed not to a need for brevity, but to these descriptions' focus on divine reception.

It is noteworthy that concern for the potential pollution of sacred space and action is marginalized in the poem. Two important designations in the Classical period regarding the worship of the gods are missing from Homer. Ἁγνός and ἅγιος are the words most commonly used to denote purity, but neither the terminology nor the concept is found in the *Iliad* in any consistent or established fashion. The implications of a related term, ἅζομαι, are lost upon Agamemnon in Khruses' appeal to the Akhaians to return his daughter: "Just set my daughter free, my dear one. Here, accept these gifts, this ransom. Honor the god who strikes from worlds away—the son of Zeus, Apollo!" (παῖδα δ' ἐμοὶ λύσαιτε φίλην, τὰ δ' ἄποινα δέχεσθαι / ἁζόμενοι Διὸς υἱὸν ἑκηβόλον Ἀπόλλωνα, *Iliad* I 20–21). Despite his use of ἁζόμενοι, Khruses is dismissed by Agamemnon, whose treatment of priests will be discussed in detail in Chapter Four. Although a few other instances in the poem express a similar concept of angering the divine with ἅζομαι, they are never in connection with animal sacrifice. In general, sacrifice, and other ritual actions designated toward the gods, are reflections of the reciprocity between mortals and immortals, which does not seem to take into account potential purificatory offenses, though this is a significant worry for Greeks in the Classical period.[49]

---

[48] *Iliad* I 449 = II 410; I 458 = II 421. Cf. Burkert 1985:66–68 on the Classical period; Killen 2001:441 observes that the majority of Mycenaean Fn tablets record allocations of barley etc. on the occasion of religious festivals.

[49] ἅζομαι occurs in three other contexts, twice used by gods in reference to other gods (*Iliad*

Homeric sacrifices do not mark a departure from the profane into the sacred realm through the use of recognized sacral space or lengthy preliminary rites. Nor do embedded sacrifices signal the start and end of the ritual process—the activity of preparing, killing, and distributing the offering—with clear signals to the audience. Enacted sacrifices, however, do have signals readily identifiable to the audience at the outset of the sacrificial scene. Rather than the *pompê*, the enacted sacrificial scene is signaled by the identification of the sacrificer (*Opferherr*), who gives the command to perform sacrifice, who may be explicitly described as providing victims for the sacrifice, and who will lead the sacrifice (make prayer, cut hairs, etc.) or specifically appoint someone in his stead.[50] The sacrificer in Homer also usually kills the victim, at times by himself, at other times sharing the activity with other participants. The English term 'sacrificer' is ambiguous, as is its Greek equivalent, *mageiros*, given the multiplicity of roles the word entails: the person initiating or instigating the ritual, the person who conducts the ritual, and the slaughterer. All of these roles could be subsumed by one individual, or distinguished according to the occasion and nature of the ceremony. Henri Hubert and Marcel Mauss offer the distinction between the person providing the victims (*le sacrifiant*) and the ritual expert who could be called upon to slaughter them (*le sacrificateur*).[51] Agamemnon is both *sacrifiant* and *sacrificateur* in four of seven enacted sacrifices. He cuts the hairs of the victims for the sacrifice (ἦ, καὶ ἀπὸ στομάχους ἀρνῶν τάμε νηλέϊ χαλκῷ, *Iliad* III 292) and slits the throat of the animal after the prayer (ἦ, καὶ ἀπὸ στόμαχον κάπρου τάμε νηλέϊ χαλκῷ, *Iliad* III 266). In the sacrifice for the councilors in *Iliad* II, he is signaled as the *Opferherr* (*Iliad* II 402) and makes the prayer (*Iliad* II 411), while the sacrificial process is shared among the group (αὐέρυσαν μὲν πρῶτα καὶ ἔσφαξαν καὶ ἔδειραν, *Iliad* II 422).

V 830; XIV 261) and once by Hektor regarding Diomedes' lack of reverence (*Iliad* V 434). The etymological relation between ἀγνός and ἅζομαι is discussed by Parker 1983:147–151; the absence of the concept and respective terminology seems to Parker to be a "coincidence," given its use in Hesiod *Works and Days* 336 (148–149).

[50] Herrenschmidt 1982 argues that the question of who pays for sacrifice is of primary importance in indicating the *sacrifiant*, the person or group on whose behalf the sacrifice is offered. In his discussion of Hindu sacrifices, he points out that the person who pays for the sacrifices is the one hoping to benefit from them. A different approach is offered by Bremmer 1996:250, who observes that, whereas all participate in scattering the barley and lustral water, the most important person initiates the *katarkhesthai*. He includes Thucydides *History of the Peloponnesian War* I 25, an account of the perceived insult when the Corinthians are not asked to lead the sacrifice at their colony, Corcyra.

[51] Hubert and Mauss 1964; cf. Casabona 1966:85; Berthiaume 1982; Detienne 1989:11–13; Osborne 2000:296n7. *Mageiros* is not used in the *Iliad*. Aristophanes *Birds* 892–893 provides an example of the possible distinctions between these roles in Peiseteiros' irritated dismissal of the priest he summoned to perform the sacrifice, which he then performs himself.

The sacrifice in *Iliad* VII is very similar, except that no prayer is made. In *Iliad* I, Agamemnon twice authorizes sacrifices performed by others; his relative removal from these sacrifices reflects his reluctance to take responsibility for the plague, which we will discuss in detail in Chapter Four. Agamemnon manages the procurement of victims for all of the enacted sacrifices, with the exception of the briefly mentioned sacrifice of the Akhaian army in *Iliad* II.

Essentially, in every enacted sacrifice an animal is killed by someone for a god. From a systematic examination of enacted sacrifices in the *Iliad*, a remarkable pattern emerges: emphasis is time and again placed on the role of the sacrificer. Leaving aside the sacrifice to Apollo at Khruse and that of the Akhaian army preceding Agamemnon's sacrifice in *Iliad* II, the following signals alert the audience that sacrifice is about to be performed:

λαοὺς δ' Ἀτρεΐδης ἀπολυμαίνεσθαι ἄνωγεν·

(*Iliad* I 313)

while the son of Atreus told his troops to purify themselves.

αὐτὰρ ὁ βοῦν ἱέρευσεν ἄναξ ἀνδρῶν Ἀγαμέμνων

(*Iliad* II 402)

But the lord of men Agamemnon sacrificed an ox,

ἐς μέσσον Τρώων καὶ Ἀχαιῶν ἐστιχόωντο.
ὄρνυτο δ' αὐτίκ' ἔπειτα ἄναξ ἀνδρῶν Ἀγαμέμνων

(*Iliad* III 266–267)

And into the middle space between Akhaian and Trojan lines they
    marched.
Then the lord of men Agamemnon rose at once

Οἱ δ' ὅτε δὴ κλισίῃσιν ἐν Ἀτρεΐδαο γένοντο,

(*Iliad* VII 313)

Soon as they had gathered within the tents of the son of Atreus,

καὶ τὰ μὲν ἐν μέσσῃ ἀγορῇ θέσαν, ἂν δ' Ἀγαμέμνων
ἵστατο·

(*Iliad* XIX 249–250)

> And they set them down in the middle of the *agora.* Then
>> Agamemnon
> rose to his feet.

The primary narrator draws little attention to Agamemnon's motives for sacrifice, focusing rather on the social function of sacrifice during Akhilleus' withdrawal, a time of crisis for the Akhaian army. The importance in Classical ritual of the sacrificer in the demonstration of social hierarchy is described by Burkert as "'lord of the sacrifice', who demonstrates his *vitae necisque potestas* ['power over life and death'].... [Each] participant has a set function and acts according to a precisely fixed order. The sacrificial community is thus a model of society as a whole."[52] Through this action, the sacrificer, who may be a king or father, could potentially re-establish his *potestas vitae.* This special religious function of kings is attested in descriptions of sacrificial ritual throughout antiquity, as well as bearing a strong similarity to the ritual role played by Near Eastern monarchs.[53] The performance of sacrifice illuminates the *potestas* of the chief Akhaian king; when this power is challenged by Akhilleus' withdrawal and instigation of divine wrath, these sacrifices re-establish Agamemnon's superiority among the army.[54] I do not mean to imply that the primary narrator depicts Agamemnon as conscious of the way sacrifice bolsters his authority; instead, we may compare Christiane Sourvinou-Inwood's observations in regard to *polis* religion: "The particular social realities of the particular *poleis* would be reflected in the articulation of their cults. This was not a matter of a 'state' manipulating religion; the unit which was both the religious body carrying the religious authority and the social body, acting through its political institutions, de-

---

[52] Burkert 1983:37; cf. 1966:112; 1985:59.

[53] The *arkhôn basileus* in Athens, according to Aristotle, was responsible for "all traditional sacrifices," as were the Spartan kings; Aristotle *Constitution of the Athenians* 3.3 (the ancestral rites), 57.1–2 (the Eleusinian mysteries, the Lenaia, and 'almost all the ancestral sacrifices' (ὡς δ' ἔπος εἰπεῖν καὶ τὰς πατρίους θυσίας διοικεῖ οὗτος πάσας); *Politics* 1285a6, 1322b; Burkert 1985:95; Drews 1983:117; page 37 above. Auffarth 1991 proposes that a pattern resembling the Babylonian New Year's Festival and the installation of a sacral king underlies the plot of the *Odyssey.* Launderville 2003 compares the practices of kings in the Homeric epics, biblical Israel, and 'old Babylonian' Mesopotamia, specifically in regard to sacrifice and prayer (316–330). He defines sacrifice as the ritual slaughter of animals for a commensal meal (325); cf. Kitts 2005:126–127.

[54] Here I will briefly describe the role of the sacrificer's identity in the structure of enacted and embedded sacrifices; the significance of Agamemnon's sacrificial authority within the framework of the *Iliad* will be the subject of Chapter Four.

ployed cult in order to articulate itself in what was perceived to be the natural way."[55]

Accordingly, sacrificial scenes are initiated on Agamemnon's order, signaled by gathering in his quarters or his standing up before the crowd, or they commence with a description of his act of sacrifice (ἱέρευσεν). The oath sacrifices performed in front of the combined Trojan and Akhaian armies and in front of the Akhaian army to mark Akhilleus' reintegration into the group are both initiated by Agamemnon's standing up (*Iliad* III 267; XIX 249–250a). Significantly, both sacrifices are marked by movement 'into the middle' (ἐς μέσσον), a signal of motion toward a politically neutral space: ἐς μέσσον signifies the "sacred interstice in the interest of common activity."[56] Since this is not a commensal sacrifice, the description of movement "into the middle" is, on one hand, a signpost to the audience for the start of the ritual action, on the other, a powerful expression of the brief unity of the two parties joined in the oath sacrifice under the auspices of Agamemnon's ritual authority: in *Iliad* III, the Akhaians and Trojans, in *Iliad* XIX, Akhilleus and Agamemnon. In both scenes, Agamemnon is accompanied by a ritual helper (Odysseus and Talthubios, respectively), and the herald, Talthubios, is sent by Agamemnon to fetch victims (*Iliad* III 118; XIX 196).

Odysseus helps Agamemnon with another sacrifice, the hecatomb for Apollo at Khruse. He is chosen by Agamemnon to lead the sacrifice in his stead, since Agamemnon's performance as *Opferherr* on this occasion would signal an admission of guilt, which he will not be prepared to make until *Iliad* IX. Odysseus clearly states that he is present with the victims at Agamemnon's behest:

> ὦ Χρύση, πρό μ' ἔπεμψεν ἄναξ ἀνδρῶν Ἀγαμέμνων
> παῖδά τε σοὶ ἀγέμεν, Φοίβῳ θ' ἱερὴν ἑκατόμβην
> ῥέξαι ὑπὲρ Δαναῶν.

> (*Iliad* I 442–444)

> Khruses, the lord of men Agamemnon sent me here
> to bring your daughter back and sacrifice a holy hecatomb to
>   Apollo
> on behalf of the Danaans.

---

[55] Sourvinou-Inwood 2000:18.

[56] Burkert 2003:16; Detienne 1967:97, who observes that the phrase also carries connotations of equal distribution of meat in commensal sacrifices (1989:13). Cf. Aristophanes *Peace* 1118: Hierokles' attempts to claim some of the *splankhna* because they are "in the middle" (ἐν μέσῳ). The oath sacrifices are discussed at length by Kitts 2005:127–156, who focuses on the order imposed by sacrifice in contrast to the disorder of the battlefield (124–126).

Even though Agamemnon is not physically present at the sacrifice to Apollo upon the return of Khruseis, Odysseus immediately signals his authority to the audience with the formulaic phrase ἄναξ ἀνδρῶν Ἀγαμέμνων 'lord of men Agamemnon', which is used in three of the five sacrifices performed by the chief king, a point to which we will return in Chapter Four.

Finally, there is one enacted sacrifice not performed by Agamemnon or explicitly in his name, that of the Akhaian army (*Iliad* II 400–401). This is the briefest enacted sacrifice in the epic and the only one not specifying victims or named deities. Nonetheless, it is Agamemnon who tells the men to go to their huts and eat in preparation for battle (*Iliad* II 369–393). They are so inspired by his speech that their shouts of approval are compared to waves crashing on rocks (*Iliad* II 394–397). They go back to the ships, prepare dinner, and each sacrifices and prays:

> κάπνισσάν τε κατὰ κλισίας, καὶ δεῖπνον ἕλοντο.
> ἄλλος δ' ἄλλῳ ἔρεζε θεῶν αἰειγενετάων,
> εὐχόμενος θάνατόν τε φυγεῖν καὶ μῶλον Ἄρηος.
> αὐτὰρ ὁ βοῦν ἱέρευσεν ἄναξ ἀνδρῶν Ἀγαμέμνων

> (*Iliad* II 399–402)

> [The troops] lit fires beside their tents and took their meal.
> Each sacrificed to one or another deathless god,
> praying to flee death and the grind of war.
> But the lord of men Agamemnon sacrificed an ox...

As it is conducted on his order, this sacrifice is also an expression of Agamemnon's overall ritual authority, extending even to the generic sacrifices of the troops. While the brief description of the army's ritual performance immediately preceding a lengthy description of Agamemnon's sacrifice ties the two actions to his ritual authority, it highlights the elite and exclusive nature of the sacrifice for the councilors. It is interesting to note that the altar "frequently used by the Akhaians," described by the complex narrator at *Iliad* VIII 249–250, is not utilized in this scene.

The link between sacrifice and centralized authority, so clear in the enacted scenes, is less certain in the embedded references, which focus more on relationships between mortals and immortals. The two sacrificers of the primary narrative-text, Agamemnon and Khruses, also remember their own sacrifices in prayers.[57] Even in embedded sacrifices, Agamemnon is still the

---

[57] Agamemnon, *Iliad* VIII 238–241; Khruses, *Iliad* I 40–41. The pattern created by embedded sacrifices will be discussed at length in Chapter Three.

sacrificer for the Akhaians at Troy, as shown in his memory of his sacrifices on the way to Troy (*Iliad* VIII 238), which may be contrasted with Nestor's memory of how "someone in Argos sacrificed" (*Iliad* XV 372). Hektor's sacrifices, although neither performed in the poem nor mentioned by the hero himself, are much discussed by others: twice by Zeus (as are those of Priam and the Trojans) and once by Apollo, as well as being imagined by Agamemnon to be harmful to the Akhaian cause and by Priam as the cause for his son's special treatment. Hektor's piety is a foil for Akhilleus' estrangement from these ceremonies, which his mother's direct influence over the plans of Zeus allows. In contrast to his son's approach to the gods, Peleus makes a vow and is remembered as a sacrificer by Nestor. In addition, Oineus, neglects Artemis in Phoinix's digression, and Akhilleus and Diomedes vow that they will personally perform sacrifices. The complex narrator also describes the vows to sacrifice of Pandaros and Meriones, whose diligence is contrasted with the absence of a vow by Teukros.[58]

In contrast to the prominence of the sacrificer in enacted scenes, some embedded sacrifices elide the role of the sacrificer through generalizing references to groups rather than a focus on one person. Iris wants to feast on the hecatombs of the Aithiopes. Phoinix describes the propitiation of gods by men in general.[59] When Akhilleus insults Lukaon, he refers to "you all" as sacrificers (ἱερεύετε, *Iliad* XXI 131–132). In memories of sacrifice, Odysseus and Nestor both refer to "us" making sacrifices (ἔρδομεν, *Iliad* II 306; XI 707), as does the Trojan priestess Theano (ἱερεύσομεν, *Iliad* VI 309), a striking promise in a vow to Athena that seems to imply that the women themselves would offer sacrifice. There are three descriptions of the Akhaian army making sacrifices: the altar used frequently by Akhaians is briefly mentioned; the lack of sacrifices by the Danaans before building the wall causes the wrath of Poseidon, who, in turn, does not single out an individual, even though Nestor alone has proposed the plan (*Iliad* VII 327–343; 450). The sacrifices of Athenian youths are alluded to in the Catalogue of Ships, and a simile describes youths performing sacrifices in honor of Poseidon Helikonios. Finally, there are embedded sacrifices that do not refer to the sacrificer at all: Aineias and Akhilleus worry about the anger of the gods over neglected sacrifices, and the struggle between Hektor

---

[58] Hektor's sacrifices: to Zeus, *Iliad* IV 48–49 (by the Trojans in general); XXII 170–172, XXIV 68–70; to the Olympians, *Iliad* XXIV 33–34; imagined by Agamemnon, *Iliad* X 46. Priam refers to 'gifts' given to the gods by his son, *Iliad* XXIV 425–428. Akhilleus: *Iliad* IX 357; Diomedes: *Iliad* X 292–294; Pandaros: *Iliad* IV 119–121; Peleus: *Iliad* XXIII 140, XI 772; Phoinix: *Iliad* IX 535–536; Teukros and Meriones: *Iliad* XXIII 863–864, 872–873.

[59] Iris: *Iliad* XXIII 206–207; Phoinix: *Iliad* IX 499–501.

and Akhilleus is compared in a simile to a contest over a *hierêion* 'sacrificial victim'.[60]

Nestor's digression in *Iliad* XI may serve as a good example of the selective presentation of details in embedded sacrifices, which can emphasize the role of the sacrificer but, unlike enacted sacrifices, do not consistently prioritize this individual. The first of three embedded sacrifices describes how "we" sacrificed around the city, without further details (ἔρδομεν, *Iliad* XI 707). Then, without distinguishing individuals, he describes sacrifices at the river bank (ῥέξαντες, *Iliad* XI 727), although he includes exact details about which victims were consecrated to which divinities (*Iliad* XI 728–729), two of whom are later attributed with his success in battle (*Iliad* XI 752–758). Nestor refers only once in the three recollections of sacrifice to a specific sacrificer, Peleus, in an attempt to persuade Patroklos to help the Akhaians (*Iliad* XI 772), an observation designed to draw attention to the current isolation of Patroklos and Akhilleus, which we will discuss further in Chapter Three.

In enacted sacrifices, the sacrificer is also the person who makes the prayer. Burkert describes the combination of ritual and prayer as the cornerstone of Greek ritual practice: "There is rarely a ritual without prayer, and no important prayer without ritual: *litai-thysiai*, prayers-sacrifices is an ancient and fixed conjunction."[61] In Plato's dialogue, Euthuphro defines piety as the knowledge of the words and actions that will be pleasing to the gods when praying and sacrificing.[62] Throughout Greek literary sources, prayer and sacrifice compliment each other in maintaining a relationship between mortals and immortals; the prayer verbalizes the request, while the sacrifice is a pleasing gift which will help persuade the deity. The success of the prayer relies on reciprocity: the god will give favor because of the sacrifice and/or honorary gifts in the past or future. In this way, prayer relies on sacrifice, and when sacrifice is not made, prayers typically emphasize past or future gifts. On the basis of literary descriptions of prayer, five methods of urging the god to heed an appeal can be identified: requests to receive the current offering, vows for future sacrifices in return for immediate help, vows for future sacrifices dependent on current success, generalized "if-ever" appeals, and "if-ever"

---

[60]   Akhaian army: *Iliad* VII 459, VIII 250, XII 6; youths: II 550–551, XX 403–405); Akhilleus: I 64–67; Aineias: V 177–178; ἱερήϊον: XXII 158–161.

[61]   Burkert 1985:73, with bibliography at 375n3. On the inexorable connection between prayer and sacrifice in the Classical period, Sourvinou-Inwood 2000: "prayers are a constituent part of all cultic acts" (44). Cf. Pindar *Olympian* 6.78.

[62]   Plato *Euthuphro* 14b: ἐὰν μὲν κεχαρισμένα τις ἐπίστηται τοῖς θεοῖς λέγειν τε καὶ πράττειν εὐχόμενός τε καὶ θύων, ταῦτ' ἔστι τὰ ὅσια. Parker 1998b:109 compares this to *Odyssey* xvi 184 and xix 397; see also Pulleyn 1997:7.

appeals with reference to sacrifice.[63] However, in the *Iliad*, only both types of vows and "if-ever" appeals can be found, which can also be categorized as "future-oriented prayers." These prayers make requests, while "past-oriented prayers" seek atonement.[64]

Prayer, followed by the sprinkling of barley grains in some scenes, completes the pre-kill phase of the ritual process in the enacted sacrifices. The special role of the sacrificer is bolstered by the act of prayer, which he makes on behalf of the group. Though most enacted sacrifices include prayer, it is not described in embedded sacrifices, such as the sacrifices of Nestor recounted to Patroklos, and sacrifice is only very rarely referred to in prayers. However, characters occasionally report the speeches of others, so it is not a generic distinction that precludes embedded sacrifice's inclusion of prayer: for example, Nestor remembers the exact speech of Menoitios to Patroklos, but restricts his description of the sacrifice to Peleus' burning of thigh bones (*Iliad* XI 765–789). A brief outline of prayers in enacted sacrifices and 'free prayers', those without accompanying offerings, which embed descriptions of sacrifice, will be set out here as parts of the ritual process presented in the poem, before giving an in-depth discussion of these speech acts as part of the pattern of embedded sacrifices in Chapter Three. In the enacted sacrifices, Agamemnon and Khruses act as spokesmen for the community, distinguishing themselves as leaders of the sacrifice and communicators with the gods:

τοῖσιν δὲ Χρύσης μεγάλ᾽ εὔχετο χεῖρας ἀνασχών

(*Iliad* I 450)

And then Khruses stretched his arms to the sky and prayed loudly
for the group

---

[63] Pulleyn 1997:4 defends reliance on literary sources, the only evidence available, for prayer; Versnel 1981:3 describes the continuity throughout antiquity of "fundamental elements and structures." "If-ever" requests are discussed in detail by Pulleyn 1997:16–38. Parker 1998b:120 notes that "if-ever" requests, while frequent in poetry, are only found in two prose authors, Lysias 2.39 and Herodotos I 87 (117).

[64] Lateiner's categories, which also include "complaints" and "miscellaneous requests" (1997:250–252). His miscellaneous requests are "unritualized wishes addressed to divinities" (252), wishes which Lang 1975:310 defines as "simple prayers," distinct from those requests embellished with reasons the god should grant them or the purpose they will serve, "complex prayers." Lateiner broadly defines prayer as any address to gods (252), but only those which make requests of gods are considered to be prayers in this study. Morrison 1991:147 adopts a similar approach. I will not attempt a detailed analysis of prayers here, but refer the reader to Lateiner 1997:246–272, a discussion of the form and context of Homeric prayers, as well as the treatments of the topic by Adkins 1969; Lang 1975; Muellner 1976; Morrison 1991. Pulleyn 1997 is a comprehensive treatment of Greek prayer, which discusses the Homeric material in depth throughout the study. He defines prayer as "an articulate request directed towards gods" (6) and discusses the complex issue of reciprocity expressed in prayers (8–38).

τοῖσιν δ' εὐχόμενος μετέφη κρείων Ἀγαμέμνων

(Iliad II 411)

And then King Agamemon raised his voice in prayer for the group

τοῖσιν δ' Ἀτρεΐδης μεγάλ' εὔχετο χεῖρας ἀνασχών

(Iliad III 275)

And then, Atreus' son stretched his arms to the sky and prayed
   loudly for the group

κάπρου ἀπὸ τρίχας ἀρξάμενος, Διὶ χεῖρας ἀνασχὼν
εὔχετο· τοὶ δ' ἄρα πάντες ἐπ' αὐτόφιν εἴατο σιγῇ
Ἀργεῖοι κατὰ μοῖραν, ἀκούοντες βασιλῆος.
εὐξάμενος δ' ἄρα εἶπεν ἰδὼν εἰς οὐρανὸν εὐρύν·

(Iliad XIX 254–257)

He cut some hairs from the boar's head, first tufts to start the rite,
   and lifting up his arms to Zeus
he prayed, while the armies held fast to their seats in silence,
in the proper way, listening to their king.
He scanned the vaulting skies as he prayed.

The people making prayer either lift their arms, voices, or both, gestures frequently found throughout literary descriptions of prayer.[65] Khruses' prayer responds to his initial communication with Apollo, which began the plague (Iliad I 35–43). This prayer and his pouring of libations while burning the thigh bones (I 462–463) are the two actions that distinguish his role from the otherwise collective performance of ritual actions. The description of Agamemon's act of praying in the final enacted sacrifice underscores the image of his power over the group, who sit "kata moiran listening to their king" (κατὰ μοῖραν ἀκούοντες βασιλῆος). The connotations of the word moira indicates propriety; it is used in Homer in contexts stretching from destiny to the appropriate distribution of sacrificial meat.[66] On the occasion of Agamemnon's last performance as Opferherr in the epic, his only performance for an army united with Akhilleus, the soldiers sitting "in the proper way" provide a striking contrast to his stature as spokesman.

---

[65] Pulleyn 1997:188–195 offers an overview of the evidence and scholarship on these gestures.

[66] On the semantics of moira in Homer, see Nagy 1979:134–135. The distribution of sacrificial meat at Nestor's meal after the group sacrifice in Pylos is twice described as κατὰ μοῖραν (Odyssey iii 40, 66).

Further, the prayers of the *Opferherr* are differentiated from those of the group in two sacrifices. Before Agamemnon's sacrifice in *Iliad* II, the members of the group are described as making individual sacrifices and prayers to survive the battle (*Iliad* II 400–401), and after the oath sacrifice, the Trojan and Akhaian armies make a prayer, the words of which are given in direct speech (*Iliad* III 319–323).[67] Agamemnon outlines a very specific plan for outcomes of the duel appropriate to the defeat of either Menelaos or Paris, while the armies pray more generally for vengeance on potential oath breakers and for everlasting friendship. But because of Thetis' request, which has essentially nullified all Akhaian prayers and sacrifices until the return of Akhilleus, Zeus denies the prayers of the army (*Iliad* III 302). The oath sacrifice marking the reintegration of Akhilleus into the group in *Iliad* XIX does not include libations, oaths, or prayers made by the army, despite the same public setting, 'into the middle' (ἐς μέσσον), and the oath made by Agamemnon. The inclusion of the army's sentiments in *Iliad* III accentuates the importance of the group, all of whom will be affected by the violation of the oath, while the oath sacrifice in *Iliad* XIX restricts the emphasis to Agamemnon as he brings Akhilleus back into the group.

Countless prayers in Homer are made without accompanying offerings or references to past offerings, in contrast to the Classical dedications and literary evidence, which suggest that such prayers are rare.[68] Out of 29 prayers and vows in the *Iliad*, speech acts making requests to gods, only three refer to sacrifice, and there are only five vows in which future sacrifices are promised.[69] The three prayers that embed sacrifices are 'free prayers', those made

---

[67] Although not in reference to sacrifice, compare Ajax's command to the army to pray openly or in silence to protect their prayers from enemy ears (*Iliad* VII 194–199), which is reported in direct speech (*Iliad* VII 200–205). De Jong has observed that the prayers of the group are included to form a contrast with those of the leader (1987a:82). Cf. the description of the army's prayers (*Iliad* XV 367–369) before focusing on the prayer of Nestor (*Iliad* XV 370–376).

[68] For instance, Pulleyn 1997:30–31 argues that prayers without offerings are the recourse of people who would like to sacrifice, but cannot: their prayers form the '*da-quia dedi*' ('if-ever') type; he also discusses "free prayers" (165). Versnel 1981:56 observes that "the element of exchange was fundamental to dealings with deities."

[69] Prayers in the *Iliad*: I 35–43, 450–457 (Khruses); II 401 (Akhaian army), 411–420 (Agamemnon); III 275–291 (Agamemnon), III 295–302, 318–324 (Akhaian and Trojan armies); III 350–354 (Menelaos); IV 101–103 (Athena about Pandaros) ~ IV 119–121 (complex narrator concerning Pandaros); V 114–121 (Diomedes); VI 304–311 (Theano), VI 475–481 (Hektor); VII 177–180, 200–205 (Akhaian army); VIII 236–246 (Agamemnon); X 272–282, 460–464 (Odysseus), X 283–295 (Diomedes); XV 370–378 (Nestor); XVI 231–252 (Akhilleus), XVI 513–527 (Glaukos); XVII 559–568 (Menelaos), XVII 645–648 (Ajax); XIX 254–265 (Agamemnon); XXIII 194–198 (complex narrator about Akhilleus); XXIII 870–873 (complex narrator concerning Meriones); XXIII 769–771 (Odysseus); XXIV 306–314 (Priam). Of these prayers, three embed past sacrifices: I 35–43 (Khruses); VIII 236–246 (Agamemnon) XV 370–378 (Nestor). Five vows promise future

without an accompanying ritual action, performed by Khruses, Agamemnon, and Nestor. Vows are made by Pandaros, Akhilleus, and Meriones, as well as by the Trojans, collectively represented by the priestess Theano. Although acts of prayer are emphasized in the enacted sacrifices, Khruses and Agamemnon do not actually refer to the sacrifices at hand to bolster the strength of their requests. Nestor seems to have a special status with regard to sacrifice; he remembers sacrifices most frequently and has a very prominent role in the *Odyssey* as the *Opferherr* in Pylos. Instead of presenting the three Akhaian vows promising future sacrifices in direct character speech, they are reported by the complex narrator: Pandaros' vow is suggested by a disguised Athena and is not successful; Iris must bring Akhilleus' vow to the attention of its intended recipients, the Winds; and Apollo's reaction to Meriones' vow is not depicted. Diomedes pronounces the only vow embedding sacrifice that seems to be successful; Theano's vow of sacrifice to Athena is denied. In comparison to the number of characters making prayer without reference to sacrifice, Agamemnon's status as the only character making enacted sacrifices and one of only three mortals to speak of them in requests addressed to gods serves as another indication that descriptions of sacrifice are restricted to specific contexts.

2.3 Kill

The "kill" phase of the ritual process is, quite simply, the slaughter of the victim, which can vary descriptively in method employed, level of detail given, and terminology used. In embedded sacrifices emphasis is not given to the kill, which is expressed only in the general terms indicative of the entire sacrificial process (e.g. ἱερὰ ῥέζειν). Enacted sacrifices, as befit primary narrative descriptions, emphasize the finite verbs for killing and the act of the slaughter; oath sacrifices draw attention to the act of killing, while commensal sacrifices describe the kill as part of the preparations for the meal. The verses describing the kill in enacted scenes are listed below:

ἔρδον δ' Ἀπόλλωνι τεληέσσας ἑκατόμβας

(*Iliad* I 315)

They sacrificed perfect hecatombs to Apollo.

---

sacrifices: IV 101–103 (Athena about Pandaros) ~ IV 119–121 (complex narrator concerning Pandaros); VI 304–311 (Theano); X 283–295 (Diomedes); XXIII 194–198 (complex narrator concerning Akhilleus); XXIII 870–873 (complex narrator concerning Meriones). The prayers and vows that embed sacrifice are discussed fully in Chapter Three, pages 112f.

αὐέρυσαν μὲν πρῶτα καὶ ἔσφαξαν καὶ ἔδειραν

(*Iliad* I 459 = II 422)

first they lifted back the heads of the victims, slit their throats,
and skinned them.

ἦ, καὶ ἀπὸ στομάχους ἀρνῶν τάμε νηλέϊ χαλκῷ·
καὶ τοὺς μὲν κατέθηκεν ἐπὶ χθονὸς ἀσπαίροντας,
θυμοῦ δευομένους· ἀπὸ γὰρ μένος εἵλετο χαλκός.

(*Iliad* III 292–294)

He spoke, and cut the lambs' throats with his ruthless dagger
and let them fall to the ground, dying, gasping away
their life breath, cut short by the sharp bronze.

τοῖσι δὲ βοῦν ἱέρευσεν ἄναξ ἀνδρῶν Ἀγαμέμνων

(*Iliad* VII 314)

in their midst the lord of men Agamemnon sacrificed
an ox,

ἦ, καὶ ἀπὸ στόμαχον κάπρου τάμε νηλέϊ χαλκῷ.

(*Iliad* XIX 266)

He spoke, and cut the boar's throat with his ruthless dagger.

Clear links between the enacted sacrifices are established through both shared vocabulary and ritual details. Verses describing the kill and post-kill are virtually identical in the two large sacrifices in *Iliad* I and II, although the earlier shared feast is a longer affair. The slaughter of the victims is described with the same formula (τάμε νηλέϊ χαλκῷ) in both oath sacrifices. The kill is doubly emphasized in Agamemnon's sacrifice in *Iliad* II, first anticipated at the start of the scene ("but the lord of men Agamemnon sacrificed an ox," αὐτὰρ ὁ βοῦν ἱέρευσεν ἄναξ ἀνδρῶν Ἀγαμέμνων, *Iliad* II 402), then reiterated at the moment of death with the verb ἔσφαξαν 'they slit their throats' (*Iliad* II 422). The first description highlights Agamemnon's authority over the entire sacrificial procedure, although the group performs the manual activity of killing the victim (ἔσφαξαν). The sacrifice in *Iliad* VII does not further elaborate on the kill after describing Agamemnon's initiative with an almost identical verse to that found at the beginning of the enacted sacrifice in *Iliad* II.

Sacrifice in the *Iliad* is not a particularly bloody affair, nor are there any clear references to the relatively bloody offerings characterized in modern reconstructions of Greek ritual as 'khthonian'.[70] The most graphic depictions of slaughter are the aforementioned oath sacrifices, which describe the slitting of different victims' throats with the same formulaic phrase (*Iliad* III 292; XIX 266). Margo Kitts has suggested that the graphic description of the slaughter in *Iliad* III, as well as the subjective description of the "ruthless dagger," likens the victims to humans dying on the battlefield, emphasizing the vengeance that the participants wish upon the potential violators of the oath.[71] However, these oath sacrifices do not engage the participants in bloody acts of conse-cration; although an essential practice for oath ceremonies in the Classical period, the Homeric participants do not dip their hands into the blood or geni-tals of the animal.[72] In *Iliad* III the armies also pour libations of wine instead of using the animals' blood, as might be expected, to guarantee that the oath-breakers' blood will spill.[73] So, even at its most bloody, sacrifice in the *Iliad* does not place a great emphasis on the violence of the animals' deaths. The sheep in *Iliad* III are described as falling lifeless to the ground, an elaboration on their death (*Iliad* III 293–294), but otherwise enacted sacrifices proceed directly to the treatment of the carcass. The frequent use of sacrifice as a metaphor, or even occasion, for murder in tragedy is not found in the *Iliad*, despite a martial backdrop that would provide ample opportunity for such comparisons.

[70] For example, Odysseus slits the throats of sheep over a βόθρος, a ditch characteristic of 'khthonic' offerings (*Odyssey* xi 35–36). A white ram and black ewe are sacrificed at *Iliad* III 103, which may be the single reference in the poem to an Olympian/khthonian duality (Burkert 1985:199–203). Scullion 1994:76 describes the distinction between Olympian and khthonian sacrifice on the basis of the latter's different occasions for offering (at night), color of victims (black), and direction of the offering (downwards), as well as its practice of entirely consuming the offering in a fire (holocaust) and its different terminology (ἐναγίζειν, ἐσχάρα, βόθρος, χοαί). None of these terms are found in the *Iliad*, except ἐσχάρα, which is once used of Trojan watch-fires (*Iliad* X 418). This may be part of a general silence regarding offerings to heroes or non-Olympian deities in the poem, on which see Kearns 2004:60–61.

[71] Kitts 2005:29–32 discusses the marked emphasis on violence in the oath sacrifices, as well as the associations between the killing of the victim and the death of men on the battlefield, as opposed to commensal sacrifices; see also Seaford 1994:46–47. Burkert 2003:87 thinks that the "paradox of ritual" is more apparent in oath sacrifice; cf. Burkert 1985:250–254.

[72] On this basis, Dietrich 1988:35 states that nothing distinguishes oath and *thusia* sacrifices in Homer (see esp. n10). Cf. Aeschylus *Seven Against Thebes* 44; Xenophon *Anabasis* VI 2.9; Herodotos VI 68; Stengel 1910:83.

[73] This substitution has been puzzled over since antiquity. Scholium T *ad Iliad* III 300 suggests that the participants knew that the oath was futile. Kirk 1985:301 suggests variable practices as the motivation. Dietrich 1988:36 argues for the creative choice at Homer's disposal.

Enacted sacrifice in the *Iliad* remains an idealized picture of Agamemnon's authoritative actions. It is ironic, and perhaps reflective of his role as *Opferherr* in the *Iliad*, that the description of his murder at a feast in the *Odyssey* compares his death to the slaughter of an ox at a trough.[74] Although a *mageiros* is not needed for Homeric sacrifices, the descriptions of the *makhaira* 'sacrificial knife' reinforce the poem's emphasis on Agamemnon's authority. Both oath sacrifices describe Agamemnon's *makhaira*:

Ἀτρεΐδης δὲ ἐρυσσάμενος χείρεσσι μάχαιραν,
ἥ οἱ πὰρ ξίφεος μέγα κουλεὸν αἰὲν ἄωρτο.

(Iliad III 271–272; XIX 252–253)

Atreus' son drew forth with his hand the *makhaira*
always slung at his battle-sword's big sheath.

The *makhaira*, a term used in the *Iliad* only in reference to the sacrificial knife as distinct from weapons used in battle, is described as a ritual equivalent to Agamemnon's sword, hanging beside the sword sheath.[75] The repeated description of Agamemnon's sacrificial knife links his military hegemony to his sacrificial authority, while emphasizing the frequency with which he sacrifices.

In keeping with the brevity of details of the kill phase in the *Iliad*, there are no descriptions of collecting the blood in a *sphageion*, nor is there mention of other items necessary for the slaughter of animals. The laborious process of sacrifice can be gleaned from the depiction on a fifth-century *kulix*, a vessel perhaps itself intended for use in a sacrificial ceremony, either as a *khernips* or to sprinkle the animal with water.[76] This depiction includes a bundle of spits, an altar with a basin (*podaniptêr*) in front of it, the *sphageion* underneath, a *makhaira* and knife case, two *hudriai*, an unidentifiable pot, and what is probably a basket: the quantity of and specialized uses for this equipment testify to the tedious procedure of slaughtering and dismembering an animal for

---

[74] *Odyssey* iv 534–535. Henrichs 2000 examines the perversion of sacrifice in tragedy with reference to the passage in the *Odyssey*: the substitution of a trough for an altar is a further perversion of the ritual.

[75] This is true in actual ritual practice as well; see Martin 1983:86, esp. n2. The Cretan youths on Akhilleus' shield have golden *makhairai* hanging from their belts (*Iliad* XVIII 590–602), which Martin believes indicates "ritual ornaments" (89). Kitts 2005:151–152 links the prominence of the *makhaira* in oath sacrifices to the emphasis on violence in these scenes, as opposed to commensal sacrifices. A more detailed discussion of the *makhaira* can be found below, pages 186f.

[76] Paris Louvre C 10.574; cf. van Straten 1995:49, 105. An *amnion* is used at *Odyssey* iii 444, identified with the *sphageion* by the scholia.

consumption. Inventories from the Mycenaean period, suggestive of sacrificial and feasting equipment, are recorded in the palace in Pylos on the occasion of the appointment of the office holder *da-ma-ko-ro*. One tablet, Ta 716, lists two gold chains, axes, swords, and a *τόρπεζαι 'table' with nine feet. The chains may have been used to restrain the animal, as seems to be depicted on the *Hagia Triadha* sarcophagus, and the other utensils are appropriate to sacrificial contexts.[77] We may compare images of restrained animals found in Classical vase painting, such as a black-figure plate on which three legs of the ox are tied.[78] The silence concerning the motions of the animals awaiting sacrifice is part of the idealization of the sacrificial process in Homer, reflective of the poem's overall bias regarding the practical aspects of cooking and eating.[79]

In addition to the silence regarding the necessary implements and steps in the sacrificial process, the menial tasks of handling and slaughtering the animals, normally performed by slaves in Classical contexts, are accomplished by the heroes themselves. When Agamemnon sacrifices for the councilors, the most prominent Akhaians in the poem with the exception of Akhilleus, they perform the slaughter and serve dinner themselves (*Iliad* II 421–432). Similarly, Nestor remembers Akhilleus and Patroklos handling the carcass while Peleus makes the offering of thigh bones and libations to the gods (*Iliad* XI 772–776). Unlike in the Classical period, a professional *mageiros* is never employed.[80] Khruses is aided by anonymous young men, who hold the spits for him (perhaps akin to the *splankhnoptēs* attested in Classical vase painting) and who also serve wine and sing the *paian*, a unique instance of music in sacrificial contexts in the poem.[81] The absence of attendant slaves further narrows the focus onto the role of individuals and the solidarity created through the sacrificial process. Agamemnon has one ritual assistant, the herald Talthubios,

---

[77] Speciale 1999; Killen 1998:421–422; he gives parallels from the Classical period for audits of temples around the time of festivals (422n93). *τόρπεζαι may be a very early reference to the use of a *trapeza*, the specialized table for ritual offerings in the Classical period unattested in Homer, on which see Gill 1974 and Jameson 1994.

[78] London B 80; cf. van Straten 1995:101, esp. n307; see also Peirce 1993:255.

[79] Bassett observes: "As the meal varies from the normal, either in circumstances or importance, the ribbon-like narrative broadens and fills with content. This, however, very rarely includes details of the food itself or of the accessories of the table" (1938:45).

[80] E.g. Menander *Duskolos* 450; cf. van Straten 1995:146–147. A *daitros* is used in the *Odyssey* for the carving of meat (*Odyssey* iv 57).

[81] *Iliad* I 463, 471–474. Van Straten 1995:134–135 gives the evidence for *splankhnoptês* from four vases: London E455, E456, Palermo V661a, and Berlin inv. 3232. Burkert 1985:43–44, 74, discusses Paian, a god in Linear B sources who is mentioned twice in Homer (*Iliad* V 401, 899), as well as the ritual cry associated with the cult of Apollo; he also discusses music in cult more generally (102–103).

who assists in both oath sacrifices: he leads forth the victims (*Iliad* III 119–120, 269; XIX 196–197), holds the boar for Agamemnon (*Iliad* XIX 251), and throws the carcass into the sea after Agamemnon cuts the throat (*Iliad* XIX 266–268). This specialized assistance to the sacrificer suggests an original function for heralds in ritual contexts.[82] Talthubios' participation in the oath sacrifices is motivated by their public visibility in politically neutral spaces, whereas the commensal sacrifices in which he does not participate, held in Agamemnon's quarters, place emphasis on unified participation.

Enacted sacrifices focus on the sacrificer, usually Agamemnon, and the social dynamics of mortals. The prominence of the action of sacrificing and, often, the subsequent feast reveal a conspicuous lack of attention to divine portion or reception. The intention of the enacted sacrifices—to communicate with the gods—is nonetheless made conspicuous by prayers and pre-kill rites. These scenes are constructed within the framework of the quarrel between Akhilleus and Agamemnon. Embedded sacrifices, on the other hand, exist entirely in the framework of relations between mortals and immortals and are specifically concerned with the power of sacrifice to influence the outcome of events positively through divine pleasure or displeasure. Having set out a framework of the sacrificial ritual process, we will now turn to the post-kill phase and the gifts offered to the gods.

---

[82] Talthubios' assistance may reflect the implicitly religious role of heralds, which is otherwise superficial in the *Iliad*. Heralds are included among other religious personnel in a Linear B tablet from Pylos (Fn 187; Killen 2001:436; Latacz 2002:121), and one of the most important religious officials for the Eleusinian Mysteries is the 'Sacred Herald' (e.g. Xenophon *Hellenika* 2.4.20; Clinton 1974), but a comprehensive study of these officials in Greek cult practice is lacking. On heralds in epic poetry, see Berthiaume 1982:7 and Latacz 2002:121.

Chapter Three
The Gift of Sacrifice

T**HE POST-KILL PHASE OF SACRIFICIAL RITUAL** can be divided into two categories: gifts for the gods and food for men.[1] Gifts for the gods are propor-
tionately meager in comparison to the feasts enjoyed by the mortal
participants. The inequality of these offerings underlies much of ancient
Greek discourse about sacrifice, as discussed in Chapter One. Hesiod's etiology
of sacrifice, instrumental to many of the theoretical interpretations summarized in Chapter One, identifies this inequality as the origin of the ritual; in his
Theogony, Prometheus attempts to deceive Zeus by camouflaging the undesir-
able portion of bones with a layer of fat:

> καὶ γὰρ ὅτ' ἐκρίνοντο θεοὶ θνητοί τ' ἄνθρωποι
> Μηκώνῃ, τότ' ἔπειτα μέγαν βοῦν πρόφρονι θυμῷ
> δασσάμενος προύθηκε, Διὸς νόον ἐξαπαφίσκων.
> τοῖς μὲν γὰρ σάρκας τε καὶ ἔγκατα πίονα δημῷ
> ἐν ῥινῷ κατέθηκε καλύψας γαστρὶ βοείῃ,
> τοῖς δ' αὖτ' ὀστέα λευκὰ βοὸς δολίῃ ἐπὶ τέχνῃ
> εὐθετίσας κατέθηκε καλύψας ἀργέτι δημῷ.
> δὴ τότε μιν προσέειπε πατὴρ ἀνδρῶν τε θεῶν τε·
> "Ἰαπετιονίδη, πάντων ἀριδείκετ' ἀνάκτων,
> ὦ πέπον, ὡς ἑτεροζήλως διεδάσσαο μοίρας."
>
> (Hesiod *Theogony* 535–545)

For when the gods and mortal man fell to disputing
at Mekone, [Prometheus] acting in a spirit of kindness,
divided and dished up a great ox, deceiving the mind of Zeus.
On the one side he put the flesh and the rich and fat inner
      parts
hidden under the skin, concealed in the paunch of the ox;
on the other side he put the ox's white bones, arranging them
well with skillful deception, concealed in silvery fat.
Then the Father of Gods and Men addressed him as follows:

---

[1]   On this division of the post-kill phase, see Stengel 1910:73–78; Meuli 1946:246–248, 268–272;
and Burkert 1985:6.

"Son of Iapetos, lord surpassing all others in glory,
ah my good fellow, how very unfairly you make this division!"[2]

Prometheus invites Zeus to choose one of the portions, and the king of the gods deliberately takes the bones, which is cited as the reason mortals offer the thigh bones of sacrificial victims to the gods (Hesiod *Theogony* 545–560).

Prometheus' attempted deception of Zeus institutes the cultic procedure that defines man's place as subordinate to that of the gods. Mortals and gods having previously dined together, the institution of sacrifice replaces such commensality with a retributive distance between the two groups and the subordination of mortals. As Jean-Pierre Vernant writes, "In the sacrificial ceremony the festive side of joyous communication with the gods can never be separated from the other aspect of the ritual—recognized and proclaimed subordination to the gods, the resigned acceptance of the mortal condition, and the permanent abdication of all claims to what lies beyond the human."[3] According to structuralist interpretations of this passage, eating defines man's mortality in contrast to the immortality of the gods; agriculture and cooked food identify man's place above animals. Commensal sacrifices, those followed by a shared meal, perfectly encapsulate this hierarchy: the civility of the cooked feast elevates mortals from animals, while the feast embodies the mortal need for food.[4] Because sacrifice recognizes man's subordination, man is able to ask for the favor of the gods. Thus sacrifice is, for men, a means of communication; for gods, a means of rewarding behavior that pleases them. Underlying the hierarchy expressed in the sacrificial process, this concept of reciprocity, an exchange between gods and men as expressed in the earliest extant etiology for the performance of sacrifice, stands at the heart of ancient Greek cult mentality. As Harvey Yunis notes, "The relationship of reciprocity may be uneven, unequal, or uncertain, but for the worshipper it must fundamentally exist."[5] Reciprocity with gods depends equally on the gift to the

---

[2] Trans. Frazer 1983.

[3] Vernant 1989:53.

[4] Vernant 1991: "Greek sacrifice differs from Vedic sacrifice in that the latter is a prototype for the act of creation, which brings forth and binds the universe together in its totality. Much more modest, Greek sacrifice recalls Prometheus' act, which alienated man from the gods" (280). However, Burkert describes the same etiology as an "admission that sacrifices could not be understood as a gift to the divinity, at any rate not as the gift of a meal" (1966:105), in refutation of the adoption of Robertson Smith's concept of commensality between men and gods created through sacrifice by Wilamowitz-Moellendorff 1931:287 and Nilsson 1967:144. On the different interpretations of the Paris School and Burkert, see pages 24f. above.

[5] Yunis 1988:53; cf. Versnel 1981:56–57; Gould 1985:1–5; Parker 1998b:105 observes that Greek cultic practice depends totally on a notion of reciprocity with gods, which is explicitly recognized in some ancient sources (e.g. Khruses' prayer, *Iliad* I 39–41, on which pages 112f. below).

gods and the divine response. Central to the performance of sacrifice is the belief that gods not only exist but also pay attention to mortals, who will be rewarded or punished according to their actions.[6] The divine machinery of the *Iliad* and the complex view offered throughout the poem of both immortal and mortal perspectives constantly raises the question of divine attention to and involvement in human affairs. Throughout the *Iliad*, the belief that sacrifice can create a reciprocal bond between men and gods is both encouraged and questioned by the opposing perspectives presented in the primary and secondary narrative-texts.

3.1 The Reciprocity of Sacrifice

Sacrifice is significant only within the context created by the primary narrator and defined by the characters themselves, whose interactions and comments dictate the Homeric world. Their perspectives on deeds and events form a "cultural grammar" which must be our decoding system for symbolic ritual actions such as sacrifice.[7] Dialogue in the poem identifies the characters' value centers and clarifies their perceptions, which are not necessarily apparent in the limited depiction of events in the primary narrative-text. For this reason, the difference between primary and secondary narrative voices is crucial to a discussion on Homeric sacrifice; the primary narrator is omniscient and can therefore accurately describe the actions of the gods, whereas characters often speak about the gods in general terms and wrongly attribute motives and feelings both to the gods and to each other. The emphasis that the primary narrative places on Agamemnon's role as sacrificer and the feast following the sacrifice expresses the social function of enacted sacrifice. Embedded scenes turn the spotlight rather on the relationship between men and gods, often focusing on gift-offerings and their reception. This distinction between narrative voices can best be appreciated through a survey of secondary narrative descriptions

---

There are different definitions of reciprocity, depending on the context (gift-giving, war, etc.) Van Wees prefaces his summary of the different definitions of this concept thus, " What makes it possible to consider one's self-interest while appearing to act in the interests of others is the principle of reciprocity, which demands that benefits bestowed must be repaid" (van Wees 1998:15).

[6] The criteria offered by Yunis 1988:56, who discusses this topic with reference to the plot of *Sisyphus* (TRGF 1 43 f 19) and the Athenian hymn to the deified Demetrios Poliorkêtês (Athenaios 253e). He observes that the belief in reciprocity does not imply that the gods are predictable or rational, but prevents them from seeming entirely unpredictable and irrational (53).

[7] "Cultural grammar" is Hammer's term (2002:11). Similar is Bakhtin's "value centers"; see Bakhtin 1981 and Felson-Rubin 1993:161. Davidson 1994 observes a similar 'grammar' in Persian epic.

of these gift-offerings for the gods, as compared to the less emphatic presentation of the post-kill stage in enacted sacrifices. The broad topic of speech acts in Homer falls outside the range of this study on sacrifice, and it is unnecessary to discuss all 39 embedded sacrifices individually. Rather, a comparison of the post-kill phase's different emphasis in enacted and embedded sacrifices will call attention to the frustration expressed in embedded sacrifices.

The diverse preferences in sacrificial terminology among the narrative voices reflect their different perspectives, as has long been observed by scholars in other contexts. For example, abstract nouns are virtually confined to character speech and the complex narrator, showing a tendency in the primary narrative-text to avoid moral judgments.[8] The major characters seem to use language specific to their individual situations, either by employing exceptional vocabulary or by applying shared vocabulary in an unusual way. An early study by Adam Parry on Akhilleus' unique use of language prompted a systematic study by Paul Friedrich and James Redfield that reveals several unique rhetorical and lexical features relevant to the hero's personality and motivation.[9] For example, the first verse of the *Iliad* describes Akhilleus' μῆνις (*mênis*), a word used in a restricted manner throughout the poem in reference to feelings about his wounded *timê* or about the wrath of the gods.[10] Jasper Griffin extends this type of lexical investigation to include the language used by Agamemnon, who utilizes unique vocabulary concerned with possessions and status.[11] On the smallest level, individual words taken from traditional epic vocabulary become significant markers of the work's central theme, representing both Agamemnon's authority and Akhilleus' wounded pride.

In the *Iliad*, sacrifice is described with verbs pinpointing the moment of the kill ('slit the throat') or noun and verb combinations, which indicate

---

[8] Shewan 1935:325 observes: "It is a familiar fact that there are considerable differences, metrical and linguistic, between the general narrative and the speeches of the *Iliad* and *Odyssey*." Griffin 1986:40, 50 describes Homer as having two languages, one for the narrator and the other for the characters. In her discussion of emotive vocabulary, de Jong 1987b:143 concludes that the exceptional occurrences outside of character speech of "evaluative and affective words/ expressions should be interpreted through the focalizing character" rather than the primary narrator.

[9] A. Parry 1956; Friedrich and Redfield 1978: for example, Akhilleus uses abusive language and emotive particles much more frequently than other characters (251–252). Martin 1989:146–230 furthers this discussion.

[10] Nagy 1979:73; see also 1979:4, which describes Homeric words as "functioning elements of an integral formulaic system inherited precisely for the purpose of expressing complexities." Muellner 1996 is a comprehensive study of *mênis* in the poem.

[11] Griffin 1986:51, with a chart on 57.

either the process more generally ('to make a sacrifice') or a specific stage of the process ('to offer thigh bones to the gods'). While the verbs ἱερεύειν 'to kill', σφάζειν 'to slit the throat', and τάμνειν 'to cut' are favored in the primary narrative-text, references to the offerings, ἑκατόμβη 'hecatomb', ἱερά 'sacrificial offerings', κνίση 'sacrificial smoke', and μηρία 'thigh bones' are used almost exclusively in embedded sacrifices. For instance, Agamemnon is described in the primary narrative-text performing an enacted sacrifice to Zeus:

> αὐτὰρ ὁ βοῦν ἱέρευσεν ἄναξ ἀνδρῶν Ἀγαμέμνων
> πίονα πενταέτηρον ὑπερμενέϊ Κρονίωνι.
>
> *(Iliad* II 402–403)
>
> But the lord of men Agamemnon sacrificed an ox,
> five years old and fat, to the son of mighty Kronos, Zeus.

In this introduction to a lengthy description of sacrifice (*Iliad* II 403–432), the primary narrator highlights the physical act of killing the ox with a finite verb (ἱέρευσε), prioritizes the sacrificer (ἄναξ ἀνδρῶν Ἀγαμέμνων), and specifies the divinity to whom the sacrifice is directed (ὑπερμενέϊ Κρονίωνι). The honorific gift of the ox to Zeus is enhanced by the description of its age and plumpness (πίονα πενταέτηρον), and Agamemnon's slaughter of the beast (ὁ βοῦν ἱέρευσε ἄναξ ἀνδρῶν Ἀγαμέμνων) signals to the audience his power and authority. However, the embedded sacrifice in Agamemnon's memory of previous sacrifices in his lengthy prayer to Zeus demonstrates a shift in emphasis:

> οὐ μὲν δή ποτέ φημι τεὸν περικαλλέα βωμὸν
> νηΐ πολυκλήϊδι παρελθέμεν ἐνθάδε ἔρρων,
> ἀλλ' ἐπὶ πᾶσι βοῶν δημὸν καὶ μηρί' ἔκηα,
> ἱέμενος Τροίην εὐτείχεον ἐξαλαπάξαι.
>
> *(Iliad* VIII 238–241)
>
> Not once, I swear, did I pass a handsome altar of yours,
> sailing my oar-swept ship on our fatal voyage here,
> but on each I burned the fat and thigh bones of oxen,
> longing to raze Troy's sturdy walls to the roots.

Agamemnon's memory defines the reciprocal relationship between mortals and immortals through sacrifice; he sacrifices often to Zeus in the hope of sacking Troy, yet the outcome of these efforts remains in doubt. The sacrifice is described not in terms of the 'kill' central to all primary narrative descriptions, but by the burnt offering of fat and thigh bones to the god (δημὸν καὶ μηρί' ἔκηα). One of the distinctive features of animal sacrifice is the "play" between sacrificer, victim, and divinity, or, more precisely, the relationship between the sacrificer and deity created by the slaughter of the victim.[12] However, in embedded sacrifices, the slaughter of the victim is almost completely elided, and a more idealistic depiction of gift-offerings summarizes the entire ceremony. Agamemnon elaborates his memory of the gift-offering with a reference to altars, which are almost never described in enacted scenes. Altars and special portions emphasize the gift-exchange aspect of sacrifice, the reason most speakers refer to sacrifice, while the shared feast that often follows sacrifices is hardly described at all. Typical of embedded sacrifices, Agamemnon's description of sacrifice on his journey to Troy underscores the element most important to him: his anxiety that help owed him in return for his piety will not be given.

Even descriptions of the same sacrifice exhibit these perspectival distinctions. We may compare Agamemnon's description of the sacrifice to Apollo at Khruse, "so that, having <u>made sacrificial offerings</u> for us you may appease the far-shooter" (ὄφρ' ἡμῖν ἑκάεργον ἱλάσσεαι <u>ἱερὰ ῥέξας</u>, *Iliad* I 147), with the description of the consecration of this hecatomb by the primary narrator: "first they lifted back the heads of the victims, slit their throats, and skinned them" (αὐέρυσαν μὲν πρῶτα καὶ ἔσφαξαν καὶ ἔδειραν, *Iliad* I 459). The subjective motivations of the characters for sacrifice are juxtaposed with the narrator's "eye-witness" presentation. Agamemnon's speech summarizes the entire procedure as an appeasement of the god, while the primary narrator depicts the process of killing the animal.[13]

Agamemnon's instructions for sacrifice embed a common designation for the sacrificial act in the poem: ἱερὰ ῥέξας 'having made sacrificial offerings'. ἱερός is a wide-ranging word indicative of divine presence, a marker of the awesome power of the gods.[14] The many applications of ἱερός, modifying a range of objects including temples, chariots, cities, and corn, indicate that it probably had an earlier unmarked meaning, such as 'strong', which then developed to include strength deriving from the infusion of divine power, as well as "that which belongs to a god."[15] When used in character speech describing

---

[12] Vernant 1991:291.

[13] Casabona 1966:77, 86 observes that the usage of θύειν, φονέιν, and κτείνειν depend on the viewpoint of the speaker. The preponderance of finite verbs in the primary narrative has been discussed by Muellner 1976:31–34 as "ritual narrative."

[14] On ἱερός in Homer, Rudhardt 1958:255; Casabona 1966:2, 19; Benveniste 1973:456–461; Vermeule 1974:95.

[15] See Casabona 1966:2; Burkert 1985:269; Benveniste 1973:45–47. West 1988:155 explores the

relations with gods, this noun always refers specifically to the gift-act, such as in Odysseus' preparation of a thanks-offering for Athena:

νηΐ δ' ἐνὶ πρύμνῃ ἔναρα βροτόεντα Δόλωνος
θῆκ' Ὀδυσεύς, ὄφρ' ἱρὸν ἑτοιμασσαίατ' Ἀθήνῃ.

(*Iliad* X 570–571)

Then away in his ship's stern Odysseus stowed the bloody gear of
    Dolon,
so that they could prepare an offering for Athena.

Although the offering is not an animal but the arms of Dolon, which are never given to Athena within the poem, this complex narrative summary of Odysseus' intention shows the focus on the act of offering implied in the term ἱρόν.[16] In embedded references to sacrifice, ἱερός means 'sacrificial offering', either standing alone as the object of the verbs ῥέζειν or ἔρδειν 'to make' or as an adjective further qualifying victims or altars as belonging to the divinity.[17] The phrase "to make sacrificial offerings" (ἱερὰ ῥέζειν/ἔρδειν) is used exclusively in character speech, as opposed to the finite verbs favored in the primary narrative-text for enacted sacrifices. For example, a character may refer to the consecration of "sacred hecatombs" (ῥέξειν θ' ἱερὴν ἑκατόμβην, *Iliad* XXIII 147), or ἱερά itself may indicate the sacrificial offering. Nestor remembers two different sacrifices, first in Pylos ("we offered victims to the gods," ἔρδομεν ἱρὰ θεοῖς, *Iliad* XI 707), then at the banks of the river Alpheios ("offering splendid victims to mighty Zeus," Διὶ ῥέξαντες ὑπερμενεῖ ἱερὰ καλά, *Iliad* XI 727). These verbs underscore the activity of making an offering (ἱερὰ καλά) to the divinity. Akhilleus speaks of future sacrifices ("tomorrow at daybreak, once I have sacrificed to Zeus," αὔριον ἱρὰ Διὶ ῥέξας, *Iliad* IX 357), and vows ἱερὰ καλά to the Winds (*Iliad* XXIII 195), repeated to the Winds by Iris (*Iliad* XXIII 209). Here ἱερά represents the god's portion and perhaps reflects the semantic meaning of divine power.

Hiera is used in embedded sacrifices as a general expression for the gift-offering. Often described are the specific victims, which may vary in species, age, number, and color.[18] When the number of victims is specified, it is a heca-

---

significance of ἱερός as 'full of impetus' as opposed to 'holy', citing analogs in the *Rig-Veda*.

[16] It is interesting that dedicatory objects, similar to vows, are also discussed or imagined in impossible or negative contexts: no vow of sacrifice or other gifts is fulfilled in the poem. Dedicatory objects in Homer are discussed by Seaford 2004:55.

[17] Burkert 1976:171 and 1985:3 explain the verbs as a reflection of the basic meaning of sacrifice in Greek religion. Cf. German *Opfer*, Latin *operari*.

[18] For victims in the Classical period, see Hermary et al. 2004; Rosivach 1994:68f., esp. 74n18, gives the testimonia for the variety of factors affecting the choice in the fourth century.

tomb or one, twelve, or fifty animals.[19] In enacted sacrifices, Agamemnon twice sacrifices an ox to Zeus (five years old and fat, *Iliad* II 403; five years old and male, VII 314). Accompanying the swearing of oaths, he sacrifices a boar (*Iliad* XIX 266) and a white ram and black ewe (*Iliad* III 103f.). A hecatomb of bulls and goats is offered to Apollo in an enacted sacrifice in *Iliad* I, which is uneaten (*Iliad* I 315), and another hecatomb for Apollo is consumed at a feast (*Iliad* I 468). 'Hecatomb' can refer to a group of specific animals or be used more generally as a term for sacrificial victims, functioning almost as a generic denomination for sacrifice rather than as a specific quantity. The number of animals involved in such an offering is a matter of debate: the offering of one hundred bulls, the meaning indicated by the etymology of ἑκατόμβη from ἑκατὸν βοῦς 'one hundred oxen', seems to have occurred at least during the Great Panathenaic festival.[20] It is difficult to know the quantity of the animals envisioned by the Homeric audience, since there are hecatombs of animals other than oxen, hecatombs of different species of animals combined, and plural hecatombs offered at one time.

The two enacted sacrifices to Apollo in *Iliad* I are the only hecatombs sacrificed in the primary narrator's descriptions, but this grandest of Homeric offerings is described in several embedded sacrifices. A single hecatomb of goats and lambs is proposed by Akhilleus as the cause of Apollo's anger. Athena encourages Pandaros to vow a hecatomb of lambs to Apollo, which he does, as does Meriones. Hektor tells the army he is heading to Troy to tell the councilors and women to vow hecatombs, which are elsewhere described as twelve unworked heifers by Helenos, Hektor himself, and Theano. Poseidon and Artemis are angry over missed opportunities to enjoy hecatombs, also a cause of anxiety for Iris. The river Sperkheios is vowed a hecatomb by Peleus. The gods as a group are described as receiving hecatombs at Aulis.[21] The verbs designating the consecration of the hecatombs illustrates the emphasis on

---

[19] Seaford 2004:45, following Laum 1924:18, comes up with the different statistic of a hundred, twelve, nine, or one; he considers Bellerophon's feast, in which nine animals are slaughtered, to be a sacrifice (*Iliad* VI 174). For my distinction between sacrifice and feast with reference to the Bellerophon story, see page 63 above.

[20] IG I³ 375.7–8 records that 5,114 drakhmai were available for a hecatomb at the Panathenaia, which would purchase at least 100 cows (van Straten 1995:178); cf. Rosivach 1994:70. Pulleyn 2000:143 argues against the probability of such a large sacrifice: "A sacrifice of 100 oxen in an archaic farming community probably would have spelled economic ruin."

[21] Apollo: *Iliad* I 65, 315, 459; IV 101, 120; XXIII 873. Athena: *Iliad* VI 115; 12 heifers: *Iliad* VI 93, 274, 308. Poseidon: *Iliad* VII 450, XII 6. Artemis: *Iliad* IX 535. Iris: *Iliad* XXIII 206. Sperkheios: *Iliad* XXIII 146. Gods: *Iliad* II 306. The adjective ἑκατόμβοιος is applied to the tassels on Athena's *aegis* and to Diomedes' armor (*Iliad* II 449 and VI 236). Seaford 2004:34–35 discusses the worth of objects in the *Iliad* described in terms of cattle.

gift-giving in embedded sacrifices: hecatombs can be given ("nor did they give a hecatomb of splendid bulls to the gods," οὐδὲ θεοῖσι δόσαν κλειτὰς ἑκατόμβας, *Iliad* VII 450 = XII 6) or eaten ("the rest of the gods had feasted full on oxen," ἄλλοι δὲ θεοὶ δαίνυνθ' ἑκατόμβας, *Iliad* IX 535). Hecatombs are also described as "accomplished" for gods with the same verbs that qualify ἱερά: in Odysseus' address to Khruseis ("perform a sacrifice of a holy hecatomb to Phoibos," Φοίβῳ θ' ἱερὴν ἑκατόμβην / ῥέξαι, *Iliad* I 443–444) and Odysseus' memory of Aulis ("we were busy offering perfect hecatombs to the immortals," ἔρδομεν ἀθανάτοισι τεληέσσας ἑκατόμβας, *Iliad* II 306).

The single occurrence of "perform a sacrifice of a hecatomb" in the primary narrative-text comes in the only purification sacrifice in the epic. As soon as he has selected an embassy and provided hecatombs for Apollo at Khruse, Agamemnon orders the men to cleanse themselves and make sacrifice ("They sacrificed perfect hecatombs of bulls and goats," ἔρδον δ' Ἀπόλλωνι τεληέσσας ἑκατόμβας / ταύρων ἠδ' αἰγῶν, *Iliad* I 315–316). The sacrifice, which Agamemnon orders anonymous characters to perform on the seashore, is a response to his delegation of responsibility for the return of Khruseis to Odysseus. Typical of enacted scenes, the eyewitness perspective of the primary narrative does not anticipate the reception of the gods. The sacrifice provides pleasurable *knisê* that swirls to heaven (κνίση δ' οὐρανὸν ἷκεν ἑλισσομένη περὶ καπνῷ, *Iliad* I 317), but does not provide a feast for the mortal participants. Another hecatomb is sacrificed to Apollo at Khruse in *Iliad* I, an enacted sacrifice that will be discussed more fully in Chapter Four. However, this offering is only designated as a hecatomb in speech and descriptions of its movement on and off the ship; the description of the sacrifice itself is not specific about the type or quantity of animals. Otherwise, hecatombs are only described in embedded sacrifices.[22]

Embedded sacrifices also describe a much greater variety of victims than enacted scenes. The species of victim is specified in eleven embedded sacrifices, varied according to the divinity. Zeus is the most frequent recipient of sacrifice in character speech: he receives an ox (*Iliad* XI 773, XV 373), oxen (*Iliad* VIII 240; XXII 170), and a ram (*Iliad* XV 373). Apollo is presented with a hecatomb of lambs and goats (*Iliad* I 65), hecatombs of lambs (*Iliad* IV 101, 120, XXIII 864, 873), and bulls and goats (*Iliad* I 41). Poseidon desires hecatombs (*Iliad* VII

---

[22] We will return to the enacted sacrifices in *Iliad* I, in pages 165f. below. Hecatombs are similarly confined to character speech in the *Odyssey*, occurring once in the narrative-text to describe the heralds' leading a hecatomb through the city (*Odyssey* xx 276); otherwise this designation for animal sacrifice is only found in embedded sacrifices (*Odyssey* i 25; iii 59, 144; iv 352, 478, 582; v 102; vii 202; xi 132; xiii 350; xvii 50, 59; xix 366; and xxiii 279).

445) and receives a bull (*Iliad* XI 728, XX 403). Erekhtheus receives bulls and rams (*Iliad* II 550). Rivers receive several offerings: a bull for Alpheios (*Iliad* XI 728), a lock of hair, hecatomb, and 50 rams promised to Sperkheios (*Iliad* XXIII 146–147), and bulls and living horses for Skamandros (*Iliad* XXI 130–131).[23] The gods as a group receive hecatombs and a combination of oxen and goats (*Iliad* II 306; XXIV 34). The practice of matching the gender of the victim to that of the divinity, well attested in the Classical period, is already present in the *Iliad*.[24] Nestor remembers *hiera kala* for Zeus and bulls for Poseidon and Alpheios, but a heifer for Athena (*Iliad* XI 728–730). Alpheios, Apollo, Erekhtheus, and Poseidon receive bulls (ταῦρος), although Zeus receives oxen (βοῦς), the gender of which are not made explicit in the embedded sacrifices. In addition to Nestor's memory of a heifer, Athena receives 12 heifers (*Iliad* VI 93, 274, 308), and one heifer (*Iliad* X 292), which in Diomedes' vow is promised to have very elaborate decorations.

In embedded sacrifices, the ritual is often specifically depicted in terms of the gifts enjoyed by the gods. The smoke from the burnt offerings (*knisê*) rising to the gods above is described only in the purification sacrifice enacted for Apollo (*Iliad* I 317), but it occurs four times in character speech. Characters describe *knisê* as part of the honors paid to the gods that reinforce the reciprocal relationship between mortals and immortals. At the start of the poem, Akhilleus wants to re-establish reciprocity with Apollo through restoration of the correct amount of hecatombs and *knisê* (*Iliad* I 65–67). Akhilleus expresses his desire to repair reciprocity by means of sacrifices described, not with the reference to the ritual slaughter prominent in enacted sacrifices, but with a reference to gifts for the gods. This conversation about divine reciprocity initiates the crisis, on the human level, between Akhilleus and Agamemnon, since it is in response to Akhilleus' query that Kalkhas reveals that Khruseis must be returned (*Iliad* I 92–100). In his lengthy speech attempting to persuade Akhilleus to give up his wrath, Phoinix describes the role of *knisê* in soothing angry gods (*Iliad* IX 500). Zeus twice describes his love for the Trojans in terms of their satisfying his hunger for the appropriate share of sacrificial smoke:

οὐ γάρ μοί ποτε βωμὸς ἐδεύετο δαιτὸς ἐΐσης,
λοιβῆς τε κνίσης τε· τὸ γὰρ λάχομεν γέρας ἡμεῖς.

(*Iliad* IV 48–49 = XXIV 69–70)

Never once did my altar lack its share of victims,
libations and the sacrificial smoke. These are our gifts of honor.

---

[23] Some historical evidence for river gods is given by Jameson 1991:202.
[24] Cf. Burkert 1985:65; Jameson 1991:203.

From Zeus' perspective, sacrifice is contextualized entirely in terms of the relations between mortals and immortals. Zeus' description of libations and *knisê* as his *geras* echoes the issue of reciprocity among mortals. *Knisê* is the gift that Zeus remembers never lacking, thanks to Trojan piety. The other well-received gift to the gods is the burning thigh bones mentioned by Zeus and Apollo in illustration of Hektor's piety (*Iliad* XXII 169–172; XXIV 33–34).[25] Both refer to the entire sacrificial process as a gift of thigh bones, a method of describing sacrifice characteristic of the focus on divine reception in embedded sacrifices. Not only do gods focus on this gift, but Khruses (*Iliad* I 40), Agamemnon (*Iliad* VIII 240), and Nestor (*Iliad* XI 773, XV 373) also encapsulate sacrifices in the act of giving thigh bones.

Thigh bones are burned for the gods and Zeus describes *knisê* (the smoke from burnt offerings) and libations as the *geras* of the gods (*Iliad* IV 48–49 = XXIV 69–70), but these gifts are not depicted consistently throughout enacted and embedded scenes. In the *Iliad* there are no holocaust sacrifices, in which an animal is burnt entirely as an offering to the gods.[26] The only entirely burnt offerings made in the poem are the bits cast into the fire by Patroklos; the word θυηλαί 'burnt offerings' (*Iliad* IX 220) is found only here in Homer.[27] After the second oath sacrifice, the victim, a boar, is thrown into the sea to be food for the fish, which may be some sort of offering (βόσιν ἰχθύσιν, *Iliad* XIX 267–268).[28] In enacted sacrifices, the thigh bones, wrapped with *knisê*, which in this context means 'animal fat', are only offered in two of the seven scenes, both times accompanied by roasted *splankhna*, which are eaten immediately. The enacted sacrifices describe the thigh bones as part of a relatively lengthy process of sacrifice, in contrast to the summary of the ritual in embedded descriptions of the thigh bones. The roasting of the *splankhna* is emphasized in Agamemnon's sacrifice in *Iliad* II as replacing the libations made by Khruses in

---

[25] On the thigh bones in Homer, see Meuli 1946:215; Burkert 1966:105n38; 1983:2; 1979:55; and Petropoulou 1986:140. We will return to Zeus and Apollo's conversation in Chapter Four, pages 191f. below.

[26] Burkert 1985:62–63 gives some examples of these offerings throughout the Greek world, which create, in his view, a seeming dichotomy with the meager offerings of "Promethean sacrificial practice". Holocaust sacrifices were performed for Zeus, Hera, and Artemis among the Olympians, and more frequently for heroes and the dead.

[27] Burkert 1976:181; Stengel 1910:4–12, and page 49 above.

[28] The disposal of the victims after the first oath sacrifice is left unclear. Priam takes away the sheep that he provides in *Iliad* III, and nothing is said of Agamemnon's sheep (*Iliad* III 310; cf. III 103–104). Burkert 1985:252 believes that the removal of the victims after the oath sacrifice in *Iliad* III suggests that they would have been consumed. Kitts 2005:127–128 discusses the differences between the choice and treatment of these oath victims and the practices attested in the Classical period.

Iliad I, neither of which is mentioned in the other commensal enacted sacrifice in *Iliad* VII:

> μηρούς τ᾽ ἐξέταμον κατά τε κνίσῃ ἐκάλυψαν
> δίπτυχα ποιήσαντες, ἐπ᾽ αὐτῶν δ᾽ ὠμοθέτησαν·
> καῖε δ᾽ ἐπὶ σχίζῃς ὁ γέρων, ἐπὶ δ᾽ αἴθοπα οἶνον
> λεῖβε· νέοι δὲ παρ᾽ αὐτὸν ἔχον πεμπώβολα χερσίν.

> (*Iliad* I 460–463)

> They carved out the thigh bones and wrapped them
> in a double layer of fat, and topped them with strips of raw flesh.
> And the old man burned these on cleft sticks and poured out glis-
>   tening wine
> while young men at his side held five-pronged forks.

> μηρούς τ᾽ ἐξέταμον κατά τε κνίσῃ ἐκάλυψαν
> δίπτυχα ποιήσαντες, ἐπ᾽ αὐτῶν δ᾽ ὠμοθέτησαν·
> καὶ τὰ μὲν ἂρ σχίζῃσιν ἀφύλλοισιν κατέκαιον,
> σπλάγχνα δ᾽ ἂρ᾽ ἀμπείραντες ὑπείρεχον Ἡφαίστοιο.

> (*Iliad* II 423–426)

> They carved out the thigh bones and wrapped them
> in a double layer of fat, and topped them with strips of raw flesh.
> And they burned these on cleft sticks, peeled and dry,
> spitted the vitals, held them over Hephaistos' flames.

Both of these enacted sacrifices in *Iliad* I and II also offer to the gods the action ὠμοθετεῖν. This verb seems to describe the placement of bits of meat on top of the thigh bones, which have been wrapped in a double layer of *knisê* 'fat'.[29] As discussed in section 1.2, the description of Khruses pouring libations over the burning thigh bones and the account of the *splankhna* in *Iliad* II are the only dissimilar verses in a block of repeated text (*Iliad* I 458–461 = II 421–424; I 464–469 = II 427–432). The sacrifice in *Iliad* II creates an image of the group roasting the thigh bones and *splankhna* together in order to highlight their group solidarity in the face of Akhilleus' withdrawal. Khruses' libation over the thigh bones is unique in an enacted sacrifice, despite the emphasis that

---

[29] The verb is only elsewhere attested at *Odyssey* iii 458 and xiv 427 and in Apollonius Rhodius *Argo-nautika* III 1033. A Classical parallel may be found in the reference to *maskhalismata* in an inscrip-tion from the Attic deme of Phrearrhioi, which is defined in the *Suda* as "pieces of meat from the shoulders that are laid on the altar beside the thigh bones in sacrifices to the gods"; van Straten 1995:127 relates this to the confusion in ancient commentators on Homer regarding the derivation of the verb from ὦμος 'shoulder' or ὠμός 'raw'; cf. Lupu 2005:166–168.

Zeus places on this rite as part of the honor given to the gods by men; here is another example of the narrow focus of the primary narrator. Elsewhere, Nestor remembers Peleus pouring libations over the burning thigh bones (*Iliad* XI 774–775), and a different sort of libation is poured out to accompany the prayer after the victims are killed in the oath sacrifice in *Iliad* III (295–296).

Gift-offerings are downplayed in the primary narrator's focus on pre-kill rites and the infrequent descriptions of gods receiving the offerings, but they are foremost in the minds of the characters, both mortal and immortal. Enacted sacrifices are followed by shared meals on three occasions, and the elaborate preparation of the meat for consumption further diminishes the emphasis on divine pleasure, leading some scholars to conclude that the presentation of sacrifice in Homer focuses on the human feast. This would tend to marginalize the gods, which complicates the overall depiction of the relations between mortals and immortals.[30] However, drawing a distinction between embedded and enacted sacrifices helps to elucidate the seeming distance between men and gods during sacrifice. Although the shared feast is not mentioned in the vast majority of embedded sacrifices, relatively lengthy descriptions of cooking meat for feasts follow the three commensal sacrifices. In each of these enacted sacrifices, the primary narrator marks the transition from the gifts for the gods to the feast for the heroes with the spitting of meat (*Iliad* I 465 = II 428; VII 317). In *Iliad* I and II, the remainder of the animal (aside from the *splankhna* and thigh bones) is cut up, put on spits, roasted, drawn off the spits, and eaten—a process slightly altered in *Iliad* VII:

αὐτὰρ ἐπεὶ κατὰ μῆρε κάη καὶ σπλάγχνα πάσαντο,
μίστυλλόν τ᾽ ἄρα τἆλλα καὶ ἀμφ᾽ ὀβελοῖσιν ἔπειραν,
ὤπτησάν τε περιφραδέως, ἐρύσαντό τε πάντα.
αὐτὰρ ἐπεὶ παύσαντο πόνου τετύκοντό τε δαῖτα,
δαίνυντ᾽, οὐδέ τι θυμὸς ἐδεύετο δαιτὸς ἐΐσης.
αὐτὰρ ἐπεὶ πόσιος καὶ ἐδητύος ἐξ ἔρον ἔντο

(*Iliad* I 464–469 = II 427–432)

Once they had burned the thigh bones and tasted the organs
they cut the rest into pieces, pierced them with spits,
roasted them to a turn and pulled them off the spits.
The work done, the feast laid out, they ate well
and no man's hunger lacked an appropriate share of the feast
When they had put aside desire for food and drink ...

30 For instance, Seaford 2004: "the Homeric sacrifice is centered on the feeding (and general participation) of the group ... without barely a mention of any continuity of *object* or *place* as a context for animal sacrifice ... and with the deity marginalized" (52); cf. Sherratt 2004:183.

τὸν δέρον ἀμφί θ' ἕπον, καί μιν διέχευαν ἄπαντα,
μίστυλλόν τ' ἄρ' ἐπισταμένως πεῖράν τ' ὀβελοῖσιν,
ὄπτησάν τε περιφραδέως, ἐρύσαντό τε πάντα.
αὐτὰρ ἐπεὶ παύσαντο πόνου τετύκοντό τε δαῖτα,
δαίνυντ', οὐδέ τι θυμὸς ἐδεύετο δαιτὸς ἐΐσης·
νώτοισιν δ' Αἴαντα διηνεκέεσσι γέραιρεν
ἥρως Ἀτρεΐδης, εὐρὺ κρείων Ἀγαμέμνων.
αὐτὰρ ἐπεὶ πόσιος καὶ ἐδητύος ἐξ ἔρον ἔντο

(Iliad VII 316–323)

They skinned the animal quickly, and cut everything up,
expertly sliced the meat into pieces, pierced them with spits,
roasted them to a turn and pulled them off the spits.
The work done, the feast laid out, they ate well
and no man's hunger lacked an appropriate share of the feast
But the lord of far-flung kingdoms, hero Agamemnon,
honored Ajax with the long savory cuts that line the backbone.
And when they had put aside desire for food and drink ...

The *Iliad* VII sacrifice differs from the earlier scenes in its focus on the preparations for cooking.[31] The thigh bones are not roasted, nor are the *splankhna*
described. Descriptions of cutting up the meat in the earlier commensal sacrifices have been altered by the replacement of τ' ἄρα τἆλλα 'the remaining bits
of the animal' (*Iliad* I 465 = II 428) with the adverb τ' ἄρ' ἐπισταμένως 'expertly'
(*Iliad* VII 317). Τἆλλα extends the description of the roasted *splankhna*: the
participants divide up "the rest" of the meat, apart from the innards and thigh
bones, which have been dedicated to the gods via having been consumed and
burned, respectively. Since the *splankhna* and thigh bones are not consumed
at *Iliad* VII, 'the remaining bits' is inappropriate in this context. Instead, the
adverb 'expertly' emphasizes the proper division of meat in anticipation of
the honorary portion for Ajax.[32]

Only in *Iliad* VII, when Agamemnon awards Ajax the chine (νῶτος), the
backbone of the animal, is any specific mention made of special portions for individuals at sacrifices. Aside from this anomaly, more emphasis is given to cooking the meat than to its actual consumption, and virtually no mention is
made of the distribution of the meat, although this is a central theme of sacrifice in both literature and historical practice as we can reconstruct it. In the

---

[31] Similar descriptions of flaying the carcass occur three times in the *Odyssey* (iii 456; xiv 427; xix
421 = *Iliad* VII 316).

[32] Cf. *Odyssey* xiv 437, where the same verse describes Eumaios' gift of the chine to Odysseus.

Classical period, the ritualized distribution of certain cuts of meat plays an essential role in the bonding of participants and the maintenance of social structure. The choicest parts of the animal would have been distributed according to rank; for example, Herodotos records that the Spartan kings, even on campaign, were given the chine and skin of the sacrificial animals.[33] Numerous sacred laws attest to the careful division of parts of the animal for the cult official, and in some cases these honorary parts served as a form of payment for holding the office.[34] The social prestige and economic benefits of sacrificial meat are extremely important elements of public sacrifices in the context of the *polis*: in Athens, for example, membership in a phratry is signified by the sharing of sacrificial meat, a symbol of belonging on all social and political levels. The *prytaneis* sacrifice, give libations, and feast together, which Demosthenes cites as the foundation for the ties that bind all public authorities together.[35] However, in the *Iliad*, the important task of dividing and apportioning sacrificial meat has a relatively restricted use in comparison to the consistent focus on the role of the sacrificer in initiating the ceremony. Agamemnon provides 'private' sacrificial feasts for his close friends and councilors in *Iliad* II and VII that seem to be by invitation only. With the exception of Odysseus and Khruses, who are identified by name, the primary narrator only describes an anonymous group of youths who share the *splankhna* and feast following the sacrifice to Apollo in *Iliad* I, the other commensal sacrifice in the poem. Sacrifices embedded in character speech and the complex narrative voice only twice mention the meal following the sacrifice, although memories of shared meals without reference to sacrifice are frequently described. The importance of the shared meal can be gleaned from Lukaon's appeal to Akhilleus before being killed: "Yours was the first bread I broke, Demeter's gift, the day you seized me from Priam's well-fenced orchard" (πὰρ γὰρ σοὶ πρώτῳ πασάμην Δημήτερος ἀκτὴν / ἤματι τῷ ὅτε μ' εἷλες ἐϋκτιμένῃ ἐν ἀλωῇ, *Iliad* XXI 76–77). Without reference to sacrifice, the youth evokes commensality as evidence of a social bond that would preclude Akhilleus' killing him. Typical of Akhilleus' subversion of these social bonds, the appeal is unsuccessful, making

---

[33] Herodotos 6.56; cf. Jameson 1991:199.

[34] Hermary et al. 2004:118–120 sets out the evidence for special divisions of the animal.

[35] [Demosthenes] 43.82; Rosivach 1994:11, 66–67; cf. Stengel 1920:105–106; Sourvinou-Inwood 2000:27–29. Demosthenes 19.190: "I know that all the *prytaneis* sacrifice together on each occasion, dine together and pour libations together. ... The *boule* does the same; at the inauguration, there is a sacrifice and communal feast, and libations and sacrifices are made by all the generals together, and almost all, so to speak, of the public officials" (ἐγὼ δ' οἶδ' ὅτι πάντες οἱ πρυτάνεις θύουσιν ἑκάστοτε κοινῇ καὶ συνδειπνοῦσιν ἀλλήλοις καὶ συσπένδουσιν ... ἡ βουλὴ ταὐτὰ ταῦτα, εἰσιτήρι' ἔθυσε, συνειστιάθη· σπονδῶν, ἱερῶν ἐκοινώνησαν οἱ στρατηγοί, σχεδὸν ὡς εἰπεῖν αἱ ἀρχαὶ πᾶσαι); cf. Rosivach 1994:47.

it an important scene to which we will return. Other than Ajax's prize portion, there are no clear indications of ritualized meat distribution according to social rank or merit in the sacrifices of the *Iliad*, although such a process is described as part of feasts, for example those at which the Lycians honor Sarpedon and Glaukos (*Iliad* XII 310–321).[36]

Although distribution of meat is not a focus of enacted sacrifices, the practice of honorific apportionment seems to be reflected in the repeated phrase "and no man's hunger lacked an appropriate share of the feast" (οὐδέ τι θυμὸς ἐδεύετο δαιτὸς ἐΐσης, *Iliad* I 468; II 431; VII 320), which has the inherent meaning 'meat apportioned according to rank'. The phrase ἐΐση δαίς indicates that everyone has received the portion equal to his merit rather than a portion equal to that of everyone else.[37] Although the emphasis on special portions for Ajax is unique, the enjoyment of the meal is identical in all three commensal sacrifices. The commensal sacrifices in *Iliad* I and II are also expanded with an additional description of the satisfaction afforded by the feast: "When they had put aside desire for food and drink" (αὐτὰρ ἐπεὶ πόσιος καὶ ἐδητύος ἐξ ἔρον ἔντο, *Iliad* I 469 = II 432). These verses, which conclude the feasts and demonstrate the thematic meaning of ἐΐση δαίς, will be discussed more fully in Chapter Four as part of the role of sacrifice in the quarrel between Akhilleus and Agamemnon.

The principle of distribution in sacrificial feasts in the *Iliad* is not at the forefront of either the primary or secondary narrator's descriptions of sacrifice. The former emphasizes Agamemnon's initiative, corresponding to his provision of victims, but does not mention the distribution of meat in the sacrifices in *Iliad* I and II. In character speech, distribution is entirely absent, with the exception of Zeus' description of his altar as never lacking his appropriate share (ἐδεύετο δαιτὸς ἐΐσης, *Iliad* IV 44–49; XXIV 68–70).[38] Instead, most characters speak about sacrifice purely in terms of the relationship between themselves and their god. Nestor's speech to Patroklos in *Iliad* XI contains the only two embedded sacrifices that also describe feasting: he

[36] Berthiaume 1982:62–69 proposes that all meat distribution was "ritualized", but distribution deriving from a sacrifice would have been marked by the god's portions. However, in the *Iliad* the enacted scenes do not focus on this process, and it is entirely absent from embedded sacrifices.

[37] This verse also follows the feast of the Olympians at *Iliad* I 602 and Patroklos' funeral feast at *Iliad* XXIII 56, on which see below pages 201f. This definition is suggested by Nagy 1979:132; see also Puttkammer's important study (1912). Seaford 2004:52 and Baudy 1983 discuss the importance of the division of sacrificial meat in relation to concepts of divisions of booty and land in Homer.

[38] Mackie 1996:130 discusses the "equal feast" as a defining characteristic of Akhaian society, in contrast to Trojan society. However, she does not note the importance of this theme in reference to Trojan sacrifices described twice by Zeus.

remembers a feast after Peleus' sacrifice (*Iliad* XI 772–780), as well as sacrifices at the river Alpheios, a description followed by the army eating dinner in its companies (*Iliad* XI 725–731). After sacrificing at the riverbank, Nestor and his comrades have supper, as does the army (δόρπον ἔπειθ' ἑλόμεσθα κατὰ στρατὸν ἐν τελέεσσι, *Iliad* XI 730), but this feast is distanced from the sacrifice, as signified by the temporal marker ἔπειτα. Furthermore, the description of the army eating in its individual companies does not evoke the commensality of the shared feast following enacted sacrifices in the primary narrative. In the memory of Peleus' sacrifice, the meal is described as an act of hospitality. The commensality of a shared meal creates essential social bonds between the participants, which Nestor wishes to evoke when remembering Peleus' hopsitality to Patroklos during the crisis faced by the Akhaian army.[39] Wanting Patroklos to remember his relationship with the other Akhaians, he recalls sacrifices as well as a shared meal in the hopes that Patroklos will feel obligated to help them.

Zeus' observation that his altar is always full of his appropriate share is one of the rare suggestions in the poem that the gods 'eat' the sacrificial offerings. Kirk observes that the Homeric gods have been "purified" or "de-carnalized," as opposed to their Near Eastern counterparts, who are imagined as consumers of food. The divine reception of sacrifice is distanced from the food of the gods, *nektar*, and even this foodstuff is only rarely consumed. A similar "de-carnalization" is also at work in the preparation of heroic food, which is idealized to fit a romanticized depiction of heroes and kings, part of the overall avoidance of mundane practicalities in the poem.[40] Sacrifices occur on a large scale, but without any of the tedium such offerings would entail. The general Homeric tendency to elevate details to the grandest, most regal scale is reflected in the consistent practice of roasting meat rather than boiling it, which occurs only once in a simile (*Iliad* XXI 361–365), and in the almost exclusively carnivorous diet of the heroes, which is unrealistic for any historical society of this time period.[41]

Animal sacrifice, when the sacrificer directs the action specifically toward the gods, is relatively infrequent, while eating is part of the daily

---

[39] See pages 120f. below.

[40] Kirk 1990:9–11; cf. Griffin 1980:187–188. Both scholars observe that ambrosia is not actually consumed by the gods in the *Iliad*. They drink *nektar* at *Iliad* I 599–604; IV 1–4; and unspecified drinks at *Iliad* XV 88; XXIV 100–102. The gods attend feasts with the Aithiopes at *Iliad* I 424; XXIII 201–207, see below pages 190f.

[41] Sheratt 2004:184. Most sacrificial meat consumed in the Classical period was probably boiled: van Straten 1995:147 discusses the evidence. Berthiaume 1982:5–9, 64–67 describes Homeric contexts for eating and food preparation.

routine of heroes, featured in nearly every day presented in both Homeric poems.[42] Eating provides an important social context, particularly in the *Iliad*, for interactions and discussion, which in turn form an essential backdrop of the poem for the audience. The feasts following enacted commensal sacrifices serve a social function similar to feasts without offerings to the gods, but cast the discourse in a context firmly associated with Agamemnon's authority in Akhilleus' absence, often providing an occasion for speechmaking and planning. For example, after the participants have enjoyed the feast, signaled by the repeated verses described above, the harmonious atmosphere leads to Nestor's announcement of a plan in *Iliad* II and VII:

τοῖς ἄρα μύθων ἦρχε Γερήνιος ἱππότα Νέστωρ·
"Ἀτρεΐδη κύδιστε, ἄναξ ἀνδρῶν Ἀγάμεμνον"

(*Iliad* II 433–434)

Among them Nestor the noble old horseman spoke out first:
"Most glorious son of Atreus, lord of men Agamemnon ... "

τοῖς ὁ γέρων πάμπρωτος ὑφαίνειν ἤρχετο μῆτιν
Νέστωρ, οὗ καὶ πρόσθεν ἀρίστη φαίνετο βουλή·
ὅ σφιν ἐὺ φρονέων ἀγορήσατο καὶ μετέειπεν·

(*Iliad* VII 324–326)

Among them first of all the old man began to weave his counsel:
Nestor, whose earlier plan had appeared best.
With good will to the lords he addressed them and spoke.

In enacted sacrifices, the sacrificial feast completes the lengthy description of the pre-kill and kill phases, creating the social harmony necessary for planning and decision-making. In *Iliad* II, the first day of combat in the poem, Nestor's speech urges the councilors to marshal the army and start battle. In *Iliad* VII, he recommends gathering the dead, burning the corpses, and building the wall. Although there is no shared feast, the oath sacrifice in *Iliad* XIX leads to Akhilleus' important speech and the end of the quarrel:

ἦ καὶ ἀπὸ στόμαχον κάπρου τάμε νηλέϊ χαλκῷ.
τὸν μὲν Ταλθύβιος πολιῆς ἁλὸς ἐς μέγα λαῖτμα
ῥῖψ' ἐπιδινήσας, βόσιν ἰχθύσιν· αὐτὰρ Ἀχιλλεὺς

---

[42] Bassett 1938: "Eating, like going to sleep and waking, is at least mentioned if not described in the account of every day presented ... " (46); Arend 1933:70 describes the Homeric "delight in hospitality" that inspires the frequent eating in the poems.

ἀνστὰς Ἀργείοισι φιλοπτολέμοισι μετηύδα.

(*Iliad* XIX 266–269)

[Agamemnon] spoke and cut the boar's throat with his ruthless
    dagger.
Talthubios whirled it round and slung it into the yawning gulf of
    the gray sea
for swarming fish to eat. Then Akhilleus
stood and addressed the Argives keen for battle.

The description of Akhilleus' authoritative act of standing (αὐτὰρ Ἀχιλλεὺς ἀνστάς) to exhort the troops to battle concludes the enacted sacrifice begun by Agamemnon standing up (ἂν δ' Ἀγαμέμνων ἵστατο, XIX 249–250). The heroes' physical stances reflect their individual spheres of authority: war and sacrifice, respectively. The positive emphasis that sacrifice places on Agamemnon's leadership is one of its important thematic functions. Sacrifice is perhaps the only activity in which Agamemnon has an obvious authority: he is certainly deficient in persuasive speechmaking, and, although he enacts all of the above sacrifices, others take advantage of the opportunity for speechmaking offered by the communal meal.[43] These speeches propose important paths of action for the plot. Nestor tells Agamemnon to start the day of battle; Nestor proposes the burial of the dead and construction of the wall; and, finally, Akhilleus suggests that they eat so that they can then rejoin battle on the last day of combat in the poem.

3.2 The Pattern of Embedded Sacrifices

Throughout the *Iliad*, mortal and immortal characters speak of sacrifices with an almost exclusive focus on its role in the creation of reciprocity. When considering these character descriptions, the pattern that emerges is one of doubt, frustration, and even anger over a perceived failure of sacrifice to create lasting bonds between men and gods. Embedded sacrifices can be grouped into roughly three general categories. Some embedded sacrifices express an idealized reciprocal relationship with gods, but are grounded in unhappy, crisis situations and establish either frustrated expectations or highlight the inconsistent success rates of sacrifice. Some either explicitly acknowledge that the ritual is unsuccessful, or express anxiety that sacrifice has gone unnoticed by the gods or has provoked them to anger. Finally, a few speeches depict

---

[43] On Agamemnon's inadequate speeches, see Martin 1989:62–63, 113–119; Taplin 1990; and pages 157f. below.

the anger of the gods toward mortals because of sacrifices. An overview of embedded sacrifices will demonstrate this overall negative impression, which forms part of the poetic depiction of the breakdown of mortal/immortal reciprocity.

In many respects the *Iliad* is concerned with retribution: misdeeds are appropriately punished. Many of the most important actions on the human level revolve around a theme of 'need–offer–rejection', such as Khruses' ransom, rejected by Agamemnon, or Agamemnon's compensation, rejected by Akhilleus.[44] Agamemnon's enacted sacrifices draw the audience's attention to the challenge presented to the Akhaian social hierarchy by Akhilleus' rejection of compensation; the embedded sacrifices draw the audience's attention to the questionable reciprocity between gods and humans that results from Akhilleus' distortion of mortal/immortal relations. To return to Yunis' definition of reciprocity in Greek worship, in the *Iliad* the gods certainly care about mortals and pay attention to them, but sacrifice does not facilitate this relationship; even when sacrifices are described as pleasing, they are nonetheless inadequate in comparison to the superior bond with the gods enjoyed by Akhilleus. As we continue to explore the presentation of sacrifice in the poem, we will see that Akhilleus' ability to influence divinities through his mother Thetis' intercession is contrasted directly with the attempts of mortals to influence them with sacrifice. While Agamemnon is associated with the controlled, ordered enacted sacrifices, embedded sacrifices problematize the ritual as a method of communicating with gods. As Oliver Taplin observes, "There is a consistent [cultic] framework, but its application, its interaction with the human world is again beset with questions. ... How does piety influence the gods?"[45]

Patterns of mortal/immortal relations are established early in the poem, partly through the false expectations created by ideal examples of reciprocity among men and gods. The prayers of Khruses and Odysseus and of Diomedes express reciprocal relationships, but the former instance is a foil for the breakdown of this type of relationship, and the latter highlights the possibility of reciprocity without recourse to sacrifice. Pandaros is encouraged by Athena to make a meaningless vow, and, though Nestor recalls sacrifices that he believes to have positively influenced the gods in his favor, they only serve to contrast the disjunction between sacrifice and divine favor at this point in the poem. At the start of the poem, Khruses makes a prayer to Apollo that establishes

---

[44] Rosner 1976:321n18 describes this theme in relation to the uses of λίσσομαι. On the themes of ransom and revenge throughout the poem, see Wilson 2002.
[45] Taplin 1992:7.

the ideal standard: a personal, reciprocal relationship is illustrated through references to past honors given the god, including sacrifice, and on this basis Khruses makes a request with a wish formula found in many prayers, "now bring my prayer to pass" (τόδέ μοι κρήηνον ἐέλδωρ):[46]

κλῦθί μεν, ἀργυρότοξ᾽, ὅς Χρύσην ἀμφιβέβηκας
Κίλλαν τε ζαθέην Τενέδοιό τε ἶφι ἀνάσσεις,
Σμινθεῦ, εἴ ποτέ τοι χαρίεντ᾽ ἐπὶ νηὸν ἔρεψα,
ἢ εἰ δή ποτέ τοι κατὰ πίονα μηρί᾽ ἔκηα
ταύρων ἠδ᾽ αἰγῶν, τόδέ μοι κρήηνον ἐέλδωρ·

(*Iliad* I 37–41)

Hear me, god of the silver bow who strides the walls of Khruse
and Killa sacrosanct—lord in power of Tenedos—
Smintheus, if ever I roofed a shrine to please your heart,
ever burned for you the fat thigh bones
of bulls and goats, now, now bring my prayer to pass.

Khruses desires revenge on the Akhaians, so, asking Apollo for his attention, he honors him with epithets, a catalog of places special to the god, and reminders of his past sacrifices and honorific deeds. As a spoken description of sacrifices, this prayer is one of the 'embedded sacrifices' that occasionally refer to past sacrifices to enhance a request, in contrast to prayers accompanying the performance of sacrifice in the *Iliad*, which neither mention past sacrifices nor refer to the current offering. Khruses' prayer is successful—Apollo hears him and unleashes the plague upon the Akhaians (*Iliad* I 43–52). But this demonstration of a reciprocal relationship with the god only comes at a moment of crisis, and it creates an even greater crisis among the Akhaian army. After the Akhaians return his daughter, Khruses officiates at a sacrifice to Apollo and revokes this original request with an address almost identical to his first, which includes even the same wish formula (μοι τόδ᾽ ἐπικρήηνον ἐέλδωρ). The only difference is the much-debated epithet *Smintheus*, which may evoke Apollo's capacity to cause a plague or have a special function in the psychology of Khruses' 'personal' relationship with the god, appropriate when he is alone on the beach but not in front of the Akhaians.[47] During the public

---

[46] Khruses' prayer is discussed at length by Pulleyn 1997:16f. as a representative of the 'if ever' type. The vocabulary of prayer is discussed by Muellner 1976; Pulleyn 1997:132–155; Lateiner 1997:246–247. Tsagarakis 1977:34 observes that, in his original prayer, Khruses prays not to get his daughter back, but for revenge.

[47] Pulleyn 2000 note *ad loc.* gives a brief summary of the ancient and modern scholarship on 'Smintheus', which may either refer to either a place, 'Sminthe', or be derived from σμίνθος, 'mouse', which could possibly connect it with the spread of plagues by mice.

performance of sacrifice, Khruses gestures more generally to Apollo's role in the maintenance of their reciprocal relationship:

κλῦθί μευ, ἀργυρότοξ’, ὃς Χρύσην ἀμφιβέβηκας
Κίλλαν τε ζαθέην Τενέδοιό τε ἶφι ἀνάσσεις·
ἠμὲν δή ποτ’ ἐμεῦ πάρος ἔκλυες εὐξαμένοιο,
τίμησας μὲν ἐμέ, μέγα δ’ ἴψαο λαὸν Ἀχαιῶν·
ἠδ’ ἔτι καὶ νῦν μοι τόδ’ ἐπικρήηνον ἐέλδωρ

(*Iliad* I 451–455)

Hear me, God of the silver bow who strides the walls of Khruse
and Killa sacrosanct—lord in power of Tenedos!
If you honored me last time and heard my prayer
and rained destruction down on all Akhaia's ranks,
now bring my prayer to pass once more ...

Although Khruses still draws on a relationship with Apollo, in this prayer *accompanying* sacrifice, he repeats neither his past gifts to the god nor the current offering, and he makes no mention of sacrifice.[48] Perhaps the present offering may require no spoken elaboration, but we might expect him to bolster his request, or at least emphasize the honor for the god, by referring to the hecatomb he is about to consecrate. Just as before, the god hears Khruses' prayer in a typical verse describing the reception of a prayer (ὣς ἔφατ’ εὐχόμενος, τοῦ δ’ ἔκλυε Φοῖβος Ἀπόλλων, *Iliad* I 43 = 457), which is apparently unaffected by the lack of reference to sacrifice.[49] The gods hear most prayers, and many are 'granted', but only two other prayers even mention past sacrifices.[50] This inconsistent representation of the importance of sacrifice in the creation of reciprocity between gods and men, and the subsequently unpredictable capability of mortals to influence the gods in the *Iliad*, creates a tension between narratives. While enacted sacrifices are painstakingly performed in the primary narrative, characters themselves neither explicitly

---

[48] The reluctance in Homeric prayers to refer to the sacrifice at hand can be contrasted with the consistency of this practice in other literary sources; cf. Trugaios' prayer to Peace during his sacrifice, in which he asks the goddess to receive his sacrifice: "Oh most holy queen, goddess, mistress Peace, queen of dances, queen of marriages, receive our sacrifice" (ὦ σεμνοτάτη βασίλεια θεά, πότνι’ Εἰρήνη, δέσποινα χορῶν, δέσποινα γάμων, δέξαι θυσίαν τὴν ἡμετέραν, Aristophanes *Peace* 974–977).

[49] The formulaic expression occurs at *Iliad* I 43, 457; V 121; X 295; XVI 249 (partly denied), 527; XXIII 771; XXIV 314.

[50] Agamemnon's and Nestor's prayers (*Iliad* VIII 240; XV 373), see below pages 118f. Morrison 1991:149 estimates that 63 percent of prayers, 19 out of 30, are given positive responses in both the *Iliad* and *Odyssey*. There are different estimations of prayers in the poem, depending on how 'prayer' is defined; I count 29 (see page 86 above).

associate sacrifice with prayer, often omitting it from requests, nor do they feel confident that sacrifice is working in their favor. Khruses does not associate Apollo's favor with sacrifice in the second prayer; he is confident that Apollo has heard him, but this ability to influence Apollo with his prayers only creates false expectations for future reciprocity. In the next sacrifice scene, performed by Agamemnon for his 'councilors', the prayer is denied by Zeus, who is bound to honor Thetis' request on behalf of Akhilleus. The expectations raised by Khruses' successful relationship with Apollo intensifies the disruption of reciprocity by Akhilleus' influence on divine activity. Khruses' initial prayer to Apollo on the beach may form an ideal model of reciprocity, but it is an ideal that is repeatedly revealed to be out of reach.

An interesting contrast between an existing reciprocal relationship with a god not based on sacrifice and the attempt to establish one with sacrifice can be found in the requests of Odysseus and Diomedes to Athena. When the men set out on the night raid, Athena sends a heron as an omen, which is immediately recognized as such by Odysseus. He responds with a prayer for Athena to give them glory and success:

> χαῖρε δὲ τῷ ὄρνιθ' Ὀδυσεύς, ἠρᾶτο δ' Ἀθήνῃ·
> "κλῦθί μευ, αἰγιόχοιο Διὸς τέκος, ἥ τέ μοι αἰεὶ
> ἐν πάντεσσι πόνοισι παρίστασαι, οὐδέ σε λήθω
> κινύμενος· νῦν αὖτε μάλιστά με φῖλαι, Ἀθήνη,
> δὸς δὲ πάλιν ἐπὶ νῆας ἐϋκλεῖας ἀφικέσθαι,
> ῥέξαντας μέγα ἔργον, ὅ κε Τρώεσσι μελήσῃ."
>
> *(Iliad* X 277–282)

> Glad at the bird omen, Odysseus prayed to Athena,
> "Hear me, daughter of aegis-bearing Zeus, standing by me always,
> in every combat mission—no maneuver of mine slips by you—
> now, again, give me your best support, Athena, comrade!
> Grant our return in glory back to the warships
> once we've done some feat that brings the Trojans pain!"

Odysseus describes an established and long-standing relationship with the goddess, who is "always" attentive to his actions. Unlike Khruses' first prayer to Apollo, Odysseus does not cite any reasons why the goddess favors him. Without relying on an unpredictable sacrifice as a method of gaining her favor, he is serenely confident in his patroness's support. Others also seem confident in her protection of Odysseus; in fact, Diomedes cites her love for Odysseus as the reason he chooses Odysseus to accompany him on the raid (*Iliad* X 245). At no point in the entire poem does Odysseus or Athena refer to sacrifice as part of the maintenance of their relationship, although his pious performance of sacrifices at Troy is cited in the *Odyssey*, along with his superior wisdom, as a reason for the divine favor shown to him there.[51]

The silence of the *Iliad* on his sacrifices, which seem to have an important place in the epic tradition, reflects the poem's restriction of the presentation of sacrifice to contexts associated with Agamemnon and Akhilleus' quarrel and its negative implications for reciprocity between men and gods: Odysseus' happy relationship with Athena still stands, but remains relatively disconnected from the thematic pattern of sacrifice in the poem. In contrast, Diomedes, in making his vow of sacrifice, seems to "piggyback" onto the guaranteed success of Odysseus' prayer with the invocation for Athena to "hear me too" at the start of his prayer:

> <u>κέκλυθι νῦν καὶ ἐμεῖο,</u> Διὸς τέκος, Ἀτρυτώνη·
> σπεῖό μοι ὡς ὅτε πατρὶ ἅμ' ἕσπεο Τυδέϊ δίῳ
> ἐς Θήβας, ὅτε τε πρὸ Ἀχαιῶν ἄγγελος ᾔει.
> τοὺς δ' ἄρ' ἐπ' Ἀσωπῷ λίπε χαλκοχίτωνας Ἀχαιούς,
> αὐτὰρ ὁ μειλίχιον μῦθον φέρε Καδμείοισι
> κεῖσ'· ἀτὰρ ἂψ ἀπιὼν μάλα μέρμερα μήσατο ἔργα
> σὺν σοί, δῖα θεά, ὅτε οἱ πρόφρασσα παρέστης.
> ὣς νῦν μοι ἐθέλουσα παρίσταο καί με φύλασσε.
> σοὶ δ' αὖ ἐγὼ ῥέξω βοῦν ἦνιν εὐρυμέτωπον
> ἀδμήτην, ἣν οὔ πω ὑπὸ ζυγὸν ἤγαγεν ἀνήρ·
> τήν τοι ἐγὼ ῥέξω χρυσὸν κέρασιν περιχεύας.

> (*Iliad* X 284–294)

> <u>Hear me too,</u> daughter of Zeus, Atrutône!
> Be with me now, just as you went with father, noble Tydeus,
> into Thebes that day he ran ahead of the Akhaians as a messenger.
> He left his armored Akhaians along the Aisopos' banks
> and carried a peaceful word to Theban cohorts.
> But turning back he devised some grand and grisly works
> with you, noble Goddess, and you stood by him, a steadfast ally.
> So come, stand by me now, protect me now!
> I will make you a sacrifice, a yearling heifer broad in the brow,
> unbroken, which has never been led under the yoke by men.
> I'll sacrifice it to you—I'll sheathe its horns in gold!

---

[51] *Odyssey* i 60–67. He does have an important ritual role as Agamemnon's stand-in at the sacrifice at Khruse; see below pages 172f.

Although Athena has directly and openly intervened in the *aristeia* of Diomedes in *Iliad* V, he mentions neither this nor any other past occasions, focusing rather on her relationship with his father. He at least assumes that he does not have a reciprocal relationship with Athena, so he seems to rely upon a vow in an attempt to get Athena's attention. The elaborate details of the victim to be sacrificed add emphasis to his desire to cultivate the same type of relationship with Athena that his father had, while the lengthy prayer, following immediately upon Odysseus' request, reflects his anxiety in anticipation of the night raid into the Trojan camp. Athena hears both prayers ("So they spoke in prayer, and Pallas Athena heard them," ὣς ἔφαν εὐχόμενοι, τῶν δ' ἔκλυε Παλλὰς Ἀθήνη, *Iliad* X 295), and her reception does not suggest any distinction, despite the differences in content.

As with prayers, vows of sacrifice do not seem to imply a more successful divine response. To illustrate this, it is worth comparing Athena's response in *Iliad* X to her face-to-face encounter with Diomedes following his prayer during his *aristeia* (*Iliad* V 115–120). In both prayers he refers to the help she gave his father, but in the prayer before the *Doloneia* he also vows a heifer, with the lavish promise to gild its horns.[52] Yet, whereas only the primary narrator and the audience are aware of her help in *Iliad* X, the goddess appears directly to Diomedes in response to his prayer in *Iliad* V. Not every embedded sacrifice is negative, and there is no indication that the vow of sacrifice is not helpful for Diomedes or desirable for the goddess. However, promises of sacrifice do not necessarily lead to divine favor, and positive examples of mortal/immortal relations remain relatively distanced from sacrifice. Another vow promises sacrifice in exchange for immediate help: upon Pandaros' homecoming, Athena encourages him to vow a hecatomb of firstborn lambs to Apollo in exchange for a successful shot at Menelaos, a vow that is repeated in indirect speech by the complex narrator (*Iliad* IV 100–103; 119–121). Here, for a vow instigated by a disguised god, no response by Apollo is given, and the primary narrator explains that the gods choose to protect Menelaos rather than Pandaros (*Iliad* IV 127–129). Athena's implication that the vow of sacrifice would elicit Apollo's

[52] See Lang 1975:311–312 on the function of the memory of Tydeus' exploits within the context. We can also compare Odysseus' presentation of the spoils of Dolon to Athena (*Iliad* X 461–464), to which no response is described, as a further example of the dissociation of immortal attention and gift-offerings within the poem. The *Doloneia* was questioned as a late addition to the poem in antiquity by the T-scholium ad *Iliad* X 1; e.g. Kirk 1962:310–312, Taplin 1992:11; Hainsworth 1993:151f. The use of gilded horns in elevating a sacrifice to an appropriate level for divine presence is paralleled in only one instance in the *Odyssey*: in response to Athena's epiphany, Nestor gilds the horns of a heifer, a sacrifice which Athena attends unbeknownst to the mortal participants (*Odyssey* iii 381–383).

help serves as an important example of the way in which the potential for idealized reciprocity created by sacrifice is continually undermined.

Among the most colorful and much-admired aspects of the *Iliad* are the 24 digressions, which speakers use to interrupt the focus on current events at Troy in order to provide paradigms in defense of a current course of action or to persuade or dissuade someone from a proposed course of action.[53] Descriptions of sacrifice are embedded in three hortatory, external analepses made by Odysseus, Phoinix, and Nestor. However, embedded sacrifices never take the form of internal analepses; although memories of sacrifices made before the embarkation for Troy are relatively frequent, characters never recall sacrifices performed in the poem or refer to earlier sacrifices at Troy. The memories of past sacrifices provide a contrast with the current desperate situation of the Akhaian army caused by Akhilleus' wrath. But sacrifice is still presented as an ineffective gift-offering to the gods, in the sense that either the sacrifices before Troy are currently nullified by Thetis' request, or they are remembered to Akhilleus and Patroklos to highlight the present predicament of the army in contrast to its previous success. Odysseus' memory of sacrifice at Aulis has been discussed in Chapter Two. The rather vague description of sacrifice, in contrast to the vivid memory of the location and portent anticipating Akhaian success, is intended to inspire confidence in the troops; this attempt at confidence is undermined by the audience's knowledge that Zeus has just made a superior arrangement with Thetis. Phoinix's embedded sacrifices demonstrate the anger of the gods, part of the most distressing examples of embedded sacrifices, which will be discussed below. Nestor's embedded sacrifices fit into the pattern of idealized reciprocity, as in Khruses' first prayer, which is at odds with the overall presentation of the efficacy of sacrifice in the poem.

Nestor gives four digressive, hortatory speeches in the *Iliad*, but only in his address to Patroklos in *Iliad* XI does he refer to sacrifice. His digressions have been well studied, particularly the possible connections between these stories and the epic cycle.[54] Nestor's digressions offer paradigms of heroic

---

[53] Gaisser 1969:2 defines digression as "tales and episodes that interrupt the flow of the action to tell of events unconnected with the main story or to give background information." She counts 24 digressions, including those set within the time of the poem, such as the shield of Akhilleus: *Iliad* II 100–109, 299–332, 494–759, 816–877; III 204–224; IV 370–400; V 381–404; VI 119–236, 407–432; VII 123–160; IX 434–605; X 254–272; XI 655–803; XIV 110–127, 313–328; XV 14–33; XVIII 37–50, 393–409, 478–608; XIX 86–136; XX 213–241; XXIII 624–650, 740–749; XXIV 599–620. See also Austin 1966:301, who counts 18 digressions dealing with material outside the poem.

[54] Kirk 1990 *ad Iliad* VII 123–160 concludes that Nestor's stories function like a "minor genre" within the poem. On the digressions of Nestor, see Austin 1966; Pedrick 1983; Dickson 1995.

virtue and bravery, intended to inspire such qualities in his addressee. As the quarrel between Agamemnon and Akhilleus begins, he intervenes with a digression on the help he gave the Lapiths against the Kentaurs, but he does not refer to sacrifice (*Iliad* I 259–274), despite the importance of this theme in the context of the quarrel. He rebukes the timidity of the Akhaians in the face of Hektor's challenge by recalling how he met the Arkadian Ereuthalion's challenge and killed him (*Iliad* VII 132–160), again without reference to sacrifice. During Patroklos' funeral games, he remembers his prowess as a youth in the funeral games of Amarunkeus, his last digression in the epic (*Iliad* XXIII 629–650). In Nestor's longest and most important hortatory digression, he convinces Patroklos to borrow Akhilleus' armor and join the battle.[55] On this occasion, he embeds three sacrifices (*Iliad* XI 706–707, 725–729, 772–775), while recalling both his strength in battles against the Epeians and the advice Menoitios gave Patroklos before he left Phthia for Troy (*Iliad* XI 656–803). The length of Nestor's digression, itself a persuasive technique, reflects its importance, and the fact that this most crucial digression is his only memory to be enhanced with embedded sacrifices is significant.[56]

Like Odysseus' digression on Aulis, Nestor's speech is drawn from personal experiences, occurs at a critical stage of Akhaian distress, and functions to encourage troops to rejoin battle, in this case, Akhilleus' contingent. Nestor's speech to Patroklos can be divided into two sections: his two battles with the Epeians (*Iliad* XI 670–761), intended as an exemplum of heroic bravery, and a second section in which he remembers visiting the house of Peleus (*Iliad* XI 761–803).[57] In the Epeian episode, Nestor remembers sacrifices "around the city" when the booty was divided up (*Iliad* XI 706–707), as well as a sacrifice before crossing the river (*Iliad* XI 727–729). The two military engagements with the Epeians create a "tricolon" pattern emphasizing Nestor's glory in battle, the collection or proper division of booty, and sacrifice to the gods.[58] The first battle is followed by sacrifices in the city and the proper division of spoils, in which Nestor remembers a positive example of reciprocity both within a

---

[55] This paradigmatic exhortation is unique in the lack of direct comparison between the speaker and person addressed, direct command, and direct connection with the present circumstances, as well as the extraordinary length; Pedrick 1983:5–60 concludes that Akhilleus is the intended addressee, a substitution that explains these anomalies.

[56] Austin's principle of *amplificatio*: "the length of the anecdote is in direct proportion to the necessity for persuasion at the moment" (1966:306).

[57] Pedrick's division (1983:57), drawing on Schadewaldt 1938:83f.; Lohmann 1970:70–75 proposes a tripartite division.

[58] Pedrick 1983: this memory of battle is Nestor's *aristeia* (63–66). Ring composition is discussed by Gaisser 1969:4–5.

community and in mortals' relations with immortals. These memories echo the connection between sacrifice in *Iliad* I and the crisis of reciprocity, and Nestor hopes to convince Patroklos to help the army in order to remedy the damage done by Akhilleus' withdrawal. He tries to tempt Patroklos with a positive example of the kind of social harmony Akhilleus' withdrawal has disrupted.

Nestor's second battle, and second memory of sacrifice, occurs in the infantry expedition against the Epeians. After the Pylians arrive at the river Alpheios, Nestor describes sacrifices made to Zeus, Alpheios, Poseidon, and Athena and the different victims offered to each divinity. On the following day, immediately preceding the battle, they offer prayers to Zeus and Athena (*Iliad* XI 736), which are not accompanied by animal sacrifice. Nestor then remembers the actions of gods amid the human fighting: Poseidon saves his sons, Zeus gives glory to the Pylians, and Athena drives back the enemy (*Iliad* XI 751–758). Finally, the battle ends with a prayer to Zeus and praise of Nestor (*Iliad* XI 761). The act of honoring the gods punctuates his description of the battle: sacrifices and the careful designation of victims for each deity empha-size the Pylians' reciprocity with their gods, and Nestor vividly remembers their help to the young hero whom he hopes will go into battle as a substi-tute for Akhilleus. Nestor's implication that divine help will follow those who are brave in battle and who make offerings to the gods proves sadly false in Apollo's opposition of Patroklos on the battlefield and Zeus' partial denial of Akhilleus' prayer for his friend's safety in *Iliad* XVI. So these descriptions of sacrifice embedded in the Epeian episode act as foils to the actual situation created by Akhilleus' withdrawal (social crisis and disruption, problematic distribution of booty and sacrifices, inability of gods to respond to requests accompanying sacrifice) and the situation created by Nestor's speech (success in battle and divine protection). Nestor's memory of sacrifice only draws atten-tion to the failure of this method in the timeframe of the primary narrative-text: strikingly, the sacrifices of both Agamemnon and Hektor are denied by Zeus the power the mortals hope they will possess.

In the latter part of his digression, Nestor recalls his arrival with Odysseus at the house of Peleus in order to raise troops for the Akhaian army, where-upon he discovers his host burning *mêria* to Zeus and pouring libations while Akhilleus and Patroklos carve the carcass:

γέρων δ' ἱππηλάτα Πηλεὺς
πίονα μηρία καῖε βοὸς Διὶ τερπικεραύνῳ
αὐλῆς ἐν χόρτῳ· ἔχε δὲ χρύσειον ἄλεισον,
σπένδων αἴθοπα οἶνον ἐπ' αἰθομένοις ἱεροῖσι.

σφῶϊ μὲν ἀμφὶ βοὸς ἕπετον κρέα, νῶϊ δ' ἔπειτα
στῆμεν ἐνὶ προθύροισι· ταφὼν δ' ἀνόρουσεν Ἀχιλλεύς,
ἐς δ' ἄγε χειρὸς ἑλών, κατὰ δ' ἑδριάασθαι ἄνωγε,
ξείνιά τ' εὖ παρέθηκεν, ἅ τε ξείνοις θέμις ἐστίν.
αὐτὰρ ἐπεὶ τάρπημεν ἐδητύος ἠδὲ ποτῆτος

(*Iliad* XI 772–780)

And the old horseman Peleus
burned the fat thigh bones of an ox to thundering Zeus,
deep in the walled enclosure of his court. He was lifting a golden
    cup
and pouring glistening wine to go with the glowing victims.
You two were busy over the flesh of the ox when we both
stood at the broad doors. Akhilleus sprang to his feet, he seemed
    startled,
clasped the two of us by the hand and led us in—He pressed us to
    take a seat
and set before us sumptuous stranger's fare, the stranger's right.
And once we had our fill of food and drink ...

The arrival of guests during the performance of sacrifice, while typical in the *Odyssey*, is not found elsewhere in the *Iliad*.[59] The image of Peleus as *Opferherr*, the only sacrificer specified in the three embedded scenes in this speech, while Akhilleus and Patroklos dismember the carcass, draws a poignant contrast between the harmonious social context of Peleus' household and the current isolation of the two young heroes, which comprises the 'argument function' of Nestor's digression. Shifting the focus away from the sacrifice to Zeus, the meal is then described as the customary honor given to guests (ἅ τε ξείνοις θέμις ἐστίν), so that the sacrificial meal serves as an example of both offerings to the gods and collective reciprocity among mortals. Using descriptions of the sacrifice and meal, Nestor again demonstrates the correct reciprocal relations between mortals and immortals and among men, this time in an effort to convince Patroklos to aid the Akhaian army. Of course, neither Patroklos nor Akhilleus will return to the home of Peleus. Their deaths in battle will prevent them from experiencing this kind of happy commensal sacrifice; again, Nestor's positive depiction of sacrifice only heightens an awareness of the contrast between these happy occasions and the crises of reciprocity in the poem.

---

[59] Although Gaisser 1969:13 describes this as a standard hospitality scene. On typical hospitality scenes, see Reece 1993.

Several embedded sacrifices either explicitly acknowledge the ritual as ineffectual or express anxiety in this regard—the second category of embedded sacrifices. The idealized reciprocity described in the embedded sacrifices of Khruses and Nestor is either worthless or absent entirely. Zeus twice laments his inability to save Troy and Hektor despite their offerings (*Iliad* IV 48–49 = XXIV 69–70), and Apollo berates the gods as a group for ignoring Akhilleus' mutilation of Hektor's corpse despite his sacrifices (*Iliad* XXIV 33–34). Hektor's sacrificial offerings are directly contrasted with Akhilleus' status as the son of a goddess in this context, which we will discuss fully in Chapter Four. Zeus expresses a more subtle contrast between the relationship between men and gods, which sacrifice ought to but cannot create, during the duel between Akhilleus and Hektor. Zeus fondly remembers Hektor's sacrifices before asking the gods if he should be saved:

> ἐμὸν δ' ὀλοφύρεται ἦτορ
> Ἕκτορος, ὅς μοι πολλὰ βοῶν ἐπὶ μηρί' ἔκηεν
> Ἴδης ἐν κορυφῇσι πολυπτύχου, ἄλλοτε δ' αὖτε
> ἐν πόλει ἀκροτάτῃ.

(Iliad XXII 169b–172a)

> My heart grieves for Hektor
> who burned so many thigh bones of oxen for me,
> on the rugged peaks of Ida, and at other times
> at the highest point of the city.

This memory and the subsequent suggestion that Hektor be spared is immediately rebuffed by Athena (*Iliad* XXII 174–181). Several scholars have argued that the *Iliad* stresses Zeus' love for mortals to generate *pathos* in the sad depiction of his powerlessness to protect them.[60] Sacrifice is an important part of this pattern: sacrifice, and the reciprocity it is supposed to entail, is not sufficient to protect Hektor, and the sadness this notion conveys is intensified by the impression of a long-standing relationship between Zeus and Hektor, who has burnt many offerings (πολλά) in different places sacred to the god. Altars feature prominently in Zeus' fond descriptions of Trojan worship (*Iliad* IV 48, XXIV 69) and are also described in the primary narrator's description of his sanctuary on Mount Ida (*Iliad* VIII 48). This suggestion of a permanent,

---

[60] Cf. Griffin 1980:128; Schadewaldt 1944:107; and Parker 1998b:116. Schein 1984:45 observes, "The Olympian gods were not the only gods with which Homer's audience would have been familiar. Their centrality in the *Iliad* and the way they are made to clarify by contrast the condition of mortals in the poem reflect the way Homer exploits and transforms the religion of the poetic tradition in accordance with the genre and the distinctive themes of his epic."

ongoing reciprocal relationship between Zeus and the Trojans, as expressed by altars that are full of sacrifices, is undermined by the imminent destruction of Troy. Even when the gods are thankful for sacrifices, the ritual is still described negatively as unable to obligate the divine recipient to help the sacrificer.

Two prayers are denied in the *Iliad*, particularly forceful examples of the negative pattern underlying embedded sacrifices. Like Khruses' prayer over the hecatomb, Agamemnon's prayer accompanying the sacrifice in *Iliad* II, which closely recalls the sacrifice to Apollo in *Iliad* I, does not acknowledge or attempt to create any special relationship with Zeus by reference to the present offering or past gifts, but proceeds straight to the request:

"Ζεῦ κύδιστε μέγιστε, κελαινεφές, αἰθέρι ναίων,
μὴ πρὶν ἐπ' ἠέλιον δῦναι καὶ ἐπὶ κνέφας ἐλθεῖν,
πρίν με κατὰ πρηνὲς βαλέειν Πριάμοιο μέλαθρον
αἰθαλόεν, πρῆσαι δὲ πυρὸς δηΐοιο θύρετρα,
Ἑκτόρεον δὲ χιτῶνα περὶ στήθεσσι δαΐξαι
χαλκῷ ῥωγαλέον· πολέες δ' ἀμφ' αὐτὸν ἑταῖροι
πρηνέες ἐν κονίῃσιν ὀδὰξ λαζοίατο γαῖαν."
Ὣς ἔφατ', οὐδ' ἄρα πώ οἱ ἐπεκραίαινε Κρονίων,
ἀλλ' ὅ γε δέκτο μὲν ἱρά, πόνον δ' ἀμέγαρτον ὄφελλεν.

(*Iliad* II 412–420)

"Zeus, most glorious, most great, lord of the dark clouds who lives
        in the bright sky,
don't let the sun go down or the night descend on us!
Not till I hurl the smoke black halls of Priam headlong—
torch his gates to blazing rubble—
rip the tunic of Hektor and slash his heroic chest to ribbons
with my bronze—and a ruck of comrades around him,
groveling facedown in the dust, gnaw on their own earth!"
And so he spoke, but the son of Kronos would not yet grant him
        fulfillment,
but he accepted the sacrifices, and increased the unenviable toil.

Agamemnon's request is stated at some length, yet any honorific titles for Zeus or argumentation based on past reciprocity is absent. He does not include any reasons why Zeus should honor his request, nor conditions for the likelihood of its fulfillment, such as found in Khruses' 'if-ever' appeal to end the plague. Zeus denies Agamemnon's prayer, presumably because of his promise to Thetis, but he does receive the sacrifice. The request is not bolstered by reference to the sacrifice, nor does the god feel obliged to honor it even if he receives the offering; the two aspects of the ceremony are seemingly disengaged. The recollection of the sacrifice in *Iliad* I overseen by Khruses, and the positive reaction of Apollo to that sacrifice, increase the negative impression created by the failure of this prayer. Although, because the request is denied, the enacted sacrifice is a failure, Agamemnon does not know this, and the primary narrative description of the social interaction following the feast is positive. The way in which sacrifice refrains from bringing mortals closer to gods or allowing them privileged access to or influence over divine intentions is reflected in the mismatched conviviality of the mortal feast versus the ominous knowledge given to the audience about Zeus' plans. Agamemnon makes two other prayers in conjunction with the enacted oath sacrifices, intending to invoke the gods in their capacity as witnesses and avengers.[61] These two oaths are described purely from an eyewitness perspective, without reference to their divine reception (*Iliad* III 275–291; XIX 254–265). However, Zeus denies the subsequent prayer made by Akhaians and Trojans (*Iliad* III 301), again because of his promise to Thetis to honor Akhilleus.

Only twice are prayers elsewhere rejected, denials that Robert Parker describes as the "grimmest moments in the *Iliad*":[62] Theano's prayer with a vow of sacrifice (*Iliad* VI 311) and Akhilleus' prayer, accompanying a libation, for Patroklos's safety (*Iliad* XVI 249), which we will return to in Chapter Four. The lengthy anticipation of the vow of the Trojan women in *Iliad* VI, remarkably forecast in three speeches by Helenos and Hektor, is a powerful example of the generally negative tone of mortal discourse with respect to sacrifice in the poem. Helenos begins the process by instructing Hektor to marshal the women to go to the temple and give Athena gifts, "then promise to sacrifice twelve heifers in her shrine, yearlings never broken, if only she'll pity Troy, the Trojan wives and all our helpless children" (καί οἱ ὑποσχέσθαι δυοκαίδεκα βοῦς ἐνὶ νηῷ / ἤνις ἠκέστας ἱερευσέμεν, αἴ κ' ἐλεήσῃ / ἄστύ τε καὶ Τρώων ἀλόχους καὶ νήπια τέκνα, *Iliad* VI 93–95). Hektor repeats to his mother these instructions (*Iliad* VI 274–276), which are finally expressed to Athena by Theano (*Iliad* VI 308–310). Helenos' and Hektor's discussion of the vow and gift-offering builds up audience anticipation, heightening Theano's scene in the temple to a significant climax. The repetition makes Athena's denial of their prayer and vow all the more power-

---

[61] For a detailed discussion of the oath rituals, Burkert 1985:250–252; Kitts 2005:115–187. Pulleyn 1997:80 describes *Iliad* III 245–313 as a 'curse-oath-sacrifice' on the grounds that oaths are more similar to curses, lacking the reciprocity inherent in prayers.

[62] Parker 1998b:117; see also Lang 1975. On Akhilleus' prayer, see pages 190–191.

ful.[63] When Theano finally speaks the vow, Athena immediately rejects it, indicating the futility of vows of sacrifice to placate angry gods.[64] Athena's denial is described with the same formulaic verse that twice describes Apollo's reception of Khruses' successful prayer, but with the substitution of a verb of denial for ἔκλυε 'he heard', the sign of acceptance: "So she spoke, making prayer. But Pallas Athena refused" (ὣς ἔφατ᾽ εὐχομένη, <u>ἀνένευε</u> δὲ Παλλὰς Ἀθήνη, *Iliad* VI 311). Similar to the rejection of Agamemnon's request, recollections of Khruses' ideal reciprocity with Apollo increase the *pathos* of these rejections.

Athena's rejection of the Trojan vow has been analyzed by Mabel Lang, who proposes that vows in Homer allow the divinity the choice of accepting or rejecting the request, since, in contrast to prayers with reference to past sacrifices, the reciprocal relationship underlying vows has not yet been established. She concludes that vows express a notion of bribery and are therefore insulting to divinities. Accordingly, the context dictates the ritual form used; Theano makes a vow rather than a *da-quia-dedi* 'give-because-I gave' prayer to help ease the impact of impending rejection, since Athena would be hard-pressed to reject a prayer made on the basis of past sacrifices.[65] However, throughout the poem there are numerous indications that sacrifice does not enhance requests or reflect the likelihood of their success: most prayers are successful, but very few refer to sacrifice, and those that do meet with mixed results. For example, during the duel consecrated by his brother's lengthy oath sacrifice, Menelaos, without reference to sacrifice, prays to Zeus for vengeance before throwing his spear at Paris: "Menelaos, son of Atreus, gave prayer to father Zeus, 'Zeus, King, give me revenge, he wronged me first!'" (Ἀτρεΐδης Μενέλαος ἐπευξάμενος Διὶ πατρί / Ζεῦ ἄνα δὸς τίσασθαι ὅ με πρότερος κάκ᾽ ἔοργε, *Iliad* III 350–351). He continues to describe Paris' wrongdoing, but does not refer to past or future sacrifices as a way of influencing the god. Menelaos throws his spear, and Paris evades it, after which Menelaos breaks his sword on the shield of his foe: his reaction to this is to blame Zeus, whom he describes at this point as the "most baneful god" (θεῶν ὀλοώτερος, *Iliad* III 365), indicating his belief that his prayer was not successful. Later, when defending the body of Patroklos, he prays to Athena for strength: "if only Pallas would

---

[63] Hektor's involvement in the relaying of Helenos' plan to Hecabe is curious. He would serve the Trojans better on the battlefield. Morrison 1991:156 interprets the whole scene as an excuse to get the hero into Troy to meet with his wife and family.

[64] On the question of Athena's rejection, attributed by ancient critics to Theano's slight adjustment to Helenos' original plan, see Kirk 1990 note *ad loc.*; Morrison 1991:152–156; Lateiner 1997:259. If we turn to the reception of Homer, we can see the tragedy of the Trojans' failed piety emphasized repeatedly throughout Book II of the *Aeneid*.

[65] Lang 1975:310. See also Morrison 1991:152.

give me power" (εἰ γὰρ Ἀθήνη / δοίη κάρτος ἐμοί, *Iliad* XVII 561–562). This request, embedded in a speech addressed to Phoinix, continues to describe the challenges posed by Hektor and does not otherwise contain any references to Athena or attempt to get her attention with honorific titles or references to sacrifice. Nonetheless, Athena is thrilled that Menelaos prayed to her first: "the grey-eyed goddess Athena rejoiced that the man had prayed to her before all other gods" (ὣς φάτο, γήθησεν δὲ θεὰ γλαυκῶπις Ἀθήνη / ὅττι ῥά οἱ πάμπρωτα θεῶν ἠρήσατο πάντων, *Iliad* XVII 567–568). This speech to Phoinix, which contains only the briefest of addresses to the goddess, thrills Athena, while other prayers promising sacrifice, such as those of the Trojan women, are coldly denied. Although both prayers come at times of crisis, Menelaos does not refer to past or future sacrifices, in marked contrast to his brother's diligent performance of such ritual actions; reference to sacrifice is not needed to reinforce requests in prayers in the *Iliad*. The vast majority of prayers, including this one, are successful even though they do not usually seem to rely on reciprocity based on gift-exchange.

Yet characters often worry that their sacrifices are unsuccessful in creating reciprocity or that gods are angry about sacrifices. Similar to Khruses' first prayer, Nestor and Agamemnon both make 'free prayers', utterances without accompanying ritual action, which refer to past sacrifices in attempts to persuade the gods for help in moments of crisis (*Iliad* VIII 236–244; XV 372–376). Both prayers refer to past sacrifices to strengthen their requests, which seem more like anxious reminders to the particular god lest he forget those sacrifices at crisis moments. Agamemnon despairs that his sacrifices on the journey to Troy did him no good, an anxious complaint only then followed by his request for help:

Ζεῦ πάτερ, ἦ ῥά τιν᾽ ἤδη ὑπερμενέων βασιλήων
τῇδ᾽ ἄτῃ ἄασας καί μιν μέγα κῦδος ἀπηύρας;
οὐ μὲν δή ποτέ φημι τεὸν περικαλλέα βωμὸν
νηῒ πολυκλήϊδι παρελθέμεν ἐνθάδε ἔρρων,
ἀλλ᾽ ἐπὶ πᾶσι βοῶν δημὸν καὶ μηρί᾽ ἔκηα,
ἱέμενος Τροίην εὐτείχεον ἐξαλαπάξαι.
ἀλλά, Ζεῦ, τόδε πέρ μοι ἐπικρήηνον ἐέλδωρ·
αὐτοὺς δή περ ἔασον ὑπεκφυγέειν καὶ ἀλύξαι,
μηδ᾽ οὕτω Τρώεσσιν ἔα δάμνασθαι Ἀχαιούς.

(*Iliad* VIII 236–244)

Father Zeus, when did you ever strike a mighty king
with such mad blindness—then tear away his glory?

Not once, I swear, did I pass a handsome altar of yours,
sailing my oar-swept ship on our fatal voyage here,
but on each I burned the fat and thigh bones of oxen,
longing to raze Troy's sturdy walls to the roots.
So, Zeus, at least fulfill this prayer for me:
Let the men escape with their lives if nothing else—
Don't let the Trojans mow us down in droves.

Agamemnon addresses Zeus directly (Ζεῦ πάτερ), but replaces the standard positive remembrance of sacrifice exhibited in Khruses' argument (the 'if-ever' formula) with his worry that Zeus did not care about these sacrifices. He uses the same wish formula as Khruses (μοι ἐπικρήηνον ἐέλδωρ), linking his prayer with that ideal model of reciprocity, but the anxiety that he does not have this kind of reciprocal relationship with Zeus replaces the more optimistic tone of Khruses' requests. Agamemnon asks the god to "at least" let the Trojans flee, an expansion to the wish formula twice used by Khruses (ἀλλὰ Ζεῦ τόδε πέρ μοι ἐπικρήηνον ἐέλδωρ). His rather pathetic request signals the Akhaian army's imminent crisis in the face of Hektor's onslaught, and he thinks that his earlier sacrifices and prayers had no effect, since conquering Troy was the request expressed while sacrificing on every altar *en route* (ἐπὶ πᾶσι βοῶν δημὸν καὶ μηρί' ἔκηα / ἱέμενος Τροίην εὐτείχεον ἐξαλαπάξαι). As discussed in Chapter Two, Agamemnon gets a seemingly positive response to this prayer, the army is cheered by Zeus' omen, but he does not seem to have the individualized reciprocal relationship shared between Khruses and Apollo, and he does not get a personal response, such as feeling stronger or faster. We can compare Athena's more obvious response to Diomedes' prayer, in which he relies on her relationship with his father and does not make reference to sacrifice: she hears him and makes his limbs light, and then she directly appears to him (*Iliad* V 115–123). The breakdown of reciprocity between Agamemnon and Zeus is a reflection of the disruption of society Agamemnon himself has caused. The audience knows that Zeus is favoring Hektor to honor the request of Thetis. Just as Agamemnon upset the balance of reciprocity within the army, Akhilleus has upset the balance of reciprocity between men and gods.

Although the emphasis on the sacrificer is not as prominent in embedded sacrifices as in enacted ones, Agamemnon's ritual authority is still reflected in his own memory of his role as sacrificer on the journey to Troy. Nestor makes a similar prayer using exactly the same request as that in Agamemnon's prayer in *Iliad* VIII (μηδ' οὕτω Τρώεσσιν ἔα δάμνασθαι Ἀχαιούς), the only other free prayer to refer to sacrifice. However, rather than drawing on a reciprocal relationship with Zeus established by his past sacrifices, he vaguely alludes to any past sacrifice performed by an Akhaian:

Ζεῦ πάτερ, εἴ ποτέ τίς τοι ἐν Ἄργεΐ περ πολυπύρῳ
ἢ βοὸς ἢ οἰὸς κατὰ πίονα μηρία καίων
εὔχετο νοστῆσαι, σὺ δ' ὑπέσχεο καὶ κατένευσας,
τῶν μνῆσαι καὶ ἄμυνον, Ὀλύμπιε, νηλεὲς ἦμαρ,
μηδ' οὕτω Τρώεσσιν ἔα δάμνασθαι Ἀχαιούς.

(*Iliad* XV 372–376)

Father Zeus! If ever someone in Argos' golden wheatlands
burned the fat thigh bones of a sheep or ox
and prayed for a homecoming and you promised with a nod—
remember it now, Olympian, save us from this ruthless day!
Don't let these Trojans mow us down in droves!

Nestor's prayer includes an 'if-ever' argument, but replaces the personal reciprocal relationship between the person making the prayer and the deity, as expressed in Khruses' prayer to Apollo, with the general hope that any past sacrifices were pleasing enough. Nestor's prayer is heard by Zeus (ὡς ἔφατ' εὐχόμενος, μέγα δ' ἔκτυπε μητίετα Ζεύς, *Iliad* XV 377), a variation on the formulaic verse describing divine reception of Khruses' and Agamemnon's prayers. Zeus thunders in response, but it inspires the Trojan army, whose refreshed onslaught, likened to a stormy sea, is described at length (*Iliad* XV 379–386). Nestor's prayer seems to have the opposite of its intended effect; the embedded sacrifice and request provoke a response from Zeus, but this response is actually harmful to the current Akhaian cause.

The references to past sacrifices by Agamemnon and Nestor contextualize the contrast between former wishes and the current situation: on the basis of the current state of affairs, they worry that the past sacrifices were meaningless. In the *Iliad*, characters make prayers for help at times of crisis, and their anxiety about past sacrifices is in part a reflection of the emergent circumstances on the battlefield.[66] However, if emergency appeals motivate reference to sacrifice in prayers, we would expect them to be much more frequent than the three prayers made by Khruses, Agamemnon, and Nestor. Simon Pulleyn suggests that the "most normal context for a prayer is accompanying a sacrifice. Where this is not so, there is usually a reference to past

---

[66] Lateiner 1997: "Homeric prayers are utilitarian speech, demands to spell immediate relief" (255).

sacrifices or promise of future ones."[67] If the use of sacrifice to enhance requests to the gods in the *Iliad* is restricted to only a few examples, and prayers accompanying sacrifice do not refer to the current offering, then the overall pattern of embedded sacrifices portrays confusion, uncertainty, and disappointment, whereas the overall pattern of prayer, without reference to sacrifice, is positive. Character references to sacrifice demonstrate the weaknesses in this system of reciprocity, which does not seem to extend into other types of prayer. The frustration expressed in embedded sacrifices stands in contrast to the consistent presentation of the care and concern of gods for mortals, which must be filtered throughout the poem by the special treatment given to Akhilleus.

Finally, embedded sacrifices describe the potential for the gods' anger over neglected sacrifices or mortal transgressions to threaten reciprocity. This anger constitutes the negative potential of sacrifice, while the power of sacrifice to please the gods is described problematically as ineffectual, as demonstrated at the beginning of the poem by Akhilleus' suggestion that the plague has been caused by the Apollo's anger over sacrifice:

εἴτ' ἄρ' ὅ γ' εὐχωλῆς ἐπιμέμφεται εἴθ' ἑκατόμβης,
αἴ κέν πως ἀρνῶν κνίσης αἰγῶν τε τελείων
βούλεται ἀντιάσας ἡμῖν ἀπὸ λοιγὸν ἀμῦναι.

(Iliad I 65–67)

He blames us either for a vow we failed, or a hecatomb.
If only he would share the sacrificial smoke of lambs and full-
grown goats,
he might be willing to save us from this plague.

Kalkhas explains the true cause of the plague, the abduction of Khruseis, which can be appeased by her return and the sacrifice of a hecatomb (*Iliad* I 93–100). Akhilleus' worry that a sacrifice could provoke Apollo's anger initiates a pattern of references to the anger of the gods throughout the poem. His worry about a vow, however, is not consistently maintained in the poem, since no vows made in the *Iliad* are fulfilled within the poem. The anger of the gods over vows is recalled only near the end of the poem, when the complex narrator describes a vow to Apollo by Meriones in contrast to Teukros' neglect:[68]

---

[67] Pulleyn 1997:40. He observes the tendency of Homeric man to complain to gods (197). Lateiner 1997:251 describes these complaints in prayers as the "most alien to Euro-Americans."

[68] Verse 864 is missing in a first-century papyrus and a few manuscripts, on which Richardson 1993 note *ad loc.*

Τεῦκρος δὲ πρῶτος κλήρῳ λάχεν. αὐτίκα δ' ἰὸν
ἧκεν ἐπικρατέως, οὐδ' ἠπείλησεν ἄνακτι
ἀρνῶν πρωτογόνων ῥέξειν κλειτὴν ἑκατόμβην.
ὄρνιθος μὲν ἅμαρτε· μέγηρε γάρ οἱ τό γ' Ἀπόλλων·

(Iliad XXIII 862–865)

And the lot fell to Teukros to shoot first. He quickly
loosed an arrow, full-draw force but never swore to the Lord
he'd slaughter a splendid hecatomb of victims, newborn lambs,
so he missed the bird—Apollo grudged him that."

σπερχόμενος δ' ἄρα Μηριόνης ἐξείρυσε χειρὸς
τόξον· ἀτὰρ δὴ ὀϊστὸν ἔχεν πάλαι, ὡς ἴθυνεν.
αὐτίκα δ' ἠπείλησεν ἑκηβόλῳ Ἀπόλλωνι
ἀρνῶν πρωτογόνων ῥέξειν κλειτὴν ἑκατόμβην.

(Iliad XXIII 870–873)

Meriones leapt to snatch the bow from his hand,
already clutching a shaft while Teukros aimed,
and quickly swore to the Far-Shooter Apollo
he'd slaughter a splendid hecatomb of victims, newborn lambs—

Meriones shoots the dove, but Apollo's reaction to his vow is not described, as opposed to the explicitly negative response to Teukros' lack of piety. Although the gods do not seem particularly inclined to heed *da-quia-dabo* 'give-because-I will give' requests, they can be galled at the lack of such offerings. The idea that sacrifice might anger gods is also expressed by Aineias, who warns Pandaros that he ought to pray to Zeus for success against Diomedes, whom he suspects may be a god angered at the Trojans over sacrifices ("unless he is some god angry at the Trojans, raging because of sacrifices," εἰ μή τις θεός ἐστι κοτεσσάμενος Τρώεσσιν / ἱρῶν μηνίσας, *Iliad* V 177–178). When the Trojans suffer on the battlefield, Aineias casts this crisis in terms of a failure of reciprocity between mortals and immortals. In a similar moment of crisis, Agamemnon also imagines that sacrifices have failed, and he tells Menelaos that Hektor's sacrifices are more persuasive than their own. When concerned about Akhaian defeats, he urges upon Menelaos the need for a new strategy:

χρεὼ βουλῆς ἐμὲ καὶ σέ, διοτρεφὲς ὦ Μενέλαε,
κερδαλέης, ἥ τίς κεν ἐρύσσεται ἠδὲ σαώσει

Ἀργείους καὶ νῆας, ἐπεὶ Διὸς ἐτράπετο φρήν.
Ἑκτορέοις ἄρα μᾶλλον ἐπὶ φρένα θῆχ' ἱεροῖσιν·

(*Iliad* X 43–46)

Tactics, my noble Menelaos. That's what we need now, you and I
both,
and cunning tactics too. Something to shield and save
our men and ships since Zeus' heart has turned—
his mighty heart is set on Hektor's offerings more than ours.

In a contrast typical of the tragic *pathos* that colors the poem, the audience knows that Zeus is not swayed by Hektor's sacrifices, but by Thetis' request that the Akhaians suffer for dishonoring Akhilleus. Hektor's sacrifices do not help him, and this irony, created by character misconceptions about the power of sacrifice and the will of the gods, is one of the most prominent aspects of embedded sacrifices. Embedded sacrifices express frustration over the failure of sacrifice to create reciprocity between gods and mortals, but when such reciprocity is imagined to exist, misunderstandings or the inapplicability of the speaker's view on sacrifice to the situation convey the same frustration to the audience: Agamemnon imagines Hektor's sacrifices are persuasive, while Zeus has already conceded to Hera that Troy will be destroyed despite their sacrifices (*Iliad* IV 48–49). In Zeus' opinion, Hektor's sacrifices are not successful in precisely the way that Agamemnon imagines them to be.

Even Akhilleus cannot gain divine assistance through vows of sacrifice. When the pyre of Patroklos fails to light, Akhilleus is described as making libations and a vow to the Winds. At this climactic moment, the vow is not given in direct speech, but is summarized by the complex narrator. Had Iris not sped Akhilleus' request to the Winds, who were themselves having dinner (*Iliad* XXIII 198–216), his vow would have gone unnoticed. When Iris tells the Winds about Akhilleus' vow, she describes her haste to attend the Aithiopian sacrifices so that she can take part in the feast:

οὐχ ἕδος· εἶμι γὰρ αὖτις ἐπ' Ὠκεανοῖο ῥέεθρα
Αἰθιόπων ἐς γαῖαν, ὅθι ῥέζουσ' ἑκατόμβας
ἀθανάτοις, ἵνα δὴ καὶ ἐγὼ μεταδαίσομαι ἱρῶν.
ἀλλ' Ἀχιλεὺς Βορέην ἠδὲ Ζέφυρον κελαδεινὸν
ἐλθεῖν ἀρᾶται, καὶ ὑπίσχεται ἱερὰ καλά.

(*Iliad* XXIII 205–209)

"No time for sitting now. I must return immediately to the Ocean's
running stream,

the Aithiopes' land, where they are sacrificing hecatombs
to the gods so that I will have my share of the offerings.
But, Boreas, blustering Zephyr, Akhilleus
begs you to come, and he promises splendid victims."

Iris' message illustrates two aspects of the negative pattern of embedded sacrifices. The negative presentation of reciprocity often found in embedded sacrifices is here alluded to in Iris' haste, in case she should miss her share, to rejoin
the banquet. There is also a worry, frequently attested in votive offerings and
inscriptions in the Classical period, that the gods will be too preoccupied to
heed prayers. Without the intervention of Iris, the messenger of the gods, the
Winds would also be too preoccupied with their dinner to notice Akhilleus'
request for help, even though he promises 'fair offerings' (ὑπίσχετο ἱερὰ καλά,
Iliad XXIII 159) and pours libations.[69] Akhilleus' special status attracts the
messenger of the gods, but not even he is assured the success of his requests
through the mortal method of prayer.

Iris' conception of sacrificial offerings as feasts for the gods (ἐγὼ μεταδαίσομαι ἱρῶν), a rare indication in the poem that the gods consume sacrificial offerings, echoes Zeus' description of his altar never lacking his share
of victims. The only other instance in the poem referring to divine consumption is Phoinix's description of Oineus' inadequate sacrifices: "Oineus offered
[Artemis] no first fruits, his orchard's crowning glory. The rest of the gods
had feasted full on oxen" (οὔ τι θαλύσια γουνῷ / ἀλωῆς Οἰνεὺς ῥέξ'· ἄλλοι δὲ
θεοὶ δαίνυνθ' ἑκατόμβας, *Iliad* IX 534–535).[70] Iris is afraid that she will miss her
share of the sacrifices; Artemis is angry that she has been overlooked. Vernant
interprets the notion that gods "consume" the sacrificial offering of smoke as
part of the invitation for gods to join the human feast usually subsequent to
sacrifice:

> Because it is directed towards the gods and claims to include them
> with the group of guests in the solemnity and joy of the celebration,
> it evokes the memory of the ancient commensality when, seated
> together, men and gods made merry day after day at shared meals.[71]

[69] Cf. Glaukos' prayer to Apollo (*Iliad* XVI 514–527), which honors the ability of the god to listen
no matter where he is. Iris is also sent to Akhilleus by Hera at *Iliad* XVIII 165–202. Arend 1933:58
observes that this is the only exception to the otherwise consistent role of Iris as a messenger
for the gods to each other or to mortals, but never otherwise for mortals to gods. A further
discussion of this unique scene is given below, pages 190f.

[70] The only other occurrence of μεταδαίνυμαι is in Andromakhe's vision of the exclusion of
orphaned Astuanax from Trojan feasts (*Iliad* XXII 498).

[71] Vernant 1989:24–25.

Although this notion of divine commensality is largely elided in representations of sacrifice in the *Iliad*, this memory of shared meals between men and gods, when evoked, shapes in part the negative connotations given to sacrifice in character speech: gods worry or are angry that they have missed their share of the feast.

Embedded sacrifices express several explicit descriptions of the gods' anger. In his long digression in *Iliad* IX, Phoinix twice describes sacrifice in reference to this anger, suited to his goal of convincing Akhilleus to give up his own wrath: first, the power of sacrifices to atone for man's transgressions, and then Artemis' above-mentioned wrath over neglected sacrifices (*Iliad* IX 499–501, 535–537). Phoinix's embedded sacrifices are not a part of his "autobiography," but derive instead from two different mythological paradigms.[72] After his autobiography (*Iliad* IX 434–495), Phoinix signals a change in the digression, describing the power of sacrifices and prayer to influence the gods, which sets the stage for his cautionary tale for Akhilleus—the Meleagros story, beginning with Oineus' neglect of sacrifices to Artemis. Phoinix describes sacrifice as a means by which man can compensate for wrong-doing, the opposite of sacrifice enhancing requests as exhibited in Khruses' prayer:

στρεπτοὶ δέ τε καὶ θεοὶ αὐτοί,
τῶν περ καὶ μείζων ἀρετὴ τιμή τε βίη τε.
καὶ μὲν τοὺς θυέεσσι καὶ εὐχωλῆς ἀγανῇσι
λοιβῇ τε κνίσῃ τε παρατρωπῶσ' ἄνθρωποι
λισσόμενοι, ὅτε κέν τις ὑπερβήῃ καὶ ἁμάρτῃ.

(*Iliad* IX 497–501)

Even the gods themselves can bend,
and theirs is the greater power, honor, strength.
Even they, with incense and soothing vows,
with libations and sacrificial smoke, men can bring them round,
begging for pardon when one oversteps the mark, does something
wrong.

In this context, sacrifice is a method of soothing angry gods rather than establishing reciprocity with them. Phoinix describes divinities as able to change

---

[72] His digression on the wrath of Meleagros exemplifies the paradigmatic digressive technique in the *Iliad*, particularly its careful adaptation and selection of traditional elements in the story, which are nonetheless ill-fitted to their purpose. I will not discuss this very complicated speech in depth, but refer the reader to Whitman 1958:190–191; Willcock 1964:149f.; Lohmann 1970:245f.; Rosner 1976; Scodel 1982b; Swain 1988. There are numerous parallels between this speech and other parts of the poem, particularly the similarities between Akhilleus and Meleagros (Lohmann 1970:261–271).

their minds in favor of forgiveness when men offer incense, vows, libations, and sacrificial smoke, a description he expands with the personification of Prayers (*Litai*) and Blindness (*Atê*), who work either for or against mortals by heeding or denying supplication (*Iliad* IX 496–512). However, this depiction of the gods is incompatible with that presented elsewhere in the poem: sacrifices do not succeed in changing the will of the gods, as we have seen already with the scant use of sacrifices embedded in prayers. Nor have sacrifices been used elsewhere in the poem to soothe the wrath of the gods. For example, Kalkhas makes clear that Apollo is not angry about sacrifices in *Iliad* I, and Athena rejects the vow of the Trojan women. Kalkhas does recommend that the return of Khruseis and a sacrifice will assuage Apollo, who is pleased by the sacrifice, but the emphasis seems to rest more on Khruses' ability to call off the god. Finally, Phoinix's analogy of the soothing sacrifices fails to convince its listener; Akhilleus is neither mollified nor persuaded to accept gifts. This failure calls into question not only Phoinix's methodology, but also his representation of the gods, who elsewhere in the poem are not swayed by sacrifices.

Phoinix's portrayal of the appeasement of the gods with sacrifice reverberates in his lengthy description of the appeasement of Meleagros' wrath with gifts. He begins with Oineus' neglect of Artemis in sacrifice: "incensed that Oineus offered her no first fruits, his orchard's crowning glory. The rest of the gods feasted full on hecatombs, but alone almighty Zeus' daughter, he gave her nothing" (χωσαμένη ὅ οἱ οὔ τι θαλύσια γουνῷ ἀλωῆς / Οἰνεὺς ῥέξ᾽· ἄλλοι δὲ θεοὶ δαίνυνθ᾽ ἑκατόμβας / οἴῃ δ᾽ οὐκ ἔρρεξε Διὸς κούρῃ μεγάλοιο, *Iliad* IX 534–536). The ire of Artemis begins a cycle of wrath and retribution: Artemis sends the Calydonian boar; once the beast is killed by Meleagros, its carcass causes strife between the Aitolians and Kouretes. Angry at his mother's curse upon him, Meleagros refuses to help defend the city. He rejects the entreaties and gifts of priests, townspeople, friends, and relatives, until he finally yields to his wife's pleading. His return to battle without gifts is meant to serve as a warning to Akhilleus to capitulate to the embassy and Agamemnon's offer (*Iliad* IX 527–605).

Like all speakers in the *Iliad*, Phoinix tailors his story to fit the situation and addressee. On this particular occasion, by omitting certain aspects well known to the audience, he attempts to make the story more persuasive. Included in these omissions, the quarrel over spoils between Atalanta and Meleagros' relatives might have led his addressee to recall the quarrel over spoils and a woman in *Iliad* I, a connection strengthened further by the instigation of angry gods in both situations.[73] Given the possibility of omission, it is all the more striking that Phoinix characterizes Artemis' wrath specifically as the result of neglected sacrifices, an error intimated even on the micro-level of its diction. According to Casabona, ἱερεύειν 'to sacrifice' places emphasis on the sacrificial animal, which is always specified in conjunction with this verb, whereas ἔρδειν and ῥέζειν 'to do' focus on the ceremony since they can be used without objects, as already evidenced in the description of the Akhaians' sacrifice (*Iliad* II 400).[74] The use of multiple references to offerings—the "first fruits" that are neglected and the hecatombs on which the other gods feast—followed by a verb that can denote sacrifice, but is here without an object, underscores Oineus' error (οἴῃ δ' οὐκ ἔρρεξε Διὸς κούρῃ μεγάλοιο). But the stress on the sacrificial act itself (ἔρρεξε) casts this error in terms of upsetting the principle of the "equal feast."

Both references to sacrifice in Phoinix's digression contend that the gods' reception can have benefits or drawbacks for mankind. However, by attempting to either provoke or appease divine wrath, embedded sacrifices inevitably address the anger of the gods, the negative reception. In both cases, sacrifice evokes notions of a breakdown in the relations between mortals and immortals, which corresponds with crises of reciprocity and kinship among mortal communities. These descriptions of sacrifice become part of an unsuccessful strategy to convince Akhilleus to give up his wrath: Akhilleus replies to Phoinix that he has no need of honor from the Akhaians since he enjoys honor directly from Zeus ("I think my honor lies in the great decree of Zeus," φρονέω δὲ τετιμῆσθαι Διὸς αἴσῃ, *Iliad* IX 608). Akhilleus' dismissal of Phoinix's request here, which has been strengthened by descriptions of sacrifice as able to appease the wrath of the gods, anticipates Akhilleus' rejection of sacrifice as he approaches his own death. The association of sacrifice with divine displeasure featured in Phoinix's digression is typical of embedded sacrifices throughout the poem.

Artemis is not the only god angry over missing sacrifices. Poseidon emphatically expresses such sentiments, warning Zeus that the Akhaians have built a wall without sacrifice, which will cause him and Apollo to lose the *kleos* of their wall (*Iliad* VII 455–463). He complains to Zeus that this wall, built without sacrifice to the gods, anticipates the demise of mortal/immortal reciprocity:

[73] Swain 1988:274; Willcock 1964:149–153.
[74] Casabona 1966:20.

Ζεῦ πάτερ, ἦ ῥά τίς ἐστι βροτῶν ἐπ' ἀπείρονα γαῖαν
ὅς τις ἔτ' ἀθανάτοισι νόον καὶ μῆτιν ἐνίψει;
οὐχ ὁράᾳς ὅτι δὴ αὖτε κάρη κομόωντες Ἀχαιοὶ
τεῖχος ἐτειχίσσαντο νεῶν ὕπερ, ἀμφὶ δὲ τάφρον
ἤλασαν, οὐδὲ θεοῖσι δόσαν κλειτὰς ἑκατόμβας;
τοῦ δ' ἤτοι κλέος ἔσται ὅσον τ' ἐπικίδναται ἠώς·
τοῦ δ' ἐπιλήσονται τὸ ἐγὼ καὶ Φοῖβος Ἀπόλλων
ἥρῳ Λαομέδοντι πολίσσαμεν ἀθλήσαντε.

(Iliad VII 446–453)

Father Zeus, is there a man on the whole wide earth
who still informs the gods of all his plans, his schemes?
Don't you see that the long-haired Akhaians
have flung that rampart up against their ships, around it
they have dug a trench and never offered the gods splendid
> hecatombs,
but its fame will spread as far as the light of dawn!
And men will forget those ramparts I and Phoibos Apollo
reared for the hero Laomedon with great struggle.

Again, sacrifice is described in terms of problems or failure. Poseidon implies that the neglected hecatombs call into question the hierarchical relationship between mankind and gods. Zeus replies that Poseidon need not fear for his *kleos* 'glory', and he tells Poseidon to destroy the wall after the Akhaians have left (*Iliad* VII 454–463). However, though Poseidon will have his vengeance, the Akhaians will never know that they have erred. The wall is brought up again in the events predicted outside of the action at Troy, in one of the two external prolepses in the complex narrative-text. In *Iliad* XII, the complex narrator describes the destruction of the Akhaian wall, which, again, is said to be motivated by the lack of sacrifice and the will of the gods (*Iliad* XII 6–33).[75] The destruction of the wall by Apollo and Poseidon is supernaturally violent and definitive: after the Akhaians leave Troy, Apollo turns the courses of rivers, Zeus supplies constant rains, and Poseidon sweeps the wall down with the waves of the ocean. Ruth Scodel, in her discussion of the allusions in this passage to Near Eastern destruction myths otherwise suppressed in the *Iliad*,

---

[75] De Jong 1987:88b suggests that this remarkable prediction emphasizes the futility of man's efforts, in contrast with the infinite power of the gods, to set the stage for the events of *Iliad* XII, which in antiquity was called the *teikhomakhia*. The other external prolepsis concerns Philoktetes (*Iliad* II 724–725). Scodel 1982b:33n1, with bibliography, refutes Page's argument that the wall is a late intrusion into the epic (1959:315–324).

finds the lack of sacrifice a flimsy excuse for such cosmic upheaval.[76] Although the cosmological destruction of the wall is certainly unanticipated in Zeus' original reply to Poseidon, the emphasis on sacrifice in this context can be better appreciated as part of a pattern, throughout the poem, of embedded sacrifice as an expression for disjunction between men and gods. The mention of the lack of sacrifice as the cause for divine wrath in both *Iliad* VII and XII ties the destruction of the wall to the association of sacrifice with the inability to create reciprocity between men and gods, either through mistakes, such as Oineus' in Phoinix's digression, or because of superior bonds between gods, such as Zeus' acquiescence to Thetis' request or Hera's desire to destroy Troy. Like that of Artemis, Poseidon's anger implies that the gods want sacrifices, but that the relationship between gods and men has broken down or is dysfunctional. Further, the Akhaians remain blissfully unaware of their error; the conversation between Poseidon and Zeus and the reference in the complex narrative 'pause' call attention to the ignorance of men regarding the motivations and intentions of gods.

Akhilleus, whose ability to influence the gods will be the subject of Chapter Four, remains singularly abreast of the gods' design. Before turning to this topic, the analysis of one final pair of similes in the complex narrative voice will complete this discussion of embedded sacrifices. Although sacrifice is never used as a metaphor for human death in the *Iliad*, two similes compare the deaths of heroes to that of sacrificial animals. James Redfield has distinguished three types of Homeric similes, in order of frequency: natural phenomena, hunting and herding, and human technology.[77] At the beginning and end of Akhilleus' rampage against the Trojans, two of his victims, Hippodamas and Hektor, are linked to sacrificial victims. Of the estimated 341 similes in the poem, these are the only two that contain embedded sacrifices.[78] Hippodamas' death cry is compared to that of a bull dragged around an altar of Poseidon, an allusion to sacrifice further qualified by the observation of Poseidon's delight (*Iliad* XX 403–405).[79] The fact that the embedded sacrifice

---

[76] Scodel 1982b: "The failure to offer hecatombs (mentioned at 7.450 and 12.6) as a reason for the gods' displeasure and the wall's eventual ruin seems like motive-hunting, a commonplace inserted to justify an action with no real cause" (34). Her argument draws on Hesiod's 'five ages' (*Works and Days* 109–201) and 'golden age' mythology, in which sacrifice plays a prominent role. We will return to this topic below, page 191.

[77] Redfield 1975:188–189.

[78] Scott's estimation (1974:191–205); there are other estimations on the basis of length, see Edwards 1991:24.

[79] Snodgrass 1971:419 gives the evidence for the cult of Poseidon Helikonios; cf. Herodotos 1.148.1. Hera rebukes Poseidon for his lack of pity for the Akhaians, despite the many offerings he receives at Helike and Aigai (*Iliad* VIII 203–204), another example of negative descriptions

compared to Hippodamas' death is described as "pleasing" for Poseidon makes the grim analogy all the more tragic:

αὐτὰρ ὁ θυμὸν ἄϊσθε καὶ ἤρυγεν, ὡς ὅτε ταῦρος
ἤρυγεν ἑλκόμενος Ἑλικώνιον ἀμφὶ ἄνακτα
κούρων ἑλκόντων· γάνυται δέ τε τοῖς ἐνοσίχθων·

(*Iliad* XX 403–405)

And he gasped his life away and bellowed, like when some bull
bellows being dragged round for the Helikonian lord
by young boys and the earthquake god delights in these things.

Poseidon's attention to his sacrifices contrasts with Akhilleus' lack of attention to the death of Hippodamas ("And the proud man's spirit left his bones behind but [Akhilleus] rushed with his spear against noble Poludoros," ὣς ἄρα τόν γ' ἐρυγόντα λίπ' ὀστέα θυμὸς ἀγήνωρ / αὐτὰρ ὁ βῆ σὺν δουρὶ μετ' ἀντίθεον Πολύδωρον, *Iliad* XX 406–407). The comparison of a man's death to the delight Poseidon takes in watching a sacrifice, similar to the importance that Artemis in Phoinix's digression and Poseidon in *Iliad* VII attach to sacrifices, implies that the god appreciates his sacrifices. In this example, despite the delight in sacrifice exhibited by the gods, the gruesome context reiterates the gap between men and gods expressed throught embedded sacrifices. At the end of his rampage, Akhilleus' pursuit of Hektor is negatively compared to a foot race for which the prize is a sacrificial victim or oxhide (οὐχ ἱερήϊον οὐδὲ βοείην, *Iliad* XXII 159). Immediately following this, another lengthy simile compares Akhilleus' chase to a horse race at funeral games (*Iliad* XXII 162–166). In these cases, the similes present the actions on the battlefield from the perspective of the gods: they watch Akhilleus and Hektor race as if they were a spectacle, a horse race for prizes.[80] With the deaths of Hippodamas and Hektor, sacrificial ritual becomes an expression of the helplessness of man in his very attempt to influence the course of events. As de Jong has observed, "The net result is that the mortality of man is placed against the background of the immortality of the gods, for whom human misery is like a tragic play, which they watch, but in which they themselves are not directly involved."[81] Although the gods insist on sacrifices and become angry if they are ignored, the benefit to mankind for offering sacrifices is made ambiguous at best and is, at times, called directly into question.

---

of offerings in the maintenance of reciprocity. What Poseidon takes pleasure in is not entirely clear: the antecedent could be either the victims or the young men, Edwards 1991 note *ad loc.*

[80]   De Jong 1987b:130f.; Griffin 1980:139.

[81]   De Jong 1987b:131.

Sacrifice surfaces as a topic of conversation because of the concern that it does not work as a mode of communication with gods. This theme is juxtaposed with the gods' relative distance in the enacted scenes, in which their response is usually either negative or omitted. The uncertainty and frustration underlying embedded sacrifices opposes the pattern of control, dominance, and established social hierarchy reinforced in Agamemnon's performance of enacted sacrifice. While Agamemnon's enacted sacrifices are performed to encourage communication and integration within the Panakhaian society, when characters, including Agamemnon, speak about sacrificial ritual, they express uncertainty about its potential for success. As we will see, Zeus and Apollo, although gods, themselves express frustration over the inability of sacrifice to create an effective reciprocal relationship: embedded sacrifices are problematized even in divine discourse. Zeus and Apollo seem troubled that the burning of *mêria*, the specific gift to the gods, is an insufficient incentive for divine favor.

The inadequacy of sacrifice, which is refuted throughout the poem as a potential support system, is one part of the wide-sweeping portrayal of mortal vulnerability pervasive in the poem, as shown by Jasper Griffin and Seth Schein, whose like-minded approaches to the Homeric "human condition" can be briefly summarized.[82] The dual presentation of mortal and immortal actions and thoughts gives greater weight to human actions: only mortals can take the risks that give their actions significance. At the same time, this creates a model of futility. The gods have such great power and control over human affairs that the audience cannot help but recognize this futility. Human actions must seem "ephemeral and pathetically limited" to the gods, who are perfect, ageless, immortal, and constantly described as "living easily".[83] The anthropomorphic nature of the gods strengthens the contrast between their power and immortality and the helplessness of the heroes, who can only hope to achieve honor and glory before their inevitable death.[84] In summary, Schein writes:

> Homer's Olympians are presented in a double perspective: they are
> frivolous and their existence is lacking in seriousness when compared
> with the tragic reality of human strivings for heroic achievement and
> meaning in life; yet in contrast to their cosmic power and perfection,
> human existence is limited and unimportant. Homer never lets his
> audience forget either side of this double view. ... At any rate Homer

[82] Schein 1984; Griffin 1980.
[83] Schein 1984:53. Cf. Griffin 1980:179–204.
[84] Griffin 1980:183–184; Schein 1984:54–55.

was responsible for the religious view, characteristic throughout the Archaic and Classical periods, that emphasized human ignorance and powerlessness in the face of a higher cosmic order even while it made human beings the subjects and objects of all significant action, suffering, and speculation.[85]

In this context of divine omnipotence and human weakness, descriptions of sacrifice embedded in character speech create a pattern of frustration and helplessness representative of this unbridgeable gap between the blessed immortals and the struggling heroes, made more tragic by the dual representation of events. Dieter Lohmann has recognized that a character's given perception of reality, as expressed in a speech, is often at odds with the reality depicted in the primary narrative-text, a tendency marked in embedded sacrifices by precisely this dual representation of divine and mortal perspectives.[86] For example, on the divine plane, we see the gods reflecting sadly on their inability to save Hektor despite his sacrifices (*Iliad* XXIV 33–76), while on the human level, Agamemnon imagines that the gods favor the sacrifices of Hektor (*Iliad* X 46), and worries that his own sacrifices are unsuccessful, as he states in his prayer to Zeus (*Iliad* VIII 238–241).

The sacrifices described by the primary narrator appear to be attempts to balance the crisis of reciprocity in Akhaian society instigated by Agamemnon's quarrel with Akhilleus in *Iliad* I: the performance of sacrifice provides a positive demonstration of Agamemnon's leadership.[87] This crisis of reciprocity then shifts to the relationship between mortals and immortals as Akhilleus persuades his mother to influence the plans of Zeus. Because of Akhilleus' direct influence on the gods, the reciprocity that should be created through sacrifice is rendered ineffective. The resulting situation creates a constant questioning of the efficacy of sacrifice by both mortals and immortals. Through the *Iliad*'s application of the sacrificial motif, the breakdown of reciprocity, the failure of sacrifice as a gift-exchange, and mortal frustration and vulnerability are brought to bear.

---

[85]   Schein 1984:62.

[86]   Lohmann 1970:196–212; a similar argument is made about the discrepancies between primary and secondary narrator-texts by Andersen 1990.

[87]   Seaford 2004: "The crisis of the *Iliad* is a breakdown of the form of reciprocity (Achilles' prize is in return for fighting) controlled by the leader (redistribution)" (44). He contrasts the communal distribution of the sacrificial feast with the irregular and unpredictable distribution of booty.

Chapter Four
The King of Sacrifice

FROM ITS OUTSET, THE *ILIAD* connects Agamemnon's power to sacrifice. Sacrifice serves simultaneously as a display of his status-based hierarchy over the Akhaian army and, contextualized in the Panakhaian society at Troy, as a show of *timê* 'honor' toward the gods. It is this principle of *timê* that guides the actions of *Iliad* I: Agamemnon slights Akhilleus' *timê* when he publicly asserts his superior authority by taking away Briseis.[1] Nestor, who here identifies himself as the wise advisor to the king, responds by advising Agamemnon not to take Briseis although it is in his power to do so. Even more strongly, Nestor cautions Akhilleus to respect the authority of a mightier king:

μήτε σὺ τόνδ' ἀγαθός περ ἐὼν ἀποαίρεο κούρην,
ἀλλ' ἔα, ὥς οἱ πρῶτα δόσαν γέρας υἷες Ἀχαιῶν·
μήτε σὺ, Πηλεΐδη, ἔθελ' ἐριζέμεναι βασιλῆϊ
ἀντιβίην, ἐπεὶ οὔ ποθ' ὁμοίης ἔμμορε τιμῆς
σκηπτοῦχος βασιλεύς, ᾧ τε Ζεὺς κῦδος ἔδωκεν.
εἰ δὲ σὺ καρτερός ἐσσι, θεὰ δέ σε γείνατο μήτηρ,
ἀλλ' ὅ γε φέρτερός ἐστιν, ἐπεὶ πλεόνεσσιν ἀνάσσει.

(*Iliad* I 275–281)

Don't seize the girl, powerful as you are—
leave her, just as the sons of Akhaia gave her, his prize from the
very first.
And you, Son of Peleus, never hope to fight it out with your king,
pitting force against his force: no one can match the honors dealt
a king, you know, a sceptered king to whom Zeus gives glory.
Strong as you are—a goddess was your mother—
he has more power because he rules more men.

Nestor contrasts Akhilleus' superior strength and divine birth with Agamemnon's regal authority, which must be obeyed. As Keith Stanley has observed, "The sequence (*Iliad* I 53–292) as a whole is organized precisely and strikingly to articulate the conflict that emerges between honor due the divinely sanctioned king and that owed the divinely favored hero."[2] This contrast is

---

[1]   Nagy 1979:72; Martin 1989:97.
[2]   Stanley 1993:41.

reflected throughout the poem in the performance of animal sacrifice, which is dominated by Agamemnon and shunned by Akhilleus. The interrelated issues of *timê* and *geras* 'honorific portion' raised between the king and warrior also function between man and god; the gods favor men who give them their proper *timê*, which Zeus defines as the *geras* of sacrifice.[3] Agamemnon is the divinely sanctioned king and therefore the only person represented as a performer of animal sacrifice, the *geras* of the gods, but he is remiss in honoring Akhilleus' *timê*. Further, when dishonored by Agamemnon, Akhilleus receives his *timê* from Zeus himself until he chooses to return to the army, which renders futile Agamemnon's gifts of honor to the gods. The contrast between Agamemnon's honoring of the gods and his mistreatment of Akhilleus forms part of the poem's depiction of the distance between mortals and immortals, while establishing the unique interstice occupied by Akhilleus, who is effectively isolated from both.

Sacrifice in the *Iliad* exists as a reaffirmation of the tense social hierarchy created by the expedition to Troy, an authoritarian construct in which various kings submit to the most powerful king, Agamemnon. Agamemnon initiates and carries out five of the seven enacted sacrifices (*Iliad* I 312–317; II 402–432; III 267–302; VII 313–323; and XIX 249–268), and sacrifice is his first action after the withdrawal of Akhilleus. He also provides victims for the sacrifice at *Iliad* I 436–474, a singular instance in which he delegates his ritual authority to Odysseus in order to avoid acknowledging responsibility for the plague. The other enacted sacrifice in the poem is performed by a group, "one and another of the Akhaians" (*Iliad* II 400–401), as a brief precursor to the large, detailed sacrificial scene led by Agamemnon (*Iliad* II 402–432). Instances of enacted sacrifice are so few in the *Iliad* that we ought to ask not why the ritual is omitted where we might expect it, but why it has been included.[4] In this chapter, an exploration of the poem's representation of Agamemnon's authority in the context of the Panakhaian community will lay the foundation for a close examination of a sacrificial framework for the quarrel in *Iliad* I. We will then look at the other sacrifices in the epic as a continuation of the pattern established in *Iliad* I, before concluding with an analysis of Akhilleus' isolation as expressed through his abstinence from and disregard for sacrifice.

The sacrificer enjoys a special religious designation as the intermediary between man and god through his connection to the sacralized offering. As

---

[3] *Iliad* IV 48–49 = XXIV 69–70, see also page 114. Hesiod *Works and Days* 134–137 describes the gods in the Silver Age as bereft of *timê* because men did not offer sacrifice; Nagy 1990b:135. On the connection between *timê* and *geras*, Nagy 1979: "As for Achilles, he loses his *timê* 'honor' specifically because Agamemnon has taken away his *geras* 'honorific portion'" (132).

[4] Stengel 1910:62 observes the paucity of animal sacrifice in Homer.

Jean-Pierre Vernant notes, "By furnishing the divinity with the consecrated object, the sacrificer expects the ceremony to produce a transformation as a result of the sacrifice and bestow on him a new religious quality."[5] The fact that six of the seven enacted sacrifices are strictly limited to performances organized by Agamemnon demonstrates his supremacy and special ritual authority. The exclusivity of this focus on Agamemnon can be seen with comparison to the large number of characters who make prayers, discussed above, or with those who pour libations for the gods, a ritual action given gift status equivalent to sacrificial *knisê* according to Zeus. Although Agamemnon never makes them, libations unaccompanied by sacrifice are made by the Trojans and Akhaians *en masse*, the Akhaian councilors, the embassy to Akhilleus, Odysseus and Diomedes, Akhilleus, and Priam.[6] While libations and prayers remain significant ritual actions dedicated to the gods, occurring at crucial junctures in the poem in response to imminent threats and crises, the restricted use of animal sacrifice in relation to the quarrel between Akhilleus and Agamemnon stands out in comparison.

Feasting is equally frequent in the poem, as described in Chapter Three, but is seldomly preceded by animal sacrifice. This selective presentation of enacted sacrifices in the primary narrative also extends to Agamemnon as *Opferherr*: only those meals provided in contexts that support his authority over the army during Akhilleus' absence include sacrifices. Therefore, when he invites the councilors to his hut in *Iliad* IX 89–91, Agamemnon merely provides a *dais* for them, which leads to Nestor's advice regarding reconciliation with Akhilleus:

> Ἀτρεΐδης δὲ γέροντας ἀολλέας ἦγεν Ἀχαιῶν
> ἐς κλισίην, παρὰ δέ σφι τίθει μενοεικέα δαῖτα.
> οἱ δ' ἐπ' ὀνείαθ' ἑτοῖμα προκείμενα χεῖρας ἴαλλον.
> αὐτὰρ ἐπεὶ πόσιος καὶ ἐδητύος ἐξ ἔρον ἕντο,
> τοῖς ὁ γέρων πάμπρωτος ὑφαίνειν ἤρχετο μῆτιν
> Νέστωρ, οὗ καὶ πρόσθεν ἀρίστη φαίνετο βουλή·

> (*Iliad* IX 89–94)

Meanwhile the son of Atreus led his councilors
  toward his quarters and set before them a feast to please their
    hearts.
They reached out for the good things that lay at hand

---

[5] Vernant 1991:291.

[6] Trojans and Akhaians (*Iliad* III 295–296, VII 480–481); Akhaian councilors (*Iliad* IX 712); the embassy to Akhilleus (*Iliad* IX 177, 656–657); Odysseus and Diomedes (*Iliad* X 579); Akhilleus (*Iliad* XVI 231–232, XXIII 196–197); Priam (*Iliad* XXIV 306).

> But when they had put aside their desire for food and drink
> Among them first of all the old man began to weave his counsel:
> Nestor, whose earlier plan had appeared best.

While this is very similar to the councilors' feasts provided by Agamemnon in *Iliad* II and VII, those events are marked by animal sacrifice. In all three scenes, the councilors congregate in Agamemnon's quarters (*Iliad* II 404–409, VII 313, IX 89) and a feast is enjoyed, described with the formulaic verse "When they had put aside desire for food and drink" (αὐτὰρ ἐπεὶ πόσιος καὶ ἐδητύος ἐξ ἔρον ἕντο, *Iliad* II 432 = VII 323 = IX 92), which then provides an opportunity for Nestor to speak (*Iliad* II 433, VII 324–325 = *Iliad* IX 93–94). The connections between the meetings in *Iliad* II and IX are further reinforced by similes comparing the consternation of men to stormy seas (*Iliad* II 144–149, IX 4–8).[7]

Why not perform sacrifice before the feast for the councilors in *Iliad* IX? I propose that animal sacrifice is limited to contexts that bolster Agamemnon's authority, whereas the embassy to Akhilleus, like the sacrifice at Khruse in *Iliad* I, could be perceived as an admission of guilt and defeat for Agamemnon. In *Iliad* I he appoints an ambassador, Odysseus, to lead the hecatomb to Khruse, similar to the embassy suggested by Nestor to announce the offer of gifts to Akhilleus. No sacrifice precedes the council session in which this embassy is planned because the occasion does not promote Agamemnon's authority and is therefore not a context for sacrifice or for any other positive symbol of his reign, for example, his scepter.[8] The embassy to Akhilleus in *Iliad* IX is a vulnerable moment for Agamemnon, and, although frequent libations and prayers are performed by the embassy, highlighted by the use of verses also found in sacrificial contexts, sacrifice is conspicuously absent. Before the embassy leaves the camp of Agamemnon, all pour libations:

> αὐτίκα κήρυκες μὲν ὕδωρ ἐπὶ χεῖρας ἔχευαν,
> κοῦροι δὲ κρητῆρας ἐπεστέψαντο ποτοῖο,
> νώμησαν δ' ἄρα πᾶσιν ἐπαρξάμενοι δεπάεσσιν.

> (*Iliad* IX 174–176)

> Heralds at once poured water on their hands,
> and the young men brimmed the mixing bowls with wine,
> and tipping first drops for the gods in every cup, they poured full
> rounds for all.

---

[7] Cf. Stanley 1993:109.

[8] Stanley 1993:109–110, comparing these two advisory meetings, remarks that Agamemnon is depicted in the *Iliad* IX scene in an "unceremonious" manner, appearing without his scepter.

Rather than references to gods, the libations before departure are combined with the drinks imbibed by the embassy, "Libations finished, when everyone had drunk to his heart's content" (αὐτὰρ ἐπεὶ σπεῖσάν τ' ἔπιόν θ' ὅσον ἤθελε θυμός, *Iliad* IX 177). On the way to Akhilleus' quarters, Ajax and Odysseus are described as praying to Poseidon:

> τὼ δὲ βάτην παρὰ θῖνα πολυφλοίσβοιο θαλάσσης
> πολλὰ μάλ' εὐχομένω γαιηόχῳ ἐννοσιγαίῳ
> ῥηϊδίως πεπιθεῖν μεγάλας φρένας Αἰακίδαο.
>
> (*Iliad* IX 182–184)

> So they made their way at once along the shore of the loud-
>   resounding sea,
> praying hard to the god who moves and shakes the earth
> that they might easily bring the proud heart of Akhilleus.

Before they leave the camp of Akhilleus, another libation is poured:

> οἱ δὲ ἕκαστος ἑλὼν δέπας ἀμφικύπελλον
> σπείσαντες παρὰ νῆας ἴσαν πάλιν· ἦρχε δ' Ὀδυσσεύς.
>
> (*Iliad* IX 656–657)

> Then each man, lifting his own two-handled cup,
> poured it out to the gods, and back they went along the ships,
>   Odysseus in the lead.

Finally, after the discussion in Agamemnon's hut, *Iliad* IX concludes with libations before bed:

> καὶ τότε δὴ σπείσαντες ἔβαν κλισίηνδὲ ἕκαστος
>
> (*Iliad* IX 12)

> pouring cups to the gods, each man sought his shelter.

Interestingly, there are no specific references to the gods as recipients of these libations, which places the focus of this scene on the tension in the Akhaian community rather than on the depiction of reciprocity between gods and men. The indirect description of the prayer to Poseidon, without his reaction given, similarly reduces the impact of this action in the creation of a bond between the people praying and the divinity. These ritual actions create an atmosphere of solemnity and highlight the anxiety of the heroes involved, but the overall context of Agamemnon's vulnerability precludes the animal sacrifices that produce a positive image of his hegemony for the audience.

A brief glance at the outline of events in *Iliad* VII provides a similar demonstration of the restricted performance of sacrifice as opposed to unmarked scenes of feasting or other ritual actions dedicated to gods.[9] The action begins with Hektor's proposal of a second duel (*Iliad* VII 67–91), reminiscent of the first duel in *Iliad* III, which was sanctified by an oath sacrifice performed by Agamemnon in front of all of the armies. However, no sacrifice marks the occasion of this second duel. The Akhaians are afraid to meet Hektor's challenge, and Nestor rebukes them with a digression on his personal experience against the Arkadian Ereuthalion (*Iliad* VII 124–160). This digression, unlike his later speech to Patroklos in *Iliad* XI, does not refer to sacrifice. Nine heroes including Agamemnon volunteer, and lots are cast. The army prays to Zeus that the lot fall to Ajax, Diomedes, or Agamemnon (*Iliad* VII 177–180). Ajax and Diomedes are consistently presented as the best substitute fighters in the absence of Akhilleus, further marked by their strong support of Agamemnon's authority.[10] For example, after the embassy has failed, it is Diomedes who encourages Agamemnon and the troops to ignore Akhilleus (*Iliad* IX 697–709). The troops choose lots; Ajax, recognizing his lot, exhorts the army to pray silently, to safeguard their prayers from the Trojans, or openly, without fear (*Iliad* VII 191–199). Looking up to heaven, they pray for either the victory of Ajax or, should Hektor be dearer to Zeus, glory for both heroes (*Iliad* VII 200–205). Ajax and Hektor duel until the fight is broken up by the approaching darkness (*Iliad* VII 206–310). The Trojans rejoice upon seeing Hektor, while Ajax is led straight to Agamemnon: "while far across the field the Akhaian men-at-arms escorted Ajax back to noble Agamemnon, thrilled with victory" (Αἴαντ' αὖθ' ἑτέρωθεν ἐϋκνήμιδες Ἀχαιοὶ / εἰς Ἀγαμέμνονα δῖον ἄγον, κεχαρηότα νίκῃ, *Iliad* VII 311–312). In this context, a harmonious meeting of the councilors and a sacrificial feast, hosted and orchestrated by Agamemnon, mark this happy occasion (*Iliad* VII 313–323). The emphasis on Agamemnon's authority is signaled by the heroes' escorting of Ajax to the chief king, and further reiterated with regard to the sacrifice in the following verses:

οἱ δ' ὅτε δὴ κλισίῃσιν ἐν Ἀτρεΐδαο γένοντο,
τοῖσι δὲ βοῦν ἱέρευσεν ἄναξ ἀνδρῶν Ἀγαμέμνων
ἄρσενα πενταέτηρον ὑπερμενέϊ Κρονίωνι.

(*Iliad* VII 313–315)

---

[9] Kirk 1990:230 gives a brief summary of the scholarship on *Iliad* VII, including a discussion about the relation of this duel to that in *Iliad* III, with bibliography.

[10] On Ajax's role as Akhilleus' stand-in, see page 184 below. Links between Diomedes and Akhilleus are established in the similar descriptions of flaming armor (*Iliad* V 4; XVIII 205; XXII 26), as well as Diomedes' outstanding prowess on the battlefield (Postlethwaite 1998:95).

> Soon as they had gathered within the quarters of the son of Atreus
> the lord of men Agamemnon sacrificed an ox in their midst,
> a male, five years old, to the towering son of Kronos, Zeus.

The resultant feast honors Ajax with the honorary portion of meat and leads to Nestor's plan to build the wall (*Iliad* VII 324–343). The narrative focus then shifts to the arguing Trojans in their *agora*: Priam sends them away to have supper, for which he provides nothing; Idaios is sent as a messenger to the Akhaian camps (*Iliad* VII 345–397), where Diomedes rejects Paris' proposal; Agamemnon agrees to a burial truce (*Iliad* VII 398–411), after which the burial of the dead is briefly described without much detail (*Iliad* VII 412–432); and then the Akhaians secretly build their wall (*Iliad* VII 433–441). Significantly, it is at this point that the linear progression of events in the primary narrative is interrupted by Poseidon's complaint to Zeus that the wall has been built without sacrifice, which Zeus promises will be avenged (*Iliad* VII 446–463). At variance with Agamemnon's exclusive sacrificial feast in honor of Ajax, divine attention here emphasizes the lack of sacrifice for this grand undertaking.

The description of the mortal affairs on the plains of Troy resumes with another Akhaian feast, which is not depicted as a sacrifice: "they slew the oxen beside their tents and took their meal" (βουφόνεον δὲ κατὰ κλισίας καὶ δόρπον ἕλοντο, *Iliad* VII 466). βουφονεῖν 'to slaughter oxen' is attested only here in Greek literature; the lack of ritual details or actions directed toward gods, as well as the specific description of the troops "taking a meal" (δόρπον ἕλοντο), distinguishes this scene from the enacted sacrifices followed by dinners. The building of the wall is concluded with a refreshing repast, followed by a unique description of the troops bartering for wine brought by ships from Lemnos and the reception of an honorary thousand measures by Agamemnon and Menelaos (*Iliad* VII 467–475). This second meal, enjoyed by the troops after their hard work in building the wall and enhanced by the description of the wine, marks a significant contrast with the exclusive sacrificial meal provided by Agamemnon. The Akhaians and Trojans are collectively described as feasting through the night until being interrupted by Zeus' thunder, which frightens the men into pouring libations before drinking. *Iliad* VII concludes with their falling asleep:

> τίθεντο δὲ δαῖτα θάλειαν.
> παννύχιοι μὲν ἔπειτα κάρη κομόωντες Ἀχαιοὶ
> δαίνυντο, Τρῶες δὲ κατὰ πτόλιν ἠδ' ἐπίκουροι·
> παννύχιος δέ σφιν κακὰ μήδετο μητίετα Ζεὺς
> σμερδαλέα κτυπέων· τοὺς δὲ χλωρὸν δέος ᾕρει·

οἶνον δ' ἐκ δεπάων χαμάδις χέον, οὐδέ τις ἔτλη
πρὶν πιέειν, πρὶν λεῖψαι ὑπερμενέϊ Κρονίωνι.
κοιμήσαντ' ἄρ' ἔπειτα καὶ ὕπνου δῶρον ἕλοντο.

(*Iliad* VII 475–482)

> ...and they made a handsome feast.
> Then all night long the long-haired Akhaians
> feasted, as Trojans and Trojan allies took their meal in Troy.
> But for both sides, all night long, the Master Strategist Zeus
> plotted fresh disaster,
> his thunder striking terror—And blanching panic swept across the
> ranks.
> They flung wine from their cups and wet the earth, and no fighter
> would dare
> drink until he'd poured an offering out to the overwhelming son
> of Kronos.
> Then down they lay at last and took the gift of sleep.

The activity of feasting is described, both in the Akhaian camps and at Troy, without reference to sacrifice. This convivial occasion is juxtaposed against the ominous divine activities represented by Zeus' thunder, part of his plan to devise disaster for the armies. In the context of Akhilleus' withdrawal, this selective presentation of sacrifice bolsters Agamemnon's authority: neither divine wrath, as represented by Zeus' thunder, nor initiation or conclusion of momentous undertakings, such as the wall, provoke the primary narrator's inclusion of enacted sacrifice. The feast celebrating Ajax, the substitute fighter in Akhilleus' absence, is a celebratory moment and is therefore marked by Agamemnon's sacrifice. The other feasts in *Iliad* VII do not form part of this pattern, making descriptions of sacrifice unnecessary.

This abbreviated summary of *Iliad* VII gives a good indication of both the poem's selective representation of ritual and the pattern of Agamemnon's special ritual dominance. Sacrifices are not performed where they might be expected—before the duel in *Iliad* VII (particularly given the prominence of the sacrifice before the duel in *Iliad* III), at burial, upon building the wall, before dinner after completion of the wall, or after the terror produced by Zeus' thunder. Nor are they mentioned in Nestor's digression, although he will describe them three times in his digression to Patroklos in *Iliad* XI.

Other ritual actions, such as prayers and libations, are performed by larger groups without any special emphasis on individuals. However, Agamemnon hosts one enacted sacrifice that the primary narrator takes pains to identify both as performed and distributed by him and as a sacrifice dedicated to the gods. In this context, Menelaos is not described as co-sacrificer or provider of sacrificial animals, though he and Agamemnon are jointly given a thousand measures of wine; the focus is restricted to Agamemnon. Mass consumption by the army is twice described, but never specifically linked to Agamemnon, in contrast to the marked demonstration of his exclusive ritual largesse after the duel. Poseidon even complains to Zeus about the lack of sacrifice, highlighting the restricted performance of this ritual action. Though Zeus frightens the men and they pour libations, sacrifice is not described again in the primary narrative until the reintegration of Akhilleus in *Iliad* XIX.

The narrative only selectively includes sacrifice, depicting it as a special event performed by Agamemnon and restricted to an elite group. More specifically, enacted sacrifice functions as an expression of Agamemnon's authority, which is constantly challenged by Akhilleus. What remains at stake is the way in which the performance of sacrifice clarifies and reinforces Agamemnon's somewhat ambiguous relationship with the other kings and the general soldiery. In order to arrive at a precise understanding of sacrificial function with respect to Agamemnon, we will briefly discuss the type of rule he holds over the Akhaians, exploring his reaction to the impact of Akhilleus' withdrawal as expressed through his performances as *Opferherr*, before examining each enacted sacrifice in detail.

4.1 The Basis for Agamemnon's Ritual Authority

To fully appreciate the significance of any particular ritual action, we must establish a working sense of that action's social context.[11] The key to understanding sacrifice, a symbolic action that may be called a social institution, is the social relationships that provide the context for its performance. Though the composition of the social network in the *Iliad* is a complicated and controversial topic, largely beyond the scope of this study, the question we must raise concerns what type of authority is represented in the figure of Agamemnon, who is one of the *basileis* 'noblemen' at Troy, but who seems to have the ability to compel the others to do as he commands and who, at least sometimes, is recognized as having superior authority. Is Agamemnon's authority greater because he is specifically identified with sacrifice, a prerogative that is his alone, or is he an absolute ruler whose complete control of goods and property

---

[11] For instance, Rosivach's study of fourth-century Athenian cult inscriptions excludes third-century material because the political changes from democracy to monarchy create a different ritual environment (1994:4).

necessitates his identity as *Opferherr*? After briefly setting out the competing interpretive models for the plausible historical influences on the Homeric poems' representations of leadership, I will address some of these questions of social hierarchy in order to demonstrate that Agamemnon is seen as the supreme king while the army is camped outside Troy and that others recognize ritual authority as part of his unique powers.

Much good work has been conducted on such Homeric social institutions as land-tenure, finance, housing, marriage, etc., but the nature of social hierarchy and human relationships remains elusive.[12] There is a central question, hampered by ambiguities in both epics, concerning whether the characters in the poems identify themselves as parts of a unified group whose identity affects their actions and decision-making. Both poems represent multiple societies, which further complicates an overall understanding of the social constructs. In the *Iliad*, there is the patchwork society created by the Panakhaian expedition, which focuses not around an *oikos,* but on individual ships and shelters erected beside them: there is the Trojan society, which revolves exclusively around the *oikos* of Priam; there is the world hinted at through numerous similes and the images on the shield of Akhilleus; and then there is the society of the gods, which is probably an idealized reflection of what we should consider the norm within the poet—a hierarchical, kinship society based upon the authority of the eldest male.[13]

Part of the wide-ranging debate on the consistency of Homeric social and moral value systems stems from the poems' questionable reflection of historical practices. The social contexts comprised of the values and social institutions recognized by the characters, which may be termed 'Homeric societies', create a complex puzzle. Although much of the *Iliad* is concerned with frictions within power structures, no formalized political institutions are consistently represented. Civic identities are problematized by tensions between the clearly demonstrated, collective awareness of a civic space that influences actions and decisions and an informal power structure based on power and wealth. This tension has led to the speculation that historical influences on the epic have been conflated, which would reflect a shift away from

---

[12] The scholarship on this topic is immense: an overview is provided by Raaflaub 1991, and a thorough bibliography is given in Raaflaub 1998:189n2. This study will only cover topics relevant to the presentation of kingship, which is covered in particular by Donlan 1979; Quiller 1981; Drews 1983; Geddes 1984; Carlier 1984 and 2006; van Wees 1992; Hammer 1997; Rose 1997; Raaflaub 1998.

[13] Gould 2001:343 gives the three alternative social models. Mackie 1996 provides an in-depth analysis of the different presentation of Trojan and Akhaian societies. For instance, the Trojans are never depicted preparing a *dais.*

a Mycenaean warrior society obligated by kinship and *philia* toward the social structure of the *polis*, and would explain the seeming mixture of these social contexts within the poem. There are aspects of the social and material culture in the *Iliad* that correspond to the picture of Mycenaean palace culture as reconstructed from archaeological evidence and the Linear B tablets: a society dominated by the king, whose household provides economic stability, food supply, and protection.[14]

An important parallel to the Mycenaean period for our study could be drawn from the Mycenaean use of sacrificial feasts as examples of royal largesse, visible demonstrations of the chief king's wealth and authority analogous to the depiction of Agamemnon's feasts. Lisa Bendall has shown the hierarchy existing in the admittance granted to guests at ritual banquets at the king's palace in Pylos, based on the distribution of *kulikes*.[15] The *wanax* is the chief king, described by Thomas Palaima as "a single elevated king at a rank above or considerably above the more numerous individuals known as *basileis*," who rules over a "palatial system of regional hierarchical authority": the *wanax* appoints a range of officials to perform administrative, economic, and supervisory tasks throughout the kingdom, while the *basileis* function on the local level, supported by the *wanax*, to whom they are subordinate and for whom they are sometimes called upon to perform tasks.[16] Bendall's study of the archaeological evidence for drinking cups at the central palace in Pylos proposes that a very elite group feasted with the *wanax* in the main room, Room 6, where a small distribution of high quality *kulikes* have been found. A larger group, of lesser status but still elite, feasted in the inner courtyard, 63, visible to Room 64 and the southwest building, where a considerable amount of fineware has been found. Finally, the lower classes feasted in the courtyard before the entrance to the main building, where a large amount of low-grade *kulikes* have been found. These finds, coupled with similar finds at Malthi, where the inhabitants seem to have imitated feasting practices at Pylos, have led Bendall to conclude that the Mycenaean banquets were structured so as to

[14] Schein 1984: "The conception and the social and political organization of these gods is anachronistically modelled on the Mycenaean society as portrayed in the *Iliad* and as evidencd by the archaeological record" (16). See also Nilsson 1932; Vermeule 1964:309. Finley, one of the strongest opponents to the reflection of the Mycenaean world in Homer, proposes that the poems reflect Dark Age societies; see Finley 1970, 1982:199–212.

[15] Bendall 2004, drawing on the work of Killen on the role of the palace in the sponsorship of sacrificial banquets (1994:71–72, 2001:437); Palaima 2005 (with an appendix of relevant tablets) outlines the process for preparing and hosting feasts at Thebes and Pylos, including the inventories in the Ta series from Pylos.

[16] Palaima 2006:55, 69, arguing on the basis of the usage of the term in Linear B tablets and Homer, a discussion to which we will return, pages 176f. below.

reinforce the social hierarchy by controlling access to the banquets. Bennet and Davis describe this as "a palace-based system ... involving, for example, state sponsored conspicuous consumption in the form of feasts associated with important transitions in the control of power or with systematic offerings to deities at particular times of the year, uniting both local and regional elites."[17] The palaces wanted to bring people together to impress upon them the palatial control over agricultural wealth, particularly by offering it to the gods, which would simultaneously emphasize the generosity of the palace and the dependence of the people upon this generosity.[18] In this way, feasting would have provided a visible demonstration of royal power and social hierarchy, similar in many ways to Agamemnon's performance of sacrifice in the *Iliad*. The similarities between reconstructions of feasting at Mycenaean Pylos and the representation of Agamemnon's feasts in the *Iliad* can provide a kind of analog to other ritual practices in the poem. [19]

Many scholars, following Moses Finley, do not recognize a political awareness or identifiable *polis* in the epics, but interpret social interactions as functioning primarily on a private level, reflective of the 'Dark Ages' societies in the tenth to ninth centuries BCE, in which the *oikos* 'household' is the primary unit, led by the senior male, who owns the property and is linked to, but autonomous from, other households by a closed society of aristocratic birth.[20] In Finley's definition, the Homeric *oikos* is comprised of "the people of the household together with its land and goods," and is the forerunner of the Classical

---

[17] Bennet and Davis 1999:107.

[18] Palmer 1994:191–195.

[19] There is no question that the Homeric poems reflect some influence from the Mycenaean period, a time of 'active generation' for the poems according to Sherratt's model, discussed in Chapter One. However, the *Iliad* makes notorious omissions of crucial Mycenaean elements, such as scribes or tablets. There is an equivalent or, by some accounts, greater amount of correspondences in material and social culture to those of the ninth to eighth centuries BCE, complicating an identification of the Homeric world as "Mycenaean." Moreover, the complete destruction of the Mycenaean strongholds at the start of the "Dark Ages" (ca. 1100–800 BCE) suggested in the archaeological record renders questionable the possible cultural continuity necessary for links between the Mycenaean period and poems in circulation in the eighth century.

[20] Finley 1977:82–89, the revised edition of his 1954 work. See van Wees 1992:26–27; Adkins 1960. Scully 1990:100–113 recognizes collective decision-making and an emerging *polis*, but thinks the lack of concepts of citizenship makes the epics "pre-political." Seaford 1994:6–7 follows Finley 1977 in allowing a degree of historicity based on the internal consistencies of the political system within the poems and its resemblance to comparable known societies. Carlier 1984 argues for the reflection of a slightly later, eighth-century world in the epics. On the *oikos*, see Finley 1977, supported recently by Edmunds 1989:27–28 and Hammer 2002, who defines Homeric society as "interdependent," formed of otherwise independent aristocratic households.

polis as the central unit that establishes social and moral values and provides security and livelihood.[21] His theory is largely drawn on the representation of social interaction in the *Odyssey* at Ithaka, where the activities in Odysseus' household are considered a matter of public interest, but external to a public sphere of action. A similar model, proposed by Robert Drews, suggests that the presentation of Homeric kingship may reflect the power vacuum created by the collapse of the Mycenaean kingdoms in the Dark Ages, leading to a consolidation of power in the hands of a few *basileis*.[22] In these interpretations, the *oikos* is usually shown to have the predominant influence over decisions and actions, whether at the expense of the nascent political consciousness of the Homeric masses, as a tool to bolster an aristocratic audience threatened by the transition, or as the only secure space for collective action before the development of political activity.[23] In these models, there is not one supreme king, but an association of equally ranked nobles, and a figure such as Agamemnon becomes a *primus inter pares* 'first among equals'. His status is slightly greater than the other *basileis* because he is the ruler of the largest kingdom, as Nestor tells Akhilleus ("he rules more men," πλεόνεσσιν ἀνάσσει, *Iliad* I 281), but he does not have an otherwise distinguishable leadership role.[24] Significantly, while denying that Agamemnon has an elevated or unique rank, even Finley recognizes that "in certain of his functions—in the Assembly, for example, or in offering sacrifices to the gods—the king in fact acted the patriarch."[25]

Finally, other scholars have suggested that Homer represents the society of the early Archaic period in which the *polis* emerged. In this view, the components of a *polis* and political activity are recognizable in the *Iliad*, which reflects the uncertain nature of political changes in the ninth and eighth centuries BCE.[26] A collective conceptualization of community, in the civic and polit-

---

[21] Finley 1977:57–58.

[22] Drews 1983:100–115, who does not think that monarchs are depicted in the poem.

[23] Taplin 1992:7 describes the "shading" of public issues into the private sphere. Hammer 2002:148 supports the arguments for the use of the *Iliad* as an ideological tool to support a threatened aristocracy; see also Raaflaub 1998:182. The security of the *oikos* at the expense of the *polis* is advocated by Scully 1990:105.

[24] Finley 1977: "While recognizing monarchy, the nobles propose to maintain the fundamental priority of their status, to keep the king on the level of a first among equals" (84). See also Murray 1980:40–41 and Edmunds 1989:27. Taplin 1992:48–57, 211, although similarly inclined regarding Agamemnon's status, does not accept the label *primus inter pares* and argues that Agamemnon, rather than being a sovereign king, is the summoner of the army, which obliges him to feast his followers.

[25] Finley 1977:83.

[26] The term *polis* is used throughout both poems to describe settlements, and is essentially synonymous with *asty*: e.g. *Odyssey* vi 117–178; see Raaflaub 1997:629. West 1966:46–47, van Wees 1992:54–58, and Taplin 1992:37 detail the evidence for the representation of late eighth- to

ical sense, would reflect the Homeric poems' location in a transitional phase between "individual achievement, dependent solely on skill and prowess, toward the idea of social class in which membership alone allowed one to claim excellence," the sort of communal identity of the Classical Athenian *polis*, for example.[27] That the development of a political mindset such as the one found in the Classical *polis* occurs in the Homeric poems can be argued on the basis of the foremost heroes' responsibility for the well-being of the overall community, as well as the dependence of heroic status on the willingness of supporters. Different social ranks have different obligations; identity and wealth are the result of fulfillment of these roles and acceptance of appropriate punishments and rewards. Kurt Raaflaub concludes: "The individual's primary focus on family and *oikos* does not exclude a high valuation of service to and responsibility for the *polis.*"[28]

These very brief summaries of extremely complex arguments may serve as glimpses into the remarkable panorama of different, plausible interpretations of communities presented in the Homeric poems. Many of the arguments sketched above depend on the multiple societies depicted in the *Odyssey* and on Telemakhos' problems in his household.[29] Since the political system represented in the *Iliad* is still informal, ritual and reciprocity play the central roles that 'co-operative virtues' will later play in the *polis.*[30] Social interactions rely on a system of communal obligations that are reciprocal, existing between kindred and non-kindred alike. They are defined both through households, starting with the king's home as a model for the community, and through social interactions such as friendship, hospitality, and 'negative reciprocity' (or

---

early seventh-century society. Quiller 1981:113, van Wees 1992:31–36, and Raaflaub 1991:239–247 give lengthy arguments for definite political structures in Homer. Kirk 1962, Long 1970, Snodgrass 1974, and Sherratt 1990 suggest that the evidence is too inconsistent to be conclusive. Raaflaub 1997:628 describes the seeming "historical context" as the creation of a "historical consciousness" that is "incidental and secondary": in his opinion, the poems reflect the world of the poet and his audience.

[27] Calhoun 1962:438; cf. Raaflaub 1997:635.

[28] Raaflaub 1997:632. Similar arguments are made by Scully 1990:109 and van Wees 1992:36, who concludes: "in spite of the fact that most men have no formal political power, a town is conceived of as a political unit of which the entire male population forms a part."

[29] For example, Finley 1977:84.

[30] There is a long-standing scholarly debate about whether virtues in Homer are cooperative (justice and generosity) or competitive (prowess in war), on which see Adkins 1960, Long 1970, Cairns 1993, and Yamagata 1994. Seaford 1998:5 argues that reciprocity transcends this distinction: generosity can be admired and then become competitive. Adkins 1997:697 concludes: "the Homeric *agathos*, as head of his *oikos*, is in a situation in which self-help must be the order of the day, so that the 'competitive excellences', and courage above all, must appear most important in a crisis…. The characters of the poems are aware of the social situation which furnishes these values with the attraction which they certainly possess in the Homeric poems."

the obligations of enmity).[31] In the affairs of the heroes, the social composition in the *Iliad* is complicated by the representation of seemingly contradictory value systems, one based on inherited wealth and power, the other a meritocracy awarding heroes for individual achievements, as has been proposed by Richard Martin.[32] In John Gould's surmise, the "reciprocal obligations owed by Akhilleus and the Greeks are made unclear by the pervasive ambiguity of social values among the Greeks at Troy."[33]

Without political institutions or other formalized systems of decision-making, Homeric leadership cannot be based upon easily identifiable institutional mechanisms such as taxation or judicial functions, and it is therefore relatively unstable. The existence of moral obligations reflective of a shared value system between kindred and non-kindred has been discussed by scholars with reference to many other contexts, such as feeling shame on the battlefield on behalf of a fallen comrade, but this value system seems less secure in regards to leadership.[34] As to an organized structure of authority binding to all heroes, Walter Donlan, who, in keeping with Finley posits a historical influence from the mid-ninth/eighth century, finds Homeric society to be largely composed of autonomous and "centrifugal" households run by chieftains or "big men." He views Homeric society as a "ranked society," between egalitarian and stratified societies, in which the chief has authority but little "coercive power": Agamemnon's power relies upon the willingness of the people to follow him.[35] So Akhilleus asserts that the Akhaians follow Agamemmnon to Troy to please him and to bring *timê* to him and Menelaos ("but you are terribly shameless—we all followed you, to please you, to win your honor back from the Trojans, for Menelaos and you, you dog-face," ἀλλὰ σοὶ, ὦ μέγ' ἀναιδές, ἅμ' ἑσπόμεθ' ὄφρα σὺ χαίρῃς / τιμὴν ἀρνύμενοι Μενελάῳ σοί τε, κυνῶπα, / πρὸς Τρώων, *Iliad* I 158–160).

However, Agamemnon's power base relies on more than the allegiance of his people. At the start of the poem, he is described by Kalkhas as "the one who

---

[31] Cf. Redfield 1983:218–247 and Gould 2001:336. Gift-giving and reciprocity are essential in gradated societies: Muellner 1996:34 and Hammer 2002:59.

[32] Martin 1989: "The problem of the *Iliad* appears to be rooted in the clash of two systems: status based *timê* and performance based judgments, the latter an almost economically pragmatic 'market-value'" (97).

[33] Gould 2001:352.

[34] See Long 1970:121–139 and Gould 2001:337.

[35] Donlan 1979, 1993:155. There are many conflicting interpretations of the nature of kingship in Homer. Cf. Geddes 1984: "The kings do not seem to have any function in the world of Homer. They do not make decisions on behalf of the people, they have no judicial function, even their command of the army seems dependent ... on their powers of persuasion and their reputation in the eyes of their men" (36).

rules mightily over the Akhaians and whom the Akhaians obey" (ὃς μέγα πάντων / Ἀργείων κρατέει καί οἱ πείθονται Ἀχαιοί, *Iliad* I 78–79). Hans van Wees
suggests that the *Iliad* projects a social model based upon subordination
to an authoritative figure, whose authority is both inherited and socially
accepted.[36] Whichever historical forms may have formed the basis for the
poetic representation of communal interactions in the *Iliad*, the social world
of the Akhaians encamped outside of Troy is a gradated society consisting of
a chief king, elite nobles, and their followers. The numerous kings gathered
together at Troy command their own groups, which act as subsections within
the larger structure of the Akhaian army under the auspices of Agamemnon:
for example, when Akhilleus withdraws, so do the Myrmidons he leads. This
authority structure works on the smaller level of "noblemen" (*basileis*) and
their followers as well as the larger level of both groups' collective subordination to Agamemnon. Therefore, most of the contingents listed in the Catalogue
of Ships are composed of men from multiple towns, led by one leader or
an occasional pair of brothers.[37] In the Catalogue of Ships, Agamemnon is
described as the one who leads the most men and is the ἄριστος 'best' (*Iliad* II
580).[38] Agamemnon offers Akhilleus a gift of seven cities on the border of Pylos, which, coupled with other references to Agamemnon's control of Argos,
suggests to van Wees that he is the supreme leader of all Akhaian states.[39] Agamemnon is not a tyrant with absolute power, but he oversees the other leaders
in an arrangement loosely under his auspices, as established at the start of
the poem: Akhilleus calls the assembly (*Iliad* I 54); he, Kalkhas, and Nestor
offer their opinions in addition to those of Agamemnon (*Iliad* I 59–303); and
Akhilleus demonstrates that the authority Agamemnon wields over the other
noblemen is not sufficient to prevent him from withdrawing (*Iliad* I 293–303).
However, although Agamemnon asks advice of other characters, his approval
must be given before any action is taken.[40] No one supersedes Agamemnon;

---

[36] Van Wees 1992:31–36, 103, 282f. On the semantics of *basileus* and *anax*, see pages 176f.
below. Hammer 1997:4 describes Agamemnon's power as based on fear and inheritance.
Pucci 1998:189 points out that Agamemnon's ability to compel obedience is never contested.

[37] Van Wees 1992:37; cf. Sherratt 1990: "The complicated, intensely agnatic structure of royal
inheritance displayed by the Atreid dynasty in the epics seems particularly characteristic of an
expansive 'heroic' society" (93).

[38] Nagy 1979:26–32 discusses the semantics of ἄριστος, only used in reference to Diomedes,
Agamemnon, Ajax, and Akhilleus. On the problems with Agamemnon's entry in the Catalogue,
see Kirk 1985:181 and Page 1959:130–132.

[39] Van Wees 1992:40; *Iliad* XI 108.

[40] In *Iliad* IX, Agamemnon calls the assembly, Diomedes and Nestor speak, and action is only taken
with Agamemnon's assent (*Iliad* IX 9–161). The assembly in *Iliad* X repeats this pattern (*Iliad* X

some characters, Kalkhas, for instance, are afraid of him, and no other kings withdraw with Akhilleus, even though we are told that they initially want to respect the request of Khruses, the priest whom Agamemnon treats with contempt (*Iliad* I 22–23). Carlier concludes that there are three political levels in the poem: the three hundred-odd subsections of the army, which he calls 'boroughs'; the 29 kingdoms that make up the military contingent; and the "Panakhaian community whose supreme leader is Agamemnon."[41]

Although there are many kings at Troy, Agamemnon has responsibility for the army, even if this power is based on accepted rather than demonstrable premises. Not all of his subordinates are happy with his rule, not least Akhilleus, nor is he presented as a flawless or ideal ruler, but his authority over the army remains beyond doubt. After another of his suggestions that the Akhaians flee Troy, Odysseus even wishes Agamemnon were not the leader of the army:

Ἀτρεΐδη, ποῖόν σε ἔπος φύγεν ἕρκος ὀδόντων·
οὐλόμεν' αἴθ' ὤφελλες ἀεικελίου στρατοῦ ἄλλου
σημαίνειν, μηδ' ἄμμιν ἀνασσέμεν, οἷσιν ἄρα Ζεὺς
ἐκ νεότητος ἔδωκε καὶ ἐς γῆρας τολυπεύειν
ἀργαλέους πολέμους, ὄφρα φθιόμεσθα ἕκαστος.
οὕτω δὴ μέμονας Τρώων πόλιν εὐρυάγυιαν
καλλείψειν, ἧς εἵνεκ' ὀϊζύομεν κακὰ πολλά;
σίγα, μή τίς τ' ἄλλος Ἀχαιῶν τοῦτον ἀκούσῃ
μῦθον, ὃν οὔ κεν ἀνήρ γε διὰ στόμα πάμπαν ἄγοιτο,
ὅς τις ἐπίσταιτο ᾗσι φρεσὶν ἄρτια βάζειν
σκηπτοῦχός τ' εἴη, καί οἱ πειθοίατο λαοὶ
τοσσοίδ' ὅσσοισιν σὺ μετ' Ἀργείοισιν ἀνάσσεις·

(*Iliad* XIV 83–94)

...What's this, Son of Atreus, this talk that slips from your clenched
    teeth?
You *are* the disaster. <u>Would to god you commanded another army
    of cowards</u>
<u>instead of ruling us,</u> the men whom Zeus decrees,
from youth to old age, must wind down
our brutal wars until we drop and die, down to the last man.
Are you so eager to bid farewell to the broad streets of Troy,

204–253); Shear 2004:155n594. Donlan 1979:53 stresses the elusive foundation of Agamemnon's power.
[41] Carlier 2006:105.

> Troy that cost our comrades so much grief?
> Quiet—lest someone else of the Akhaians hear this
> speech, which no man should ever let pass his lips,
> <u>no man who has the sense to speak suitably and</u>
> <u>who is a sceptered king, whom so many obey</u>
> <u>as many as you command among the Argives.</u>

Although Odysseus shows contempt for Agamemnon's plan for retreat, he fully acknowledges that it is Agamemnon upon whose word their actions depend. His wish that Agamemnon "commanded" (σημαίνειν) another army, "instead of ruling us" (μὴ δ' ἄμμιν ἀνασσέμεν), and his plea for him to think of the countless fighters he "rules over" (σὺ ἀνάσσεις) make clear the overriding superiority Agamemnon has over the troops, whether he is fit for such rule or not. In addition, Odysseus refers to him as a "sceptered-king" (σκηπτοῦχος), the same phrase used by Nestor to describe Agamemnon when warning Akhilleus not to challenge his superior authority; indeed, the scepter is the object most symbolic of his special, inherited sovereignty.[42] While he does not have absolute control over the Akhaians, Agamemnon does preside over the community created in the encampment outside of Troy. Akhilleus withdraws and even threatens to go home (*Iliad* IX 356–361), but when he or any of the other soldiers are part of the Akhaian army community, they are all at least nominally under Agamemnon's command, as Akhilleus himself recognizes in *Iliad* XIX, which we shall discuss in detail below.

The might with which Agamemnon rules is threatened by Akhilleus' special semi-divine status at the start of the poem: although Akhilleus cannot supplant or remove Agamemnon's control over the Akhaian military, he can influence the gods to thwart Agamemnon's plans. The vulnerability of his authority, in addition to various character foibles, has tarnished Agamemnon's reception by modern critics. Oliver Taplin has proposed on the basis of his character flaws in Homer that, rather than a clear hierarchy, a "centrality" exists based on mutual obligation and the fact that Agamemnon is Menelaos' elder brother.[43] Others have argued that Agamemnon is deliberately portrayed negatively in the poem—in Charles Segal's description, as "the most wantonly cruel of the Greeks."[44] Indeed, if two criteria important for social standing in the heroic community of the *Iliad* are powers of persuasion and reputation, Agamemnon seems neither able to speak persuasively nor is he

---

[42] The adjective is only used elsewhere at *Odyssey* xiv 93; the hereditary passage of Agamemnon's scepter from Zeus through to Thuestes is described at *Iliad* II 100–108.

[43] Taplin 1990:62–69.

[44] Segal 1971:11; see also Whitman 1958:156 and Schadewaldt 1944:4.

the best warrior.[45] The characterization of Agamemnon within the poem does not appear to develop or progress except in the context of the withdrawal of Akhilleus.[46] Nonetheless, Agamemnon is the chief leader, and it is the special character of this leadership that is expressed in his provision of feasts for an exclusive group of nobles and his performances of sacrifice for both this private group and the army as a whole. Richard Seaford describes the power of a Homeric leader as based upon "wealth, prestige, and military prowess, an informal authority over the other like-named chiefs (*basileis*), and on his ability to act as a redistributor," components that must be actively sustained in order for the leader to maintain his power base, even if this power base is inherited and socially accepted.[47] Sacrifice, along with feasting, is an important component of this constant reaffirmation of his might, prestige, and wealth through redistribution.

Agamemnon is advised by a sort of King's privy council, usually described as *gerontes* 'elders', comprised of Lokrian Ajax, Telamonian Ajax, Diomedes, Idomeneus, Nestor, Menelaos, Odysseus, and Meges.[48] As the chief king, Agamemnon is obligated to provide food and drink for his councilors, as expressed by Nestor:

Ἀτρεΐδη, σὺ μὲν ἄρχε· σὺ γὰρ βασιλεύτατός ἐσσι.
δαίνυ δαῖτα γέρουσιν· ἔοικέ τοι, οὔ τοι ἀεικές.
πλεῖαί τοι οἴνου κλισίαι, τὸν νῆες Ἀχαιῶν
ἠμάτιαι Θρήκηθεν ἐπ᾽ εὐρέα πόντον ἄγουσι·
πᾶσά τοί ἐσθ᾽ ὑποδεξίη, πολέεσσι δ᾽ ἀνάσσεις.

(*Iliad* IX 69–73)

Then Atreides, lead the way—you are the most noble—
spread out a feast for all your councilors. That is your duty, a
        service that becomes you.
Your shelters overflow with the wine Akhaian ships
bring in from Thrace, daily, down the sea's broad back.

---

[45] Taplin 1990:72, 75; on the battles, see Fenik 1968:15, 84. Martin 1989:59–60 discusses Agamemnon's inability to enact a *muthos* before the Akhaians.

[46] Despite his frequent occurrences in the poem, his situation does not change (Beck 2005:205). Redfield 1975:12–15 discusses the characterization of Agamemnon as a response to Akhilleus.

[47] Seaford 1994:22. We shall return to the active promotion of these values at pages 164f. below. For a discussion of Agamemnon's rule as inherited, van Wees 1992:32 and Appendix 3; Hammer 2002:84, *contra* Geddes 1984:36 and Quiller 1981:115–118. Launderville 2003:84 notes that Odysseus' royal authority in Ithaka is not a sufficient basis for power without the wealth that the suitors covet.

[48] The council is enumerated twice, including Meges only in the latter (*Iliad* II 405–408 and X 108–110); Carlier 2006:103–104.

Grand hospitality is yours, you rule so many men.

Nestor emphasizes that Agamemnon has a special authority, "you are the most noble" (σὺ γὰρ βασιλεύτατός ἐσσι), and he associates this leadership with Agamemnon's superior wealth, here described as an outcome of his chief rule. As we will see, this special and distinctive role as provider requires Agamemnon also to be the *Opferherr*, sometimes providing food, as in *Iliad* II and VII, while at other times providing sacrificial animals and performing a ceremonial role as the spokesperson, on behalf of the army, to the gods, as in *Iliad* III and XIX. Trojan social interactions provide a marked contrast to the primary narrator's descriptions of the Akhaian councilors and army: Hektor does not provide dinner for his councilors and seems to pay his allies, whereas no payment is mentioned in connection with Agamemnon.[49]

Owing partly to Agamemnon's shortcomings and partly to the tenuous nature of leadership in Homeric society, he must constantly identify and define his authority. Along these lines, Norman Austin concludes, "Among the kings there is one acknowledged superior, but he is not the superior in either fighting or planning; his superior authority is merely accepted."[50] The most conspicuous display of Agamemnon's authority can be found in his performance of animal sacrifice. Sacrificial ritual plays a crucial role in all ancient Greek political systems. Detienne, in reference to the Classical *polis*, states that "political power cannot be exercised without sacrifice."[51] As a necessarily group action, sacrifice brings together members of the community, but it distinguishes the sacrificer. As a highly visible action, sacrifice provides a clear, unassailable demonstration of Agamemnon's dominance over the other kings, which is questionable in areas of leadership where other heroes seem better equipped. Accordingly, Agamemnon's assertion of authority in the primary narrative-text of the *Iliad* is reflected by a clear pattern of sacrificial practice. As demonstrated in Chapter Two, all enacted sacrifices are performed or ordered by Agamemnon.

Sacrificial animals in antiquity would have been expensive and would function not only on the religious/cultic level of influencing the gods favorably toward the group but also practically, when the sacrifice was followed by a

---

[49] Van Wees 1992:40; the Trojan payment of allies is implied at *Iliad* XVIII 288–292.

[50] Austin 1975:109. It is important to distinguish between authority and power, as does Hammer 2002:85; Agamemnon's authority remains intact, but the withdrawal of Akhilleus weakens his power.

[51] Detienne 1989:3. Compare the anthropological studies summarized in Bourdillon 1980, in which sacrifice is recognized as a political tool in other cultures, such as the human sacrifices in traditional Benin that enhance the king's power or the Swazi royal rituals involving confiscation of oxen from the people.

shared feast, as provisions for meals. The important value of sacrificial victims in the Homeric world is demonstrated in the simile comparing the race for Hektor's life to races for prizes of sacrificial victims (*Iliad* XXII 159–160). I have proposed that Agamemnon's control over the distribution of food, sometimes in sacrificial contexts, is an important symbol of his hegemony; however, a question remains concerning the origin of these resources. Van Wees suggests that Agamemnon acts as a redistributor for goods contributed by the members of his community.[52] He points, for example, to Menelaos' exhortation for the troops to protect the body of Patroklos in *Iliad* XVII, as well as to his scolding them in reference to their wine drinking:

ὦ φίλοι Ἀργείων ἡγήτορες ἠδὲ μέδοντες,
οἵ τε παρ' Ἀτρεΐδης, Ἀγαμέμνονι καὶ Μενελάῳ,
δήμια πίνουσιν καὶ σημαίνουσιν ἕκαστος
λαοῖς·

(Iliad XVII 248–251)

Friends—Lords of the Argives, O my captains,
all who join the Sons of Atreus, Agamemnon and Menelaos
who drink wine at the king's expense (*dêmia*) and hold command
of your own troops,

At this critical moment in the poem, Menelaos encourages the men by reminding them of an obligation to Agamemnon in the context of feasting. Lokrian Ajax and Idomeneus, two of the councilors summoned by Agamemnon to the sacrificial feast in *Iliad* II, and Idomeneus' companion Meriones are the first three to respond to Menelaos' call (*Iliad* XVII 256–259). This exhortation recalls feasts for which Agamemnon seems to have provided the provisions. A similar emphasis structures Agamemnon's rebuke that Menestheus and Odysseus are "the first to hear the call of my *dais*, whenever we Akhaians prepare the *dais* for the councilors" (πρώτω γὰρ καὶ δαιτὸς ἀκουάζεσθον ἐμεῖο, ὁππότε δαῖτα γέρουσιν ἐφοπλίζωμεν Ἀχαιοί, *Iliad* IV 343-344); the emphasis here is on the possessive, "my feast." In all of the feast scenes in the poem, descriptions of Agamemnon as providing for or hosting meals and sacrificial feasts are specifically in reference to the councilors, as implied in Menelaos' exhortation.

Agamemnon does not act as a redistributor for the entire army. When he commands the army to feast in *Iliad* II, they scatter off to their huts where they are described as praying, sacrificing, and eating. Agamemnon simultane-

---

[52] Van Wees 1992:32.

ously hosts a sacrificial feast in his quarters for the councilors (*Iliad* II 402). After the duel in *Iliad* VII, we find a similar distinction between the description of the whole army feasting and Agamemnon's private sacrificial dinner. The social hierarchy has a "trickle-down" effect: Agamemnon provides for the councilors, and, although the exact origin of these provisions is elided—part of the Homeric avoidance of mundane practicalities in food preparation—his prominence as the *Opferherr* suggests that he not only provide the provisions but also control their distribution. He authorizes the hecatombs in *Iliad* I and appoints a delegate to lead the second offering to Khruse. Agamemnon provides commensal sacrifices for the elite group of councilors in *Iliad* II and VII, who might then be expected to provide for their own men, just as he commands the leaders of the army, who are then expected to command their own troops, as in Menelaos' speech above. However, for the oath sacrifices in *Iliad* III and XIX performed on behalf of the army, Agamemnon summons Talthubios to fetch the victims, which we may assume he provides from the same stock as the other meals. This type of royal largesse, which Agamemnon distributes appropriately, can be seen as a contrast to his distribution of booty: the men initially give Briseis to Akhilleus (*Iliad* I 162), but Agamemnon exhorts them to give him another prize (*Iliad* I 135). His quarrel with Akhilleus begins when he takes away prizes that have been previously distributed. Even Akhilleus tells Agamemnon that, by reversing the principles of redistribution, he undermines his own authority (*Iliad* I 150–151).[53]

Though Agamemnon uses sacrifice to demonstrate his supreme authority, its performance does not establish the special relationship with Zeus that would further enhance his standing with the army; in fact, as we have seen in Chapter Three, the discussion of sacrifice throughout the poem undermines the notion that reciprocity with the gods makes a person more powerful or likely to succeed. The *Iliad* does not present Zeus as arbiter of Agamemnon's sacrificial authority, the kind of divine sanction alluded to in the description of his inherited scepter. Nestor, often the spokesman in promotion of Agamemnon's rule, attributes Agamemnon's authority over the army to Zeus, via the scepter:

> Ἀτρεΐδη κύδιστε, ἄναξ ἀνδρῶν Ἀγάμεμνον,
> ἐν σοὶ μὲν λήξω, σέο δ' ἄρξομαι, οὕνεκα πολλῶν
> λαῶν ἐσσι ἄναξ καί τοι Ζεὺς ἐγγυάλιξε
> σκῆπτρόν τ' ἠδὲ θέμιστας, ἵνα σφίσι βουλεύῃσθα.

---

[53] Muellner 1996:106.

(*Iliad* IX 96–99)

Most glorious son of Atreus, lord of men Agamemnon,
with you I will end, with you I will begin, since
you are king over many warriors and Zeus has placed in your
     hands
the scepter and time-honored laws, so you will advise them well.

Although Nestor alludes to the divine sanction behind Agamemnon's rule, he defines this rule in terms of the number of men Agamemnon controls, as well as by the scepter and laws overseen by Zeus. The phraseology "beginning and ending with you" is very similar to that found in the Homeric *Hymns* for addressing gods, which suggests to Robert Mondi that Agamemnon enjoyed a "divine kingship."[54] The depiction of Agamemnon's ritual authority is important in synchronizing the councilors during Akhilleus' withdrawal, but a personal relationship with Zeus is not clearly established in this regard, particularly in comparison to the god's oft-expressed gratitude for Trojan sacrifices. The *Iliad* focuses not on Zeus' role in establishing Agamemnon's authority, but on Agamemnon's wealth and power.[55] The primary narrator depicts Agamemnon as the sole distributor of sacrificial meat, which is a highly valued symbol of honor, and therefore as the community spokesperson to the gods, but it does so without characterizing any special influence over the gods. Though Agamemnon's power over men is linked to the king of the gods at critical junctures (*Iliad* I 175, XIX 87–144), this does not extend to a special relationship with or influence over divinities, which remains the unique privilege of Akhilleus.

4.2 Ritual Authority and Exclusion

Agamemnon's special authority in the poem is intensified by the challenge presented by Akhilleus' defiance. This challenge arises from the tension between status-based *timê*, which must be recreated and reaffirmed—typically through persuasive speech—and honor acquired through performance-based

---

[54] Mondi 1980:206. Cf. Burkert's description of the godlike role taken on by priests in Greek ritual (1985:97). Frazer 1911:344–367 derives sacrifice from the symbolic killing of a divine king: originally, a priest-king would be sacrificed on behalf of the community to atone for a transgression, to avert a plague, etc.

[55] Van Wees 1992:276f. discusses the symbolism of the scepter in the context of passing judgement, see Carlier 1984:193, 202–203; however, Launderville 2003:41–42, 74 observes that it is Odysseus, not Agamemnon, who effectively uses the scepter to restrain the Akhaians from flight (*Iliad* II 186ff.).

judgments.[56] A social standing based on ability, which must be established on the honor or deference given to a hero because of a certain skill, stands in contrast to the inherited status-based prestige possessed by the king, although an individual may merit both types of honor. For example, Nestor's acknowledged talent in speechmaking persuades others to listen to him, an example of performance-based judgment, while he has a separately identifiable status-based *timê* as king of Pylos and leader of a military contingent at Troy. *Timê* is the essential concept for a hierarchical society in which individuals are not equal, but are identified in terms of perceived rank, based on inherited status, performance, or a combination of the two.[57] On the one hand, Agamemnon is the chief king on the basis of his inherited status. On the other, Akhilleus can challenge Agamemnon's authority on the basis of his own ability: his military prowess is ultimately the key to Greek victory.

Dean Hammer, drawing on the work of Victor Turner, creates a definition of Homeric society as a "political field" for "social drama."[58] 'Political field' is a very useful phrase in describing not a structure or function, but an activity created by the interactions of the characters within structures or functions. It is the discussions of characters in the political field that raise questions of community organization, identity, relationships, and value systems. Hammer defines 'social drama' as "a sequence of social interactions of a conflictive, competitive, or agonistic type."[59] Sacrifice is one such social interaction, a representation of status that can take on an agonistic aura when used to maintain a leader's authority in times of crisis. Walter Burkert has described the importance of ritual as a tool for overcoming anxiety:

> [Ritual] signals and creates situations of anxiety in order to overcome them, it leads from the primal fear of being abandoned to the establishment of solidarity and the reinforcement of status, and in this way it helps to overcome real situations of crisis by substituting diverted activity for the apathy which remains transfixed in reality.[60]

Tension created by the quarrel between the men and their leader results in a constant need for Agamemnon to recreate and reassert his leadership, his inherited *timê*.[61] From the start of the poem, the interplay between enacted

---

[56] Martin 1989:97.
[57] Nagy 1979:72–73, 118, 149; See also Muellner 1996:28–29, 50.
[58] Hammer 2002:12; Turner 1988:33.
[59] Hammer 2002:14.
[60] Burkert 1985:54–55.
[61] Martin 1989:97. In contrast, Donlan 1979:55 believes that the collectivity of a group comprised of equals does not require the chief leader to re-establish his authority.

and embedded sacrifices emphasizes Agamemnon's authority. The quarrel begins and ends with sacrifice: Kalkhas' recommendation that Khruseis be returned with a propitiatory sacrifice initiates the quarrel; the oath sacrifice in *Iliad* XIX, the final enacted sacrifice, reunites Akhilleus with the army. Akhilleus and Agamemnon are both thematically linked to sacrifice, but in very different ways: Akhilleus through his deviation from normal ritual practice and Agamemnon through his manipulation and control of these same rituals. The theme of Agamemnon's ritual authority is established by the repeated emphasis on his role as sacrificer, in addition to the placement of sacrificial scenes within the primary narrative. When Akhilleus challenges Agamemnon by withdrawing from the army community, the embedded and enacted sacrifices provide a framework for his withdrawal. Adam Parry points out that, rather than being explicitly stated, Akhilleus' individuality and isolation are conveyed on numerous levels of diction and characterization.[62] Sacrifice is an important part of this conveyance: the seven enacted sacrifices directly relate Agamemnon's ritual authority to the central action—Akhilleus' anger.[63]

The first Assembly scene in *Iliad* I establishes the 'political field' through the introduction of the main characters, their relationships to one another within their society, and the role played by *timê* in social relationships. Agamemnon's *timê* is most obviously represented by his ability to command others because of his economic control over them. It is in this context that we get the first sacrifices of the epic, which are as much a part of Agamemnon's domination as the unequivocal prizes he claims from the booty (*Iliad* I 163–168).[64] A close examination of the sacrificial framework surrounding Akhilleus' withdrawal will enable us to appreciate fully the thematic connection between sacrifice and the quarrel, on both the macro-level of the narrative ordering of events and on the micro-level of diction.

The events of *Iliad* I are set out below, with the scenes involving sacrifice underlined to demonstrate the function of this ritual in the evolution of the quarrel. To summarize briefly, Agamemnon must authorize a sacrifice to appease Apollo and return Khruseis to her father. This decision, suggested first by Kalkhas and then supported by Akhilleus, leads to the quarrel between Agamemnon and Akhilleus. The primary narrator describes Odysseus boarding

---

[62] A. Parry 1956:6.

[63] Compare the observation in Muir 1981: "Although civic rituals often served the ruler's interests they were not just propaganda and did not pass messages in only one direction" (5). I differ from Kitts, who proposes that commensal sacrifices, which she equates with other feasts, are presented as a respite from tension (2002:31, 2005:14); she refers to the "commensal sacrifices" in *Iliad* I, IX, and XXIV at 1999:44 and 2002:28–30.

[64] Seaford 2004:40 observes that animal sacrifice and booty are equivalent forms of redistribution.

165

Table I. An Outline of Sacrifice in *Iliad* I

Invocation to the Muse, summary of theme   (1–7)
Khruses' request of Agamemnon   (8–32)
   Khruses' request of Apollo   (33–42)
Apollo smites the Akhaians   (43–52)
[Assembly, 53–305]
   Kalkhas advises sacrifice and the return of Khruseis   (53–120)
Quarrel begins   (121–139)
   Agamemnon decides to send an embassy for the sacrifice   (140–147)
Quarrel Resumes   (148–305)
Akhilleus goes to his huts   (306–307)
   Agamemnon loads and launches the ship for Khruse   (308–311)
   Agamemnon commands the men to sacrifice   (312–317)
Briseis taken from Akhilleus   (318–356)
Akhilleus and Thetis   (357–430a)
   Sacrifice at Khruse   (430b–474)
Return to Akhaian camp   (475–487)
Akhilleus stays apart   (488–492)
Events on Olympus   (493–611)

and Agamemnon launching the ship for the sacrifice to Apollo. Then Akhilleus goes to his huts, but, rather than immediately depicting the conversation he has with his mother, the narrative describes the disembarkation of the embassy, immediately followed by the purificatory sacrifice led by Agamemnon. The seizure of Briseis and Akhilleus' conversation with Thetis follow; then the narrative shifts to the sacrifice at Khruse, before returning to the movements of Thetis and her supplication of Zeus. The primary focuses of *Iliad* I, the alienation of Akhilleus and the threat to Agamemnon's supremacy, are thus encircled with the performance of this sacrifice.

Homeric society is reinforced through the performance of sacrifice, a display of the social cohesion between its performer and the other participants. It is fitting that *Iliad* I is more concerned with sacrifice than any other part of the poem, since it serves as an introduction to the value and belief systems that structure the Homeric world.[65] With every major event followed

[65] Latacz 2002:120f. observes that this separate presentation of simultaneous events (the sacrifice and Akhilleus' conversation with Thetis) amplifies the presentation of the quarrel between Akhilleus and Agamemnon. Stanley 1993:39 has analyzed the structure of *Iliad* I as an interlocking series of events relating to wrath and divine will (*boulê*).

by a reference to or performance of sacrifice, the enacted and embedded sacrifices provide a framework for Akhilleus' wrath, which is made vivid by the insertion of Akhilleus' conversation with Thetis between the preparation for the sacrifice on Khruse (and Agamemnon's purificatory sacrifice) and its performance. This narrative structure illustrates the impact of Akhilleus' isolation from the Akhaian community via his abstention from sacrifices in which all other Akhaians participate. Further, his appeal to Thetis is presented with many elements typical of prayers to gods, an ominous parallel to the simultaneous Akhaian prayer to Apollo.[66] It also highlights Akhilleus' semi-divine status in contrast to the Akhaian sacrifices: his mother's influence over Zeus, whose promise to her will guide the Trojans to victory until the death of Patroklos in *Iliad* XVI, is starkly juxtaposed against Agamemnon's sacrifices.

The social drama of *Iliad* I is initiated by Agamemnon's domineering behavior toward the priest Khruses. The old priest responds to Agamemnon's denial of his request, the leader's first authoritative act in the poem, by retreating to the seashore and praying to Apollo, which begins the plague that can only be stopped by the return of Khruseis and a sacrifice.[67] Khruses' disagreement with Agamemnon leads to the wrath of Apollo, which in turn leads to the quarrel between Agamemnon and Akhilleus and the wrath of Akhilleus. Lord summarizes the overriding thematic pattern thus: "The wrath of Khruses-Apollo caused the wrath of Agamemnon, which caused the wrath of Akhilleus-Thetis-Zeus, the main tale of the *Iliad*."[68] To Lord's summary may be added the role of the seer Kalkhas, whose revelation of Apollo's wrath leads to the quarrel.[69] The first references to sacrifice in the poem, in Khruses' prayer and then the discussion in the assembly scene leading up to Agamemnon's instructions for sacrifice, result from Agamemnon's refusal to acknowledge the religious authority of a priest and a seer. This refusal is an expression of Agamemnon's own religious authority through ritual domi-

---

[66] πολλὰ δὲ μητρὶ φίλῃ ἠρήσατο χεῖρας ὀρεγνύς (*Iliad* I 350); Latacz 2002:127; Morrison 1991. There are verbal echoes between Khruses' prayer on the seashore to Apollo and Akhilleus' address on the seashore to Thetis, first noticed by Havelock 1978:14.

[67] On the *loimos*, which kills both men and animals, see Pulleyn 2000:138 and Kirk 1985:58.

[68] Lord 1960:188, who cites Lévi-Strauss 1955:433 on the comparison of patterns. Wilson 2002:40–53 discusses the exchange between Agamemnon and Khruses in terms of the Homeric value system and the thematic correspondences between this encounter, the encounter between Akhilleus and Agamemnon, and that between Akhilleus and Priam.

[69] Kalkhas' role in *Iliad* I has been interpreted by Latacz 1996:95 as a deliberate counterweight to the authority of Agamemnon and as a relic of a longer account of fighting between the two men.

nance. His contempt for priests creates anticipation for the ritual acts that he will himself orchestrate.[70]

Agamemnon's treatment of Khruses, his first action in the *Iliad*, is so brutish that Aristarkhos athetized *Iliad* I 29–31, believing the scene to be inappropriate to the leader's character.[71] Khruses' special status as a priest is clearly described (*Iliad* I 14–15), and he is signified by a golden staff with ribbons, which is the only reference to priestly costume in the poem. This special status is explicitly dismissed by Agamemnon, who tells Khruses that the staff and ribbons of Apollo will not protect him (*Iliad* I 28–29).[72] Agamemnon's refusal to recognize priestly status is further reinforced by his addressing of Khruses as an old man (γέρον, *Iliad* I 26), whereas the other Akhaians refer to him as a priest (ἱερεύς, *Iliad* I 23). This behavior is not only irreverent, but it clearly contradicts the unanimous view of the troops, who want the priest's wish to be respected (*Iliad* I 22–23).[73] When he initiates the plague, Khruses reminds Apollo of past sacrifices and honors in order to persuade the god to help. As discussed above, Simon Pulleyn has observed that this type of prayer is most often spoken in lieu of sacrifice.[74] We may assume that Khruses cannot sacrifice on the shore outside of the Akhaian camps, but one wonders why he does not return to the sanctuary he "has roofed for Apollo" (ἐπὶ νηὸν ἔρεψα, *Iliad* I 39) in order to make his request with an accompanying sacrifice. Sacrifice is instead immediately associated with Agamemnon's authority. Rather than an air of general impiety, Agamemnon's attitude reflects his special status as sacrificer and anticipates his dominance as *Opferherr*. We next see Khruses at Khruse, but his performance here as *Opferherr* is undermined by Odysseus' initial speech, specifying that Agamemnon has sent this embassy and provided the sacrificial victims (*Iliad* I 442–445). The priests who interact

---

[70] Mackie 1996:33 notes that Trojan Poludamas does not fare much better at the hands of Hektor at *Iliad* XII 230–250. Compare the reverence expressed toward the priest Maron by Odysseus (*Odyssey* ix 197–201).

[71] Scholium A *ad Iliad* I 29–31; cf. Kirk 1985:56; Bassett 1938:48–49; Erbse 1969 *ad loc*. On the scene in general, Muellner 1996:98–99. Scully 1986:140 argues that Agamemnon has no regard for "religiously sanctified customs of heroic society," which forces Akhilleus to seek justice from a higher power—the gods. Kitts 2005:29 contrasts the "ritual savvy" of Nestor, Akhilleus, and Odysseus with Agamemnon's "undisguised and obtuse" attempts.

[72] Bassett 1938:48–49; Edwards 1980:6; and Scully 1986:139 think that the emphasis on Khruses' priestly garb highlights Agamemnon's folly in rejecting him.

[73] On the value system in operation here, see Wilson 2002:43, who observes that the reaction of the Akhaians in response to Agamemnon's behavior is not a consequence of the violation of religious sanctions or compensation, but a form of social pressure that anticipates the support for Khruses that Apollo will provide.

[74] Pulleyn 2000:133; 1997:16–39; see pages 83f. above.

with Agamemnon are systematically given marginalized, subservient roles. Accordingly, when Agamemnon orders the sacrifice to appease Apollo and accompany the return of Khruseis, he wants a "council-bearing" man to go, but does not think of appointing Kalkhas or another religious expert.[75]

The other notable features of Khruses' interaction with Agamemnon are the brevity of this supplication scene in comparison to the others in the *Iliad* and its lack of many of the distinguishing characteristics of Homeric supplication, particularly when compared to the embassies to Akhilleus in *Iliad* IX and XXIV.[76] Mark Edwards attributes the lack of detail in Khruses' supplication to a desire for swiftness and a need to demonstrate Agamemnon's distance from the army, emphasized by the focus on the Akhaians' reaction to Khruses rather than on that of Agamemnon himself.[77] Certainly, the initiation of the plague is brief when compared to its resolution by way of the sacrifice at Khruse. That the focus here remains on the sacrifice, rather than the meeting between the priest and Odysseus or even the return of Khruses' daughter, underscores the crucial difference between these two events: the intervening withdrawal of Akhilleus.

Agamemnon's insulting behavior toward Khruses leads to the plague, which instigates Kalkhas' recommendation that Khruseis be returned with an accompanying sacrifice. Although it was Kalkhas who initially suggested the sacrifice to Apollo (*Iliad* I 53–100), it is ultimately Agamemnon who *orders* the sacrifice (*Iliad* I 140–147), an action directly tied to his claim on another man's prize, which causes Akhilleus to withdraw. Agamemnon's response to Kalkhas' suggestion clarifies his own ritual authority in the context of his supremacy over Akhilleus:

> ἀλλ' εἰ μὲν δώσουσι γέρας μεγάθυμοι Ἀχαιοί,
> ἄρσαντες κατὰ θυμόν, ὅπως ἀντάξιον ἔσται·
> εἰ δέ κε μὴ δώωσιν, ἐγὼ δέ κεν αὐτὸς ἕλωμαι
> ἢ τεὸν ἢ Αἴαντος ἰὼν γέρας, ἢ Ὀδυσῆος

---

[75] It is interesting to compare Peirce's and Gebauer's work on the iconography of sacrifice, as they have pointed out that often identifications of "priests" in vase painting are more probably members of the group who have been depicted with a special significance, such as we might expect of the sacrificer. These individuals are clearly meant to be distinguished from the group, but do not have any of the recognizable symbols usually found with "priests" (Peirce 1993:231; Gebauer 2002:471–478).

[76] Discussed by Edwards 1980:4–6 and Wilson 2002:42. Kakrides 1971:125 has a more optimistic interpretation of Khruses' approach as "gentle." On Homeric supplication in general, see Thornton 1984. Kirk 1985:55 details the highly formulaic language of Khruses' speech, which further links this scene with other supplications in Homer.

[77] Edwards 1980:6.

ἄξω ἑλών· ὃ δέ κεν κεχολώσεται ὅν κεν ἵκωμαι.
ἀλλ' ἤτοι μὲν ταῦτα μεταφρασόμεσθα καὶ αὖτις,
νῦν δ' ἄγε νῆα μέλαιναν ἐρύσσομεν εἰς ἅλα δῖαν,
ἐν δ' ἐρέτας ἐπιτηδὲς ἀγείρομεν, ἐς δ' ἑκατόμβην
θείομεν, ἂν δ' αὐτὴν Χρυσηΐδα καλλιπάρῃον
βήσομεν· εἷς δέ τις ἀρχὸς ἀνὴρ βουληφόρος ἔστω,
ἢ Αἴας ἢ Ἰδομενεὺς ἢ δῖος Ὀδυσσεὺς
ἠὲ σύ, Πηλεΐδη, πάντων ἐκπαγλότατ' ἀνδρῶν,
ὄφρ' ἡμῖν ἑκάεργον ἱλάσσεαι ἱερὰ ῥέξας.

(Iliad I 135–147)

But if our generous Argives will give me a prize,
a match for my desires, equal to what I've lost, well and good.
But if they give me nothing, I will take a prize myself—
either your own, or Ajax's or Odysseus' prize—
I'll commandeer her myself, and let that man I go to visit choke
      with rage!
Enough. We'll deal with all this later, in due time.
Now come, let's haul a black ship down to the bright sea,
gather a decent number of oarsmen along her locks and put
      aboard a hecatomb,
and Khruseis herself, in all her beauty...
we embark her too. Let one of the leading men take command,
either Ajax, or Idomeneus, or trusty Odysseus,
or you, Akhilleus—the most violent man alive—
so, having performed sacrifice for us, you may appease the
      Far-Shooter.

Agamemnon links his control over Akhilleus to his sacrificial authority with a tripartite command outlining how he will take the *geras* of his choosing, his instructions for the preparation of the hecatomb, and the appointment of an ἀρχὸς ἀνήρ 'leading man' to escort it. This speech demonstrates that only Agamemnon can order the sacrifice to be performed, just as only he can decide to give back Khruseis. It is also framed with threats: to take the prize of Akhilleus, Ajax, or Odysseus, and to appoint Ajax, Idomeneus, Odysseus, or Akhilleus to take the hecatomb. In both threats Agamemnon emphasizes Akhilleus, making him the first potential victim of greed and designating an entire verse to the possibility that he will be forced to make amends with Khruses and Apollo (ἠὲ σὺ Πηλεΐδη, πάντων ἐκπαγλότατ' ἀνδρῶν, *Iliad* I 146).

Ἐκπαγλότατος 'most violent man' is a rare word in the poem, used again only by Iris when rousing Akhilleus to protect the body of Patroklos and by Akhilleus when vaunting over the corpse of Iphition (*Iliad* XVIII 170, XX 389). The impact of the word in Iris' speech resonates with Agamemnon's description of Akhilleus as the possible envoy for the sacrifice: his refusal to fight, provoked by Agamemnon in this speech, will cause the deaths of many Akhaians, and his wrath over the death of Patroklos will cause the deaths of many Trojans. Akhilleus is mentioned by Agamemnon first when it comes to the danger of losing of his *geras* ("your own, or Ajax's or Odysseus' prize," I 138) and last when it comes to the duty of leading the embassy to Khruse ("Ajax, Idomeneus, trusty Odysseus, or you, Akhilleus," I 145–146), thereby creating a ring that links Akhilleus, the removal of the *geras,* and the sacrificial embassy.

It is Agamemnon's speech authorizing both the removal of *geras* and the sacrificial embassy that sets the 'quarrel' with Akhilleus in motion. Akhilleus focuses only on the issue of *geras* and his perception of the imbalance between workload and recognized honor from his peers. His reaction provokes Agamemnon to narrow his threat down to the substitution of Briseis directly for Khruseis. The quarrel continues, as outlined above, until the Assembly is disbanded and Akhilleus withdraws. His departure to his hut is directly followed by the disembarkation of the sacrificial embassy:

> Πηλεΐδης μὲν ἐπὶ κλισίας καὶ νῆας ἐΐσας
> ἤϊε σύν τε Μενοιτιάδῃ καὶ οἷς ἑτάροισιν·
> Ἀτρεΐδης δ' ἄρα νῆα θοὴν ἅλαδὲ προέρυσσεν,
> ἐν δ' ἐρέτας ἔκρινεν ἐείκοσιν, ἐς δ' ἑκατόμβην
> βῆσε θεῷ, ἀνὰ δὲ Χρυσηΐδα καλλιπάρῃον
> εἶσεν ἄγων· ἐν δ' ἀρχὸς ἔβη πολύμητις Ὀδυσσεύς.

(*Iliad* I 306–311)

> The son of Peleus strode off to his trim ships and shelters
> together with the son of Menoitios and their comrades;
> and Agamemnon had a vessel hauled down to the sea,
> he picked out twenty oarsmen to man her locks,
> put aboard the hecatomb for the god and led Khruseis in all her
>   beauty
> amidships. Versatile Odysseus took the helm as captain.

If, following the work of Egbert Bakker, we consider Homeric poetry as a stylized representation of spoken discourse, then the diction supports the thematic structure of events, here reinforcing the association between Akhilleus' wrath and Agamemnon's performance of sacrifice.[78] Regarding the particles found at the beginning of most Greek sentences, Bakker has observed that "the Greek language provides a number of particles and other devices that enable speakers to let their listeners keep track of the flow of discourse in which they find themselves, by inviting them to make a step, or look forward, jointly with the speaker."[79] In the context of performance poetry, the particles μέν/δέ focus the attention of the audience on the second action, thereby giving the latter part of the clause an increased emphasis.[80] In the above passage, Akhilleus' movement toward his camp is marked as the first part of the action (Πηλεΐδης μέν), which is concluded with the phrase Ἀτρεΐδης δέ, directly linking Agamemnon's preparations to Akhilleus' withdrawal. We may also note the accumulation of third person singular verbs (ἔκρινεν 'he picked out', ἐς βῆσε 'he put aboard', εἷσεν 'he led') referring to Agamemnon's individual authority in orchestrating the arrangements for the sacrifice in Khruse. Agamemnon delegates authority for this sacrifice, just as he does with the embassy for Briseis; he is not prepared at this point to take personal responsibility for his mistakes. Odysseus acts as Agamemnon's 'second in command' in ritual contexts, also standing by his side in the oath sacrifice (*Iliad* III 267-268), and he is Agamemnon's delegate again as part of the apologetic embassy to Akhilleus (*Iliad* IX 169).

Following the verse that describes Odysseus boarding the ship as the 'leading captain', another μέν/δέ clause links the embarkation of the ship with Agamemnon's instructions for the purification of the army, the first enacted sacrifice of the poem:

> Οἱ μὲν ἔπειτ' ἀναβάντες ἐπέπλεον ὑγρὰ κέλευθα,
> λαοὺς δ' Ἀτρεΐδης ἀπολυμαίνεσθαι ἄνωγεν·
> οἱ δ' ἀπελυμαίνοντο καὶ εἰς ἅλα λύματα βάλλον,
> ἔρδον δ' Ἀπόλλωνι τεληέσσας ἑκατόμβας

---

[78] Bakker, who agrees with Lord's model for oral dictation in the transmission of the text to a written medium, persuasively argues against the imposition on Homeric poetry of a modern dichotomy between writing and speaking: "…writing in the sense of composition was a form of speaking…. The poet actually produced every sound of which the poem consists and his thought processes, and hence the presentation and structure of his discourse, were not in any way governed by writing in our conceptional sense" (1997:26).

[79] Bakker 1997:61. He explains the English translation of δέ as 'and' (51); μέν, as an indication of something more important that will follow, in most cases cannot be translated into English. He also observes the different connotations of these particles as marking contrasts in Attic texts (81).

[80] Bakker 1997:62–71, 82.

ταύρων ἠδ' αἰγῶν παρὰ θῖν' ἁλὸς ἀτρυγέτοιο·
κνίση δ' οὐρανὸν ἷκεν ἑλισσομένη περὶ καπνῷ.

(*Iliad* I 312–317)

The party launched out on the sea's foaming lanes
<u>and</u> the son of Atreus told his troops to purify themselves.
They purified themselves and threw the filth in the surf
and sacrificed to Apollo perfect hecatombs
of bulls and goats along the beaten shore of the fallow barren sea
and savory smoke went swirling up the skies.

The first sacrifice expresses the theme of his special ritual authority with a μέν clause describing the men's procession to the place of sacrifice, the shore, *"and"* the son of Atreus instructing the men to purify themselves (ἄνωγεν, *Iliad* I 313); the anticipated δέ emphasizes his name (<u>δ'</u> Ἀτρεΐδης). This purificatory sacrifice is then directly followed by the removal of Briseis from Akhilleus and his conversation with Thetis, an interruption in the linear progression of the narrative, which resumes when the ship arrives at Khruse. So the seizure of Briseis stands in the middle of two enacted sacrifices—one a hecatomb organized and dispatched by Agamemnon to Khruse, the other a purificatory sacrifice performed at his orders. The activities of the men in the purificatory sacrifice are summarized, before the intentions of Agamemnon are made known: "So the men were engaged throughout the camp. But Agamemnon would not stop the quarrel, the first threat he hurled at Akhilleus" (ὣς οἱ μὲν τὰ πένοντο κατὰ στρατόν· οὐδ' Ἀγαμέμνων / λῆγ' ἔριδος, τὴν πρῶτον ἐπηπείλησ' Ἀχιλῆϊ, *Iliad* I 318–319). Agamemnon sends the heralds to fetch Briseis, and Akhilleus then retreats to the shore. Just after one group of his mortal counterparts attempts to influence the gods through sacrifice, and immediately before another sacrifice to Apollo, the narrative structure ties in the isolated Akhilleus' own dissident method of communication with divinities: the direct summoning of his mother to act on his behalf. After the scene between Akhilleus and Thetis (*Iliad* I 348–430), the progression of the hecatomb to Khruse resumes, redirected by way of a combination of the conjunction αὐτὰρ 'but' and Odysseus' name at the end of the verse:

ὣς ἄρα φωνήσασ' ἀπεβήσετο, τὸν δὲ λίπ' αὐτοῦ
χωόμενον κατὰ θυμὸν ἐϋζώνοιο γυναικός,
τήν ῥα βίῃ ἀέκοντος ἀπηύρων· αὐτὰρ Ὀδυσσεὺς
ἐς Χρύσην ἵκανεν ἄγων ἱερὴν ἑκατόμβην.

(*Iliad* I 428–431)

> So saying she went away and left [Akhilleus] there, alone,
> his heart inflamed for the sashed and lovely girl
> they'd wrenched away from him against his will. But Odysseus
> drew in close to Khruse, leading a holy hecatomb.

The combination of Odysseus' name and the conjunction, Αὐτὰρ ᾿Οδυσσεύς 'but Odysseus', alerts the audience that a prior action has been resumed: the episode between Akhilleus and Thetis has been an interjection in the midst of the hecatomb's progression to Khruse.[81] In this way the sacrificial framework around Akhilleus' withdrawal is signposted on the macro-level of narrative movement and on the micro-level of diction.

Although Agamemnon is absent at Khruse, Odysseus immediately notifies Khruses of his authority as they stand around the altar preparing to sacrifice:

> ἐκ δ᾿ εὐνὰς ἔβαλον, κατὰ δὲ πρυμνήσι᾿ ἔδησαν·
> ἐκ δὲ καὶ αὐτοὶ βαῖνον ἐπὶ ῥηγμῖνι θαλάσσης,
> ἐκ δ᾿ ἑκατόμβην βῆσαν ἑκηβόλῳ ᾿Απόλλωνι·
> ἐκ δὲ Χρυσηῒς νηὸς βῆ ποντοπόροιο.
> τὴν μὲν ἔπειτ᾿ ἐπὶ βωμὸν ἄγων πολύμητις ᾿Οδυσσεὺς
> πατρὶ φίλῳ ἐν χερσὶ τίθει, καί μιν προσέειπεν·
> "ὦ Χρύση, πρό μ᾿ ἔπεμψεν ἄναξ ἀνδρῶν ᾿Αγαμέμνων
> παῖδά τε σοὶ ἀγέμεν, Φοίβῳ θ᾿ ἱερὴν ἑκατόμβην
> ῥέξαι ὑπὲρ Δαναῶν, ὄφρ᾿ ἱλασόμεσθα ἄνακτα,"

> (*Iliad* I 436–444)

> And out went the mooring-stones—cables fast astern—
> and out went the crew themselves in the breaking surf,
> and out they lead the hecatomb for the far-shooter Apollo,
> and out of the deep-sea ship Khruseis stepped too.
> Then tactful Odysseus led her up to the altar,
> placing her in her loving father's arms, and said,
> Khruses, the lord of men Agamemnon sent me here
> to bring your daughter back and sacrifice a holy hecatomb
> to Apollo on behalf of the Danaans, so we can appease the god."

This is the only lengthy scene not specifying the sacrificer along with details of the victims and divine recipient. As in other enacted scenes, the location is described first, followed by the victims and the god, in this instance all closely

---

[81] Cf. Bakker's "syntax of activation": he discusses this scene as an example (1997:109); on the development and possible etymologies of αὐτάρ, see 1997:96n18.

linked by the repetition of ἐκ δέ. Only the sacrificer is missing, as Odysseus explains: he, Odysseus, is present as the delegate of Agamemnon. The accumulation of third person plural verbs describing the removal of the hecatomb from the ship (ἔβαλον, ἔδησαν, βαῖνον, βῆσαν) recalls the emphasis on Agamemnon's individual authority in the loading of the ship (*Iliad* I 308-311). In this sense, Odysseus does not stand in for Agamemnon, but the group will collectively enact the sacrifice at Agamemnon's behest. Therefore, uniquely, Odysseus and Khruses share the role of sacrificer. Odysseus brings the victims and initiates the sacrifice, but Khruses makes the prayer and pours libations on the god's portion (*Iliad* I 450-457, 462-463). Nowhere else in either the *Iliad* or the *Odyssey* does a priest or seer conduct a sacrifice, despite Kalkhas' manifest presence in *Iliad* I and II. Furthermore, Odysseus refers to Agamemnon as ἄναξ ἀνδρῶν Ἀγαμέμνων 'lord of men Agamemnon', the special noun-epithet formula associated with the quarrel and Agamemnon's role as sacrificer, as discussed below.

The structural framework surrounding the sacrifice at Khruse anchors it between Akhilleus' withdrawal and Thetis' request to Zeus: ordinary mortals, stung by the temporary loss of their best fighter, offer gifts to Apollo while Akhilleus' mother contrives another divine plot against them. The unusual length of this sacrifice scene creates a sense of foreboding, prolonging the audience's suspense as to the effect Akhilleus' withdrawal will have on the Akhaian army. This is also one of three instances in which Agamemnon's managerial role is given added emphasis by a delay between his instruction for the necessary sacrificial provisions or descriptions of their procurement and the start of the sacrifice. Agamemnon gives the order to prepare for the sacrifice at Khruse (*Iliad* I 140-147), but the sacrifice itself is postponed until *Iliad* I 430f., after the seizure of Briseis from Akhilleus and his conversation with Thetis. The *teikhoskopia*, the second instance, intervenes between Agamemnon and Hektor's instructions for the oath sacrifice (*Iliad* III 116-120) and the start of the sacrifice (*Iliad* III 264). Finally, the instruction speech given by Agamemnon for the oath sacrifice to reintegrate Akhilleus (*Iliad* XIX 196-197) is followed by a series of speeches before the sacrifice begins at *Iliad* XIX 249. These instruction speeches are important verbal commands, generating audience anticipation of the actual performance of the sacrifice and highlighting Agamemnon's role as *Opferherr*.

After the sacrificial feast is completed, the Akhaians return to their camps with a favorable wind sent by Apollo. Their actions form a contrast to the lonely Akhilleus, who sits raging: "But he raged on, grimly encamped by his fast fleet, the royal son of Peleus, the swift runner Akhilleus" (Αὐτὰρ ὁ μήνιε νηυσὶ παρήμενος ὠκυπόροισι / διογενὴς Πηλῆος υἱὸς, πόδας ὠκὺς Ἀχιλλεύς·, *Iliad* I 488–489). The segue between the movements is again marked by αὐτάρ. This juxtaposition of the return of the troops after a sacrifice on Khruse and the isolation of Akhilleus forms the culmination of human events in *Iliad* I; the remainder takes place on Olympus. The ease with which Thetis can bend the ear of Zeus creates an acute contrast to the elaborate procedure of sacrifice, just as Zeus' universal control provides a foil to Agamemnon's fractured dominion.

4.3 The Language of Sacrificial Authority

To continue our discussion of how enacted sacrifices reinforce thematic meaning in the context of the quarrel, let us look at the phraseology of Agamemnon's special ritual authority. When Odysseus informs Khruses that he is present at Agamemnon's behest, he uses the specialized noun-epithet formula ἄναξ ἀνδρῶν Ἀγαμέμνων 'lord of men Agamemnon', which also initiates the sacrifice in four of the six enacted sacrifices:

> ὦ Χρύση, πρό μ' ἔπεμψεν ἄναξ ἀνδρῶν Ἀγαμέμνων
>
> (*Iliad* I 442)
>
> Khruses, the lord of men Agamemnon sent me here...

> αὐτὰρ ὃ βοῦν ἱέρευσε ἄναξ ἀνδρῶν Ἀγαμέμνων
>
> (*Iliad* II 402)
>
> But the lord of men Agamemnon sacrificed an ox,

> ὄρνυτο δ' αὐτίκ' ἔπειτα ἄναξ ἀνδρῶν Ἀγαμέμνων
>
> (*Iliad* III 267)
>
> And lord of men Agamemnon rose at once...

> τοῖσι δὲ βοῦν ἱέρευσεν ἄναξ ἀνδρῶν Ἀγαμέμνων
>
> (*Iliad* VII 314)
>
> And in their midst the lord of men Agamemnon sacrificed
> an ox...

This is the noun-epithet, specifically linked to Agamemnon's sacrificial authority, by which he is most often described, starting with his first mention at

Iliad I 7.[82] The theme and meter have a reciprocal relationship, so that one does not necessitate the other so much as they develop simultaneously as part of the same process. Meter may be regarded as a 'regulator' or basic precondition for the formula, but the context is equally important. The epithet chosen for the particular event being described is the audience's key to understanding the meaning of the event. Gregory Nagy has written that the epithets "evoke the persona provided by the tradition"; John Miles Foley has explained that the noun-epithet formula acts as a "metonymic pathway to the poetic conjuring of personalities."[83]

This noun-epithet formula is doubly significant in the context of enacted sacrifices as emphatically expressive of both Agamemnon's name, rather than a designation such as a patronymic or pronoun, and the phrase 'lord of men'. Since an overtly expressed subject is not required in Greek, it is therefore introduced as a signpost for a separate unit, a device for drawing attention.[84] Proper names are used in Homer to channel the discourse and make "sure that a given event is seen in the right perspective."[85] The persona needed for the theme of sacrifice is that of the top leader of the Akhaians, Agamemnon, but the narrative is careful to emphasize his ritual role, specifically in terms of his broader responsibility for the army, with the phrase 'lord of men' (ἄναξ ἀνδρῶν). All of the Argives at Troy are described *en masse* as *basileis* 'noblemen' (*Iliad* VII 106, X 195), as are Nestor (*Iliad* I 277) and Akhilleus (*Iliad* I 176) on an individual basis. Agamemnon is twice called *basileus*, followed by a possessive genitive, 'King of gold-rich Mykenae' (*Iliad* VII 180, XI 46), still reflective of his special superiority, as these are the only instances where the noun is followed by a specification of the land ruled.[86] Although frequently used in regard to divinities in the Classical period, *basileus* is not applied in this way in Homer.

---

[82] Parry 1971:39 lists 37. Using the TLG, I find 44 in reference to Agamemnon: *Iliad* I 7, 172, 442, 506; II 373, 402, 434, 441, 612; III 81, 267, 455; IV 148, 255, 336; V 38; VI 33; VII 162, 314; VIII 278; IX 96, 114, 163, 672, 677, 697; X 64, 86, 103; XI 99, 254; XIV 64, 103, 134; XVIII 111; XIX 51, 76, 146, 172, 184, 199; XXIII 49, 161, 895. Carlier 2006:101 attests 56 in all of Homer, but does not list them. In addition, the phrase describes Ankhises (*Iliad* V 268), Aineias (*Iliad* V 311), Augeias (*Iliad* XI 701), and Eumelos (*Iliad* XXIII 288). In Chapter One, I have referred to the excellent scholarship regarding the significance of formulaic noun-epithet phrases: Lord 1960:148; Nagy 1996b:50; 2003:40; and Havelock 1971:53, who describes noun-epithet phrases as a process of "continual anticipation."

[83] Nagy 1990b:23; Foley 1990:23. See also Nagy's review of Foley (1996c). Bakker 1997:162 attributes the changing nuances of the epithets to their contexts and the audience's ability to recognize the meaning in the context of the event.

[84] Meillet and Vendryes 1924:598; cf. Bakker 1997:97.

[85] Bakker 1997:93–94.

[86] βασιλῆα πολυχρύσοιο Μυκήνης. Cf. Drews 1983:101; Gschnitzer 1966:101n8. Skherie has at least thirteen *basileis* (*Odyssey* viii 390-391) and the suitors are twice called by this title (*Odyssey* i 386, 392).

Basileus implies a high social rank, but not the top position, which seems to be that of the *anax*, a word that may be used in different contexts, but always with the meaning 'one-man rule', whether in reference to the master of a house or town. So, in reference to Agamemnon, ἄναξ ἀνδρῶν refers to his hegemony over the Akhaian army.[87]

Scholars since Aristarkhos have noticed the difference between particularized and generic epithets.[88] The particularized noun-epithet formula ἄναξ ἀνδρῶν Ἀγαμέμνων is used in three contexts: sacrifice, the *aristeia*, and speech contexts describing Agamemnon's own speech, his responses to others' speeches, and in honorific address to him by other speakers. All three contexts express the social status and importance of the heroes, the central issues raised by the poem. ἄναξ ἀνδρῶν is not only the formulaic phrase by which Agamemnon is most often described, but also that most closely linked with the central action of Akhilleus' withdrawal, as it is used in the description of the quarrel at the start of the poem:

> ἐξ οὗ δὴ τὰ πρῶτα διαστήτην ἐρίσαντε
> Ἀτρεΐδης τε ἄναξ ἀνδρῶν καὶ δῖος Ἀχιλλεύς

(*Iliad* I 6–7)

> from the time when the two first broke and clashed,
> the son of Atreus lord of men and god-like Akhilleus.

The repeated epithet highlights Agamemnon's leadership, his defining feature, whereas δῖος can be taken as a reference to Akhilleus' divine parentage.[89] The use of this epithet in the first description of the quarrel establishes it as Agamemnon's most important identification: Bakker has written of the "quintessential identity" reflected in a "quintessential name," which for Agamemnon

---

[87] This word is mainly used with Agamemnon, but there are exceptions: Nestor is called *anax* of Pylos at *Iliad* II 77, as is Agamemnon's Trojan equivalent Priam at *Iliad* II 373, as well as Aineias, Ankhises, Augeias and Eumelos, see above. Nestor is prominently depicted as the ritual authority at Pylos in the *Odyssey*, which may be a reflection of some sort of special status. Carlier 2006:101 discusses the uses of the term and concludes that it refers to 'one-man rule', whether over a household or larger group. He advocates the translation 'lord' as reflective of the similar range of meanings in this word in Greek as found in English or French *seigneur*. Van Wees 1992:31 notes that *anax* can be used in Homer in reference to cities, houses, slaves, and animals, as well as of the gods. Drews 1983:101, drawing heavily on Gschnitzer 1966:99–112, argues that Homeric *basileus* can be synonymous with *anax*, but that the political system is undergoing radical changes at the time. A bibliography on the topic is given by van Wees 1992:31n23.

[88] The evidence is summarized by Parry 1971:120.

[89] Kakrides 1971:129.

is ἄναξ ἀνδρῶν.[90] In this way the proem anticipates Agamemnon's role as *Opferherr* in the context of the quarrel and Akhilleus' thematic opposition to sacrifice as the child of a goddess.

This thematic association with the quarrel in the use of the phrase ἄναξ ἀνδρῶν Ἀγάμεμνον continues throughout the poem. The phrase occurs most often in *Iliad* IX (96, 114, 163, 672, 677, 697) and *Iliad* XIX (51, 76, 146, 172, 184, 199), the books most concerned with the quarrel. In addition, this phrase can be lengthened to a full-verse ornamental address, Ἀτρεΐδη κύδιστε, ἄναξ ἀνδρῶν Ἀγάμεμνον 'Son of Atreus, most glorious, the lord of men Agamemnon', which is used eight times in the *Iliad*, all specifically in the context of the quarrel (*Iliad* II 434; IX 96, 163, 677, 697; X 103; XIX 146, 199).[91] For instance, when Akhilleus insults Agamemnon, he replaces the honorific formulaic verse Ἀτρεΐδη κύδιστε, ἄναξ ἀνδρῶν Ἀγάμεμνον 'Son of Atreus, most glorious, lord of men Agamemnon' with Ἀτρεΐδη κύδιστε, φιλοκτεανώτατε πάντων 'Son of Atreus, most glorious, most covetous of all men' (*Iliad* I 122). Obviously, an epithet meaning 'lord of men" would have been associated with authority figures, but there are other ways of expressing this notion, such as κρείων 'ruler', used 40 times of Agamemnon, or phrases like ὄρχαμε λαῶν 'leader of the people', used to describe Menelaos (*Iliad* XVII 12).[92] The fact that Akhilleus alters this particular verse when challenging Agamemnon indicates its importance as an acknowledgment of his authority. When the two men are finally reconciled, preceding the oath sacrifice, Akhilleus twice addresses Agamemnon with the full honorific verse Ἀτρεΐδη κύδιστε, ἄναξ ἀνδρῶν Ἀγάμεμνον (*Iliad* XIX 146, 199).[93] Nestor addresses Agamemnon thus when beginning a series of advisory speeches: after the sacrifice (*Iliad* II 434), about the embassy (*Iliad* IX 96), in response to Agamemnon's list of gifts (*Iliad* IX 163), and about Agamemnon's surprise night visit (X 103). This verse is also used by Odysseus to tell of Akhilleus' withdrawal (*Iliad* IX 677), reiterated by Diomedes (*Iliad* IX 697). The repetition of ἄναξ ἀνδρῶν Ἀγάμεμνον links the enacted sacrifices together as a group, showing the role of sacrifice as a distinct demonstration of Agamemnon's authority during Akhilleus' withdrawal. Of particular importance is the repetition of αὐτὰρ ὁ βοῦν ἱέρευσε ἄναξ ἀνδρῶν Ἀγαμέμνων (*Iliad*

---

[90] Bakker 1997:170.

[91] Only Zeus and Agamemnon are κύδιστε, another signifier of Agamemnon's supreme authority (Scodel 2002:21).

[92] κρείων Ἀγαμέμνων: *Iliad* I 102, 130, 285, 355, 411; II 100, 369, 411, 477, 576; III 118, 178; IV 153, 188, 204, 283, 311, 356, 368; V 537; VI 63; VII 107, 322, 405; IX 62, 368; X 42; XI 107, 126, 153, 177, 238; XIII 112; XIV 41; XVI 58, 72, 273; XVIII 445; XXIII 110, 887.

[93] Whallon 1969:3.

II 402, VII 313), where the sacrificial performance replaces Ἀτρεΐδη κύδιστε ἄναξ.

After *Iliad* XIV, this formula is used of Agamemnon exclusively in contexts directly linked with Akhilleus. In fact, the entire conversational exchange in *Iliad* XIX is marked by its use: when Agamemnon approaches the Assembly (*Iliad* XIX 51), at the beginning of his apology speech (*Iliad* XIX 76), in Akhilleus' response (*Iliad* XIX 146), in Odysseus' comments (*Iliad* XIX 172), when Agamemnon gives the instructions to prepare the sacrifice (*Iliad* XIX 184), and Akhilleus' final response to Agamemnon (*Iliad* XIX 199). On such repetition Nagy writes, "Each occurrence of a theme (on the level of content) or of a formula (on the level of form) in a given composition in performance refers not only to its immediate context but also to all the other analogous contexts remembered by the performer or by any member of the audience."[94] In this way, the use of the epithet in the context of sacrifice is an important key to understanding this theme in the *Iliad*.

So, at *Iliad* I 442, the authority of Agamemnon is reiterated through this formula, despite his physical absence. In delegating Agamemnon's authority, Odysseus describes him with the epithet most clearly tied with its theme:

τὴν μὲν ἔπειτ' ἐπὶ βωμὸν ἄγων πολύμητις Ὀδυσσεὺς
πατρὶ φίλῳ ἐν χερσὶ τίθει, καί μιν προσέειπεν·
"ὦ Χρύση, πρό μ' ἔπεμψεν ἄναξ ἀνδρῶν Ἀγαμέμνων"

(*Iliad* I 440–442)

The tactful Odysseus led her up to the altar,
placing her in her loving father's arms, and said,
"Khruses, the lord of men Agamemnon sent me here..."

The noun-epithet phrase is not only significant in and of itself, but its position at the end of the verse also ensures the audience's appropriate response.[95] Different verbalizations are associated with different ranks in the narrative, and the narrator has carefully emphasized Agamemnon's authority, even his special ritual authority, by repeatedly using this particular epithet.[96]

---

[94] Nagy 1996b:50. Lord 1960:45–46 argues that the oral tradition made little use of purely ornamental epithets, describing themes in Homer as having a *suprameaning*, a resonance acquired from all past uses and contexts.

[95] The noun-epithet formula at the end of the verse is used to distinguish certain heroes; cf. Kahane 1994:135–141.

[96] Bakker 1997:111 discusses the different ways in which the narrative can express characterization.

4.4 Agamemnon's Sacrificial Authority in Akhilleus' Absence

The *Iliad* as a whole is composed of intricately balanced parallel scenes and episodes, incorporated into a larger framework of sections (which we call 'Books'), following a complex pattern of ring composition.[97] As a consequence, the entire poem is structured around *Iliad* I by a sophisticated series of echoes and recurrent motifs, a trend especially prominent with respect to enacted sacrifices. The delegated sacrifice at Khruse and Agamemnon's grand sacrifice for the councilors in *Iliad* II are linked by the exact repetition of ten verses, *Iliad* I 458–461 = *Iliad* II 421–424 and *Iliad* I 464–469 = *Iliad* II 427–432. The narrative links these scenes to emphasize Agamemnon's role as sacrificer: his delegation of authority in *Iliad* I anticipates his shift to sacrificer in the similar scene in *Iliad* II. Agamemnon's elaborate sacrifice is preceded by a short description of the men sacrificing at his command, a command so moving that the shouts of his subordinates are compared to waves stirred by the south wind (*Iliad* II 394–397). The narrative focuses attention on both Agamemnon's authority (only he can give the command for sacrifice) and the grand scale on which he performs the ritual, which is juxtaposed against the brief, anonymous Akhaian sacrifice:

> κάπνισσάν τε κατὰ κλισίας, καὶ δεῖπνον ἕλοντο.
> ἄλλος δ' ἄλλῳ ἔρεζε θεῶν αἰειγενετάων,
> εὐχόμενος θάνατόν τε φυγεῖν καὶ μῶλον Ἄρηος.
> αὐτὰρ ὁ βοῦν ἱέρευσεν ἄναξ ἀνδρῶν Ἀγαμέμνων
> πίονα πενταέτηρον ὑπερμενέϊ Κρονίωνι
>
> (*Iliad* II 399–404)

[the troops] lit fires beside their tents and took their meal.
Each sacrificed to one or another deathless god,
each man praying to flee death and the grind of war.
But the lord of men Agamemnon sacrificed an ox,
fat rich, five years old, to the son of mighty Kronos, Zeus.

In the above instance, as at several junctures in the *Iliad*, the comments or actions by anonymous Akhaians are provided as a contrast to the actions of their leader.[98] The men's prayers to escape death act as a foil to Agamemnon's

---

[97] Whitman 1958:87; see also Schein 1984:31–32, Lowenstam 1993:12. Stanley 1993 is a full-length study on the topic of ring composition in the *Iliad*; he discusses the 'Book' divisions throughout (with conclusions at 249f.).

[98] See de Jong 1987a. Kirk 1985 *ad Iliad* II 402–403 points out the similarities between the contrasting dinners of the army and the councilors represented here and on the shield of Akhil-

detailed and grandiose sacrifice of oxen to Zeus, which is accompanied by a prayer asking that he be permitted to conquer Troy.[99] The full verse introduction to Agamemnon's first commensal sacrifice (*Iliad* II 402) markedly combines his specialized epithet ἄναξ ἀνδρῶν Ἀγαμέμνων and the particle αὐτάρ. Whereas αὐτάρ would usually sufficiently signal the audience on its own and would not be accompanied by a noun-epithet formula,[100] its presence distinguishes *Iliad* II 402 from the preceding anonymous Akhaian sacrifice (*Iliad* II 400-401). Acting as an indicator, the particular combination of αὐτάρ and ὁ directs the audience to the change of subject from the Akhaians to Agamemnon.[101]

The primary narrator directs special attention to the exclusive nature of Agamemnon's sacrifice with an extended description of the invitation he extends to the councilors:

> κίκλησκεν δὲ γέροντας ἀριστῆας Παναχαιῶν,
> Νέστορα μὲν πρώτιστα καὶ Ἰδομενῆα ἄνακτα,
> αὐτὰρ ἔπειτ' Αἴαντε δύω καὶ Τυδέος υἱόν,
> ἕκτον δ' αὖτ' Ὀδυσῆα, Διὶ μῆτιν ἀτάλαντον.
> αὐτόματος δέ οἱ ἦλθε βοὴν ἀγαθὸς Μενέλαος·
> ᾔδεε γὰρ κατὰ θυμὸν ἀδελφεὸν ὡς ἐπονεῖτο.

(*Iliad* II 404-409)

and he called the excellent elders of all the Argive forces:
Nestor first and foremost, then lord Idomeneus,
but then the two Ajaxes and Tydeus' son
and Odysseus sixth, a mastermind like Zeus.
The lord of the war cry Menelaos came uncalled,
he knew at heart what weighed his brother down.

Agamemnon's directive is presented as part of the ritual action, following the two verses that signal the start of the sacrifice (*Iliad* II 402-403). The description of the councilors as "excellent elders of the Panakhaians" at this juncture is unique, drawing the audience's attention to the importance of this event and creating a sense of anticipation for the sacrifice.[102] The councilors are

---

leus. Here, the army takes its dinner while Agamemnon provides a luxurious feast; on the shield, the harvesters eat porridge while the heralds prepare an ox for the king (*Iliad* XVIII 556-560).

[99] The contrast between the wishes of the leaders and their followers is potentially relevant to the performance context (Launderville 2003:295-296; Raaflaub 1989:4).

[100] Bakker 1997:110; cf. Gunn 1971:23.

[101] Bakker 1997:62.

[102] Kirk 1985:158 discusses the ancient commentary on this passage, which had troubled commen-

then described as standing around the bull while Agamemnon prays (*Iliad* II 410–418). Zeus rejects the prayer and receives the sacrifice (*Iliad* II 419–420). The councilors sprinkle barley after the prayer, and all help with the sacrifice, preparation of meat, and handling of the carcass. The feast follows, which in turn leads to Nestor's counsel (*Iliad* II 421–433).

The day of battle begins with Agamemnon's grand sacrifice in *Iliad* II and ends in *Iliad* VII with an honorary banquet for Ajax, Akhilleus' replacement as champion of the Akhaians. This sacrifice also initiates advice from Nestor, recalling the scene in *Iliad* II in both design and structural function:[103]

οἱ δ' ὅτε δὴ κλισίῃσιν ἐν Ἀτρεΐδαο γένοντο,
τοῖσι δὲ βοῦν ἱέρευσεν ἄναξ ἀνδρῶν Ἀγαμέμνων
ἄρσενα πενταέτηρον ὑπερμενέϊ Κρονίωνι.

(*Iliad* VII 313–315)

Soon as they had gathered within the quarters of the son of
    Atreus,
in their midst the lord of men Agamemnon sacrificed an ox,
a male, five years old, to the towering son of Kronos, Zeus.

Here, in the final commensal sacrifice of the epic, the established theme of Agamemnon's ritual authority is again specially emphasized. Like *Iliad* II, the sacrifice begins by localizing the performance in Agamemnon's quarters. δέ is followed by both ὅτε, a signal for audience participation, and δή, which suggests that the audience is in step with the narrative goals.[104] Then the same verse that identifies Agamemnon as the sacrificer in *Iliad* II is repeated, II 402 ~VII 314, with the substitution of τοῖσι δέ 'in their midst' for αὐτὰρ ὁ 'but he'. This substitution reflects the expectation that the audience be familiar with this theme, which uses Agamemnon's gift of the best meat to Ajax to reiterate his ritual largesse (*Iliad* VII 321–322). Significantly, the sacrifice in *Iliad* VII frames the ritual performance with statements about Agamemnon's authority:

Οἱ δ' ὅτε δὴ κλισίῃσιν ἐν Ἀτρεΐδαο γένοντο,
<u>τοῖσι δὲ βοῦν ἱέρευσεν ἄναξ ἀνδρῶν Ἀγαμέμνων</u>
ἄρσενα πενταέτηρον ὑπερμενέϊ Κρονίωνι.
τὸν δέρον ἀμφί θ' ἕπον, καί μιν διέχευαν ἅπαντα,

---

tators with its description of Menelaos coming of his own accord.
[103] See Stanley 1993:56; Bassett 1938:49. I discuss the intervening oath sacrifice in *Iliad* III in Chapter Two, pages 88f. above.
[104] Bakker 1997:75, 79.

μίστυλλόν τ' ἄρ' ἐπισταμένως πεῖράν τ' ὀβελοῖσιν,
ὤπτησάν τε περιφραδέως, ἐρύσαντό τε πάντα.
αὐτὰρ ἐπεὶ παύσαντο πόνου τετύκοντό τε δαῖτα,
δαίνυντ', οὐδέ τι θυμὸς ἐδεύετο δαιτὸς ἐΐσης·
νώτοισιν δ' Αἴαντα διηνεκέεσσι γέραιρεν
ἥρως Ἀτρεΐδης εὐρὺ κρείων Ἀγαμέμνων.
αὐτὰρ ἐπεὶ πόσιος καὶ ἐδητύος ἐξ ἔρον ἕντο,

(*Iliad* VII 313–323)

Soon as they had gathered within the tents of the son of Atreus
in their midst the lord of men Agamemnon sacrificed an ox,
a male, five years old, to the towering son of Kronos, Zeus.
They skinned the animal quickly, and cut everything up,
expertly sliced the meat into pieces, pierced them with spits,
roasted them to a turn and pulled them off the spits.
The work done, the feast laid out, they ate well
and no man's hunger lacked an appropriate share of the feast
But the lord of far-flung kingdoms, hero Agamemnon,
honored Ajax with the long savory cuts that line the backbone.
And when they had put aside desire for food and drink...

The framing of the honorary sacrifice with the formulaic noun-epithet formulas expressing leadership (*Iliad* VII 314, 322) makes the significance of this action clear to the audience. The details of the animal's sacrifice and the subsequent treatment of the carcass have been abbreviated in comparison to the sacrifices in *Iliad* I and II, further emphasizing that this happy social occasion is under the auspices of Agamemnon's authority.

Agamemnon uses sacrifice at this critical juncture to honor Akhilleus' substitute, Ajax, whose important role during Akhilleus' withdrawal is introduced in the Catalogue of Heroes. In the Catalogue, Agamemnon is described as "bearing himself triumphantly...preeminent amongst all the warriors, because he was the best (ἄριστος), and he led the most men" (*Iliad* II 579–580). At the end of the Akhaian catalogue, the posed question, "who was the best (ἄριστος) of the Akhaians?" (*Iliad* II 761), is followed by a description of the best being Ajax, whereas Akhilleus is said to have maintained his wrath (*Iliad* II 768–769). Agamemnon is singled out as the best (ἄριστος) in terms of leadership, Akhilleus and Ajax as the best warriors. The Catalogue also highlights the tension between Agamemnon and Achilles, as noted by Keith Stanley: "Within the catalogue, the juxtaposition of Agamemnon and Akhilleus at equivalent positions in the series (in the second and next to last sections) demonstrates an interest less in consistent geographical logic than in placement of two conflicting elements in a formal balance that reflects and emphasizes the dramatic polarity established in *Iliad* I."[105] The entire poem is, in many ways, situated around the conflict between the hero Akhilleus and his king. Steven Lowenstam has described the plot of the *Iliad* as motivated by a "central question": what does it mean to be 'preeminent' in the *Iliad*? He concludes that the poem demonstrates leadership and gallantry in coexistence, but recognizes the impossibility of these two notions being expressed in one person.[106] The *Iliad* then becomes, as Dean Hammer pronounces, in essence, a poem about the nature of authority.[107] Sacrifice establishes the link between the characters chosen to manifest these attributes in the poem.

Enacted sacrifices achieve thematic significance in *Iliad* I as a symbol of the social drama created by the quarrel between Akhilleus and Agamemnon. The strife begins when Kalkhas, encouraged by Akhilleus not to fear Agamemnon, explains that, although Apollo is angry not about hecatombs but by Agamemnon's treatment of Khruses, he will be assuaged only by a hecatomb and the return of the girl (*Iliad* I 92–104). The consequent agonistic exchange between Akhilleus and Agamemnon introduces the overall questioning of reciprocity and *timê* that guide much of the poem's action.[108] Because Agamemnon takes Akhilleus' prize, Akhilleus will not take part in the sacrifice, which initiates his pattern of abstinence from Agamemnon's sacrifices. Though the sacrifice to assuage Apollo is a small feature of the heated debate in the Akhaian *agora*, it establishes the important association between Agamemnon's superiority over the army and his status as the *Opferherr*. Through the delegation of the sacrificial embassy, Agamemnon uses an association to sacrifice to elevate the importance of Ajax and Odysseus: Ajax will be honored in a sacrificial context for performing his role as substitute best fighter, and Odysseus will be Agamemnon's ritual assistant, leading the sacrifice to Khruse and standing beside the king at the oath sacrifice in *Iliad* III. Agamemnon's dutiful attendance to divine rites contrasts bitterly with the crisis he has instigated with Akhilleus.

Agamemnon's threat, "If they give me nothing, I will take a prize myself, your own, or Ajax's, or Odysseus' prize," (εἰ δέ κε μὴ δώωσιν ἐγὼ δέ κεν αὐτὸς ἕλωμαι / ἢ τεὸν ἢ Αἴαντος ἰὼν γέρας, ἢ Ὀδυσῆος, *Iliad* I 137–138) is part of an

---

[105] Stanley 1993:24.

[106] Lowenstam 1993:139.

[107] Hammer 1997:2.

[108] This is a complex and well-explored topic: see Taplin 1992:50–51, Postlethwaite 1998, and the definitive study in Wilson 2002.

instruction speech that precedes the sacrifice at Khruse. He gives a similar command for sacrifice to be prepared as an introduction to the oath sacrifice that marks Akhilleus' reintegration into the group. After publicly admitting his error in removing Briseis, Agamemnon offers to present Akhilleus with all of his promised gifts (*Iliad* XIX 78–144). His speech to Akhilleus has been much discussed by scholars, for the most part with respect to his clever avoidance of direct apology, his delayed recognition of Akhilleus until the end of the speech, and his unprecedented claim to understand the minds of the gods.[109] Akhilleus refuses the gifts in his haste for battle, but, in addition to an oath by Agamemnon regarding Briseis, Odysseus urges nourishment for the army before battle (*Iliad* XIX 145–182). Agamemnon readily agrees to the oath and gives the orders for the sacrifice to be prepared to accompany the gift presentation:

> Ταλθύβιος δέ μοι ὦκα κατὰ στρατὸν εὐρὺν Ἀχαιῶν
> κάπρον ἑτοιμασάτω, ταμέειν Διί τ' Ἠελίῳ τε.
>
> (*Iliad* XIX 196–197)

Here among the wide army of the Akhaians let Talthubios quickly prepare a wild boar for me—to sacrifice to Helios and Zeus.

Similar to the oath sacrifice in *Iliad* III, Agamemnon will perform a visible demonstration, in front of the whole army, of his role as spokesman to the gods, reiterating his ritual authority as he offsets the threat posed by Akhilleus' withdrawal. On the one hand, Agamemnon attempts to compete with Akhilleus through an aristocratic gift-exchange by imposing gifts, which Akhilleus rejects.[110] On the other hand, Agamemnon intends to sanctify these gifts with an oath sacrifice, a suggestion that Akhilleus completely ignores. He again tells Agamemnon that he would rather do battle unfed (*Iliad* XIX 205–207), although Agamemnon mentions nothing about feasting, referring only to the presentation of the gifts and the oath sacrifice, which is customarily uneaten. This oath sacrifice is the last sacrifice enacted in the epic. Before making the prayer to which all Akhaians silently listen, Agamemnon draws his sacrificial knife:

> Ἀτρεΐδης δὲ ἐρυσσάμενος χείρεσσι μάχαιραν,
> ἥ οἱ πὰρ ξίφεος μέγα κουλεὸν αἰὲν ἄωρτο.
>
> (*Iliad* XIX 252–253 = III 271–272)

---

[109] Rabel 1997:82 is a good discussion of this speech as Agamemnon's personal description of the plot of the poem; see also Lohmann 1970:173–174; Arend 1933:117; Dodds 1951:1–27; and Edwards 1991 note *ad loc.*

[110] Mackie 1996:157.

And Atreus' son drew forth with his hands the dagger
always slung at his battle-sword's big sheath.

In this context, Agamemnon's final demonstration of ritual authority concludes the quarrel with Akhilleus. Akhilleus' use of Agamemnon's full ornamental address in the discussions preceding the oath sacrifice ("Son of Atreus, most glorious, lord of men Agamemnon," Ἀτρεΐδη κύδιστε, ἄναξ ἀνδρῶν Ἀγάμεμνον, *Iliad* XIX 146, 199) signals his acceptance of Agamemnon's superiority. Akhilleus then observes the final enacted sacrifice. Since sacrifice is used at early stages in the poem to define human relationships within Homeric society, once these relationships are no longer contested, enacted sacrifice is no longer needed.[111]

Just as in *Iliad* III, the *makhaira* 'sacrificial knife' always hanging beside Agamemnon's sword emphasizes his role as chief king and *Opferherr*—both aspects that Akhilleus directly opposes throughout the poem. The theme of Akhilleus' opposition to the *Opferherr* may have very deep roots: the importance of the *makhaira* in other traditions relating the Trojan War, especially in association with Akhilleus, has been explored by Nagy, who observes the general suppression of connections between murder, sacrifice, and feasting in the *Iliad*, although they are prominent in other depictions of the family of Akhilleus. Peleus' marriage to Thetis is a feast attended jointly by gods and mortals, the setting for Eris' (Strife's) instigation of the quarrel among the gods, leading to the judgement by Paris. A song by the Phaiakian singer Demodokos in the *Odyssey* describes a quarrel between Akhilleus and Odysseus at a sacrifice:

νεῖκος Ὀδυσσῆος καὶ Πηλεΐδεω Ἀχιλῆος,
ὥς ποτε δηρίσαντο θεῶν ἐν δαιτὶ θαλείῃ
ἐκπάγλοις ἐπέεσσιν, ἄναξ δ' ἀνδρῶν Ἀγαμέμνων
χαῖρε νόῳ, ὅ τ' ἄριστοι Ἀχαιῶν δηριόωντο.

(*Odyssey* viii 75–78)

the quarrel between Odysseus and Peleus' son, Akhilleus,

---

[111] Muellner 1996:141–142 argues for the establishment of social bonds in this scene. Social relationships may no longer be publicly contested, but they are still not harmonious. Postlethwaite 1998:100–101 proposes that, after *Iliad* XIX, Agamemnon is presented as subordinate to Akhilleus. He sees the feast scene with Priam as an extension of Akhilleus' animosity towards Agamemnon, "overriding conventions of balanced reciprocity...and [continuing] to declare his own authority and to demean his old adversary" (103). For a similar view, see Wilson 2002. Nagy 1979:132–134 discusses the reintegration of Akhilleus at the *dais* suggested by Odysseus in *Iliad* XIX, but also important is Akhilleus' participation in Agamemnon's oath sacrifice; cf. Griffin 1980:14–15.

how these once contended, at the god's generous feast
with words of violence, so that the lord of men, Agamemnon,
was happy in his heart that the best of the Akhaians were quarreling.

The quarrel takes place at a sacrificial *dais,* while in the *Iliad* the sacrificial context is replaced with the *agora.* In the *Iliad,* the quarrel leads to sacrifices to assuage Apollo, and Agamemnon relies on sacrifice to demonstrate his authority during the crisis caused by Akhilleus; sacrifice is still central to the quarrel, but is motivated by Akhilleus' absence. The thematic connection between Akhilleus and the *dais* has been moderated in the *Iliad* by the change of the context of the quarrel from a sacrifice to the *agora,* but it has retained the same semantic notions of apportionment and honor found in sacrificial feast settings. The terms *geras* 'honorific portion', *timê* 'honor', *dateomai* 'to divide', and *moira* 'portion, fate, destiny' can be applied to the allotment of sacrificial meat at the "equal feast," as well as to Akhilleus' loss of *geras* and *timê* in *Iliad* I and, most importantly, to his short life.

The special negative association of sacrifice with the family of Akhilleus is most emphatically represented in the traditions of the death of his son Purrhos during a sacrifice at Delphi. In Pindar *Paian* 6, Purrhos quarrels with the attendants distributing meat after a sacrifice at Delphi and is killed by Apollo. In another poem, Pindar describes Purrhos' death as the result of a quarrel with a man carrying a *makhaira* over cuts of sacrificial meat. It is significant that, in this version, Purrhos is bringing 'first fruit' offerings from the spoils of Troy to the god.[112] On the basis of the continued negative connection between Akhilleus' son and sacrifice, it is tempting to draw a deeper thematic association between the family of Akhilleus and aberrant sacrifices: Purrhos is killed while trying to act as an *Opferherr* with Trojan spoils, the role which belongs to Agamemnon in the *Iliad* and which is instrumental in his quarrel with Akhilleus. Following in his father's footsteps, Purrhos causes quarrels in sacrificial settings. Akhilleus' association with feasting has been understated and 'stylized', but it can still be seen in the frequent depictions of Akhilleus' short life in terms associated with divisions of meat, which are then actualized in the death of Purrhos over sacrificial meat. The thematic connections

---

[112] Pindar *Paian* 6.117–120; *Nemean* 7.40–43; Nagy 1979:123–141; cf. Martin 1983:88. The death of Purrhos is also described in Asklepiades *FGrH* 12.15; Kallimakhos f. 229.7 (Pfeiffer); Pausanias 10.7.1; Strabo 421. Akhilleus refers to a son, Neoptolemos, at *Iliad* XIX 327; he is also a topic of conversation between Akhilleus and Odysseus in the underworld scene at *Odyssey* xi 505–537. On the double name Purrhos/Neoptolemos, see *Kupria* fragment 14, Allen and Nagy 1979:119n1.

between *neikos* 'quarrel', the division of meat at feasts, and the figures of Peleus, Akhilleus, and Purrhos is summarized by Nagy:

> "For the Achilles of our *Iliad*, the restoration of *timê* happens at a *dais*—but the same does not hold for the Strife Scene where he had originally lost that *timê*. Pyrrhos, on the other hand, has his Strife Scene on account of his *timai* at an overt sacrifice; furthermore, his actions mirror closely on the level of myth the proceedings of the sacrifice on the level of ritual. To put it another way, our story of Pyrrhos is much closer to a ritual quarrel over cuts of sacrificial meat than our story of Achilles, where the narrative elements have been considerably stylized—especially in *Iliad* I."[113]

There is a second aspect of Akhilleus' special negative association with the *dais:* his savage perversion of the feast.[114] Akhilleus' murderous rampage after his reintegration in *Iliad* XIX is often compared to a savage *dais*: he wishes he could eat Hektor raw, and Apollo compares his slaughter of Trojans to a lion's *dais* of sheep (*Iliad* XXII 346–347, XXIV 41–43). Outside of battle, Akhilleus' abstention from food symbolizes his grief and isolation. When urged to eat by the councilors, he refuses, remembering how Patroklos used to prepare food for him in his hut (*Iliad* XIX 315–318).[115] He refers to the ἐίση δαίς shared by the army as a στυγερὴ δαίς (*Iliad* XXIII 48, 56), and he rejects Lukaon's plea based on their once having shared a meal together (*Iliad* XXI 74–113). The last image of Akhilleus is his shared meal with Priam; ironically, this forced feast with the enemy, conspicuously lacking sacrifice, is also the resolution of his savage temper (*Iliad* XXIV 618–619).

4.5 The Isolation of Akhilleus between Men and Gods

Having established the use of enacted sacrifices as a positive demonstration of Agamemnon's kingship, I shall conclude with a brief discussion of Akhilleus' abstinence from normative sacrificial procedure as symbolic of his unique intermediary status between gods and mortals. Akhilleus' withdrawal in *Iliad* I can be described as a reversal of the "traditional values of a competitive system

---

[113] Nagy 1979:134.

[114] On the specific case of Akhilleus, see Segal 1971:40f.; Hekabe calls Akhilleus the "raw-eater," *Iliad* XXIV 207. Griffin 1980:18–20 observes the displacement of cannibalism in the frequent heroic boast that wild animals will eat the enemy's corpse.

[115] Postlethwaite 1998: "Akhilleus' abstention from food, and particularly the communal feast, is indicative of his continued alienation from the fellowship of heroic society" (99).

in which men are judged by their success and failure in visible action."[116] His separation from the group, the inevitable result of his status as the son of a goddess, entitles him to special treatment, which in turn becomes a source of his anger at the group: Akhilleus' mother has given him special knowledge of his imminent death, whereas the others may hope for a homecoming. Constantly identified by other characters as the son of a goddess, he is the only hero to speak face to face with the gods. Akhilleus' wrath is described as *mênis* 'anger', a term elsewhere used only of divinities. He is revived with ambrosia, the ointment of the gods, and is given immortal horses and armor.[117] Thanks to his mother, Akhilleus has an extraordinary knowledge of plot events and other characters' motives. His unique, elevated status is implied by his pairing with a divine opponent, Skamandros, as well as in the special help he receives from Athena, Poseidon, Hephaistos, and Hera.

However, all of the special features likening Akhilleus to the gods serve also to emphasize his mortality: he is distanced from mortal heroes by special divine treatment and superhuman knowledge of the future, but, as a mortal hero condemned to die, he is equally distanced from immortals.[118] The *Iliad* has suppressed all of the invulnerable and immortal characteristics usually associated with Akhilleus as a mythical figure, such as the tradition maintaining that Thetis tried to make him immortal.[119] It is this intermediate status as mortal, but as isolated from other mortals through exceptional qualities suggestive of divinities, that the portrayal of sacrifice reflects. For instance, Akhilleus' prayer and vow to the Winds is uniquely transmitted through the help of Iris, who is herself *en route* to feast with the Aithiopes (*Iliad* XXIII 205–209). The

[116] Stanley 1993:43. Cf. Latacz 1996, in reference to the singing competitions: "Naturally (in the Homeric world) there are competitions not only at the festival contests; in daily life, in every occupation, at every moment, it is a matter of winning out and excelling" (31).

[117] On his identification as the son of a goddess, see *Iliad* I 280; XXI 24, 99, et al.; Schein 1984:91. He speaks to Athena at *Iliad* I 195ff. and to Thetis throughout the poem. Muellner 1996:114 notes that after Athena's intervention, "it is plausible even to say that he has given up his ties to the Akhaian community in the name of his ties to the divine one." *Mênis* of Akhilleus: *Iliad* IX 517; XIX 35, 75. *Mênis* of gods: *Iliad* I 75; V 34, 178, 444; XIII 624; XV 122; XVI 711; XXI 523. The exception is Aineias' anger towards Priam, *Iliad* XIII 460, on which see Nagy 1979:73. Zeus sends Athena to nourish Akhilleus by instilling nektar and ambrosia into his chest, XIX 349–355. The divine horses of Akhilleus: XVI 148ff.; XVII 426ff. The ironic inability of the divine armor to protect the mortal bearer is remarked on by Hephaistos, *Iliad* XVIII 464-467 (Griffin 1980:187–188).

[118] Martin 1989:235; Schein 1984:81. Scully 1990:121 observes that, after the death of Patroklos, Akhilleus faces his own imminent death with "objective clarity and impersonal indifference that parallels the Olympian view."

[119] On the mythic traditions of Akhilleus' death, see Gantz 1993:625–628. Although Thetis' attempts to make the baby invulnerable are not attested until Apollonius Rhodius IV 869ff., Schein 1984:91n3 defends the evidence for an early tradition of invulnerability on the basis of vase painting.

unique assistance given so that Akhilleus' prayer may reach the ears of its intended recipient draws attention to his special status. At a rare moment in which Akhilleus relies on traditional mortal methods of communicating with the gods, the divine messenger of the gods becomes his message bearer as well. Akhilleus never performs the sacrifices he promises to the Winds. In fact, he neither remembers past sacrifices, nor performs sacrifice in the context of the poem, but alludes rather to future sacrifices, which the audience knows will be precluded by his imminent death. His only other appeal to the gods in the mortal mode occurs in his libation to Zeus for the safety of Patroklos (*Iliad* XVI 220–250).[120] When concerned about his mortal friend, Akhilleus applies mortal methods of communication. When he wants something for himself, however, he appeals directly to his mother. Nonetheless, since despite his special status not even Akhilleus can bend the will of Zeus, his libation for the life of Patroklos is unsuccessful.

In her haste to join the Aithiopes, who still feast with the gods, Iris brings to mind an image of the 'Golden Age', a time of commensality between men and gods, to which Thetis' marriage to a mortal also belongs.[121] Akhilleus seems to have an intermediary status similar to that of the Aithiopes. This tacit comparison of Golden Age commensality between men and gods with the ineffecient system of animal sacrifice as a means of communication between the two groups is made explicit in the final discussion of Akhilleus by the Olympian gods. Apollo, in his characteristically hostile approach to Akhilleus, berates the other gods for allowing him to mistreat Hektor's body:

σχέτλιοί ἐστε, θεοί, δηλήμονες· οὔ νύ ποθ' ὑμῖν
Ἕκτωρ μηρί' ἔκηε βοῶν αἰγῶν τε τελείων;
τὸν νῦν οὐκ ἔτλητε νέκυν περ ἐόντα σαῶσαι,
ᾗ τ' ἀλόχῳ ἰδέειν καὶ μητέρι καὶ τέκεϊ ᾧ
καὶ πατέρι Πριάμῳ λαοῖσί τε, τοί κέ μιν ὦκα
ἐν πυρὶ κήαιεν καὶ ἐπὶ κτέρεα κτερίσαιεν.
ἀλλ' ὀλοῷ Ἀχιλῆϊ, θεοί, <u>βούλεσθ'</u> ἐπαρήγειν,

(*Iliad* XXIV 33–39)

Hard-hearted you are, you gods, you live for cruelty!
Did Hektor never burn in your honor thigh bones of oxen and
flawless, full-grown goats?

---

[120] He uses the same wish formula (τὸ δέ μοι κρήηνον ἐέλδωρ) as Khruses and Agamemnon, as well as in Thetis' speech to Zeus: *Iliad* I 41, 455 (Khruses), 504 (Thetis); VIII 242 (Agamemnon); XVI 238 (Akhilleus).

[121] Scodel 1982a discusses allusions to "Golden Age" ideology in Homer; see also Nagy 1979:130.

> Now you cannot bring yourselves to save him—even his corpse—
> so his wife can see him, his mother and his child,
> His father Priam and Priam's people: how they'd rush
> To burn his body on the pyre and give him burial rites!
> But murderous Akhilleus—you gods, you <u>choose</u> to help Akhilleus.

Sacrifice is here contrasted directly with Akhilleus' special status. Apollo draws attention to the pious performance of sacrifice by Hektor, whom the gods ought to help, in contrast to Akhilleus, whom they choose to help (βούλεσθ' 'you all choose'). Apollo's directive concerning Akhilleus' savagery refers to the hero as ὀλοός 'destructive, murderous', a rare application of this powerful adjective to a person.[122] Hera's response to Apollo clearly focuses Akhilleus' status: he is the child of a goddess whom she herself has reared and therefore cannot be compared to Hektor (*Iliad* XXIV 58–60). Hera refers specifically to the marriage of Peleus and Thetis, which all the gods attended (*Iliad* XXIV 62–63). This image of gods and mortals celebrating together, similar to Iris' feasting with the Aithiopes, again recalls Golden Age commensality. In both instances, Akhilleus' liminality is emphasized by references to cheerful occasions in which the gap between gods and men does not yet exist. Sacrifice, such as that made by Hektor, is the post-Golden Age attempt by men to communicate with gods, a symbol of the lingering divide between mortals and immortals. In this sense, Akhilleus stands as a symbol of thematic opposition to sacrifice.

Zeus replies to Hera that Hektor and Akhilleus are not equals, but that Hektor is nonetheless a favorite mortal, repeating his earlier statement about his well-fed altar and the *geras* of the gods:

> οὐ μὲν γὰρ τιμή γε μί᾽ ἔσσεται· ἀλλὰ καὶ Ἕκτωρ
> φίλτατος ἔσκε θεοῖσι βροτῶν οἳ ἐν Ἰλίῳ εἰσίν·
> ὣς γὰρ ἐμοί γ᾽, ἐπεὶ οὔ τι φίλων ἡμάρτανε δώρων.
> οὐ γάρ μοί ποτε βωμὸς ἐδεύετο δαιτὸς ἐΐσης,
> λοιβῆς τε κνίσης τε· τὸ γὰρ λάχομεν γέρας ἡμεῖς.
>
> (*Iliad* XXIV 66–70)

> These two can never attain the same degree of honor.
> Still, the immortals loved prince Hektor dearly, best of all mortals
> > born in Troy;
> so I loved him, at least: he never stinted with gifts to please my
> > heart.

---

[122] *Iliad* XXIV 39; cf. Segal 1971:58.

Never once did my altar lack its share of victims,
libations and the sacrificial smoke. These are our gifts of honor.

Like Apollo, Zeus explicitly compares Hektor's sacrifices to Akhilleus' semi-divine status: Hektor's act of giving the immortals their proper *geras* cannot equate him with the son of Thetis. This striking description of the meaning of sacrifice for Zeus recalls the quarrel between Akhilleus and Agamemnon over *geras*. Fittingly, the context in which the word is most often used is Thetis' description of Briseis as Akhilleus' *geras* (*Iliad* I 507).[123] Zeus then concedes to Akhilleus the singular honor of being informed of the will of the gods—that Hektor should be returned to Priam. This is the kind of direct communication that the other heroes so clearly lack and that they attempt to establish through sacrifice.

One of the greatest achievements of the poem lies in the fact that Akhilleus' semi-divine status is constantly contrasted with his impending death.[124] As we have seen, from the perspective of the gods, Akhilleus is presented in opposition to mortal sacrificers. Significantly, Akhilleus himself, assuming a divine ability to deny sacrifice, rejects the power of sacrifice on two occasions, both signposts of his own impending doom: the rejection of Trojan sacrifices over the corpse of Lukaon and his revocation of Peleus' vow at the funeral of Patroklos. Akhilleus kills Lukaon despite the youth's lengthy supplication, the longest in the epic before that of Priam, and his subsequent treatment of the corpse, which is flung into the river to be food for the fish, is described in terms that closely recall oath sacrifice,[125] another way in which Akhilleus perverts normative sacrificial ritual. The entire exchange between the two heroes locates Akhilleus outside the norms of human behavior, and the conventions of battlefield speech are manipulated to stress this detachment. For example, Akhilleus' response is uniquely framed in terms of its reception by Lukaon, the only time the verb προσηύδα 'address, speak to' appears in a speech introduction rather than conclusion (*Iliad* XXI 97–98).[126] Akhilleus focuses specifically

---

[123] *Geras* is used in reference to Bruseis/Khruseis: *Iliad* I 118, 120, 123, 133, 135, 138, 161, 163, 167, 185, 276, 356, 507; II 240; IX 111, 344, 367; XVI 54, 56; XVIII 444; XIX 89. See Nagy 1979:132. *Geras* is only used elsewhere in the poem in reference to funerary rites (*Iliad* XVI 457, 675; XXIII 9) and the right of elders to persuade younger men (*Iliad* IV 323; IX 422), though a unique usage occurs in reference to Akhilleus' account of Aineias' hope to inherit Priam's power (*Iliad* XX 182).

[124] Schadewaldt 1944:260f.; Griffin 1980:191.

[125] Lukaon is one of several victims of Akhilleus whose death is depicted as a sort of mock oath sacrifice: Kitts 2005:162–166 explores the latent oath sacrifice imagery in this scene.

[126] See Beck 2005:171–175, who describes Akhilleus' behavior as "disengaged, berserk" (174).

on the futility of sacrifice to save the Trojans, just as the gods later conclude concerning Hektor's fate:

οὐδ' ὑμῖν ποταμός περ ἐΰρροος ἀργυροδίνης
ἀρκέσει, ᾧ δὴ δηθὰ πολέας ἱερεύετε ταύρους,
ζωοὺς δ' ἐν δίνῃσι καθίετε μώνυχας ἵππους.

(*Iliad* XXI 130–132)

Not even your silver-whirling, mighty-tiding river
can save you —not for all the bulls you've sacrificed to it for years,
the living, single-footed stallions you cast into its eddies.

Akhilleus assimilates himself to divinity by expressing a god-like perspective in his rejection of the efficacy of sacrifice; his rejection of cult worship demonstrates a self-conscious removal from mortal society and the value systems therein. Further, Akhilleus' speech provokes the anger of Skamandros, the sacrifices to whom he rejects as meaningless (*Iliad* XXI 136–138), culminating in the battle encompassing the remainder of *Iliad* XXI. Though his speech is part of the pattern of embedded sacrifices, which express anxiety or despair that sacrifices are not working, his intermediate status empowers him to adopt a divine perspective: similar to the laments by Zeus and Apollo that sacrifices cannot save mortals, Akhilleus casts Lukaon's death in terms of failed sacrifices. This speech also reflects the depth of his superhuman wrath, which the encounter with the Trojan youth has provoked by aggravating the acute awareness of his own imminent death.[127] The boast to kill Trojans in spite of any divine protection is part of his overall refusal of Lukaon's supplication, a reaction instigated by his remorse over Patroklos' death, the aforementioned knowledge of his own death, and his subsequent lack of sympathy for any other mortal. All of these reactions are part of the questioning of value systems initiated by the breakdown of reciprocity in *Iliad* I.[128] As we have already seen, sacrifice has been used to reassert Agamemnon's status among the Akhaian army in response to the breakdown of reciprocity. But here it is used contrarily to demonstrate Akhilleus' isolation, through his renunciation of normative ritual practices as he heads toward his own death.

Akhilleus' deviation from sacrificial ritual is most dramatically expressed in his slaughter of the Trojan youths at the funeral of Patroklos (*Iliad* XXIII 175–176).[129] This ritual process is not animal sacrifice since it is not a gift-

---

[127] Segal 1971:30–131; Scully 1986:140; Fenik 1968:213. Lohmann 1970:106 argues that Akhilleus sees his own death in that of Lukaon; cf. Stanley 1993:205.

[128] The breakdown of reciprocity is discussed by Seaford 2004:35–37.

[129] Lukaon predicts his own death at the hands of Akhilleus with this verb (σὺ δ' ἄμφω δειροτο-

offering to deities. Yet the primary narrator describes the gifts offered in such a way as to recall normative animal sacrifice, further contrasting Akhilleus' variance from accepted practice. Akhilleus slaughters sheep and cattle, which he flays (ἔδερον, *Iliad* XXIII 167), a verb also used to describe this process after sacrifice (*Iliad* I 459 = II 422). Whereas Agamemnon and the councilors wrap the thigh bones with fat from the victims (*knisê*, *Iliad* I 460–461 = II 423–424), Akhilleus wraps Patroklos' corpse in fat (*dêmos*, *Iliad* XXIII 169–170), adding jars of honey and oil, four living horses, and two dogs, before he slaughters twelve Trojan youths (*Iliad* XXIII 171–173):

κα̣ὶ μὲν τῶν ἐνέβαλλε πυρῇ δύο δειροτομήσας,
δώδεκα δὲ Τρώων μεγαθύμων υἱέας ἐσθλοὺς

(*Iliad* XXIII 174–175)

He slit the throats of two [dogs], threw them onto the pyre
and then a dozen brave sons of the proud Trojans...

The use of the verb δειροτομεῖν recalls Lukaon's death, linking these deaths to Akhilleus' supra-mortal wrath against the Trojans. In addition to his use of terminology associated with animal sacrifice, twelve is one of four possible quantities of animals used for sacrifices.[130] Patroklos' funeral is performed only after Akhilleus, with Agamemnon's approval, is reintegrated into the community, and it remains a private affair. The extreme savagery of this slaughter is described thus by Seth Schein:

> The greatest lapse into savagery in the *Iliad* is Achilles' sacrifice at the pyre of Patroklos of 12 Trojan youths...such deliberate savagery, however, really is not animalistic but distinctively human in its planned brutality and its perversion of an activity (sacrifice) that is supposed to bring humans closer not to animals but to the gods. Clearly Homer is portraying Achilles at this stage of the poem as beyond a boundary that humans in the *Iliad* normally do not cross.[131]

An enormous sense of *pathos* is created by the representation of superhuman qualities at the funeral of Patroklos, since this burial prefigures Akhilleus' own

---

μήσεις, *Iliad* XXI 89): Kitts 2005:157–158; see also Petropoulou 1988 and Saïd 1998 on the burial customs in this scene.

[130] Previously, he promised to kill (ἀποδειροτομεῖν) the Trojan youths (*Iliad* XVIII 336–337). This verb is also used of Odysseus' sacrifice of sheep to the dead (*Odyssey* xi 35). On the quantity of animals in Homeric sacrifice, see pages 99f. above.

[131] Schein 1984:79.

funeral. When he appears to urge Akhilleus to perform the funeral, Patroklos' ghost specifically asks that their bones be buried together, as they lived together in Peleus' house:

καὶ δὲ σοὶ αὐτῷ μοῖρα, θεοῖς ἐπιείκελ' Ἀχιλλεῦ,
τείχει ὕπο Τρώων εὐηφενέων ἀπολέσθαι.
ἄλλο δέ τοι ἐρέω καὶ ἐφήσομαι, αἴ κε πίθηαι·
μὴ ἐμὰ σῶν ἀπάνευθε τιθήμεναι ὀστέ', Ἀχιλλεῦ,
ἀλλ' ὁμοῦ, ὡς ἐτράφημεν ἐν ὑμετέροισι δόμοισιν,
εὖτέ με τυτθὸν ἐόντα Μενοίτιος ἐξ Ὀπόεντος
ἤγαγεν ὑμέτερόνδ' ἀνδροκτασίης ὕπο λυγρῆς,
ἤματι τῷ ὅτε παῖδα κατέκτανον Ἀμφιδάμαντος
νήπιος οὐκ ἐθέλων ἀμφ' ἀστραγάλοισι χολωθείς·
ἔνθά με δεξάμενος ἐν δώμασιν ἱππότα Πηλεὺς
ἔτραφέ τ' ἐνδυκέως καὶ σὸν θεράποντ' ὀνόμηνεν·
ὣς δὲ καὶ ὀστέα νῶϊν ὁμὴ σορὸς ἀμφικαλύπτοι
χρύσεος ἀμφιφορεύς, τόν τοι πόρε πότνια μήτηρ.

(*Iliad* XXIII 80–92)

And you too, your fate awaits you too, godlike as you are,
        Akhilleus—
to die in battle beneath the proud rich Trojans' walls!
But one thing more. A last request—grant it, please.
Never bury my bones apart from yours, Akhilleus,
Let them lie together, just as we grew up together in your house,
after Menoitios brought me there from Opoeis, and only a boy,
but banished for bloody murder the day I killed Amphidamas' son.
I was a fool—I never meant to kill him, quarreling over a dice
        game.
Then the horseman Peleus took me into his halls,
he reared me with kindness, appointed me your aide.
So now let a single urn, the gold two-handled urn
your noble mother gave you, hold our bones—together!

Patroklos reminds Akhilleus that he too will die at Troy, preventing any return to the happy home of Peleus.[132] The memory of Akhilleus and Patroklos in Peleus' house recalls Nestor's memory of his arrival in Phthia, upon which he found Peleus making sacrifice and Akhilleus and Patroklos busy preparing the meat for a meal. Likewise, Nestor remembers Menoitios' instructions that

---

[132] On this scene, see van der Valk 1964:446 and Petropoulou 1988:485.

Patroklos help Akhilleus. This is contextualized in the speech against a backdrop of a sacrifice (*Iliad* XI 785–790), the memory of which persuades Patroklos to go into battle, ultimately to his death.[133] The pleasurable occasions of shared meals are also associated with Patroklos by Akhilleus, who refuses to eat because it reminds him of meals once prepared by Patroklos (*Iliad* XIX 315–318). The ghost of Patroklos does not mention sacrifice, but focuses on the heroes "sitting apart" from their dear friends (φίλων ἀπάνευθεν ἑταίρων, *Iliad* XXIII 77). The references to the home in Nestor's memory have been replaced in the ghost's speech with the isolation and early death of the two heroes at Troy.

When Akhilleus performs Patroklos' funeral, revoking a vow made by his father to Sperkheios and giving the lock of hair to Patroklos instead, his isolation and his rejection of sacrifice are directly linked to the anticipation of his own death:

Σπερχεί', ἄλλως σοί γε πατὴρ ἠρήσατο Πηλεὺς
κεῖσέ με νοστήσαντα φίλην ἐς πατρίδα γαῖαν
σοί τε κόμην κερέειν ῥέξειν θ' ἱερὴν ἑκατόμβην,
πεντήκοντα δ' ἔνορχα παρ' αὐτόθι μῆλ' ἱερεύσειν
ἐς πηγάς, ὅθι τοι τέμενος βωμός τε θυήεις.
ὣς ἠρᾶθ' ὁ γέρων, σὺ δέ οἱ νόον οὐκ ἐτέλεσσας.
νῦν δ' ἐπεὶ οὐ νέομαί γε φίλην ἐς πατρίδα γαῖαν,
Πατρόκλῳ ἥρωϊ κόμην ὀπάσαιμι φέρεσθαι.

(*Iliad* XXIII 144–151)

Sperkheios! All in vain my father vowed to you
that there, once I had journeyed home to my own dear fatherland,
I'd cut this lock for you and offer a holy hecatomb,
and sacrifice fifty ungelded rams
to your springs, there at the spot where your grove and smoking
  altar stand!
So the old man vowed—but you've destroyed his hopes.
Now, since I shall not return to my fatherland,
I'll give this lock to the hero Patroklos to bear it on his way.

Just as with the vaunt over the corpse of Lukaon, Akhilleus, standing over the corpse of Patroklos, assumes a divine ability to reject sacrifices. Revoking Peleus' vow and standing over the corpse of Lukaon are the only times Akhilleus uses the verb ἱερεύειν 'to sacrifice'. He will not return home, as he

[133] On this memory, see pages 121f. above.

and the audience well know, and his estrangement and early death are signified in this refutation of the normative mortal approach to divine power over life and death.

The Trojan sacrifices to Skamandros (ἐν δίνῃσι 'in the eddies') will not save them, nor will Peleus' promise to sacrifice to Sperkheios (ἐς πηγάς 'to your springs') bring Akhilleus home. The unfulfilled sacrifice to Sperkheios and the rejection of sacrificial power as a means to avert death are linked, an association made more plaintive by replacing homecoming and the possibility of reciprocity with the gods with Akhilleus' commitment to share a funeral urn with Patroklos. Sacrifice now stands as a symbol of his isolation from ritual as a result of his young death, which also signifies his acquiescence to the *kleos* of epic poetry; were he not fated to die, Akhilleus would be performing sacrifice.[134] The complex irony of the impending death of a semi-divine hero is rendered more pathetic in his abstinence from sacrifice: his semi-divine status *as well as* his impending death preclude his performance of sacrifice. Akhilleus even ponders not fighting with Hektor and leaving the next day after having performed sacrifices:

> νῦν δ᾽ ἐπεὶ οὐκ ἐθέλω πολεμιζέμεν Ἕκτορι δίῳ,
> αὔριον ἱρὰ Διὶ ῥέξας καὶ πᾶσι θεοῖσι,
> νηήσας εὖ νῆας, ἐπὴν ἅλαδε προερύσσω,
>
> (*Iliad* IX 356–358)

Since I have no desire to battle glorious Hektor,
tomorrow at daybreak, once I have sacrificed to Zeus and all the
  gods
having loaded up my holds and launched out onto the breakers...

This sacrifice is never performed because he will never leave Troy, as the audience knows, and this statement serves to link Akhilleus' conspicuous absence from Akhaian sacrifices with his impending doom.

I will conclude this book with a final note on the contrast in the poem between Agamemnon's normative enacted sacrifices and Akhilleus' isolation. When Akhilleus withdraws from society, he enters a liminal realm, no longer a functioning member of the community, but acutely needed by it. He describes his treatment by Agamemnon as that appropriate to a μετανάστης (*Iliad* IX 648, XVI 59), a word that has been variously translated, perhaps best as 'migrant',

---

[134] Nagy has shown the thematic exchange of the *kleos* 'glory' of poetry for the *timê* 'honor' of cult in the case of Akhilleus: heroes in cult receive sacrifices after their death, the greatest sacrificial reward. Nagy 1979:118–141, esp. 137–138.

a foreigner living among others but outside the protection of the community. This is the condition Akhilleus creates upon his departure. Aristotle cites this passage as evidence that Akhilleus is excluded from the civil privileges of the *polis*, which, from Aristotle's perspective, would have included sacrifice.[135] In this isolation, Akhilleus' relationships with others are no longer governed by the accepted ordering principles of society. In his striving for self-sufficiency, his behavior is "articulating a notion of autonomy," and he withdraws to an extra-cultural, semi-divine world.[136]

It is interesting that we find Akhilleus, when his withdrawal is directly challenged in *Iliad* IX, instructing Patroklos to perform a unique variation on animal sacrifice, recalling Agamemnon's typical actions, but with a very different meaning appropriate to the context. After the animals have been slaughtered, cooked, salted, and served (*Iliad* IX 205–217), Akhilleus commands Patroklos to throw θυηλαί 'offerings' into the fire:

> αὐτὸς δ' ἀντίον ἷζεν Ὀδυσσῆος θείοιο
> τοίχου τοῦ ἑτέροιο, θεοῖσι δὲ θῦσαι ἀνώγει
> Πάτροκλον, ὃν ἑταῖρον· ὁ δ' ἐν πυρὶ βάλλε θυηλάς.
> οἱ δ' ἐπ' ὀνείαθ' ἑτοῖμα προκείμενα χεῖρας ἴαλλον.
> αὐτὰρ ἐπεὶ πόσιος καὶ ἐδητύος ἐξ ἔρον ἔντο,
>
> (*Iliad* IX 218–222)

> Then face-to-face with noble Odysseus he took his seat
> along the farther wall, he told Patroklos, his friend, to
> > make burnt offering to the gods
> and Patroklos threw the offerings in the fire.
> They reached out for the good things that lay at hand
> and when they had put aside desire for food and drink...

The verb ἀνώγει 'to command' recalls Agamemnon's instructions (ἄνωγεν) to the men to purify themselves before the sacrifice of hecatombs (*Iliad* I 313). No prayer or other ritual complement to the action of burning meat for the gods is listed. What is more, this offering is subsequent to the consumption of food, in contrast to normative sacrifice, in which offerings are given to the gods before the preparations for the mortal feast. Unlike Agamemnon, Akhilleus neither performs a sacrifice with pre-kill rites, nor

---

[135] Aristotle *Politics* 1278a37; Hammer 2002:94; Gschnitzer 1966; and West 1966:274, 276. Mackie 1996:139 draws comparisons between Akhilleus' language and the ideology of the poems of Hesiod. Turner 1974:23–59 describes the "liminal realm."

[136] Hammer 2002:96; cf. Friedrich and Redfield 1978:285 and Schein 1984:109. Similar opinions are expressed by Redfield 1975:93 and Nagler 1974:157–158.

does he make prayer or perform other honorary actions toward the gods. Instead, he instructs Patroklos to throw θυηλαί 'offerings' into the fire, which are then entirely consumed by the flames, not shared by the participants as are the *splankhna* in *Iliad* II 427. The absence of the expected features of sacrifice is emphasized in the description of spits, ἀμφ' ὀβελοῖσιν ἔπειρε 'pierce on spits' (*Iliad* IX 210), which are elsewhere used only in reference to *splankhna* (*Iliad* I 464 = II 427). Also, the phrase κατὰ πῦρ ἐκάη 'the fire burned' (*Iliad* IX 212) deliberately recalls the expected κατὰ μῆρε κάη 'burn the thigh bones' (*Iliad* I 464 = II 427), the ritual offering of thigh bones to the gods, also conspicuously absent from Akhilleus' feast.[137] Although Agamemnon hosts a feast without an offering to the gods earlier in *Iliad* IX, verses reminiscent of specific stages in the sacrificial process such as these found in Akhilleus' meal are not used. The primary narrative highlights Akhilleus' unique attempt at animal sacrifice with verses closely recalling the grand *thusia* sacrifices under Agamemnon's direction in *Iliad* I and II. As discussed in Chapter One, sacrificial vocabulary is used in reference to Akhilleus' meals, without reference to the gods, to highlight his abstinence from the expected sacrificial procedure.

Akhilleus attempts to recreate the kind of sacrificial feast and counseling session that Agamemnon has enacted in *Iliad* II and VII, both of which function as positive displays of authority among the leading men in his army. However, Akhilleus does not offer normative sacrifice. Odysseus explicitly compares this meal to those hosted by Agamemnon, remarking that they do not lack an "appropriate share of the feast" either in the quarters of Agamemnon or Akhilleus:

> χαῖρ', Ἀχιλεῦ· δαιτὸς μὲν ἐΐσης οὐκ ἐπιδευεῖς
> ἠμὲν ἐνὶ κλισίη Ἀγαμέμνονος Ἀτρεΐδαο
> ἠδὲ καὶ ἐνθάδε νῦν· πάρα γὰρ μενοεικέα πολλὰ
> δαίνυσθ'.

(Iliad IX 225–228)

> Cheers, Akhilleus! We do not lack our appropriate share of the
>   feast
> in the quarters of Agamemnon, the son of Atreus,
> or here and now, for you have provided many abundant things.[138]

---

[137] Stallings 1984:129.

[138] There are several variations in modern translations and textual emendations, which are discussed by Hainsworth 1993 note *ad loc.*

Scholars are divided in their opinion of the meaning of *dais* and the socio-economic function of ἐΐση δαίς 'appropriate share of the feast'. Some have argued that the *dais* emphasizes collectivity and harmony, while others posit that the Homeric *dais* is an elite affair, an exclusive meal for kings.[139] Although Akhilleus attempts to establish his independence through providing feasts in *Iliad* IX and XXIV, his feasts are compared by Odysseus to those of Agamemnon, whose hospitality is the model for this activity.[140] Significantly, neither this meal with the embassy nor the meal with Priam is described with the formulaic phrase οὐδέ τι θυμὸς ἐδεύετο δαιτὸς ἐΐσης 'no man's hunger lacked his share of the appropriate feast', a social event which only Agamemnon can enact. The redistribution of meat at communal feasts is a demonstration of central authority, which in the *Iliad*, when it is expressed through this formulaic phrase, is embodied in Agamemnon. All enacted sacrifices, the only feasts to be described thus, relate to the threats to and questioning of Agamemnon's authority implicit in Akhilleus' withdrawal.

The only occurrences of this formulaic phrase outside of the sacrifices in *Iliad* I, II, and VII are in reference to the feasts of the gods or to Akhilleus' funeral feast for Patroklos (the only time this phrase is used of his meals). The gods' banquet is described thus at *Iliad* I 602, and with the subsition of Zeus' altar for *thumos* at *Iliad* IV 48 = XXIV 69.[141] In the first of these banquets, the gods seem to have prepared a feast for themselves on Olympus, whereas Zeus refers to having received his "appropriate share" thanks to Trojan sacrifices at his altar (*Iliad* IV 48 = XXIV 69). Finally, the funeral feast for Patroklos provides "appropriate shares of the feast" for all (*Iliad* XXIII 56). The narrator describes Akhilleus as providing a τάφον μενοεικέα δαίνυ 'satsifying funeral feast' (*Iliad* XXIII 29), a meal described by Akhilleus to Agamemnon as a στυγερὴ δαίς 'wretched feast' (*Iliad* XXIII 48). Rather than giving him the pleasure and satisfaction usually accompanying a feast, Akhilleus' preparation, for which bulls, goats, sheep, and pigs are slaughtered, is hateful to him (*Iliad* XXIII 30–34.) To highlight this contrast, the consumption of this feast is described using the formulaic verses familiar from three enacted sacrifices:

---

[139] See Schmitt-Pantel 1990:22, followed by Mackie 1996:130 on the collectivity of the *dais*; the distribution of meat is discussed by Donlan 1993:163-164. Cunliffe 1924 and Stanley 1993:311n36, following Collins 1988:71, propose that the *dais* is for the elite.

[140] Kitts recognizes a difference between the feasts provided by Agamemnon and Akhilleus, describing the former as "*laos*-directed feasts and acts of munifience" and the latter as "*oikos*-directed" feasts, which emphasize hospitality (2002:29).

[141] Cf. also the feast (ἐΐση δαίς) for the gods at *Iliad* XV 95.

δαίνυντ', οὐδέ τι θυμὸς ἐδεύετο δαιτὸς ἐΐσης.   (*Iliad* I 468 = II 431 =
VII 320 = XXIII 56)
αὐτὰρ ἐπεὶ πόσιος καὶ ἐδητύος ἐξ ἔρον ἕντο   (*Iliad* I 469 = II 432 =
XXIII 57)

They feasted, nor did any man's spirit lack his appropriate share
of the feast.
But when they had put aside their desire for food and drink...

All four feasts depict the distribution of appropriate shares of meat, and the
commensal sacrifices in *Iliad* I and II are expanded with an additional description of the satisfaction afforded by the feast, which is elsewhere found only
in the funeral feast, yet another sign of the thematic association between
Agamemnon, Akhilleus, the quarrel, and sacrifice. Agamemnon's enacted
commensal sacrifices are contrasted with the 'wretched feast' (στυγερὴ δαίς,
Iliad XXIII 48) Akhilleus provides at a moment of great mourning. The verse
"when they had put aside desire for food and drink" (αὐτὰρ ἐπεὶ πόσιος καὶ
ἐδητύος ἐξ ἔρον ἕντο), is found on its own in contexts exclusively associated with Akhilleus: in the feast for the councilors preceding the embassy
to Akhilleus in *Iliad* IX, in Akhilleus' feast for the embassy, and in his meal
with Priam.[142] These verses create thematic links between Agamemnon's
enacted sacrifices, performed only in Akhilleus' absence, and feasts that form
a pattern of echoes to highlight Akhilleus' isolation from normative social
procedures.

Akhilleus' feast here is contextually and thematically very different from
the three enacted sacrifices connected with Agamemnon. First, no details of
the kill are given, nor do we know exactly who performed the task. Second,
such variety of animals is something not witnessed elsewhere in Homeric
enacted sacrifices, though it is often found in reference to the suitors' meals in
the *Odyssey*. The suitors are described as slaughtering cows, sheep, and goats
(βοῦς ἱερεύοντες καὶ ὄϊς καὶ πίονας αἶγας, *Odyssey* ii 56 = xvii 180 = xvii 535 = xx
250), and Alkinoos kills (ἱέρευσεν) 12 sheep, eight boars, and two oxen on one
occasion (*Odyssey* viii 59). The emphasis in these descriptions is on indulgent
or luxurious feasts without any specific sacral connotations. Third, Akhilleus
explicitly views this occasion as a funeral meal, focusing the audience's attention on that aspect of the ceremony. His perverse relationship with the *dais* is
clearly demonstrated; he seems disgusted with the idea of feasting, a contrast
to the description of characters satisfying their hunger with their 'appro-

---

[142] *Iliad* IX 92, 222; XXIV 628.

priate share'. This disparity with Agamemnon's sacrifices is another demonstration of the tension between hero and king. Odysseus' comparison of the "equal feast" enjoyed in the huts of Agamemnon to that provided by Akhilleus provides a poignant summary of the central conflict in the poem.

Bibliography

Adkins, A. W. H. 1960. "Honour and Punishment in the Homeric Poems." *Bulletin of the Institute of Classical Studies* 7:23–32.

———. 1969. "EUXOMAI, EUXWLH, and EUXOS in Homer." *Classical Quarterly* 19: 20–33.

———. 1972. "Homeric Gods and the Values of Homeric Society." *Journal of Hellenic Studies* 92:1–19.

———. 1997. "Homeric Ethics." In Morris and Powell 1997:694–714.

Ahl, F. and Roisman, H. M. 1996. *Odyssey Re-Formed.* Ithaca.

Andersen, Ø. 1987. "Myth, Paradigm, and 'Spatial Form' in the *Iliad.*" In Bremer et al. 1987:1–13.

———. 1990. "The Making of the Past in the *Iliad.*" *Harvard Studies in Classical Philology* 93:25–45.

Arend, W. 1933. *Die typischen Scenen bei Homer.* Berlin.

Aretz, S. 1999. *Die Opferung der Iphigeneia in Aulis: Die Rezeption des Mythos in antiken und modernen Dramen.* Stuttgart.

Armstrong, J. 1958. "The Arming Motif in the *Iliad.*" *American Journal of Philology* 79: 337–354.

Auerbach, E. 1953. *Mimesis: The Representation of Reality in Western Literature,* trans. W. R. Trask. Princeton.

Auffarth, C. 1991. *Der drohende Untergang: "Schöpfung" in Mythos und Ritual im alten Orient und in Griechenland am Beispiel der Odyssee und des Ezechielbuches.* Berlin.

Austin, N. 1966. "The Function of Digressions in the *Iliad.*" *Greek, Roman, and Byzantine Studies* 7:259–312.

———. 1975. *Archery at the Dark of the Moon: Poetic Problems in Homer's Odyssey.* Berkeley.

Bakhtin, M. M. 1981. *The Dialogic Imagination: Four Essays by M. M. Bakhtin* (ed. M. Holquist), trans. C. Emerson and M. Holquist. Austin.

Bakker, E. 1988. *Linguistics and Formulas in Homer: Scalarity and the Description of the Particle Per.* Amsterdam.

——. 1997. *Poetry in Speech: Orality and Homeric Discourse.* Ithaca.

Bakker, E. and Fabbricotti, F. 1991. "Peripheral and Nuclear Semantics in Homeric Diction: The Case of Dative Expressions for 'Spear'." *Mnemosyne* 44:63–85.

Bal, M. 1985. *Narratology: Introduction to the Theory of Narrative,* trans. C. van Boheemen. Toronto.

Bassett, S. E. 1938. *The Poetry of Homer.* Berkeley.

Baudy, G. 1983. "Hierarchie oder: die Verteilung des Fleisches." *Neue Ansätze in der Religionswissenschaft* (eds. B. Gladigow and H. G. Kippenberg) 131–174. Munich.

Beattie, J. H. M. 1980. "On Understanding Sacrifice." In Bourdillon and Fortes 1980: 29–44.

Beck, D. 2005. *Homeric Conversation.* Washington.

Bendall, L. M. 2004. "Fit for a King? Hierarchy, Exclusion, Aspiration and Desire in the Social Structure of Mycenaean Banqueting." In Halstead and Barrett 2004:105–131.

Bennet, J. and Davis, J. 1999. "Making Mycenaeans: Warfare, Territorial Expansion, and Representations of the Other in the Pylian Kingdom." *Polemos: Le contexte guerrier en Egée à l'âge du Bronze; actes de la 7e Recontre égéene internationale, Université de Liège, 14–17 avril 1998* (ed. R. Laffineur) 105–120.

Benveniste, E. 1973. *Indo-European Language and Society,* trans. E. Palmer. London. = 1969. *Le vocabulaire des institutions indo-européennes. I. Economie, parenté, société. II. Pouvoir, droit, religion.* Paris.

Bergquist, B. 1988. "The Archaeology of Sacrifice: Minoan-Mycenaean versus Greek. A Brief Survey into Two Sites with Contrary Evidence." In Hägg et al. 1988:21–34.

Bernabé, A. 1987. *Poetarum epicorum Graecorum testimonia et fragmenta.* Leipzig.

Berthiaume, G. 1982. *Les rôles du mágeiros: étude sur la boucherie, la cuisine et le sacrifice dans la Grèce ancienne.* Leiden.

Beye, C. R. 1964. "Homeric Battle Narratives and Catalogues." *Harvard Studies in Classical Philology* 68:345–373.

——. 1993. *Ancient Epic Poetry: Homer, Apollonius, Virgil.* Ithaca.

Blegen, C. and Rawson, M., eds. 1966–1973. *The Palace of Nestor at Pylos in Western Messenia.* Princeton.

Block, E. 1982. "The Narrator Speaks: Apostrophe in Homer and Vergil." *Transactions of the American Philological Association* 112:7–22.

Boardman, J. 1974. *Athenian Black Figure Vases*. New York.

Bonner, R. J. and Smith, G. 1930. *The Administration of Justice from Homer to Aristotle* I. Chicago.

Bourdillon, M. F. C. 1980. "Introduction." In Bourdillon and Fortes 1980:1–27.

Bourdillon, M. F. C. and Fortes, M., eds. 1980. *Sacrifice*. London.

Bowie, A. M. 1995. "Greek Sacrifice: Forms and Functions." *The Greek World* (ed. A. Powell) 463–482. London.

Bowra, C. M. 1930. *Tradition and Design in the Iliad*. Oxford.

Bremer, J. M., de Jong, I. J. F., and Kalff, J., eds. 1987. *Homer: Beyond Oral Poetry. Recent Trends in Homeric Interpretation*. Amsterdam.

Bremmer, J. N. 1996. "Modi di communicare con il divino: la preghiera, la divinazione, il sacrificio nella civiltà greca." *I Greci: Storia, cultura, arte, società* I (ed. S. Settis) 239–283. Turin.

———. 1998. "'Religion', 'Ritual', and the Opposition 'Sacred vs. Profane.'" In Graf 1998:9–32.

Burkert, W. 1966. "Greek Tragedy and Sacrificial Ritual." *Greek, Roman, and Byzantine Studies* 7:87–121.

———. 1976. "Opfertypen und antike Gesellschaftsstruktur." *Der Religionswandel unserer Zeit im Spiegel der Religionswissenschaft* (ed. G. Stephenson) 168–187. Darmstadt.

———. 1979. *Structure and History in Greek Mythology and Ritual*. Berkeley.

———. 1981. "Glaube und Verhalten: Zeichengehalt und Wirkungsmacht von Opfer-ritualen." In Rudhardt and Reverdin 1981:91–125.

———. 1983. *Homo Necans: the Anthropology of Greek Sacrificial Ritual and Myth*, trans. P. Bing. Berkeley.

———. 1985. *Greek Religion*, trans. J. Raffan. Cambridge, MA.

———. 2003. *Die Griechen und der Orient: Von Homer bis zu den Magiern*. Munich.

Buxton, R., ed. 2000. *Oxford Readings in Greek Religion*. Oxford.

Cairns, D. L. 1993. *Aidōs: The Psychology and Ethics of Honour and Shame in Ancient Greek Literature*. Oxford.

———, ed. 2000. *Oxford Readings in Homer's Iliad*. Oxford.

Calhoun, G. M. 1962. "The Homeric Picture." In Wace and Stubbings 1962:431–452.

Cantilena, M. 1982. *Ricerche sulla dizione epica, I: Per uno studio della formularità degli Inni omerici.* Rome.

Carlier, P. 1984. *La royauté en Grèce avant Alexandre.* Strasbourg.

——. 2006. "ἄναξ and βασιλεύς in the Homeric Poems." In Deger-Jalkotzy and Lemos 2006:101–110.

Casabona, J. 1966. *Recherches sur le vocabulaire des sacrifices en grec, des origines à la fin de l'époque classique.* Aix-en-Provence.

Chadwick, J. 1976. *The Mycenaean World.* Cambridge.

Chantraine, P. 1932. "Remarques sur l'emploi des formules dans le premier chant de l'*Iliade*." *Revue des études grecques* 45:121–154.

Chatman, S. 1978. *Story and Discourse: Narrative Structure in Fiction and Film.* Ithaca.

Cleary, J., ed. 1989. *Proceedings of the Boston Area Colloquium in Ancient Philosophy IV.* Lanham, MD.

Clinton, K. 1974. "The Sacred Officials of the Eleusinian Mysteries." *Transactions of the American Philosophical Society* 64.3:1–143.

——. 2005. "Pigs in Greek Rituals." In Hägg and Alroth 2005:167–179.

Coldstream, J. N. 1985. "Greek Temples: Why and Where?" In Easterling and Muir 1985:67–97.

Collins, L. 1988. *Studies in Characterization in the Iliad.* Frankfurt.

Connelly, J. 2007. *Portrait of a Priestess: Women and Ritual in Ancient Greece.* Princeton.

Connor, W. R. 1988. "'Sacred' and 'Secular': Ἱερὰ καὶ ὅσια and the Classical Athenian Concept of the State." *Ancient Society* 19:161–188.

Cunliffe, R. J. A. 1924. *A Lexicon of the Homeric Dialect* ed. 2. Norman, OK.

Davidson, O. M. 1994. *Poet and Hero in the Persian Book of Kings.* Ithaca.

De Jong, I. J. F. 1987a. "The Voice of Anonymity: Tis-Speeches in the *Iliad*." *Eranos* 85:69–84.

——. 1987b. *Narrators and Focalizers: The Presentation of the Story in the Iliad.* Amsterdam.

——. 1997. "Homer and Narratology." In Morris and Powell 1997:303–325.

——, ed. 1999. *Homer.* London.

De Jong, I. and Nünlist, R., eds. 2004. *Narrators, Narratees, and Narratives in Ancient Greek Literature: Studies in Ancient Greek Narrative.* Leiden.

——. 2004. "Narrators, Narratees, and Narratives in Ancient Greek Literature." In de Jong and Nünlist 2004:545–554.

Deger-Jalkotzy, S. and Lemos, I. S., eds. 2006. *Ancient Greece: From the Mycenaean Palaces to the Age of Homer.* Edinburgh Leventis Studies 3. Edinburgh.

Detienne, M. 1967. *Les maîtres de vérité dans la Grèce archaïque.* Paris.

——. 1989. "Culinary Practices and the Spirit of Sacrifice." In Detienne and Vernant 1989:1–20.

Detienne, M. and Vernant, J. P., eds. 1989. *The Cuisine of Sacrifice among the Greeks,* trans. P. Wissing. Chicago.

Deubner, L. 1932. *Attische Feste.* Berlin.

——. 1982. "Ololyge und Verwandtes." *Kleine Schriften zur klassischen Altertumskunde. Beiträge zur Klassischen Philologie* 140:607–634. Königstein/Ts.

Dickson, K. 1995. *Nestor: Poetic Memory in Greek Epic.* New York.

Dickinson, O. 1986. "Homer, the Poet of the Dark Age." *Greece and Rome* 33:20–37.

Dietrich, B. 1988. "The Instrument of Sacrifice." In Hägg et al. 1988:35–40.

Dillon, M. 2002. *Girls and Women in Classical Greek Religion.* London.

Dodds, E. R. 1951. *The Greeks and the Irrational.* Berkeley.

Doherty, L. 1995. *Siren Songs: Gender, Audiences, and Narrators in the Odyssey.* Ann Arbor.

Donlan, W. 1979. "The Structure of Authority in the *Iliad.*" *Arethusa* 12:51–70.

——. 1993. "Dueling with Gifts in the *Iliad*: As the Audience Saw It." *Colby Quarterly* 24:155–172.

Drews, R. 1983. *Basileus: Evidence for Kingship in Geometric Greece.* New Haven.

Duckworth, G. E. 1933. *Foreshadowing and Suspense in the Epics of Homer, Apollonius, and Vergil.* Princeton.

Durand, J. 1989. "Ritual as Instrumentality." In Detienne and Vernant 1989:119–128.

Durkheim, E. 2001. *The Elementary Forms of Religious Life,* trans. C. Cosman. Oxford. = 1915. *Formes élémentaires de la vie religieuse: Le système totémique en Australie.* Paris.

Easterling, P. E. and Muir, J., eds. 1985. *Greek Religion and Society.* Cambridge.

Edmunds, L. 1989. "Commentary on Raaflaub." In Cleary 1989:26–33.

Edwards, M. 1975. "Type-Scenes and Homeric Hospitality." *Transactions of the American Philological Association* 105:51–72.

———. 1980. "Convention and Individuality in *Iliad* 1." *Harvard Studies in Classical Philology* 84:1–28.

———. 1987. *Homer: Poet of the Iliad.* Baltimore.

———. 1991. *The Iliad: A Commentary, Volume 5: Books 17–20.* Cambridge.

———. 1997. "Homeric Style and 'Oral Poetics'." In Morris and Powell 1997:261–284.

Eitrem, S. 1915. *Opferritus und Voropfer der Griechen und Römer.* Kristiania [Oslo].

———. 1938. "Mantis und Sphagia." *Symbolae Osloenses* 18:9–30.

Erbse, H. 1969. *Scholia Graeca in Homeri Iliadem I-VII.* Berlin.

Fagles, R., ed. 1990. *The Iliad.* New York.

Felson-Rubin, N. 1993. "Bakhtinian Alterity, Homeric Rapport." *Arethusa* 26:159–171.

Fenik, B. 1968. *Typical Battle Scenes in the Iliad: Studies in the Narrative Techniques of Homeric Battle Description.* Hermes Einzelschriften 21. Wiesbaden.

———. 1977. Review of M. Nagler, *Spontaneity and Tradition: A Study in the Oral Art of Homer* (Berkeley, 1974). *Classical Philology* 72:60–65.

Finley, M. I. 1970. *Early Greece: The Bronze and Archaic Ages.* London.

———. 1977. *The World of Odysseus.* Revised ed. 2. New York.

———. 1982. *Economy and Society in Ancient Greece.* New York.

Fisher, N. and van Wees, H., eds. 1998. *Archaic Greece: New Approaches and New Evidence.* London.

Foley, H. 1985. *Ritual Irony: Poetry and Sacrifice in Euripides.* Ithaca.

Foley, J. M. 1990. *Traditional Oral Epic: The Odyssey, Beowulf, and the Serbo-Croatian Return Song.* Berkeley.

———. 1991. *Immanent Art: From Structure to Meaning in Traditional Oral Epic.* Bloomington.

———. 1997. "Oral Tradition and its Implications." In Morris and Powell 1997:146–173.

———. 2002. "Editing and Translating Oral Epic: The South Slavic Songs and Homer." In Worthington and Foley 2002:3–28.

Ford, A. 1992. *Homer: The Poetry of the Past.* Ithaca.

Fowler, R., ed. 2004. *The Cambridge Companion to Homer.* Cambridge.

——. 2004. "The Homeric Question." In Fowler 2004:220–232.

Fränkel, H. 1975. *Early Greek Poetry and Philosophy: A History of Greek Epic, Lyric, and Prose to the Middle of the Fifth Century,* trans. M. Hadas and J. Willis. New York.

Frazer, J. 1911. *The Golden Bough: A Study in Magic and Religion* ed. 3. London.

Frazer, R. M. 1983. *The Poems of Hesiod.* Norman, OK.

Friedrich, P. and Redfield, J. M. 1978. "Speech as Personality Symbol: The Case of Achilles." *Language* 54:263–288.

Furley, W. 1981. *Studies in the Use of Fire in Ancient Greek Religion.* New York.

Gaisser, J. 1969. "A Structural Analysis of the Digressions in the *Iliad* and the *Odyssey.*" *Harvard Studies in Classical Philology* 73:1–43.

——. 1970. "Homeric Speech Introductions." *Harvard Studies in Classical Philology* 74:1–36.

Gantz, T. 1993. *Early Greek Myth: A Guide to Literary and Artistic Sources.* Baltimore.

García, J. F. 2002. "Ritual Speech in Early Greek Song." In Worthington and Foley 2002:29–54.

García López, J. 1970. *Sacrificio y sacerdocio en las religiones micenica y homerica.* Manuales y Anejos de "Emerita" 26. Madrid.

Garland, R. S. J. 1984. "Religious Authority in Archaic and Classical Athens." *Annual of the British School at Athens* 79:75-123.

Gebauer, J. 2002. *Pompe und Thysia: Attische Tieropferdarstellungen auf schwarz- und rotfigurigen Vasen.* Beiträge zur antiken Bildersprache 7. Münster.

Geddes, A. C. 1984. "Who's Who in Homeric Society." *Classical Quarterly* 34: 17–36.

Genette, G. 1980. *Narrative Discourse: An Essay in Method,* trans. J. E. Lewin. Ithaca.

Gigon, O. et al. 1946. *Phyllobolia, für Peter von der Mühll zum 60. Geburtstag am 1. August 1945.* Basel.

Gill, C., Postlethwaite, N., and Seaford, R., eds. 1998. *Reciprocity in Ancient Greece.* Oxford.

Gill, D. 1974. "Trapezomata: A Neglected Aspect of Greek Sacrifice." *The Harvard Theological Review* 67:117–137.

Gillies, M. 1925. "Purification in Homer." *Classical Quarterly* 19:71–74.

Girard, R. 1977. *Violence and the Sacred*, trans. P. Gregory. Baltimore.

Gordon, R. L., ed. 1981. *Myth, Religion, and Society: Structuralist Essays.* Cambridge.

Gould, G. P. 1977. "The Nature of Homeric Composition." *Illinois Classical Studies* 2:1–34.

Gould, J. 1985. "On Making Sense of Greek Religion." In Easterling and Muir 1985:1–33.

——. 2001. *Myth, Ritual, Memory, and Exchange: Essays in Greek Literature and Culture.* Oxford.

Graf, F., ed. 1998. *Ansichten griechischer Rituale: Geburtstags-Symposium für Walter Burkert, Castelen bei Basel, 15. bis 18. März 1996.* Stuttgart.

——. 2002. "What is New about Greek Sacrifice." *Kykeon: Studies in Honour of H. S. Versnel* (eds. H. F. J. Horstmanshoff et al.) 113–125. Leiden.

Griffin, J. 1978. "The Divine Audience and the Religion of the *Iliad*." *Classical Quarterly* 28:1–22.

——. 1980. *Homer on Life and Death.* Oxford.

——, ed. 1995. *Iliad IX.* Oxford.

——. 1986. "Homeric Words and Speakers." *Journal of Hellenic Studies* 106:36–57.

Gschnitzer, F. 1966. "BASILEUS. Ein terminologischer Beitrag zur Frühgeschichte des Königtums bei den Griechen." *Festschrift Leonhard C. Franz zum 70. Geburtstag* (eds. O. Menghin and H. M. Ölberg). *Innsbrucker Beiträge zur Kulturwissenschaft* 11:99–112.

Gunn, D. M. 1971. "Thematic Composition and Homeric Authorship." *Harvard Studies in Classical Philology* 75:1–31.

Hägg, R. and Alroth, B., eds. 2005. *Greek Sacrificial Ritual, Olympian and Chthonian: Proceedings of the Sixth International Seminar on Ancient Greek Cult, Göteborg University, 25-27 April 1997.* Sävedalen.

Hägg, R., Marinatos, N., and Nordquist, G., eds. 1988. *Early Greek Cult Practice: Proceedings of the Fifth International Symposium at the Swedish Institute at Athens, 26-29 June, 1986.* Stockholm.

Hainsworth, J. B. 1969. *Homer.* Oxford.

——. 1993. *The Iliad: A Commentary, Volume 3: Books 9-12.* Cambridge.

Halstead, P. and Barrett, J., eds. 2004. *Food, Cuisine and Society in Prehistoric Greece.* Oxford.

Halstead, P. and Isaakidou, V. 2004. "Faunal Evidence for Feasting: Burnt Offerings from the Palace of Nestor at Pylos." In Halstead and Barrett 2004: 136–154.

Hamerton-Kelly, R. 1987. *Violent Origins: Walter Burkert, René Girard and Jonathan Z. Smith on Ritual Killing and Cultural Formation.* Stanford.

Hammer, D. 1997. "'Who Shall Readily Obey?': Authority and Politics in the *Iliad.*" *Phoenix* 51:1–24.

—— 2002. *The Iliad as Politics: The Performance of Political Thought.* Norman, OK.

Havelock, E. 1971. *Prologue to Greek Literacy.* Cincinnati.

——. 1978. "The Alphabetization of Homer." In Havelock and Hershbell 1978:2–23.

Havelock, E. and Hershbell, J. P., eds. 1978. *Communication Arts in the Ancient World.* New York.

Henrichs, A. 1981. "Human Sacrifice in Greek Religion: Three Case Studies." In Rudhardt and Reverdin 1980:195–235.

——. 1987. *Die Götter Griechenlands: Ihr Bild im Wandel der Religionswissenschaft.* Bamberg.

——. 1998. "Dromena und Legomena: Zum rituellen Selbstverständnis der Griechen." In Graf 1998:33–71.

——. 2000. "Drama and Dromena: Bloodshed, Violence, and Sacrificial Metaphor in Euripides." *Harvard Studies in Classical Philology* 100:173–188.

——. 2003. "Writing Religion: Inscribed Texts, Ritual Authority, and the Religious Discourse of the Polis." *Written Texts and the Rise of Literate Culture in Ancient Greece* (ed. H. Yunis) 38–50. Cambridge.

——. 2005. "'Sacrifice as to the Immortals': Modern Classifications of Animal Sacrifice and Ritual Distinctions in the *Lex Sacra* from Selinous." In Hägg and Alroth 2005:47–60.

——. 2008. "What is a Greek Priest?" *Practitioners of the Divine: Greek Priests and Religious Officials from Homer to Heliodorus* (eds. B. Dignas and K. Trampedach) 1–14. Washington.

Hermary, A. et al. 2004. "Les sacrifices dans le monde grec." *Thesaurus cultus et rituum antiquorum* I:60–132. Basel.

Herrenschmidt, O. 1982. "Quelles fêtes pour quelles castes?" *L'Homme* 22:31–55.

Heubeck, A. 1954. *Der Odyssee-Dichter und die Ilias.* Erlangen.

——. 1974. *Die Homerische Frage: Ein Bericht über die Forschung der letzten Jahrzehnte.* Darmstadt.

Heubeck, A., West, S., and Hainsworth, J. B. 1988. A *Commentary on Homer's Odyssey Volume I: Introduction and Books I-VIII.* Oxford.

Hoekstra, A. 1965. *Homeric Modifications of Formulaic Prototypes: Studies in the Development of Greek Epic Diction.* Amsterdam.

Horrocks, G. 1997. *Greek: A History of the Language and its Speakers.* London.

Hubert, H. and Mauss, M. 1964. *Sacrifice: Its Nature and Functions,* trans. W. D. Halls. Chicago.

Isaakidou, V. et al. 2002. "Burnt Animal Sacrifice at the Mycenaean 'Palace of Nestor.'" *Antiquity* 76:86–92.

Jaeger, W. 1960. *Humanistische Reden und Vorträge* ed. 2. Berlin.

——. 1965. *Paideia: The Ideals of Greek Culture,* trans. G. Highet. Oxford.

Jameson, M. 1988. "Sacrifice and Animal Husbandry in Classical Greece." *Pastoral Economies in Classical Antiquity* (ed. C. R. Whittaker) 87–119. Cambridge.

——. 1991. "Sacrifice Before Battle." *Hoplites: The Classical Greek Battle Experience* (ed. V. D. Hanson) 197–227. London.

——. 1994. "Theoxenia." *Ancient Greek Cult Practice from the Epigraphical Evidence: Proceedings of the Second International Seminar on Ancient Greek Cult, organized by the Swedish Institute at Athens, 22–24 November 1991* (ed. R. Hägg) 35–57. Stockholm.

Janko, R. 1992. *The Iliad: A Commentary, Volume 4: Books 13-16.* Cambridge.

Jones, P. V. 1992. "The Past in Homer's *Odyssey.*" *Journal of Hellenic Studies* 112: 74–90.

Kadletz, E. 1984. "The Sacrifice of Eumaios the Pig Herder." *Greek, Roman, and Byzantine Studies* 25:99–105.

Kahane, A. 1994. *The Interpretation of Order: A Study in the Poetics of Homeric Repetition.* Oxford.

Kakrides, J. T. 1971. *Homer Revisited.* Lund.

Kearns, E. 1982. "The Return of Odysseus: A Homeric Theoxeny." *Classical Quarterly* 32:2–8.

——. 2004. "The Gods in the Homeric Epics." In Fowler 2004:59–73.

Killen, J. T. 1994. "Thebes Sealings, Knossos Tablets, and Mycenaean State Banquets." *Bulletin of the Institute of Classical Studies* 39:67–84.

——. 1998. "The Pylos Ta Tablets Revisited." *Bulletin de correspondance hellénique* 122:421–422.

——. 2001. "Religion at Pylos: The Evidence of the Fn Tablets." In Laffineur and Hägg 2001:435–443.

Kirk, G. S. 1962. *The Songs of Homer.* Cambridge.

——. 1974. *The Nature of Greek Myths.* Harmondsworth.

——. 1976. *Homer and the Oral Tradition.* Cambridge.

——. 1981. "Some Methodological Pitfalls in the Study of Ancient Greek Sacrifice (In Particular)." In Rudhardt and Reverdin 1981:41–90.

——. 1985. *The Iliad: A Commentary, Volume 1: Books 1–4.* Cambridge.

——. 1990. *The Iliad: A Commentary, Volume 2: Books 5–8.* Cambridge.

Kitts, M. 1999. "Killing, Healing, and the Hidden Motif of Oath-Sacrifice in *Iliad* 21." *Journal of Ritual Studies* 13:42–57.

——. 2000. "The Wide Bosom of the Sea as a Place of Death: Maternal and Sacrificial Imagery in *Iliad* 21." *Literature and Theology* 14:103–124.

——. 2002. "Sacrificial Violence in the *Iliad.*" *Journal of Ritual Studies* 16:19–39.

——. 2005. *Sanctified Violence in Homeric Society: Oath-Making Rituals and Narratives in the Iliad.* Cambridge.

Kullmann, W. 1985. "Gods and Men in the *Iliad* and *Odyssey.*" *Harvard Studies in Classical Philology* 89:1–23.

Laffineur, R. and Hägg, R., eds. 2001. *POTNIA: Deities and Religion in the Aegean Bronze Age. Proceedings of the 8th Internationl Aegean Conference/8e Recontre Egéene Internationale, Göteborg, Göteborg University, 12–15 April 2000.* Liège and Austin.

Lang, M. 1975. "Reason and Purpose in Homeric Prayers." *Classical World* 68:309–314.

Latacz, J. 1975. "Zur Forschungsarbeit an den direkten Reden bei Homer." *Grazer Beiträge* 3:395–422.

——. 1996. *Homer: His Art and His World*, trans. J. P. Holoka. Ann Arbor.

——. 2002. *Homers Ilias. Gesamtkommentar I.* Leipzig.

Lateiner, D. 1997. "Homeric Prayer." *Arethusa* 30:241–272.

Lattimore, R., ed. 1967. *The Odyssey of Homer.* New York.

Laum, B. 1924. *Heiliges Geld: Eine historische Untersuchung über den sakralen Ursprung des Geldes.* Tübingen.

Launderville, D. 2003. *Piety and Politics: The Dynamics of Royal Authority in Homeric Greece, Biblical Israel, and Old Babylonian Mesopotamia.* Grand Rapids, MI.

Lehrs, K., ed. 1964. *De Aristarchi studiis Homericis.* Reprint of 1882 ed. Leipzig.

Lesky, A. 1967. *Homeros.* RE Supplementum IX:687–846. Stuttgart.

Lévi-Strauss, C. 1955. *Tristes tropiques.* Paris.

Lloyd-Jones, H. 1971. *The Justice of Zeus.* Berkeley.

Lohmann, D. 1970. *Die Komposition der Reden in der Ilias.* Untersuchungen zur antiken Literatur und Geschichte 6. Berlin.

Long, A. A. 1970. "Morals and Values in Homer." *Journal of Hellenic Studies* 90:121–139.

Lord, A. 1960. *The Singer of Tales.* Cambridge.

Lorimer, H. L. 1950. *Homer and the Monuments.* London.

Lowenstam, S. 1993. *The Scepter and the Spear: Studies on Forms of Repetition in the Homeric Poems.* Lanham, MD.

Lupu, E. 2005. *Greek Sacred law: A Collection of New Documents (NGSL).* Leiden.

Lynn-George, M. 1988. *Epos: Word, Narrative and the Iliad.* Basingstoke.

Mackie, H. 1996. *Talking Trojan: Speech and Community in the Iliad.* Lanham, MD.

Malinowski, B. 1948. *Magic, Science, and Religion, and Other Essays.* Boston.

Marinatos, N. 1988. "The Imagery of Sacrifice: Minoan and Greek." In Hägg et al. 1988:1–19.

Martin, R. 1983. *Healing, Sacrifice, and Battle: Amechania and Related Concepts in Early Greek Poetry.* Innsbruck.

——. 1989. *The Language of Heroes: Speech and Performance in the Iliad.* Ithaca.

——. 1993. "Telemachus and the Last Hero Song." *Colby Quarterly* 29:222–240.

Mauss, M. 1954. *The Gift: Forms and Functions of Exchange in Archaic Societies,* trans. I. Cunnison. Glencoe, IL.

——. 1968. *Oeuvres* I. Paris.

Mazarakis Ainian, A. 1988. "Early Greek Temples: Their Origin and Function." In Hägg et al. 1988:105–119.

Meillet, A. 1923. *Les origines indo-européennes des mètres grecs.* Paris.

Meillet, A. and Vendryes, J. 1924. *Traité de grammaire comparée des langues classiques.* Paris.

Meuli, K. 1946. "Griechische Opferbräuche." In Gigon et al. 1946:185–288.

——. 1975. *Gesammelte Schriften* I, II. Basel and Stuttgart.

Mikalson, J. D. 2005. *Ancient Greek Religion.* Malden, MA.

Mondi, R. 1980. "Σκηπτοῦχοι Βασιλεῖς: Divine Kingship in Early Greece." *Arethusa* 13:203–216.

Monro, D. B., and Allen, T. W., eds. 1920. *Homeri Opera* ed. 3. Oxford.

Morris, I. 1986. "The Use and Abuse of Homer." *Classical Antiquity* 5:81–138.

———. 1988. "Tomb Cult and the 'Greek Renaissance': The Past in the Present in the 8th Century B.C." *Antiquity* 62:750–761.

———. 1992. "Poetics of Power: The Interpretation of Ritual Action in Archaic Greece." *Cultural Poetics in Archaic Greece: Cult, Performance, Politics* (eds. C. Dougherty and L. Kurke) 15–45. Cambridge.

Morris, I. and Powell, B., eds. 1997. *A New Companion to Homer.* Leiden.

Morris, S. 1997. "Homer and the Near East." In Morris and Powell 1997:599–623.

Morrison, J. 1991. "The Function and Context of Homeric Prayers: A Narrative Perspective." *Hermes* 119:145–157.

Motte, A., Pirenne-Delforge, V., and Wathelet, P., eds. 1992–1998. *Mentor: A Bibliographical Survey of Greek Religion.* Liège.

Motto, A. L. and Clark, J. R. 1969. "*Ise Dais*: the Honor of Achilles." *Arethusa* 2:109–125.

Muellner, L. 1976. *The Meaning of Homeric Euchomai through its Formulas.* Innsbruck.

———. 1996. *The Anger of Achilles: Mênis in Greek Epic.* Ithaca.

Muir, E. 1981. *Civic Ritual in Renaissance Venice.* Princeton.

Murray, O. 1980. *Early Greece.* Brighton.

———, ed. 1990. *Sympotica: A Symposium on the Symposium.* Oxford.

Nagler, M. N. 1974. *Spontaneity and Tradition: A Study of the Oral Art of Homer.* Berkeley.

Nagy, G. 1974. *Comparative Studies in Greek and Indic Meter.* Cambridge, MA.

———. 1979. *The Best of the Achaeans: Concepts of the Hero in Archaic Greek Poetry.* Baltimore.

———. 1990a. *Pindar's Homer: The Lyric Possession of an Epic Past.* Baltimore.

———. 1990b. *Greek Mythology and Poetics.* Ithaca.

———. 1993. "Alcaeus in Sacred Space." *Tradizione e innovazione nella cultura greca da Omero all' età ellenistica. Scritti in onore di Bruno Gentili* (ed. R. Pretagostini) 221–225. Rome.

———. 1996a. *Homeric Questions.* Austin.

———. 1996b. *Poetry as Performance: Homer and Beyond.* Cambridge.

———. 1996c. Review of J. M. Foley, *Traditional Oral Epic: The Odyssey, Beowulf, and the Serbo-Croatian Return Song* (Berkeley, 1990). *Classical Journal* 91:93–94.

———. 2002. *Plato's Rhapsody and Homer's Music: The Poetics of the Panathenaic Festival in Classical Athens.* Washington.

———. 2003. *Homeric Responses.* Austin.

Naiden, F. 2007. "The Fallacy of the Willing Victim." *Journal of Hellenic Studies* 127:61–73.

Nilsson, M. P. 1932. *The Mycenaean Origin of Greek Mythology.* Berkeley.

———. 1967. *Geschichte der griechischen Religion, erster Band, bis zur griechischen Weltherrschaft* ed. 3. Munich.

Nosch, M. L. and Perna, M. 2001. "Cloth in the Cult." In Laffineur and Hägg 2001:471–477.

Obbink, D. 1988. "The Origin of Greek Sacrifice: Theophrastus on Religion and Cultural History." *Theophrastean Studies: Natural Science, Ethics, Religion, and Rhetoric* (eds. W. Fortenbaugh and R. W. Sharples) 272–295. New Brunswick.

Ong, W. J. 1982. *Orality and Literacy: The Technologizing of the Word.* London.

O'Nolan, K. 1969. "Homer and Irish Heroic Narrative." *Classical Quarterly* 19:1–19.

Osborne, R. 2000. "Women and Sacrifice in Classical Greece." In Buxton 2000:294–313.

Page, D. L. 1959. *History and the Homeric Iliad.* Berkeley.

Palaima, T. 2005. "Sacrificial Feasting in the Linear B Documents." In Wright 2005:97–126.

———. 2006. "*Wanaks* and Related Power Terms in Mycenaean and Later Greek." In Deger-Jalkotzy and Lemos 2006:53–72.

Palmer, R. 1994. *Wine in the Mycenaean Palace Economy.* Liège.

Parke, H. W. 1977. *Festivals of the Athenians.* London.

Parker, R. 1983. *Miasma: Pollution and Purification in Early Greek Religion.* Oxford.

———. 1996. *Athenian Religion: A History.* Oxford.

———. 1998a. "Sacrifice and Battle." In van Wees 1998:299–314.

——. 1998b. "Pleasing Thighs: Reciprocity in Greek Religion." In Gill et al. 1998: 105–126.

——. 2005. *Polytheism and Society at Athens.* Oxford.

Parry, A. 1956. "The Language of Achilles." *Transactions of the American Philological Association* 87:1–7.

Parry, M. 1936. Review of W. Arend, *Die typischen Scenen bei Homer* (Berlin, 1933). *Classical Philology* 31:357–340.

——. 1971. *The Making of Homeric Verse: The Collected Papers of Milman Parry* (ed. A. Parry). Oxford.

Pedrick, V. 1983. "The Paradigmatic Nature of Nestor's Speech in *Iliad* 11." *Transactions of the American Philological Association* 113:55–68.

Peirce, S. 1993. "Death, Revelry, and Thysia." *Classical Antiquity* 12:219–266.

Petropoulou, A. 1986. "The Thracian Funerary Rites (Her. 5.8) and Similar Greek Practices." *Talanta* 18:29–47.

——. 1987. "The Sacrifice of Eumaeus Reconsidered." *Greek, Roman, and Byzantine Studies* 27:135–149.

——. 1988. "The Internment of Patroklos (*Iliad* 23.252–57)." *American Journal of Philology* 109:482–495.

Postlethwaite, N. 1998. "Akhilleus and Agamemnon: Generalized Reciprocity." In Gill et al. 1998:93–104.

Pötscher, W. 1964. *Theophrastus: Peri Eusebeias.* Leiden.

Pritchett, W. K. 1979. *The Greek State at War, Part 3: Religion.* Berkeley.

Pucci, P. 1987. *Odysseus Polutropos: Intertextual Readings in the Odyssey and the Iliad.* Ithaca.

——. 1998. *The Song of the Sirens: Essays on Homer.* Lanham, MD.

Pulleyn, S. 1997. *Prayer in Greek Religion.* Oxford.

——, ed. 2000. *Homer's Iliad I.* Oxford.

Puttkammer, F. 1912. *Quo modo Graeci victimarum carnes distribuerint.* Doctoral Diss., University of Königsberg.

Quiller, B. 1981. "The Dynamics of the Homeric Society." *Symbolae Osloenses* 56:109–155.

Raaflaub, K. 1989. "Homer and the Beginning of Political Thought in Greece." In Cleary 1989:1–25.

——. 1991. "Homer und die Geschichte des 8. Jhs. v. Chr." *Zweihundert Jahre Homer-Forschung* (ed. J. Latacz) 205–256. Stuttgart.

——. 1997. "Homeric Society." In Morris and Powell 1997:624–648.

——. 1998. "An Historian's Headache: How to Read 'Homeric Society'." In Fisher and van Wees 1998:169–193.

Rabel, R. 1997. *Plot and Point of View in the Iliad.* Ann Arbor.

Radcliffe-Brown, A. R. 1933. *The Andaman Islanders.* Revised ed. Cambridge.

Ready, J. 2006. Review of M. Kitts, *Sanctified Violence in Homeric Society: Oath-Making Rituals and Narratives in the Iliad* (Cambridge, 2005). *Bryn Mawr Classical Review* 2006.06.09, http://ccat.sas.upenn.edu/bmcr/2006/2006-06-09.html.

Redfield, J. 1975. *Nature and Culture in the Iliad: The Tragedy of Hektor.* Chicago.

——. 1983. "The Economic Man." *Approaches to Homer* (eds. C. A. Rubino and C. W. Shelmerdine) 218–247. Austin.

Reece, S. 1993. *The Stranger's Welcome: Oral Theory and the Aesthetics of the Homeric Hospitality Scene.* Ann Arbor.

Reese, D. S. 1989. "Faunal Remains from the Altar of Aphrodite Ourania, Athens." *Hesperia* 58:63–70.

Richardson, N. 1993. *The Iliad: A Commentary, Volume 6: Books 21–24.* Cambridge.

Richardson, S. D. 1990. *The Homeric Narrator.* Nashville.

Robertson Smith, W. 1889. *Lectures on the Religion of the Semites, First Series: The Fundamental Institutions.* Edinburgh.

Rose, H. J. 1962. "Religion." In Wace and Stubbings 1962:463–477.

Rose, P. 1997. "Ideology in the *Iliad*: Polis, *Basileus, Theoi*." *Arethusa* 30:151–199.

Rosivach, V. 1994. *The System of Public Sacrifice in Fourth-Century Athens.* Atlanta.

Rosner, J. 1976. "The Speech of Phoenix: *Iliad* 9.434–605." *Phoenix* 30:314–327.

Rudhardt, J. 1958. *Notions fondamentales de la pensée religieuse et actes constitutifs du culte dans la Grèce classique; étude préliminaire pour aider à la comprehension de la piété athénienne au IVme siècle.* Geneva.

Rudhardt, J. and Reverdin, O., eds. 1981. *Le sacrifice dans l'Antiquité: huit exposé s suivis de discussions: Vandœuvres-Genève, 25-30 août.* Entretiens Fondation Hardt 27. Vandœuvres-Geneva.

Ruijgh, C. J. 1957. *L'élément achéen dans la langue épique.* Assen.

Rundin, J. 1996. "A Politics of Eating: Feasting in Early Greek Society." *American Journal of Philology* 117:179–215.

Russo, J. 1997. "The Formula." In Morris and Powell 1997:238–260.

Rutkowski, B. 1986. *The Cult Places of the Aegean.* New Haven.

Säflund, G. 1980. "Sacrificial Banquets in the 'Palace of Nestor'." *Opuscula Atheniensia* 13:237–246.

Saïd, S. 1979. "Les crimes des prétendants, la maison d'Ulysse et les festins de l'*Odyssée.*" *Études de littérature ancienne* 1:9-49.

———. 1998. "Tombes épiques d'Homère à Apollonios." *Nécropoles et pouvoir: idéologies, pratiques et interprétations: actes du colloque Théories de la nécropole antique, Lyon 21-25 janvier 1995* (eds., S. Marchegay, M.-T. Le Dinahet, and J.-F. Salles) 9–20. Paris.

Schadewaldt, W. 1938. *Iliasstudien.* Leipzig.

———. 1944. *Von Homers Welt und Werk: Aufsätze und Auslegungen zur Homerischen Frage.* Leipzig.

Schein, S. 1984. *The Mortal Hero: An Introduction to Homer's Iliad.* Berkeley.

Schmitt-Pantel, P. 1990. "Sacrificial Meal and Symposion: Two Models of Civic Institutions in the Archaic City?" In Murray 1990:14–33.

Scodel, R. 1982a. "The Achaean Wall and the Myth of Destruction." *Harvard Studies in Classical Philology* 86:33–50.

———. 1982b. "The Autobiography of Phoenix: *Iliad* 9.444-95." *American Journal of Philology* 103:128–136.

———. 2002. *Listening to Homer: Tradition, Narrative, and Audience.* Ann Arbor.

Scott, W. C. 1974. *The Oral Nature of the Homeric Simile.* Leiden.

Scullion, S. 1994. "Olympian and Chthonian." *Classical Antiquity* 13:75–119

Scully, S. 1986. "Studies of Narrative and Speech in the *Iliad.*" *Arethusa* 19:135–153.

———. 1990. *Homer and the Sacred City.* Ithaca.

———. 2003. "Reading the Shield of Achilles: Terror, Anger and Delight." *Harvard Studies in Classical Philology* 101:29–47.

Seaford, R. 1989. "Homeric and Tragic Sacrifice." *Transactions of the American Philological Association* 119:87–95.

———. 1994. *Reciprocity and Ritual: Homer and Tragedy in the Developing City-State.* Oxford.

———. 1998. "Introduction." In Gill et al. 1998:1–12.

———. 2004. *Money and the Early Greek Mind: Homer, Philosophy and Tragedy.* Cambridge.

Segal, C. 1971. *The Theme of the Mutilation of the Corpse in the Iliad.* Leiden.

———. 1994. *Singers, Heroes, and Gods in the Odyssey.* Ithaca.

Shapiro, H. A. 1994. *Myth into Art: Poet and Painter in Classical Greece.* London.

Shear, I. M. 2004. *Kingship in the Mycenaean World and Its Reflections in the Oral Tradition.* Philadelphia.

Sherratt, E. S. 1990. "'Reading the Texts': Archaeology and the Homeric Question." *Antiquity* 64:807–824.

———. 2004. "Feasting in Homeric Epic." In Wright 2004:181–217.

Shewan, A. 1935. *Homeric Essays.* Oxford.

Shive, D. 1987. *Naming Achilles.* New York.

Snodgrass, A. 1971. *The Dark Age of Greece: An Archaeological Survey of the Eleventh to the Eighth Centuries B.C.* Edinburgh.

———. 1974. "An Historical Homeric Society?" *Journal of Hellenic Studies* 94: 114–125.

———. 1987. *An Archaeology of Greece: The Present State and Future Scope of a Discipline.* Berkeley.

Sokolowski, F. 1955. *Lois sacrées de l'Asia Mineure.* Paris.

———. 1962. *Lois sacrées des cités grecques, supplément.* Paris.

———. 1969. *Lois sacrées des cités grecques.* Paris.

Sourvinou-Inwood, C. 1993. "Early Sanctuaries, the Eighth Century and Ritual Space: Fragments of a Discourse." *Greek Sanctuaries: New Approaches* (eds. N. Marinatos and R. Hägg) 1–13. London.

———. 1995. *'Reading' Greek Death: To the End of the Classical Period.* Oxford.

———. 1997. "Tragedy and Religion: Constructs and Readings." *Greek Tragedy and the Historian* (ed. C. B. R. Pelling) 161–186. Oxford.

———. 2000. "What is Polis Religion?" In Buxton 2000:13–37.

———. 2005. *Hylas, the Nymphs, Dionysos and Others: Myth, Ritual, Ethnicity. Martin P. Nilsson Lecture on Greek Religion, Delivered 1997 at the Swedish Institute in Athens.* Stockholm.

Sparkes, J. 1975. "Illustrating Aristophanes." *Journal of Hellenic Studies* 95:122–135.

Speciale, M. 1999. "La tavoletta PY Ta 716 e i sacrifici di animali." *Epi ponton plazomenoi: simposio italiano di studi egei dedicato, a Luigi Bernabò Brea e Giovanni Pugliese Carratelli: Roma, 18-20 Febbraio* (eds. V. La Rosa, D. Palermo, L. Vagnetti) 291–297. Rome.

Stallings, J. 1984. *Scenes of Eaten Sacrifice in the Iliad (Formulae and Function).* Doctoral Diss., Johns Hopkins University.

Stanford, W. B., ed. 1947-1948. *The Odyssey of Homer.* London.

Stanley, K. 1993. *The Shield of Homer: Narrative Structure in the Iliad.* Princeton.

Stengel, P. 1910. *Opferbräuche der Griechen.* Leipzig.

———. 1920. *Die griechischen Kultusaltertümer* ed. 3. Handbuch der klassischen Altertumswissenschaft 5.3. Munich.

Stocker, S. and Davis, J. 2004. "Animal Sacrifice, Archives, and Feasting at the Palace of Nestor." In Wright 2004:59-76.

Swain, S. C. R. 1988. "A Note on *Iliad* 9.524-99: The Story of Meleager." *Classical Quarterly* 38:271-276.

Tambiah, S. 1979. "A Performative Approach to Ritual." *Proceedings of the British Academy* 65:113-169.

Taplin, O. 1990. "Agamemnon's Role in the *Iliad.*" *Characterization and Individuality in Ancient Greek Literature* (ed. C. B. R. Pelling) 60-82. Oxford.

———. 1992. *Homeric Soundings.* Oxford.

———. 2000. "The Shield of Achilles in the *Iliad.*" In Cairns 2000:342-364.

Thomson, G. 1943. "The Greek Calendar." *Journal of Hellenic Studies* 43:52-65.

Thornton, A. 1984. *Homer's Iliad: Its Composition and the Motif of Supplication.* Göttingen.

Tsagarakis, O. 1977. *Nature and Background of Major Concepts of Divine Power in Homer.* Amsterdam.

———. 1982. *Form and Content in Homer.* Wiesbaden.

Turner, V. 1967. *The Forest of Symbols: Aspects of Ndembu Ritual.* Ithaca.

———. 1974. *Drama, Fields, and Metaphors: Symbolic Action in Human Society.* Ithaca.

———. 1988. *The Anthropology of Performance.* New York.

Van der Valk, M. 1963-1964. *Researches on the Text and Scholia of the Iliad.* Leiden.

Van Straten, F. T. 1995. *Hierà Kalá: Images of Animal Sacrifice in Archaic and Classical Greece.* Religions in the Greco-Roman World 127. Leiden.

Van Wees, H. 1992. *Status Warriors: War, Violence and Society in Homer and History.* Amsterdam.

———. 1998. "The Law of Gravity. Reciprocity in Anthropological Theory." In Gill et al. 1998:13-49.

———, ed. 2000. *War and Violence in Ancient Greece.* London.

Ventris, M. and Chadwick, J. 1973. *Documents in Mycenaean Greek* ed. 2. Cambridge.

Vermeule, E. 1964. *Greece in the Bronze Age.* Chicago.

——. 1974. *Götterkult.* Archaeologica Homerica 3. Göttingen.

Vernant, J.-P. 1980. *Myth and Society in Ancient Greece,* trans. J. Lloyd. New York.

——. 1989. "At Man's Table: Hesiod's Foundation Myth of Sacrifice." In Detienne and Vernant 1989:21–86.

——. 1991. *Mortals and Immortals: Collected Essays* (ed. F. Zeitlin). Princeton.

Versnel, H. S., ed. 1981. *Faith, Hope, and Worship: Aspects of Religious Mentality in the Ancient World.* Studies in Greek and Roman Religion 2. Leiden.

——. 1981. "Religious Mentality in Ancient Greek Prayer." In Versnel 1981:1–63.

——. 1990–1993. *Inconsistencies in Greek and Roman Religion.* Leiden.

Vidal-Naquet, P. 1986. *The Black Hunter: Forms of Thought and Forms of Society in the Greek World,* trans. A. Szegedy-Maszak. Baltimore.

Visser, E. 1988. "Formulae or Single Words? Towards a New Theory on Homeric Verse-Making." *Würzburger Jahrbücher* 14:21–37.

Vivante, P. 1982. *The Epithets in Homer: A Study in Poetic Values.* New Haven.

Von Prott, I. and Ziehen, L. 1988. *Leges Graecorum sacrae e titulis collectae.* Reprint of 1896–1906 ed. Chicago.

Wace, A. and Stubbins, F. H., eds. 1962. *A Companion to Homer.* London and New York.

Watkins, C. 1977. "A propos de μῆνις." *Bulletin de la société de linguistique de Paris* 72:187–209.

West, M. L., ed. 1966. *Hesiod. Theogony.* Oxford.

——. 1973. "Greek Poetry 2000–700 B.C." *Classical Quarterly* 23:179–192.

——. 1988. "The Rise of the Greek Epic." *Journal of Hellenic Studies* 108:151–172.

——. 1997a. "Homeric Meter." In Morris and Powell 1997:218–237.

——. 1997b. *The East Face of Helicon: West Asiatic Elements in Greek Poetry and Myth.* Oxford.

——. 1998–2000. *Homeri Ilias* I, II. Stuttgart.

Whallon, W. 1969. "The Homeric Epithets Are Significantly True to Individual Character." *Formula, Character, and Context: Studies in Homeric, Old English, and Old Testament Poetry* (ed. W. Whallon) 1–19. Washington.

Whitman, C. 1958. *Homer and the Heroic Tradition.* Cambridge, MA.

Wilamowitz-Moellendorff, U. 1931. *Der Glaube der Hellenen* I. Berlin.

Willcock, M. M. 1964. "Mythological Paradeigma in the *Iliad.*" *Classical Quarterly* 14:141–154.

Wilson, D. 2002. *Ransom, Revenge, and Heroic Identity in the Iliad.* Cambridge.

Worthington, I. and Foley, J. M., eds. 2002. *Epea and Grammata: Oral and Written Communication in Ancient Greece.* Leiden.

Wright, J. C., ed. 2004. *The Mycenaean Feast.* Princeton.

Yamagata, N. 1994. *Homeric Morality.* Leiden.

Yavis, C. G. 1949. *Greek Altars: Origins and Typology Including the Minoan-Mycenaean Offertory Apparatus; An Archaeological Study in the History of Religion.* St. Louis.

Yunis, H. 1988. *A New Creed: Fundamental Religious Beliefs in the Athenian Polis and Euripidean Drama.* Göttingen.

Zanker, G. 1998. "Beyond Reciprocity: The Akhilleus-Priam Scene in *Iliad* 24." In Gill et al. 1998:73–92.

Ziehen, L. 1939. "Opfer." *RE* 18:579–627.

Zielínski, T. 1899–1901. "Die Behandlung gleichzeitiger Ereignisse im antiken Epos." *Philologus Supplementband* 8:405–449.

Index

Agamemnon:
  advisors, 36, 76, 143–144, 159
  as *Opferherr*, viii, 2, 15–16, 27, 29,
    35, 37, 47, 51, 56, 66–68, 72–73,
    75, *77–81*, 84–88, 90–92, 95, 97,
    100–101, 106–107, 110–111,
    115, 123, 126–127, 130, 139,
    141–142.
  conflict with Akhilleus, 51,
    53–55, 64–66, 92, 102, 108, 112,
    116, 119, 134, 140–141
  embedded sacrifices, 97–98, 103,
    114
  and Hektor's sacrifices, 82, 131,
    140
  makhaira, 30, 186–187
  prayers, 124, 126–128
  tests the army, 75
  unique language, 96
  and Zeus, 65, 120, 123, 163
Akhilleus:
  armor, 12–13, 52–54, 90, 150
  assembly in Book I, 35, 64, 66,
    141, 162, 166, 168, 170–171
  death, 11
  feasting, 189, 197
  funeral for Patroklos, 5, 194–196
  influences divinities, 112, 115,
    118, 122, 124, 127, 129, 131,
    140, 173, 175–176, 190, 193,
    198
  and Lukaon, 107
  military prowess, 164
  prayer, 2, 75, 87, 143, 191
  reintegration, 80, 85–86, 111,
    149, 165, 180, 186–187

and sacrifice, 18, 33, 47, 49, 53,
    55, 59–60, 65, 70, 82–83, 92,
    99–100, 102, 110, 116, 121, 132,
    137–138, 142, 167, 174, 179,
    185, 188, 192, 194–195
  unique language, 96
  withdrawal, viii, 56, 79, 104, 120,
    144–145, 148, 156–160, 163,
    169, 178, 184
  wrath, 7, 133–135
altar, 28, 48–49, 71–74, 81, 97–98,
    102, 122, 132, 197, 201
ἄναξ ἀνδρῶν Ἀγάμεμνον, 110, 162,
    176–180
Apollo:
  and Akhilleus, 11, 129, 189,
    191–193
  destroys the Akhaian wall, 136
  Glaukos' prayer, 132
  and Hektor, 67, 82, 122
  and Khruses, 35, 112–115, 125,
    127–128, 168
  opposition to Patroklos, 120
  paian, 91
  plague, 15–16
  recipient of sacrifice, 29, 37, 47,
    59, 66, 75–76, 78, 80, 85, 87, 98,
    100–103, 107, 117, 123–124,
    130, 134, 139, 165–167,
    169–170, 173–175, 185, 188,
    194
  temples, 7, 70–71
Arend, Walter, 9, 13–15, 43, 50, 56,
    60, 66, 69, 110, 132

barley grains, 14–15, 18, 21, 27–29,
    45, 75–77
βουφονεῖν, 147

δειροτομεῖν, 195
Diomedes, 67, 77, 82, 86–87, 100,
    102, 115–117, 127, 130, 143,
    146–147, 156, 159, 179

ἔΐση δαίς, 14, 48, 58, 108, 189, 201
ἐς μέσ(σ)ον, 78, 80, 86

hecatomb, 29, 68, 72, 74, 80, 87, 97,
    100–102, 114, 134–135, 144,
    162, 170–171, 173, 197, 199
Hektor, 65, 70, 75, 82, 122, 124,
    126–127, 130–131, 140, 138,
    146, 160, 191–194, 198
herald, 80, 91–92

ἱερεύειν, 42–43, 48, 50–54, 80, 82,
    97, 135, 197, 202
ἱερός, 33, 72, 87, 97–99, 101–102,
    132
Iris, 35, 82, 87, 131–132, 171,
    190–192

Kalkhas, 34–35, 74–75, 129, 134,
    155–157, 165, 167, 169, 15, 185
katarkesthai, 21, 29, 68, 75, 77
Khruses, 15–16, 34–35, 70–71, 76,
    81, 84–85, 91, 103–104, 107,
    112–115, 122, 125, 127–128,
    133, 157, 167–169, 174–176,
    180, 191

kingship:
    basileus, 149, 151, 153, 156, 159,
        177–178
    wanax, 151
knisê, 30, 49, 97, 101–104, 143, 193,
    195

libations, 2, 16, 18, 20, 28, 29,
    49–50, 60, 75, 85–86, 89, 91,
    102–105, 107, 120, 132–134,
    143, 145, 147–149, 175, 191,
    193
Lukaon, 30–31, 107, 189, 193, 197

makhaira, 21, 27, 30, 90, 186–188
μετανάστης, 198

Nestor:
    advises Agamemnon, 36,
        110–111, 141, 143–144, 156,
        159, 179, 182–183
    embedded sacrifices, 32–33,
        60, 67, 70, 76, 82–87, 91, 99,
        102–103, 105, 108–109, 112,
        114, 119–122, 196–197
    prayers, 126–127
    sacrifices in the *Odyssey*, 3, 25,
        28–29, 87, 117, 178
    speeches, 64, 146, 148, 164
    supports Agamemnon, 153, 158,
        160, 162–163

Odysseus:
    as Agamemnon's ritual assis-
        tant, 15, 66, 68, 80–81, 107,
        142, 144, 165, 169, 172–176,
        185

and Agamemnon, 157–159, 161,
163, 170–171, 179–180, 182,
186
and Akhilleus, 187–188, 199,
200–201, 203
altar, 73
and Athena, 3, 70, 99
Aulis, 34, 71, 74–75, 101, 119
embedded sacrifices, 67, 76, 82,
118, 120
libations, 143
prayer, 86, 112, 115–117, 145
sacrifice and feasting in the
Odyssey, 42–47, 89, 106, 120,
195
ὠμοθετεῖν, 14, 30, 48, 104

Phoinix, 49, 55–56, 64, 67, 82, 102,
118, 126, 132–135, 137–138
Poseidon:
and Akhilleus, 190
anger over Akhaian wall, 82,
100–101, 135–137, 147, 149
in Mycenaean religion, 36–37, 51
recipient of prayer, 145
recipient of sacrifices, 32–33,
102, 120, 138
sanctuaries, 70
prayer, 2, 18, 33, 45–47, 55, 63–64,
73, 75, 77, 83–87, 92, 112–116,
124–129, 133, 143–145, 148,
168, 175, 191, 199–200
Priam, 29, 35–36, 56–58, 64, 74–75,
82, 86, 103, 107, 123, 143, 147,
150, 178, 190, 192–193
mantis, 33–35
meal with Akhilleus, vii, 17–18,
56–58, 167, 187, 189, 201–202
purification, 75–76
religious professionals: 34–35

priest, 35–36, 168–169

sacrifice:
enacted and embedded sacrifices defined, 65–67, 95, 97,
103
interpretations of, 23–30
kill phase, 87–92
oath sacrifices, 31, 38, 41, 66, 68,
75, 80, 86–87, 89, 103, 110, 124,
146, 162, 165, 175, 186
Opferherr, 26–27, 77, 79, 83–84,
86–87, 92, 121, 188
post-kill phase, 93–94
pre-kill phase, 43, 45, 47, 55, 75,
92, 110, 199
purificatory, 29, 101–102, 167,
173
sacrificial process, 20, 27–29, 42,
67–68, 76
sacrificial ritual in the *Iliad*
defined, 9, 19, 39, 46–48, 50,
54, 56, 59
sphagia, 32–33, 39
thusia, 36, 39, 48–50, 54, 71, 83,
98, 200
splankhna, 14–15, 18, 20, 46, 48, 58,
103–107, 200
defined, 22
σφάζειν, 18, 45, 48–50, 54–56, 97

temenos, 69–70
temple, 69–70, 72
Theano, 35–36, 87, 124–125
thigh bones (*mêria*), 14, 21–22, 25,
30, 36–37, 48, 58, 67, 85, 91,
97–98, 103, 106, 120, 139, 195,
200

θύειν, 36, 48–50, 54, 98

θυηλαί, 199–200

type scenes, 9, 12, 15–16, 18, 38, 46, 48, 62, 67

Vernant, Jean-Pierre, 1, 22, 24–25, 27–28, 94, 98, 132, 143

victims, sacrificial, 33, 68, 80, 89, 98, 99–100, 102–103, 161, 168, 174

vow, 64, 70, 82–84, 86, 87, 99, 102, 112, 117, 124–125, 129, 131, 197

Zeus:

  and Agamemnon's authority, 141, 158, 163, 179

  and Akhilleus, 135, 142, 190–191

altars, 71, 73

anger over the Akhaian wall, 136–137, 149

deception at Mekone, 22, 93–94

honor of sacrifice for gods, 60, 67, 103, 105, 108, 132, 143, 201

in Linear B tablets, 37

recipient of prayer, 72, 85, 86, 125–128, 130, 140, 146

recipient of sacrifice, viii, 21, 32–33, 51, 59, 66, 97, 99–102, 109, 120–121, 139, 147, 162, 181–184, 186, 198

sacrifices of Hector, 65, 82, 122–123, 131, 192–194

sanctuaries, 49, 69

and Thetis, 75, 115, 118, 124, 166–167, 175–176

thunder, 148

Index Locorum

Aeschylus
    Agamemnon 218–249: 74
    Seven Against Thebes 44: 89
Apollonius Rhodius
    Argonautica 3.1033: 104; 4.689:
        190
Aristophanes
    Birds 892–893: 77
    Peace 937–938: 71; 974–977: 114;
        1118: 80
Aristotle
    Constitution of the Athenians 3.3:
        79; 57.1–2: 79
    Politics 1278a37: 199; 1285a6: 79;
        1322b: 79
Asklepiades
    FGrH 12.15 (Jacoby): 188
Athenaios
    Deipnosophistai 253e: 95
Demosthenes
    19 On the False Embassy 190: 107
    43 Against Makartatos 82: 107
Herodotus
    1.87: 84; 6.56: 107; 6.68: 89
Hesiod
    Theogony 535–560: 93–94
    Works and Days 134–137: 142;
        336: 77
Homer
    Iliad I 1–611: 166–176; I 6–7:
        177–178; I 11: 34; I 14: 69; I
        20–23: 76, 157; I 35–44: 29,
        37–38, 67, 71, 85–86, 94, 101,
        103, 113–114, 191; I 43–52:

113; I 59–303: 156; I 62–67:
        35, 67, 83, 100–102, 129; I 75:
        190; I 78–79: 156; I 92–104: 34,
        67, 102, 179, 185; I 118–123:
        179, 193; I 130: 179; I 133–138:
        162, 185; I 150–151: 162; I 154:
        156; I 158–160: 155; I 161–168:
        162, 165, 193; I 172: 177; I 175:
        163; I 185: 193; I 195: 190; I
        259–281: 64, 119, 141, 153, 190,
        193; I 285: 179; I 308–319: 29,
        47, 66–67, 72, 75, 87, 100–102,
        142, 173, 199; I 355: 179; I 356:
        193; I 370: 34; I 411: 179; I
        422–474: 14–16, 19, 37, 46, 55,
        58, 66–69, 71, 75, 80, 84–86, 88,
        91, 100–101, 104–106, 108–109,
        114, 176–177, 180–181, 191,
        195, 200; I 504: 191; I 506–507:
        177, 193; I 599–604: 109; I 602:
        108, 201
    Iliad II 77: 178; II 100–109: 118,
        158, 179; II 110–141: 75; II
        144–149: 144; II 186: 163; II
        238–240: 71, 193; II 299–332:
        118; II 303–330: 34, 67, 71, 74,
        82, 100–102; II 369–404: 67,
        81, 177–179, 181; II 400–434:
        13–16, 19, 29, 31, 43, 46, 51, 58,
        66–67, 72, 77–78, 81, 85–86,
        88, 91, 97, 100, 104–106,
        108, 110, 123, 135, 142, 144,
        159, 161, 176–177, 179–180,
        181–183, 195, 200; II 441:
        177; II 449: 100; II 477: 179; II
        494–759: 118; II 550–551: 67,

83; II 576: 179; II 579–580: 184, 156; II 612: 177; II 696: 69; II 724–725: 136; II 768–769: 184; II 816–877: 118; II 858: 35

Iliad III 81: 177; III 103–104: 89, 100, 103; III 116–120: 80, 92, 175, 179; III 178: 179; III 204–224: 118; III 245: 29; III 264–311: 29–30, 38, 67, 92, 72, 75, 77–78, 85–86, 88–90, 103, 105, 124, 142–143, 172, 175–177, 186; III 319–324: 86; III 328–338: 12; III 350–354: 86, 125; III 365: 125; III 455: 177

Iliad IV 1–4: 109; IV 44–49: 67, 71, 82, 102–103, 108, 122, 131, 142, 201; IV 100–103: 67, 86, 100–101, 117; IV 119–121: 67, 82, 86, 100–101, 117; IV 127–129: 62, 117; IV 148: 177; IV 153: 179; IV 188: 179; IV 204: 179; IV 255: 177; IV 283: 179; IV 311: 179; IV 323: 193; IV 336: 177; IV 343–344: 161; IV 356: 179; IV 368: 179; IV 370–400: 118

Iliad V 4: 146; V 34: 190; V 38: 177; V 114–123: 86, 114, 117, 127; V 149: 35; V 177–178: 67, 83, 130, 190; V 268: 177; V 311: 124, 177; V 381–404: 118; V 401: 91; V 434–444: 77, 190; V 537: 179; V 899: 91

Iliad VI 33: 177; VI 42–83: 49; VI 63: 179; VI 74: 100; VI 89: 36; VI 93–98: 51, 67, 100, 102; VI 110–115: 67, 100; VI 117–178: 153; VI 119–236: 118; VI 174: 51–52; VI 194: 70; VI 236: 100; VI 266–270: 49, 75; VI 274–278: 67, 51, 100, 102; VI 298–311: 30, 36, 51, 67, 70, 82, 86, 102,

124–125; VI 407–432: 118; VI 475–481: 86

Iliad VII 12: 179; VII 67–91: 70, 146; VII 107: 179; VII 123–160: 118–119, 146; VII 162: 177; VII 177–180: 86; VII 191–323: 146, 179; VII 194–205: 86; VII 219: 5; VII 313–326: 13, 66–67, 72, 78, 88, 100, 105–106, 110, 142, 144, 176–177, 180, 183–184; VII 324–482: 82, 147–148; VII 405: 179; VII 445–463: 67, 82–83, 100–102, 135–136; VII 480–481: 143

Iliad VIII 48: 49, 69, 71, 122; VIII 203–204: 70, 138; VIII 236–250: 67, 71–72, 81–83, 86, 97, 101, 103, 140, 126, 191; VIII 278: 177; VIII 493: 5; VIII 548–552: 66

Iliad IX 4–8: 144; IX 9–161: 156; IX 12: 145; IX 62: 179; IX 69–73: 159; IX 89–94: 143–144, 202; IX 96–99: 162, 177, 179; IX 111: 193; IX 114: 177, 179; IX 163: 177, 179; IX 169: 172; IX 174–177: 75, 144–145; IX 182–184: 145; IX 205–228: 103, 199–200, 202; IX 344: 193; IX 356–361: 67, 82, 99, 158, 198; IX 367: 193; IX 368: 179; IX 422: 193; IX 434–495: 133; IX 434–605: 118; IX 444–469: 55–56; IX 496–512: 49, 67, 82, 133–134; IX 517–518: 70, 190; IX 527–608: 67, 70, 82, 100–101, 132–135; IX 648: 198; IX 656–657: 145; IX 672: 177, 179; IX 677: 177, 179; IX 697–709: 146, 177, 179; IX 712: 143

Iliad X 42: 179; X 43–46: 67, 82,
131; X 64: 177; X 86: 177; X
103: 177, 179; X 108–110: 159;
X 245: 115; X 254–272: 118; X
272–282: 86, 115; X 283–295:
67, 82, 86, 102, 114, 116–117;
X 418: 89; X 460–464: 70, 86,
117; X 570–571: 67, 70, 99; X
579: 143

Iliad XI 15–46: 12; XI 99: 177;
XI 107: 179; XI 108: 156; XI
126: 179; XI 153: 179; XI 177:
179; XI 238: 179; XI 254: 177;
XI 655–803: 118–119; XI 701:
177; XI 706–707: 67, 82–83, 99,
119; XI 725–736: 32, 67, 70, 83,
99, 109, 119–120; XI 751–758:
83, 120; XI 761–789: 84, 120;
XI 772–780: 60, 67, 70, 82, 91,
101–103, 105, 109, 119, 121;
XI 785–790: 197; XI 806–808:
71–73

Iliad XII 6–33: 67, 83, 100–101,
136; XII 228–250: 35, 168; XII
313: 70; XII 320–321: 108

Iliad XIII 70: 35; XIII 112: 179; XIII
624: 190; XIII 460: 190

Iliad XIV 41: 179; XIV 64: 177;
XIV 83–94: 157; XIV 103: 177;
XIV 110–127: 118; XIV 134:
177; XIV 313–328: 118

Iliad XV 14–33: 118; XV 88: 109;
XV 122: 190; XV 367–386: 67,
82, 86, 101, 103, 126, 128

Iliad XVI 54–56: 193; XVI 58: 179;
XVI 59: 198; XVI 72: 179; XVI
130–144: 12; XVI 148: 190;
XVI 220–252: 75, 86, 114, 124,
143, 191; XVI 238: 191; XVI
273: 179; XVI 457: 193; XVI
513–527: 86, 114, 132; XVI 675:
193; XVI 711: 190

Iliad XVII 218: 35; XVII 248–251:
124, 161; XVII 256–259: 161;
XVII 426: 190; XVII 559–568:
86, 126; XVII 645–648: 86

Iliad XVIII 37–50: 118; XVIII 111:
177; XVIII 165–202: 132; XVIII
170: 171; XVIII 205: 146; XVIII
288–292: 160; XVIII 336–337:
195; XVIII 393–409: 118; XVIII
444: 193; XVIII 445: 179; XVIII
464–467: 190; XVIII 478–608:
118; XVIII 550: 70; XVIII
556–560: 43, 51–52, 182

Iliad XIX 35: 190; XIX 51:
179–180; XIX 75–76: 177,
179–180, 190; XIX 78–144: 186;
XIX 146: 177, 179; XIX 86–136:
118, 193; XIX 87–144: 163; XIX
146: 179–180, 187; XIX 172:
177, 179–180; XIX 184: 177,
179–180; XIX 196–197: 80, 92,
175; XIX 199: 177, 179–180,
187; XIX 205–207: 186; XIX
248–268: 29–30, 52, 66–67, 72,
75, 78, 80, 85–86, 88–90, 92,
100, 103, 111, 124, 142, 175,
186, 196–197; XIX 315–318:
189, 197; XIX 327: 188; XIX
349–355: 190; XIX 364–391:
5, 12

Iliad XX 182–184: 70, 193; XX
213–241: 118; XX 389: 171; XX
391: 70; XX 403–407: 31, 67, 83,
102, 137–138

Iliad XXI 24: 190; XXI 74–113:
107, 189; XXI 89: 195; XXI
97–99: 190, 193; XXI 130–138:
51, 53, 67, 70, 82, 102, 94; XXI
361–365: 109; XXI 523: 190

Iliad XXII 158–166: 67, 83, 138;
XXII 169–172: 67, 82, 101–102,
122; XXII 174–181: 122; XXII

206: 146; XXII 346–347: 189;
XXII 358–360: 11; XXII 498:
132
Iliad XXIII 9: 193; XXIII 29–34:
55, 201; XXIII 48: 189, 201–202;
XXIII 49: 177; XXIII 56: 108,
189, 201; XXIII 80–92: 196;
XXIII 110: 179; XXIII 140–151:
49, 51, 67, 69–70, 82, 99, 100,
102, 197; XXIII 159: 132; XXIII
161: 177; XXIII 167–175: 195;
XXIII 175–176: 194; XXIII
194–198: 33, 67, 86, 99, 143;
XXIII 201–209: 67, 82, 99, 100,
109, 131, 190; XXIII 288: 177;
XXIII 305: 71; XXIII 624–650:
118–119; XXIII 740–749: 118;
XXIII 769–771: 86, 114; XXIII
826–835: 5; XXIII 862–873: 67,
82, 86, 100–101, 130; XXIII 887:
179; XXIII 895: 177
Iliad XXIV 33–39: 67, 82, 102, 122,
191; XXIV 33–76: 140; XXIV
41–43: 189; XXIV 66–70: 67,
71, 82, 102–103, 108, 122, 142,
192, 201; XXIV 95: 201; XXIV
100–102: 109; XXIV 123–125:
43, 51, 53; XXIV 207: 189;
XXIV 220–221: 35; XXIV 261:
77; XXIV 305–314: 75, 86, 114,
143; XXIV 425–428: 82; XXIV
599–628: 13, 17, 57–58, 118,
189, 202
Odyssey i 25: 101; i 60–67: 116; i
325–359: 6; i 386: 177; i 392:
177
Odyssey ii 56: 51, 202
Odyssey iii 4–9: 3, 31, 38, 46; iii
30–385: 3, 19; iii 40: 85; iii 59:
101; iii 66: 85; iii 144: 101; iii
381–383: 117; iii 418–472: 25;
iii 419: 13, 38; iii 435–446:

3, 28, 38, 90; iii 450: 29; iii
457–463: 17, 104; iii 461: 46
Odyssey iv 57: 91; iv 352: 101; iv
478: 101; iv 534–545: 90; iv 582:
101; iv 761: 28
Odyssey v 102: 101
Odyssey vii 186–190: 3; vii 202:
101
Odyssey viii 59: 202; viii 61–83:
6, 187; viii 266–369: 6; viii
363: 46; viii 390–391: 177; viii
471–543: 6
Odyssey ix 197–201: 168; ix 231:
50; ix 473–491: 8
Odyssey xi 35–36: 89, 195; xi 132:
101; xi 505–537: 188
Odyssey xii 353–365: 13, 17, 25, 46
Odyssey xiii 350: 101
Odyssey xiv 9: 51; xiv 28: 42, 51;
xiv 74–80: 42–43, 45; xiv 93:
158; xiv 149–409: 44; xiv 162:
31; xiv 419–438: 13, 38, 42,
44–45; xiv 426–427: 42, 104;
xiv 432–446: 38, 46, 50; xiv
767: 29
Odyssey xv 222: 50–51; xv 261:
50–51
Odyssey xvi 180–181: 51; xvi 184:
72; xvi 535: 51
Odyssey xvii 50: 101; xvii 59: 101;
xvii 180: 202; xvii 210–211: 72;
xvii 535: 202
Odyssey xviii 5: 89
Odyssey xix 198: 51; xix 306: 31;
xix 366: 101; xix 397: 72
Odyssey xx 3: 51; xx 250–252: 46,
51, 202; xx 276: 101; xx 312: 51;
xx 391: 51
Odyssey xxi 145:35
Odyssey xxii 318–321: 35
Odyssey xxiii: 279: 101

Odyssey xxiv 215: 51
Kupria f. 14 (Allen): 188
Lysias
  Funeral Oration 2.39: 84
Menander
  Duskolos 450: 91
Pindar
  Nemean Odes 7.40–43: 188
  Olympian Odes 6.78: 83
  Paians 6.117–120: 188

Plato
  Euthuphro 14b: 83
  Sisyphus TrGF 1 43 f (Snell,
    Kannicht, Radt): 19
Strabo
  Geography 421: 188
Thucydides
  1.25: 77
Xenophon
  Anabasis 6.2.9: 89
  Hellenika 2.4.20: 92

CPSIA information can be obtained at www.ICGtesting.com
Printed in the USA
BVOW030153240912

300997BV00006B/15/P